THE BILL MONROE READER

MUSIC IN AMERICAN LIFE

A list of books in the series appears at the end of this book.

THE
Bill Monroe
READER

EDITED BY TOM EWING

UNIVERSITY OF ILLINOIS PRESS

Urbana and Chicago

First paperback edition, 2006
© 2000 by the Board of Trustees of the University of Illinois
All rights reserved
Manufactured in the United States of America
∞ This book is printed on acid-free paper.

Title page: Bill Monroe at a festival in Stumptown, West Virginia,
August 18, 1974. Photograph by Carl Fleischhauer

The Library of Congress catalogued the cloth edition as follows:
The Bill Monroe reader / edited by Tom Ewing.
p.   cm. — (Music in American life)
Includes bibliographical references and index.
ISBN 0-252-02500-8
1. Monroe, Bill, 1911– —Criticism and interpretation.
I. Ewing, Tom, 1946– . II. Title. III. Series.
ML420.M5595B55   2000
781.642'092—dc21   00-008015
1 2 3 4 5 C P 5 4 3 2 1

PAPERBACK ISBN 0-252-07399-1 / 978-0-252-07399-1

To the memory of Ralph Rinzler,
July 20, 1934–July 2, 1994

Contents

Illustrations follow pages 50 and 182

Acknowledgments

I'm grateful to have had the opportunity to edit this book. Many thanks to Neil Rosenberg for recommending me for the job, to Judy McCulloh for offering it to me, and to both of them for helping me in many ways thereafter.

I'm thankful to have had the assistance of two other people in particular. Many thanks to Gwen McReynolds for her computer expertise and for her patience, sense of humor, and understanding, and to Sandy Rothman for his expert proofreading of my retyped versions of the selections and for his comments, suggestions, and encouragement.

I sincerely appreciate the help of many others. Thanks especially to: Dana Cupp for figuring out mandolin tunings; David Davis for providing information on the Davis family; Charlie Derrington for patiently explaining the fine points of mandolin repair; Frank Godbey for reading an early version of the book and for his suggestions; Marty Godbey for sending me all those articles about Bill; Pete Kuykendall for helping me find several authors and for making it easy to include the selections from *Bluegrass Unlimited;* Julia LaBella for discussing her relationship with Bill; Tim Lynch for taking me to see Bill in 1963; Ed Neff for figuring out mandolin tunings; Ronnie Pugh for guiding me in my search of the Country Music Foundation Library; Kate Rinzler for permitting me to read her as-yet unfinished biography of her late husband Ralph Rinzler; Mike Seeger for taking Ralph Rinzler to see Bill in 1954 and for his efforts to answer my questions; Hazel Smith for helping secure permissions for the *Country Music* selections; Charles Wolfe for his interest in the project and for his suggestions.

Thanks also to: Tom Adler, Wendell Allen, Anna Lea Barry, Jim Bessire, Homer Bradley, Erika Brady, the late Jimmy Campbell, Margo Chaney, Jacky Christian, Tim Dillman, Brad Ewing, Sam Ewing, Carl Fleischhauer, Joy Ford, Bob Good, Doug Green, Frances Harvey, Mark Hembree, Paul Kingsbury, John Jewel Lockhart, Billy Logsdon, Gene Lowinger, Betty McInturff, Luke McKnight, the late Arreta June McReynolds, Bill Millsaps, Erik Moore, Sonny Osborne, Fred and Denise Painter, Evan Reilly, John Rumble, Earl Scruggs, Billy Smith, Terry Smith, the late Earl Snead, Steve Spence, Alan Stoker, Eddie Stubbs, Ron Stuckey, Clarence "Tater" Tate, Butch Waller, Lawrence and Hazel Waltman, Harry West, Ronnie Whitten, Blake Williams, Mac Wiseman, and all of those whose wonderful work is included herein.

Introduction

A Personal Perspective

I first heard of Bill Monroe when I read his name in the liner notes of an album, sometime in the winter of 1961–62. I was a fifteen-year-old fan of folk groups like the Weavers and the Kingston Trio, and on one of my weekly visits to a record store across the street from the campus of Ohio State University in Columbus, Ohio, I happened to find a new Vanguard release called *New Folks*. It was a sampler with four or five songs by each of several different folk artists, including a group called the Greenbriar Boys (John Herald, guitar; Ralph Rinzler, mandolin; Bob Yellin, banjo). They were the first ones up on side one, and I will never forget the thrill that shot through me when I heard them. It was the first time I'd heard bluegrass, and as I searched the liner notes for an explanation I read: "Many city folk musicians try to impose their own style on the folk songs they perform. The Greenbriar Boys, on the other hand, attempt to adapt themselves to a style which might be considered traditional. This style, derived from the old-time hillbilly band, named after the section of the country where it was first evolved (Kentucky) and the band which first played it (Bill Monroe and his Blue Grass Boys), is called 'Bluegrass.'"[1]

I recall telling myself that I needed to find a record by this Bill Monroe. But when I did, several months later, I was too distracted by all those fiddles wailing away on his new *Blue Grass Ramble*[2] album to enjoy it. Seeing him in person in 1963 didn't seem to help, since he didn't sound anything like his album, and, anyway, I was really more into the Greenbriar Boys by then, learning to play guitar and trying to sing like John Herald. Thankfully, someone eventually told me about an article in an issue of *Sing Out!* that I'd somehow missed, an article about Bill Monroe written by one of the Greenbriar Boys. More curious about this coincidence than anything else, I headed straight for Ohio State's Main Library, where I knew I could find back issues of the "folk music bible" of the time.

Reading "Bill Monroe—'The Daddy of Blue Grass Music,'" by Ralph Rinzler, I discovered that there was a very good reason why Bill Monroe and his Blue Grass Boys were "the band which first played it":[3] bluegrass had originated with Bill, based on influences he'd absorbed while growing up and his resolve to play music better than anyone else. The history of Bill's career, as set forth in Rinzler's wonderfully clear prose, was enough to deepen my interest, let alone to know that Bill's "respect for and belief in his music are . . . as profound as a religious belief."[4] It was then that I decided to give *Blue Grass Ramble* another listen.

As it turned out, Rinzler's article was the beginning of a lifelong quest for me to know more about Bill and his music. The photocopy I made that day of "Bill Monroe—'The Daddy of Blue Grass Music'" became the first of an ever-growing collection of articles and books about him, and after *Blue Grass Ramble* it seems I couldn't rest until I'd heard every one of his recordings, no easy task in those pre-CD days. About twenty years later, in 1986, I was privileged to join the Blue Grass Boys, singing, playing, and traveling around the world for ten years with this truly great and uniquely talented man.

Much more importantly, I now realize, Rinzler's article was a turning point in Bill's life. Fiercely proud of all he'd accomplished and unwilling to trust just anyone with the complexity of his story, the 1962 interview that preceded the article was, incredibly, the first time Bill had ever spoken at length to any writer about his life and career. And only after the article was published (and Rinzler became his manager) did he begin to emerge from the relative obscurity that his silence had helped create for him in the late 1950s and early 1960s.

The benefits of "Bill Monroe—'The Daddy of Blue Grass Music'" were many. Thanks to it and the success that followed with a new, urban audience, the man who had always let his music speak for him realized that the time had come for him to speak for his music. Bill began to open up, and, by the beginning of the 1970s, he was formally recognized as the father of a new style of music. In the years to come, writers and interviewers would find him to be more accessible than he'd ever been before, and they too would benefit from Rinzler's article. And, as their work would permit us to know Bill better than we'd ever known him before, so would we.

Concerning This Book

The Bill Monroe Reader is a collection of writings (including articles, transcribed interviews, excerpts from books, liner notes, and poems), most of them published between 1937 and 1998 (two are previously unpublished), that are about or at least relate to the Father of Bluegrass Music, Bill Monroe. It is not by any means a collection of all or even most of the writings about him, nor is it necessarily a collection of "the best" writings about him, although many of the selections could easily qualify in that exalted category. Rather, it is a collection of some of the most informative and/or enlightening writings available to be read about him while he was living and some of the most meaningful writings to appear in the three years following his passing in 1996.

The idea for *The Bill Monroe Reader* originated with Judith McCulloh, the assistant director and an executive editor of the University of Illinois Press. She suggested a book containing "the most significant, interesting, readable, influential, and responsible" writings about Bill, a limited collection of "the things you'd most like to have on the proverbial desert island, or in the only little briefcase you could take with you around the world by freighter, or on the plane to Antarctica for a long winter's stay,"[5] from a wide variety of sources.

The choice of the contents of that "little briefcase" was left up to me. My task as editor was made easier by the fact that I'd avidly read most of the widely circulated articles about Bill that had appeared over the years since 1963 and had kept a record of their locations in various publications. Photocopies of many lesser-known items were already in my personal collection, several having been sent to me by friends in various parts of the country who knew of my interest in reading about Bill. Other writings, particularly those from before 1963, are few in number and were easily located amid the vast holdings of the Country Music Foundation Library in Nashville. The main difficulty came with limiting the possibilities to the space available, challenging me to choose only those that were the most specifically about, related to, or illustrative of Bill.

After some initial confusion about the best way to present the resulting selections (a biographical ordering was seriously considered, beginning with writings about Bill's childhood, and so forth), a straightforward chronological order, based on publication date, was finally decided upon. Presented in this order, one can clearly see the sketchy, semi-fictional quality of the earliest writings about Bill, observe the subtle improvements as the world was just beginning to understand his accomplishments, and, hopefully, gain a greater appreciation for what happened after the formerly too-proud and aloof fifty-year-old let down his guard and began to tell his story.

Concerning the Selections

Of the sixty-five selections in *The Bill Monroe Reader,* over half (thirty-four) were originally published in music periodicals, mainly magazines. The first source to provide detailed information about Bill's life and career, beginning with Rinzler's *Sing Out!* article in 1963, music magazines continued to supplement the historical record until the early 1980s, when coverage of his current activities became the norm. Generally, articles were written by fans for fans with a fascination for Bill's past in common and even in later days would occasionally contain some historical revelation. Music magazines also specialized in publishing transcribed interviews, which offered invaluable insights supplied by the man himself.

The second largest number of selections (fifteen) come from newspapers or news magazines. Newspapers introduced Bill to the general public, making a significant contribution to his nationwide, and eventual worldwide, renown. Seldom "in the news" until recent years, some aspect of his life or career usually underwent analysis in feature stories, written in conjunction with a review of his latest performance or the release of a new album. When based on a recent interview and written by a knowledgeable and caring writer, the results could be quite enlightening. Bill was rarely featured in news magazines, and his appearances there were not so much informative or enlightening as they were evidence of his acceptance by Middle America. Heralding his arrival in that domain was "Pickin' and Singin'" from the June 29, 1970, issue of *Newsweek*.

Eight of the remaining sixteen selections are excerpts from books. Five of the eight are among the selections published before 1963, prime examples of what was available to be read about Bill during the first twenty-eight years of his sixty-two-year musical career. In this "age of information" it may be hard to believe, but aside from a few other writings, none of which tell as much about Bill, these selections were the main print sources of information about him between 1934 and 1962. The three remaining selections in this category are excerpts from books written by scholars for the serious fan. Published after the first biography of Bill (Jim Rooney's *Bossmen: Bill Monroe and Muddy Waters*) in 1971 and before Neil Rosenberg's *Bluegrass: A History* in 1985, only one of the three (Rosenberg's *Bill Monroe and His Blue Grass Boys: An Illustrated Discography*) dealt with Bill exclusively. (Excerpts from more recent books that have enjoyed wide circulation have not been included here in order to provide space for writings that deserve similar exposure.)

Most of the selections are reprinted here as they were originally published. Only a few texts have been abridged or edited, and these changes are noted in the editor's comments that follow the selections. Fewer have had punctuation added, and then only for the sake of clarity or readability. Spelling errors have been "silently" corrected throughout to avoid distracting from the content with the all-too-familiar "[sic]." These corrections include the now-accepted spelling of "Vandiver" instead of "Vanderver," the correct "Shultz" rather than the incorrect "Schultz," and the often improperly conjoined "Blue Grass" in the name of Bill's band. At the time of publication, the correct spelling of the surname of the first bassist with the Blue Grass Boys (Walter "Amos" Garren) had yet to be confirmed, so it appears here as each author spelled it: Garen, Garin, Garren, or even Garrett!

Errors of fact are noted throughout. Corrections for these errors, as well as brief explanations or other related information, can be found in the footnotes accompanying the selections. Footnotes that deserve further comment are discussed at length in the editor's comments, and directions to specific paragraphs are provided with these footnotes.

In Conclusion

It is hoped that readers may have already read at least one other book that includes a chapter on bluegrass or is specifically about the music and/or Bill (a list of these can be found in the selected bibliography), since some knowledge of bluegrass and Bill's life and career is presumed here. Although a great deal can be learned about him from *The Bill Monroe Reader,* it doesn't begin to tell the full story, and a greater appreciation for its contents can be gained by reading about Bill elsewhere (*and* listening to the wonderful music he left behind).

Notes

1. Author unknown, *New Folks,* Vanguard Recording Society, VRS-9096, released Dec. 1961.
2. Bill Monroe and His Blue Grass Boys, *Blue Grass Ramble,* Decca Records, DL 4266, released June 1962.
3. Author unknown, *New Folks.*
4. Page 22, this volume.
5. Judith McCulloh, letter to the editor, Aug. 9, 1998.

The Monroe Brothers: Their Life, Their Songs (excerpt)

AUTHOR UNKNOWN

Meet Charlie and Bill

Charlie's birthday is celebrated by millions because he first saw the light of day on July 4, 1903, back in Rosine, Kentucky. He stands six feet two in his stocking feet, has blue eyes, black hair, and is quite dark in complexion. Most men (and ladies too, for that matter) agree that he's quite handsome. He weighs 198 pounds and not an ounce is fat—he's hard and rugged and can take a round or two on with the best of them. Charlie wears riding habits mostly, likes race horses, pretty dogs, home life, and fried chicken . . . is always jolly, seldom gets blue, doesn't smoke or drink, and enjoys writing songs when he can spare a moment from his show duties. Thinks the best guy in the world is his brother Bill and wouldn't trade him for the best mandolin player in the world, because Bill to him is the best world could ask for. . . .

Bill is the younger of the two. He was born at the old homestead in Kentucky too, eight years later on September 13th. He's five feet 11 inches tall, weighs 215 pounds and every ounce of him shakes when he laughs. Like Charlie, he likes to wear riding habits in public and they're always well-tailored and made of the best cloth. Both boys wear mountaineer hats, not because they like to attract attention, but because they can't get used to the smaller headpieces worn in the city. Bill, off work, likes baseball, movies, and racing cars. He's Charlie's biggest rival when it comes to eating fried chicken . . . and can sleep twelve hours a night if undisturbed. He's never angry, doesn't smoke or drink, and enjoys helping Charlie write new songs. His blue eyes, brown hair, and pinkish complexion make many a lady look twice, but his hat still fits in spite of his good looks.

How They Began

If nights out in the Kentucky mountains hadn't been so lonesome and if there had been other things to hear besides hoot owls after sundown, maybe your friends, THE MONROE BROTHERS, would never have met you or you'd never have heard of them. But as it was, Kentucky nights were long and lonely. Families lived far apart up there in the hills where Charlie and Bill were born. Neighbors dropped in only once a week or less. And shows were things only to be read of in far-off cities. But the Monroe family did get a mail order catalogue every year and to the two growing youngsters of the household, bright-colored pictures of guitars and mandolins in their big book made them dream of happier hours. So they worked in the fields raising crops, chopped down trees and sold lumber, hunted for skins, and saved penny by penny until finally they had enough money to buy those first precious instruments. And buy them they did, together with an instruction book. No teacher for the Monroe Brothers. No songs either, except those sung by their own mountain people. And day by day, month by month, they practiced, until at last folks started talking about the swell music that kept coming from the Monroe homestead. Neighbors began driving up to visit, parties were arranged, barn dances, and always Charlie and Bill[1] were named to play. All this was taking place in the mountains, but it didn't take long for news to leak down into the valley and that was about the time hillbilly music was starting a new radio fad. WWAE in Hammond, Indiana, heard of them and offered them a job. From there they appeared on the famous Alka-Seltzer National Barn Dance,[2] and then their fame was made. The Monroe Brothers were in radio to stay. America liked them and when America says you're O.K., that's all you need to know.

Their Life

Their lives have been so closely woven together and they have become so inseparable as brothers wherever they go, the history of one reads almost like that of the other. Anyhow, both Charlie and Bill are Kentucky mountaineers.[3] Charlie, the oldest, was born on July 4, 1903. Bill, his kid brother, came along a few years later on September 13, 1911. Their mother and father were pioneers in the mountains. They came over the divide back in the covered wagon days,[4] built their home at what is now Rosine, and raised their boys on this same old homestead. While they weren't too prosperous and far from wealthy, the Monroes always had enough to live on and divide with neighbors less fortunate. Charlie and Bill were brought up as Christian gentlemen, God-fearing, kind, sympathetic, living clean, wholesome lives. As children they attended mountain school, Charlie always taking up for Bill, who was much smaller then, when bullies tried to start trouble. They learned rapidly, worked hard after school in the fields, studied at night, and were devoted to their parents, caring for them until their death. But their schooling, far back in the hills, naturally was limited, and what things they learned of the outside world had to come mostly

1. Charlie appears to have been the dominant one of the two. See the editor's comments, second paragraph.
2. The Monroe Brothers did not appear on the National Barn Dance. They (and brother Birch) were square dancers with a touring version of the famed radio show.
3. Charlie and Bill were not "mountaineers." See the editor's comments, third paragraph.
4. Charlie and Bill's parents were born in Kentucky. See the editor's comments, third paragraph.

by self-teaching. Hard-earned money paid for their first musical instruments. Long hours of practice enabled them to learn to play their beloved mountain songs. And the encouragement of their friends made them go on and on, improving each week until finally they were the talk of folks all over the mountains of Kentucky. Everybody knew the Monroe Brothers. Everybody danced to their music, sang with them the happy and sad songs of the hills. And such entertainment was soon to be desired by the world beyond those tall pine trees that embraced their home. Offers of jobs came to them, their ambition was aroused, and when the right offer came along, they took it and set out to face the world. First it was radio station WWAE in Hammond, Indiana, and their success was instantaneous. Then they got a break and appeared at the National Barn Dance at WLS in Chicago. That was all the Monroe Brothers needed to push them ahead. Radio stations throughout the Midwest clamored for them. They had to make personal appearances. Theatres wanted to sign them up. And Charlie and Bill did as much work in the years to come as they had done all their young lives back in the Kentucky mountains. WJKS in Gary, Indiana, got them to sign the station on the air every day at 5:00 A.M. and their audience grew with this early morning program. They've always liked to get up early. A sponsor out in Omaha, Nebraska, heard of them and had them audition for him while he listened hundreds of miles away. They made a hit and he took them on, sending them from station to station advertising his product: KFNF, Shenandoah, Iowa; WAAW, Omaha, Nebraska; WIS, Columbia, South Carolina; WBT, Charlotte, North Carolina; WFBC, Greenville, South Carolina; and WPTF, Raleigh, North Carolina.[5] Thousands of people knew them, thousands more had heard of them, and it was only natural that a recording manufacturer contacted them to see if they wouldn't like to make records of their songs. Why not, they asked, if it'll help make people any happier? And they did. Right now they have no way of knowing how many thousands of their recordings have been sold all over the country, but a safe guess would be far above 10,000. They get a kick out of playing; they never tire of their shows, which they change often because they appear in the same communities within a few weeks; they're still unspoiled by their success, and are just as happy and industrious now as they were long years ago before radio made them the famous MONROE BROTHERS.

Excerpted from Charlie and Bill Monroe, *The Monroe Brothers: Their Life, Their Songs* (Raleigh, N.C.: By the authors, 1937), 3–5.

EDITOR'S COMMENTS

Self-published in Raleigh, North Carolina, in 1937, the Monroe Brothers' second songbook was prefaced with this anonymously written introduction, which included

---

5. The brothers' broadcasts were sponsored by Texas Crystals at the first four and, changing sponsors at WBT, by Crazy Water Crystals. Both companies sold a laxative product.

what was probably the first writing of substance about Bill. Charlie and he had been working together as a duo for about three years at this point.

It appears, based on clues provided here, that Charlie was the dominant one of the pair. Notice that it is "Charlie and Bill" throughout, not once "Bill and Charlie," the usual order these days. Charlie is "hard and rugged," while "every ounce of" Bill, the heavier of the two, "shakes when he laughs." Later, as if to remove any doubt, twenty-six-year-old Bill is dubbed Charlie's "kid brother." It's likely that Bill, strong-willed and independent, was chafing in his subordinate position, and it's also likely that the issue of who was in charge ultimately drove the two apart about a year later, while they were still working in Raleigh.

Fact was almost overwhelmed by fiction in the "How They Began" and "Their Life" sections. Prominent among the fictions was the mountain setting, with the brothers being characterized as "Kentucky mountaineers." Actually, the Monroe family lived in the relatively flat foothills of the western part of the Blue Grass State. Also exaggerated is the portrayal of Bill and Charlie's parents as "pioneers" who "came over the divide back in covered wagon days." Their father and mother, James and Malissa Monroe, were both born in Kentucky, descendants of those heroic early settlers.

A Story of the Grand Ole Opry (excerpt)

GEORGE D. HAY

Bill Monroe

Many states are represented in the Grand Ole Opry. It long since became one of the largest national centers for American folk music and homespun entertainment. We receive applications from boys and girls from sixteen to sixty and these letters are postmarked from almost every state in the Union. Our regular weekly audition day is Wednesday, beginning about ten in the morning, during which time we try to help young people with their talent problems. They are so eager and hopeful that it almost breaks our hearts to tell them that the Opry is filled to running over, but their names are filed in the office for future reference. In addition to that we try to make helpful suggestions which will enable them to obtain the necessary experience to work in big time radio. Indeed, WSM is one of the big time stations of America, employing several hundred people at various times throughout the year.

One morning in October 1939, a big, good-looking fellow came up to see us.[1]

---

1. Bill and the Blue Grass Boys auditioned on a Monday. See the editor's comments, second paragraph.

He had his own band with him. His name is Bill Monroe and he gave us a sample of folk music "as she should be sung and played." Bill and his boys have been with us ever since as one of the feature acts on the show. Bill came to us with several years of radio and recording experience. He is a native of Kentucky and has been "pickin' and singin'" since he was a small boy. There is that authentic wail in his high-pitched voice that one hears in the evening in the country when Mother Nature sighs and retires for the night. His handling of "blues" numbers is stellar and his biggest hit to date on the Opry is the "Mule Skinner Blues," during the rendition of which he hits the top of the barn. For several years his first lieutenant was Clyde Moody,[2] from North Carolina, who is now doing a single act on the Opry. Clyde has a rich country baritone and is doing a fine job. Bill's other boys have come and gone, but he maintains a good act, capable of filling any theatre or auditorium you might mention this side of Madison Square Garden in New York, and he could do well there with some help.

Bill Monroe was born on a farm near Rosine, Kentucky, on September 13, 1911. He is the youngest or nearly the youngest of a large family.[3] When each of the boys reached the age of twenty-one their father offered them the choice of a horse or one hundred dollars. If memory serves us right, Bill took the horse.[4] He acquired a small farm[5] and worked it for some time and then struck out for Chicago, where eventually he picked up his mandolin and became a professional entertainer. He worked with his older brother, Charlie, as The Monroe Brothers for some time, but decided to organize his own group, which he did sometime before coming to WSM. Recently, another brother, Birch Monroe, joined Bill and is a big help to him. Bill Monroe married Miss Carolyn Brown in 1934.[6] They have two children, Melissa, born in 1936,[7] and James William, born in 1941.[8] Mr. and Mrs. Monroe bought a good-sized farm just north of the city of Nashville[9] recently and have a very comfortable American home, the kind one reads about but seldom sees. Bill Monroe is a good citizen and the longer one knows him the better one likes him.

Excerpted from *A Story of the Grand Ole Opry* (Nashville: By the author, 1945), 51–52. Reprinted by permission of the estate of George D. Hay.

---

2. Bill's lead singer and guitarist for most of the time between September 1940 and February 1945.

3. Hay didn't know for sure that Bill was the youngest, but he didn't seem overly concerned about it.

4. Hay may not have known that Bill was sixteen when his father died.

5. Bill farmed but didn't buy a farm before leaving Kentucky.

6. Bill and Carolyn met in 1934 and married in 1936.

7. Melissa Kathleen, September 17.

8. March 15.

9. Probably Bill's first farm, forty-four acres just north of the present-day intersection of Dickerson Road and Old Hickory Boulevard, now part of Cedar Hill Park.

EDITOR'S COMMENTS

After Bill and the Blue Grass Boys joined the cast of WSM's Grand Ole Opry in 1939, six years would pass before anything longer than brief reports of their appearances would be written about them. Finally, after the end of World War II in late 1945, Opry founder Hay self-published *A Story of the Grand Ole Opry,* a forerunner of later Opry souvenir "History-Picture" books. It included sketchy biographies of all the emerging stars of the show, including this one of Bill.

It would later be revealed that Bill and the band arrived in Nashville on a Monday (October 23, 1939) but were granted an audition anyway. It seems that Hay may have intended to tell this here, then opted not to, rather than admit that an exception had been made for Bill.

At the time that *A Story of the Grand Ole Opry* was published (ca. October 1945), Lester Flatt had been with the Blue Grass Boys about six months. Earl Scruggs would join the band just before the end of the year.

Oddly, when Hay's modestly sized (5½" x 8½") book was reprinted in a larger format with photographs in 1953, the text of Bill's biography remained the same.

Bill Monroe's WSM Grand Ole Opry Song Folio No. 1 (excerpt)

GEORGE D. HAY AND GENE DUDLEY

Testimonials

Bill Monroe is one of the most authentic representatives of homespun music—more properly known as American Folk Music—that I have met in a quarter of a century.[1] He sings straight from the heart and his voice carries a lilt which is truly refreshing in these modern days.

Bill is a sturdy farmer from the grand State of Kentucky and has rubbed elbows with his fellow men throughout these United States.

Personally, I count him as one of my best friends. He is a straight shooter and a grand fellow to know. Any songbook that Bill Monroe puts out will be a genuine article because Bill is a genuine guy.

George D. Hay
"The Solemn Old Judge"

1. Country music was often referred to as "folk music" in those days.

To his many friends and fans across the country, Bill Monroe wishes to take this opportunity to thank his friends for their loyal support in the eight years he has been at the Grand Ole Opry and on other stations. Without their support, he fully realizes that his efforts would have been in vain. It has been his fans writing thousands of letters to WSM and coming to see him on his personal appearances that has made him top star in his style of music. It has been a pleasure for Bill to work for the public and he sincerely hopes the public will keep him where they have put him.

In this folio of songs, you will find a number of Bill's original songs, many of which have been recorded—more of which are to be recorded as time goes on. Look for them at your favorite record shop. We believe you will like these songs, as do many other thousands, and also believe you will like the way Bill and his Blue Grass Boys have done them on Columbia records.

Bill Monroe came to the Grand Ole Opry eight years ago, after playing on stations all over the country. He has fast risen to be one of the top stars on WSM. He is heard over the Grand Ole Opry every Saturday night, besides his early morning programs. He has a band known as the Blue Grass Boys on the air and on personal appearances, which is backing him. They consist of Lester Flatt from way up in the Cumberland Mountains, who has his own style of singing solos. Lester plays a guitar and also sings duets with Bill. Next we have Chubby Wise, the Swanee River Fiddle Player, who hails from Lake City, Florida, and plays top fiddle. Also Earl Scruggs, the boy from North Carolina, who makes the banjo talk.[2] And last, but not least, comes Chick Stripling, who we think is one of the finest comedians in the country.

Besides the Blue Grass Boys, there is the famous Blue Grass Quartet, which consists of Bill, Lester, and Earl, and last but not least, Bill's brother, Birch, who sings bass. Bill was born on a farm near Rosine, Kentucky, on September 13, 1911, and started playing and writing songs when he was only a boy. In 1934, Bill met and married Miss Carolyn Brown.[3] They have two children, Melissa, born in 1936, and a boy, James William, born in 1941. They have a good-sized farm just north of the city of Nashville, where Bill raises some of the finest horses in the country.[4] When not playing music, Bill spends much of his time taking care of his horses. He is fond of all outdoor sports, but his favorite is baseball. He keeps balls and gloves in his bus and when on personal appearance, he can be found before show time out playing ball.[5] Bill and his brother, Birch, have a special hobby of raising game chickens. They have one of the largest and finest collections in the country and anytime any of you friends are in Nashville, you are invited to stop by and inspect this fine collection of game.[6]

---

2. These were probably the first comments in print about "the original bluegrass band." See the editor's comments, second paragraph.

3. They married in 1936.

4. Most of this information was derived from Hay's biographical sketch in *A Story of the Grand Ole Opry.*

5. Bill's involvement with baseball is understated here. See the editor's comments, third paragraph.

6. This was the first time Bill's interest in game chickens was mentioned. See the editor's comments, fourth paragraph.

In closing we would like again to thank you for your kind letters and requests which these songs have been selected from. The boys have spent a lot of time on this book, putting through every effort to please you. If this has been accomplished, they have reached their goal. Again let me speak for Bill Monroe, and say thanks a million and let us know how you like the book.

Gene Dudley
Agent for Bill Monroe

Excerpted from *Bill Monroe's WSM Grand Ole Opry Song Folio No. 1* (New York: Peer International, 1947), 4. Reprinted by permission of the estate of George D. Hay.

EDITOR'S COMMENTS

Bill's first songbook was published by the music publishing giant Peer International in 1947. Unlike the self-published Monroe Brothers songbook of ten years earlier, which included only the lyrics to the songs, Bill's songbook was a top-quality product featuring the words *and* music to twenty-one songs, with a center section of photos and these "Testimonials." An endorsement from the Grand Old Man of the Grand Ole Opry and the remarks of an agent to speak for him were clear indicators of Bill's music business success.

Dudley was probably the first to comment at length in print on the members of what has come to be called "the original bluegrass band." The songbook, in fact, celebrated the band, including ten of the songs they recorded and a photo in which Flatt, Scruggs, and Wise were identified by name. (The legendary James "Chick" Stripling worked with the band very briefly, filling in for bassist Howard Watts.)

The casual mention of baseball belies the fact that games featuring the band versus local teams contributed greatly to the success of Bill's tent show appearances in the early forties. In the later forties Bill began hiring young ballplayers, and at one time he sponsored two professional teams, the Blue Grass Ball Club and the Blue Grass All-Stars.

Bill's lifelong interest in game chickens is mentioned here for the first time. Although cockfighting is illegal in Tennessee, and the state has outlawed raising the birds for fighting, it's permissible to raise them as a "hobby" and to sell them to those who "stop by" from other states where cockfighting may be legal. These days, some rare breeds sell for as much as $3,000 each.

The first recordings to be released by "the original bluegrass band," "Mansions for Me" and "Mother's Only Sleeping" (Columbia 20107), were released on March 24, 1947, shortly before this songbook was published. Both songs were included in the songbook.

Two other Bill Monroe songbooks were published: *Bill Monroe's Blue Grass Country Songs* (1950) included an introduction with the main bit of new information being that "Monroe began musically as a singer in church work when he was a boy. As a result, many of his most popular melodies today are hymns and songs of a religious nature."[1] Otherwise, Bill's increased involvement with baseball was discussed. *Bill Monroe's Grand WSM Ole Opry Song Folio No. 2* (New York: Peer International, 1953) was basically a reprint of the popular *No. 1,* with nine fewer songs and the number 2 printed over the number 1 on the cover.

Note

1. Anonymous introduction, *Bill Monroe's Blue Grass Country Songs* (Hollywood, Calif.: Bill Monroe Music, 1950), inside cover.

Grand Ole Opry (excerpt)

WILLIAM R. McDANIEL AND HAROLD SELIGMAN

Bill Monroe

Bill Monroe joined the Grand Ole Opry in 1939, together with his band which he calls the Blue Grass Boys. Although Bill himself is the featured singer, several other members of the group are also featured, both singly and together with Bill, as a quartet.

Bill Monroe was born in Rosine, Kentucky, one of eight brothers and sisters.[1] He began as a singer in church when he was a small boy, and this may have some bearing on the fact that a great many of the songs his group sing have considerable religious significance.[2] Other than sacred songs, he depends largely upon his state's stock of old-time folk tunes and some of his own compositions. He sings fewer new songs than most of the Opry artists.[3] In addition to their playing and singing, the group is capable of some good country comedy acts, which they present in personal appearances more often than on radio. Bill has sold more than 6,000,000 phonograph records.[4]

Bill plays a mandolin expertly and is the possessor of a fine tenor voice, which he often pitches into a high falsetto, especially when singing in the group.[5]

This group wears neither Western costumes nor hillbilly garb. Instead they wear large white hats like Kentucky plantation owners, plaid shirts, riding pants, and riding boots.[6]

---

1. This was the first time that a major printed source accurately reported the number.

2. From *Bill Monroe's Blue Grass Country Songs* (Hollywood, Calif.: Bill Monroe Music, 1950).

3. This was an increasingly true perception. See the editor's comments, second paragraph.

4. This figure probably includes sales of Eddy Arnold's 1951 chart-topping rendition of Bill's "Kentucky Waltz."

5. This was the first time (and one of the few times) that Bill's mastery of falsetto was noted.

6. Not long after this, riding pants and boots were discontinued as a band uniform.

Bill owns a large farm in Kentucky,[7] where he raises walking horses and game roosters as a hobby in addition to the normal operation of the farm.[8]

He and his group make many personal appearances, usually traveling in a large bus.[9] During the summer months they are accompanied by Bill's professional baseball team, which he calls the Blue Grass Ball Club. They are a well-trained, fast team which plays local teams wherever Bill and the band are appearing.[10]

Excerpted from *Grand Ole Opry* (New York: Greenberg Publishers, 1952), 47.

EDITOR'S COMMENTS

Published in New York City in 1952, *Grand Ole Opry* was probably the first formal attempt to explain the southern phenomenon to northern readers. Styled after Hay's *A Story of the Grand Ole Opry* of seven years earlier, it also included brief biographies of all of the show's major stars.

The observation that Bill "sings fewer new songs than most of the Opry artists" was an increasingly true perception. The number of older songs he was recording, including old standards, Jimmie Rodgers songs, and remakes of songs he'd recorded before, was on the increase from 1950 to 1952. Although Bill continued to write exciting new material during that time, his creativity appears to have leveled off somewhat compared to 1945–49, when thirty-six of forty recordings bore his name as composer. Also, given the "old-timey" sound of the newest of his songs, it's easy to see how he might even have been perceived as a performer who specialized in old songs.

"Bluegrass Background: Folk Music with Overdrive"

ALAN LOMAX

While the aging voices along Tin Pan Alley grow every day more querulous, and jazzmen wander through the harmonic jungles of Schönberg and Stravinsky,[1] grassroots guitar and banjo pickers are playing on the heartstrings of America. Out of

---

7. In Tennessee.

8. From *Bill Monroe's WSM Grand Ole Opry Song Folio No. 1* (New York: Peer International, 1947) and *Bill Monroe's Blue Grass Country Songs*.

9. Actually, an airport limousine or "stretch limo," often called a "bus" in those days.

10. From *Bill Monroe's Blue Grass Country Songs*.

---

1. Distinctly modernist composers.

the torrent of folk music that is the backbone of the record business today, the freshest sound comes from the so-called Bluegrass[2] band—a sort of mountain Dixieland combo in which the five-string banjo, America's only indigenous folk instrument, carries the lead like a hot clarinet. The mandolin plays bursts reminiscent of jazz trumpet choruses; a heavily bowed fiddle supplies trombone-like hoedown solos; while a framed guitar and slapped bass make up the rhythm section. Everything goes at top volume, with harmonized choruses behind a lead singer who hollers in the high, lonesome style beloved in the American backwoods. The result is folk music in overdrive[3] with a silvery, rippling, pinging sound; the State Department should note that for virtuosity, fire, and speed, our best Bluegrass bands can match any Slavic folk orchestra.

Bluegrass style began in 1945, when Bill Monroe, of the Monroe Brothers, recruited a quintet that included Earl Scruggs (who had perfected a three-finger banjo style now known as "picking scruggs")[4] and Lester Flatt (a Tennessee guitar picker and singer); Bill led the group with mandolin and a countertenor voice that hits high notes with the impact of a Louis Armstrong trumpet. Playing the old-time mountain tunes, which most hillbilly pros had abandoned, he orchestrated them so brilliantly that the name of the outfit, "Bill Monroe and his Blue Grass Boys," became the permanent hallmark of this field. When Scruggs and Flatt left to form a powerful group of their own, Don Reno joined Monroe, learned Bluegrass, departed to found his own fine orchestra, too. Most of the Bluegrass outfits on Southern radio and TV today have played with Monroe or one of his disciples—with the noteworthy exception of the Stanley Brothers, who play in a more relaxed and gentle style.[5]

Bluegrass is the first clear-cut orchestral style to appear in the British-American folk tradition in five hundred years; and entirely on its own it is turning back to the great heritage of older tunes that our ancestors brought into the mountains before the American Revolution. A century of isolation in the lonesome hollows of the Appalachians gave them time to combine strains from Scottish and English folk songs and to produce a vigorous pioneer music of their own. The hot Negro square dance fiddle went early up the creek-bed roads into the hills; then in the mid-nineteenth century came the five-string banjo; early in the twentieth century the guitar was absorbed into the developing tradition. By the time folk song collectors headed into the mountains looking for ancient ballads, they found a husky, hard-to-kill musical culture as well. Finally, railroads and highways snaked into the backwoods, and mountain folk moved out into urban, industrialized, shook-up America; they were the last among us to experience the breakdown of traditional family patterns, and there ensued an endless stream of sad songs, from "On Top of Old Smokey" to

---

2. Capitalized by Lomax, this was the new name given to the music Bill had developed.

3. This article is the source of this famous description of bluegrass. See the editor's comments, third paragraph.

4. Rather, "Scruggs picking."

5. Actually, Carter Stanley worked with Bill briefly in 1951. His brother Ralph filled in with the Blue Grass Boys but was not formally a member.

"The Birmingham Jail." Next in popularity were sacred songs and homiletic pieces warning listeners against drink and fast company; and in the late thirties, the favorite theme for displaced hillbillies was "No Letter Today."

Talented mountaineers who wanted to turn professional have had a guaranteed income since the day in 1923 when Ralph Peer skeptically waxed an Atlanta fiddler[6] playing "The Old Hen Cackled and the Rooster's Going to Crow," and Victor sold half-a-million copies to the ready-made white rural audience. Recording companies sent off field crews and made stars of such singers as Jimmie Rodgers, Uncle Dave Macon, Gid Tanner, the Carter Family, and Roy Acuff.

Countless combinations of hillbillies have coalesced and dispersed before radio microphones since WSB in Atlanta began beaming out mountainy music on its opening day.[7] Grand Ole Opry has been broadcasting from Nashville for thirty-three years; the WWVA Jamboree has gone on for twenty-seven. In the beginning, performers sang solo or with one accompanying instrument; but before microphones they felt the need of orchestras, which, while originally crude, developed with the uncritical encouragement of local audiences.

By now there has grown up a generation of hillbilly musicians who can play anything in any key, and their crowning accomplishment is Bluegrass. When the fresh sound of New Orleans Dixieland combos hit the cities some fifty years ago, it made a musical revolution first in America, then the world. Today we have a new kind of orchestra suitable for accompanying the frontier tunes with which America has fallen in love. And now anything can happen.

Originally published in *Esquire* 52:4 (Oct. 1959): 108. Reprinted by permission of *Esquire* magazine. © Hearst Communications, Inc. *Esquire* is a trademark of Hearst Magazines Property, Inc. All rights reserved.

EDITOR'S COMMENTS

By October 1959, when this article appeared in *Esquire* magazine, a "folk music revival" was in full swing in the United States. Popularized by performers like Pete Seeger, the Weavers, and the Kingston Trio, and promoted by folklorists like John Lomax and his son Alan, the folk music "craze" eventually encompassed a wide range of interest in whatever was considered to be "authentic," including traditional ballads, blues, cowboy songs, old-time music, five-string banjo picking, and bluegrass. According to Neil Rosenberg in *Bluegrass: A History,* Alan Lomax in this article "perceived [bluegrass] as an updated form of the music he'd heard in the southern mountains back in the thirties and forties,"[1] and in this widely-read piece, Lomax interpreted Bill's role in its development as being an orchestrator, or arranger, for "the original bluegrass band."

"Bluegrass," the name given by fans and disc jockeys to the music Bill had developed, was still relatively new when this article was published. According to Rosen-

---

6. "Fiddlin' John" Carson.
7. In 1922.

berg, the word had been used to refer to the music for the first time in print barely two years earlier by a young man named Ralph Rinzler[2] in the introductory notes for the first bluegrass album, *American Banjo Scruggs Style.*[3] The landmark album was produced by Mike Seeger (Pete Seeger's half-brother), who, incidentally, introduced Lomax to bluegrass music.

This article is the source of the famous description of bluegrass as "folk music in overdrive." A post–World War II innovation, the overdrive gear of an automatic transmission reduces an engine's power output (and fuel consumption) when a vehicle is driven at high speed. Lomax was apparently alluding to the fast tempos (speeds) that bluegrass is sometimes played in, an important characteristic of the music to the novice fan. Lomax's description is expressed differently (and perhaps more realistically) in the title of his article, as if overdrive was an option.

On Saturday night, October 31, 1959, Bill celebrated his twentieth anniversary on the Grand Ole Opry.

Notes

1. Neil V. Rosenberg, *Bluegrass: A History* (Urbana: University of Illinois Press, 1985), 151.
2. Ibid., 111.
3. *American Banjo Scruggs Style,* Folkways Records, FA 2314, released in early 1957 (currently available on Smithsonian/Folkways SF 40037).

Official WSM Grand Ole Opry
History-Picture Book (excerpt)

AUTHOR UNKNOWN

NAME: BILL MONROE

HOMETOWN: Rosine, Kentucky.

BIRTHDAY: September 13.

BACKGROUND: As a young boy, was a church vocalist; has continued to sing religious and gospel songs during his professional career;[1] learned to play the fiddle from his uncle Pen; started playing an early form of the mandolin;[2] in 1927 formed a band with two of his brothers and played throughout several states;[3] made first radio appearance in 1930[4] and in 1938 left his brothers' band[5] and formed the "Blue

1. From *Bill Monroe's Blue Grass Country Songs* (Hollywood, Calif.: Bill Monroe Music, 1950).
2. Rather, an early *kind* of mandolin, a round-back model, called a "tater bug" or "potato bug" for its resemblance to the round-back potato beetle.
3. The brothers toured several states in the early 1930s, but not as a band.
4. This was one of the first mentions of this bit of information.
5. The author was apparently unaware of the Monroe Brothers.

Grass Boys"; the next year joined the Grand Ole Opry; considered one of the first musicians to play bluegrass music; is known as the "King of Bluegrass Music."[6]
FAMILY: Bill lives in Nashville; his two children, Melissa, 24, and William,[7] 20, also live in Nashville.
RECORD LABEL: Decca Records.
MOST POPULAR RECORDS: "Mule Skinner Blues"
"Blue Moon of Kentucky."[8]
INTERESTS: Owns an amusement park[9] in Bean Blossom, Indiana, where Grand Ole Opry stars appear; maintains farms near Nashville[10] and owns a pack of trained fox hounds.

"Uncle Pen" was Bill Monroe's idol. Not only was he a "real" uncle (his mother's brother) who lived close by, but, and this was the most important of all, he was the finest fiddle player in the country. He had a million and one tunes in his head and he was ready to play them any time he could get anyone to listen to them. To Bill Monroe and his five brothers and two sisters, it didn't matter how hard or how long you worked on the farm during the day, as long as you knew Uncle Pen would be dropping by in the evening to fiddle to the accompaniment of crickets and hoot owls. It was Uncle Pen who taught Bill to pick guitar—to play a fiddle and the "tater" mandolin.[11] And it was from Uncle Pen that he learned the tunes that would someday become the ground roots of Bluegrass Music. Between chores, Bill practiced diligently on the guitar, hoping someday to be good enough to "back up" Uncle Pen's flying bow and fingers. The day finally came and from then on, as soon as the sun went down, Bill would throw a feed sack on the horse, put his guitar in a grass sack, and Uncle Pen, his fiddle in a case, and away they'd go, riding "double." They were quite a pair and by far the most popular "pickers" in the county, in constant demand for square dances, corn huskings, and "get-togethers." They'd play all night for two, three, and sometimes as much as five dollars . . . but no matter what it was . . . Uncle Pen always gave half of it to Bill! Many years have passed since then, but the memories of those days and Bill's "Idol" will live on forever in a number written by Bill and appropriately titled UNCLE PEN![12]

Originally published in the *Official WSM Grand Ole Opry History-Picture Book* 2:2 (1961): 85. Reprinted by permission of WSM, Inc.

---

6. Bill's role in the development of bluegrass was still not understood. See the editor's comments, second paragraph.

7. James William.

8. These were not Bill's most popular records. See the editor's comments, third paragraph.

9. This park contained the Brown County Jamboree and was later the site of Bill's festivals. See the editor's comments, fourth paragraph.

10. Bill purchased his second farm in 1954, 288 acres in nearby Goodlettsville. Apparently he still owned both farms in 1961.

11. Correctly, a "tater bug" mandolin.

12. The Uncle Pen feature story is surprisingly accurate. See the editor's comments, fifth paragraph.

EDITOR'S COMMENTS

In 1961, WSM published the second edition of its softcover souvenir booklet for fans attending the show, which could also be mail-ordered by listeners. This quasi-dossier-style entry was a great improvement over the first edition (1957), which, for example, described Bill's mandolin playing thusly: "Somewhere along the route, Bill mastered the art of playing old-time favorites on his ever-present mandolin, on which he registers listenable melodies such as his trademark, 'Mule Skinner Blues.'"[1]

Bill's main role in the development of bluegrass was still not understood. He was just "one of the first musicians to play bluegrass music" (reminiscent of the *New Folks* liner notes of that year, mentioned in the introduction). Yet, for some reason not made clear here, he was also "known as the 'King of Bluegrass Music.'" (This title would continue to be applied to Bill occasionally through the mid-1970s, later to be adopted by former Blue Grass Boy Jimmy Martin.)

According to *Billboard* country singles chart results, Bill's two most popular *records* were "Kentucky Waltz" and "Footprints in the Snow,"[2] (the versions recorded in 1945 and released in 1946). "Mule Skinner Blues" and "Blue Moon of Kentucky," although two of his most popular *songs,* never charted for Bill.

The "amusement park" in the Brown County, Indiana, town of Bean Blossom contained the Brown County Jamboree, one of the state's first country music venues. Originally founded in 1940–41, performances were held there in a tent until a "show barn" was built on the site around 1942. Bill purchased the property in 1951 and, beginning in 1967, his bluegrass festivals were held on the grounds. (Folklorist and banjo player Tom Adler is currently doing research for a book on the subject.)

The Uncle Pen feature story is surprisingly accurate, an indication that the writer probably interviewed Bill about the background of his popular song. "Uncle Pen" was already well known to country music fans via recordings by Bill (1950) and Porter Wagoner (1956). This was the first attempt, feeble but nonetheless meaningful, to assess his uncle's influence on Bill. (Notice that the hoot owls had migrated from the Monroe Brothers songbook, joined here by crickets.)

Bill's oldest sister, Maude Bell Monroe, born on November 17, 1898, died at age sixty-three on December 26, 1961. His brother John Monroe, born on May 17, 1896, died at age sixty-five on February 11, 1962.

Notes

1. *Grand Ole Opry History-Picture Book* 1:2 (1957): 33.
2. Joel Whitburn, *Top Country Singles: 1944–1993* (Menomenee, Wis.: Record Research, Inc., 1994): 245.

"Bill Monroe—'The Daddy of Blue Grass Music'"

RALPH RINZLER

Blue grass[1] music does not come from the Blue Grass region of Kentucky, but from the Western region of the state known as the "Pennyrile" (folk pronunciation of "pennyroyal," a type of mint which is evidently found in great abundance in that area). Nonetheless, the entire state is known as the "Blue Grass State," and it was with the thought of identifying his music with his state of origin that Bill Monroe, the man known as the "father of blue grass music,"[2] chose to name his band the "Blue Grass Boys."

The term "blue grass music" came into popular usage in the early 1950s, taken up by disc jockeys and country music fans to describe the music of string bands which were following a trend established by Bill Monroe in the early 1940s and maintained by him on the Grand Ole Opry since that time.

The music itself has been criticized by some city folk music enthusiasts as being nothing more than mere commercial hillbilly music. Others take from it the instrumental techniques (banjo, guitar, and mandolin—few citybillies tackle the fiddle) and overlook the subtle and equally unusual vocal styles. Most are unaware of the wide variety of different traditions, folk and otherwise, on which innovator Bill Monroe drew when establishing "his music" on the Opry some twenty-three years ago.

Perhaps a glance at a few of these traditional elements will clarify this point. The fiddling style characteristic of blue grass music blends the Scots-Irish with the little-known Negro fiddling tradition. The song repertoire draws on the Anglo-American ballad and folksong tradition, on the urban commercial tradition of "heart" (or sentimental) songs of the 19th and early 20th centuries, and on the recently established tradition of White and Negro commercial country music (generally dated from Ralph Peer's first recording of Fiddling John Carson in 1923). The vocal style developed by Bill Monroe reflects childhood influences: listening to songs and styles of neighbors and family and singing in Methodist and Baptist churches; and it reflects a long-established feeling for both Negro and White blues singing. The banjo style generally identified with Earl Scruggs is actually a development of the three-finger style of picking first popularized on records by Charlie Poole (North Carolina Ramblers) and Dock Walsh (Carolina Tar Heels) in the Twenties and Thirties, later improved upon by Fisher Hendley (Aristocratic Pigs) and Snuffy Jenkins and

---

1. At this point Rinzler preferred to spell the name of the music with two words.
2. This was not the first reference to Bill as the Father of Bluegrass. See the editor's comments, second paragraph.

brought to its final form and current prominence by Scruggs himself when he started his professional career with Bill Monroe in 1944.[3] In contrast to this, the style of mandolin picking associated with blue grass music is radically different from any approach to the instrument which existed prior to Monroe's appearance.

Bill Monroe, the youngest child in a family of eight (six boys and two girls) was born in Rosine, Kentucky, September 13, 1911. His father, James Buchanan Monroe, was of Scots ancestry—a descendant of James Monroe, fifth president of the United States.[4] He farmed, cut and hauled timber, operated his own saw mill, and mined coal on his six-hundred-acre farm located between Beaver Dam and Rosine, Ohio County, Kentucky. Although his father did not sing or play music, Bill recalls that he was a fine dancer and enjoyed doing a local dance known as the Kentucky backstep.[5] Bill's mother, Malissa Vandiver Monroe, sang old songs and ballads in a clear, pure voice, and also played the fiddle, harmonica, and accordion. As a young boy, Bill learned to read music from shape note hymnals while attending singing schools. Bill recalls learning the essentials of guitar and mandolin at eight or nine years of age, but it was not until he was twelve or perhaps thirteen that he took a serious interest in learning music.

There are two distinct influences which Bill Monroe recalls from this period of his life, and both of these are clearly manifested in his unique musical style. His mother's brother, Pen Vandiver, was a fiddler of considerable talent and local renown. It was he who taught Bill the essentials of the guitar, fiddle, and mandolin, and from the age of twelve, Bill would travel riding double with his uncle Pen, sometimes as often as twice a week to play the guitar behind the older man's fiddling at country dances.

At one such dance, Bill met a Negro fiddler and guitar picker, Arnold Shultz, a man whose name is almost legendary in that country. (Shultz influenced Kennedy Jones, who in turn influenced Mose Rager, the man from whom Merle Travis learned to play the guitar during his boyhood.) Shultz played the fiddle in a "bluesy," syncopated fashion, getting notes and sounds that were not commonly heard in country fiddling. His guitar style also set forth a musical language which Bill was not to forget; the young boy would frequently play guitar behind Shultz's fiddling at dances. Shultz did not sing, but Bill recalls he could "whistle the blues" better than anyone around.

There were many opportunities that young Monroe found to stand by and listen to Negro workers "whistle the blues" while they plowed fields, lined track, and did other forms of labor in the area of Rosine and Beaver Dam. Surrounded by these sounds in his daily life, Bill Monroe resolved, at the age of thirteen, to play the mandolin in a way that nobody else had ever played it and to play his music clean-

---

3. December 1945.

4. Bill's father was not a descendant of President James Monroe. See the editor's comments, third paragraph.

5. Also called the double backstep in other areas, the Kentucky backstep is a particular kind of dance step, not a dance. Usually only the best dancers are capable of doing it.

er and better than anyone. The few people around home who did play the mandolin simply chorded it as an accompaniment to singing.

Bill and his older brother Charlie played and sang around home, finally winning a singing contest with the song "He Will Set Your Fields on Fire."[6] In 1927 they formed a band with their older brother Birch playing lead on the fiddle, Charlie singing lead and picking the guitar, and Bill chording the mandolin and singing tenor (he was then sixteen years old). After touring for three years, they settled in Hammond, Indiana, in 1930 and for several years performed on radio stations in the area.[7] When Birch left the group in 1934, Charlie and Bill worked at various radio stations as "The Monroe Brothers" (WAAW, Omaha, 1934–35; WBT, Charlotte, 1935–36) gathering considerable renown and polish.

When Victor first approached them to make records they refused, thinking the returns would be slight. After their second refusal they received a wire from Victor Bluebird representative Oberstein[8] saying, "MUST HAVE THE MONROE BROTHERS," and he would not take "no" for an answer. In Charlotte on February 7, 1936,[9] Bill and Charlie recorded ten songs (among them "Nine Pound Hammer," "You've Got to Walk That Lonesome Valley," "Darling Corey," and "This World Is Not My Home"),[10] and within a few weeks their first record, "What Would You Give in Exchange for Your Soul," sold 100,000 copies. They continued recording for the Bluebird label until January 28, 1938 (thirty-one records were released, some of which are soon to be reissued on the Camden label).[11]

During these years, Bill and Charlie worked at radio stations WFBC, Greenville, South Carolina (1936–7) and WPTF, Raleigh, North Carolina (1937–8). In 1938 the brothers separated, and Bill went to Little Rock, Arkansas, forming his first band, the "Kentuckians." They played for station KARK for three months, but Bill felt this would lead to nothing significant, and went off to Atlanta, home of the "Crossroad Follies" (a popular country music show), put an ad in the paper indicating that Bill Monroe was recruiting musicians for a band, and subsequently chose Cleo Davis (guitar and lead voice), Art Wooten (fiddle), and Amos Garin (string bass).

It was at this time that Bill began to sing lead on some songs. He rehearsed this band with great care, and after six weeks the "Blue Grass Boys" made their first radio appearance in Asheville, South Carolina.[12] Soon after this Bill set out to establish himself with a permanent spot on a leading radio station, and his first stop was at WSM, Nashville. He was auditioned by the Stone brothers and George Hay ("The Solemn Old Judge," initiator of the Grand Ole Opry), and was hired with the words,

---

6. Recorded by the Monroe Brothers in 1937 and by Bill and the Blue Grass Boys in 1954.

7. Rinzler's discussion of the events of 1927–33 is not correct. See the editor's comments, fourth paragraph.

8. Eli Oberstein.

9. February 17, 1936.

10. "You've Got to Walk That Lonesome Valley" and "Darling Corey" were recorded at their second session, June 21, 1936.

11. *Early Blue Grass Music by the Monroe Brothers*, RCA Camden, CAL-774, released June 1963.

12. WWNC, Asheville, *North* Carolina.

"If you ever leave the Opry, it'll be because you've fired yourself."[13] The following Saturday night (in October 1939)[14] Bill Monroe and his Blue Grass Boys played their first show on the Opry, starting with a song which is still one of Monroe's most popular, the "Mule Skinner Blues." In time a banjo picker was added to the group, and with this addition the blue grass band took its final form. "Stringbean,"[15] Monroe's first banjo picker, played old-time, two-finger style banjo and did comedy as well.

In the ensuing years Bill Monroe and the Blue Grass Boys were heard on the Opry every Saturday that they were not touring,[16] and the sound of blue grass music was heard on radios, juke boxes, and phonographs throughout the country. Bill has always trained the musicians who worked for him with the result that, regardless of the change in personnel over the years, the driving rhythm and characteristic fiddling style (which Monroe imparts to his fiddlers) have been ever present in the music heard on records and in performances of the group. Most of the leading musicians in blue grass music have at one time gone through their period of "apprenticeship" with Monroe: Flatt and Scruggs, Carter Stanley, Don Reno, Mac Wiseman, Jimmy Martin, Sonny Osborne, and Gordon Terry, to mention a few.

In conversation as well as in performance Bill Monroe's respect for and belief in his music are immediately apparent. It is this conviction, as profound as a religious belief, which has enabled Monroe to resist the trends of Nashville and to retain his remarkably unique musical style throughout more than twenty years of constant exposure. This same conviction, imparted to other musicians and to audiences, is responsible for the endurance and significance of the traditional folk strain in commercial country music.

At this point it is an easy task to evaluate the contribution of Bill Monroe. It was the combination of musical traditions, both the Anglo-Scots and the Negro, meeting as they did in that area of Kentucky, which enabled Monroe to blend these two powerful strains in his own instrumental and vocal style. In his choice of instrumental treatment and repertoire, it was Monroe who set the trend to play traditional songs on traditional instruments, and this he did at a time when the trend in commercial country music among performers of his generation was directly opposed to him. The searing tenor harmonies, dependent upon intervals of the fourth and fifth, which Monroe features, are reminiscent of those found in the old shape note hymnals from which he learned as a child.

Monroe pioneered mandolin virtuosity and forged the driving rhythms and tempos (characteristic of his music from the time of his first recordings with Charlie in 1936: "My Long Journey Home," B6422, "Roll in My Sweet Baby's Arms," B6773, for example). Bill Monroe is still the most dynamic and subtle singer in the field of blue grass music, exhibiting a vocal style which could only have developed from a background of rich and varied musical styles.

---

13. This was the first appearance of this well-known quote.
14. The exact date, October 28, 1939, had not yet been determined.
15. Stage name of David Akeman.
16. In the early years, performers were required to perform on the Opry every Saturday night.

But more important than his function as an instrumentalist, vocalist, creator, and preserver, Bill Monroe is a spiritual force. In his ability to sing and play with fire and inspiration characteristic of only a great musician, he draws people to him and to his music. In the fashion of the best traditional folk singers, Bill Monroe never sings a song the same way twice; each performance is a creative challenge and thus his songs never lose the excitement which is the burning soul he has imparted to his music.

> If you're singing a song to satisfy your heart and feeling, you won't sing it the same way every time.

(I should like to acknowledge with gratitude the contributions and assistance of Bessie Lee and Bill Monroe,[17] Ed Kahn, D. K. Wilgus, and Richard Rinzler.—R.R.)

Originally published in *Sing Out!* 13:1 (Feb.–Mar. 1963): 4–8. Reprinted by permission of the publisher.

EDITOR'S COMMENTS

This selection, as I mention in the introduction, was the first full-length biographical article about Bill ever published *and* the first to discuss his primary role in the development of bluegrass. It appeared in the February–March 1963 issue of *Sing Out!* about a year after the magazine published an article in which Earl Scruggs was called "the undisputed master of Bluegrass music."[1]

Three major print sources had referred to Bill as the Father of Bluegrass before Rinzler's article: In 1959, in the extensive notes for the *Mountain Music Bluegrass Style* album[2] (recommended by Rinzler in the original; not included here), producer Mike Seeger wrote that Bill was "called the father of bluegrass"[3] (Seeger recalled recently that he first saw the title on a show poster sometime in the early fifties). In the 1961 edition of *A History and Encyclopedia of Country, Western, and Gospel Music,* editor Linnell Gentry noted that Bill was "called 'The Father of Blue Grass Music.'"[4] And in October 1962, RCA Victor's Camden label released an album of Bill's early recordings titled *The Father of Blue Grass Music.*[5]

Recent genealogical research has proven that Bill's father was not a descendant of President James Monroe.[6] It is possible, in genealogical terms, that they were collaterally related (they had an ancestor in common). Their kinship, however, was not along direct lines.

Rinzler's discussion of the events of 1927–33, based on information from the previous selection and only one interview with Bill, is not correct. Briefly: Birch and Charlie had left home for their second trip north in 1927 and were working in Hammond, Indiana, when their father died in 1928. Bill left Kentucky in 1929, joining

---

17. Rinzler apparently thought that Bill and his bassist/companion, Bessie Lee Mauldin, were legally married at this point.

them in nearby Whiting, where he found work at a Sinclair Oil refinery, and the three brothers played music on the side, including making their radio debut in Hammond at WWAE. In 1932, while living in East Chicago, Indiana, they joined a touring WLS National Barn Dance show as square dancers. As part of this show, they danced at the Chicago World's Fair in 1933.

Notes

1. Pete Welding, "Earl Scruggs—and the Sound of Bluegrass," *Sing Out!* 12:2 (Apr.–May 1962): 4.

2. *Mountain Music Bluegrass Style,* Folkways Records, FA 2318, released 1959 (currently available on Smithsonian/Folkways SF 40038).

3. Mike Seeger, liner notes for *Mountain Music Bluegrass Style.*

4. Linnell Gentry, ed., *A History and Encyclopedia of Country, Western, and Gospel Music* (Nashville: McQuiddy Press, 1961): 273.

5. Bill Monroe and His Blue Grass Boys, *The Father of Blue Grass Music,* RCA Camden, CAL-719, released Oct. 1962.

6. Based on research by Anna Lea Barry, Columbus, Ohio, 1984. See also Richard D. Smith, "Monroes of Rosine, Kentucky—A Family History," *Bluegrass Unlimited* 31:7 (Jan. 1997): 24.

"First Bluegrass Festival Honors Bill Monroe"

MAYNE SMITH

The First Annual Bluegrass Festival was held on Labor Day weekend, 1965, near Roanoke, Virginia.[1] The names of the musicians present—they include most of the major bluegrass artists—and the size of the mixed northern and southern audience can easily be set down, but the real meaning of this festival must finally escape expression in words. Committed musicians are suspicious of writers, and they have good reason. If music could be talked, men would always speak rather than make music. But music is something quite different from language, and the man who writes about music inevitably falls short of the truth. As Don Reno put it, "Music expresses thoughts that people can't put into words and sometimes would be afraid to speak, even if they could." Particularly is this true in the realm of American country music where little academic jargon has developed, and where music so often relates to the central experiences of life: religion, love, death.

Bluegrass is the intimate, personal music of a single man, Bill Monroe. Many great musicians have produced top-notch bluegrass, but in calling it "bluegrass" they acknowledge that their style is founded on the private creative impulse that has patterned the music of Monroe's Blue Grass Boys since the early 1940s. There are

---

1. About ten miles north of Roanoke, near the town of Fincastle.

many, in fact, who feel that only Bill Monroe can inspire and consistently perform music in true bluegrass spirit.

One of these is Carlton Haney, who, with Ralph Rinzler's help, produced the Bluegrass Festival. This short, solid man, whose modest size is coupled to a personal humility and warmth that attract all who meet him, has been involved in bluegrass less than ten years. As a friend of Clyde Moody, one of Monroe's earliest and best guitarists, Carlton met Bill in the middle 1950s. At the time, Haney says, he did not understand bluegrass, and would even turn off the radio when Monroe's band came over the air.

Nevertheless, he entered the music business "for the money," to become Bill's booking agent in 1954. After a year or so, he began to perform the same job for the Don Reno–Red Smiley band, still mainly motivated by financial interest but increasingly curious about the music.

A 1957 trip to Nashville provided his basic answer, he says. One day in November, Haney helped put together an informal music session backstage at the Grand Ole Opry. Present were Bill Monroe, Don Reno, Red Smiley, Jimmy Martin, Bobby Hicks (one of Monroe's greatest fiddlers), and some others. Haney's own words tell the rest:

> Bill, Don, Red, and Jimmy were going to play "Live and Let Live" and Jimmy started his guitar in his "Good 'N' Country" time (the beat associated with Martin's Sunny Mountain Boys band). But at the end of the first line, Bill started tuning his mandolin—which means "You're not right." The men stopped playing and Bill said, "I'll start it, boys." And he started it in bluegrass time; and then I knew what bluegrass was.

This event was a revelation to Haney which, he says, immediately explained to him just how all the different musicians related to the basic Monroe style. Then and there he began to plan for a festival that would help others to understand as he had.

Although in the popular mind bluegrass banjo playing is one of the outstanding features of bluegrass music, to Haney it is the rhythmic features of the music which make it a unique style. And talks with Monroe make it clear that the refinement of Snuffy Jenkins' three-finger banjo style by Don Reno and Earl Scruggs, the development of the tense, high-pitched singing style, the melodic kinship of bluegrass fiddle and mandolin with the blues—all these elements are subordinate in Bill's mind to the beat and time of bluegrass. The right beat, says Monroe, is close to modern rock and roll, and was first recorded on the early "Mule Skinner Blues," a record on which Monroe played guitar himself so as to insure the proper rhythm. Carlton Haney further discussed the problem of bluegrass beat:

> The beat of bluegrass is provided by the bass and guitar—it is the basis of all the rest. The time is what you do with the beat of the music (involving the rhythmic placement of specific notes). Only Bill Monroe can play the music in this manner that we call bluegrass. Other groups have the beat, but Bill is the only man that has the true time, and the only man you can learn it from so that people will pay to hear it.

This matter of making money at bluegrass is no mere economic factor, either. Bluegrass demands great technical skill and constant creative ingenuity. You cannot devote your full attention to music unless you are making your living at it. Furthermore, if you can live from playing music, it shows you're reaching your audience—at least in the bluegrass field, where very few musicians are doing this successfully. Haney believes that only talent and great sincerity will insure long-term financial success in bluegrass:

> The people know when you're transferring your mind through your hands to them, and that's when you're playing bluegrass. And that's what we did yesterday—to thousands, which has been my dream—and that's why we had the festival. I saw men crying; one time I had to leave the stage myself.

Haney was speaking of the climax of the festival weekend, the History of Bluegrass show[2] which took up five hours of Sunday afternoon. Many of the listeners had been at Cantrell's Horse Farm, on the scene of the festival, since Friday afternoon—constantly bombarded by bluegrass coming from a record-seller's loudspeaker, from the stage, and from groups of pickers scattered all over the 240-acre grounds. They might have been expected to be somewhat desensitized by four long instrumental workshops, three lengthy concerts, and countless hours of informal discussion and music. Perhaps, in fact, they were.

But Sunday's final show broke all such temporary barriers between musicians and audience. On the stage, before better than three thousand people, the history of Monroe's band was partially recreated as he was joined by the greats of bluegrass in the order in which they had appeared in his band over the past twenty-five years. Some important figures were missing, like Flatt and Scruggs, Rudy Lyle, Bobby Hicks, Vassar Clements, Kenny Baker (curiously, fiddlers seemed rare at this festival). But onto that rough board stage in the afternoon heat strode Clyde Moody, Don Reno, Benny Martin, Mac Wiseman, Jim Eanes, Carter Stanley, Jimmy Martin, and Larry Richardson. To follow, there was an unprecedented series of songs with Bill Monroe and the Stanley Brothers performing together (Ralph Stanley has never before worked with Monroe[3]), and finally a group of numbers by Bill's current Blue Grass Boys: Pete Rowan (guitar), Gene Lowinger (fiddle), Lamar Grier (banjo), and Bill's son, Jimmy (bass). Lowinger had been playing a good part of the afternoon along with great alumni of the band, and it was a revelation for many to see how inspired Gene's music became. If there was ever an ideal opportunity to learn bluegrass fiddle, it arose for Lowinger, and he profited magnificently.[4] Bill's other present members, like Lowinger, are city boys (Lowinger, New York; Rowan, Massachusetts; Grier, Washington, D.C.). All drew the praise of observers for their ability to work with their leader, and later in the

---

2. Advertised as "The Blue Grass Music Story."

3. Ralph Stanley had filled in with the band in the fifties.

4. Shortly after this article was published, Lowinger left the Blue Grass Boys, replaced in February 1966 by Richard Greene.

evening, Monroe and Haney predicted that this would be one of Bill's best bands, not only because the boys are talented, but because they deeply want to master bluegrass under Monroe's tutelage.

The mere fact that missing major bluegrass groups can easily be listed—Flatt and Scruggs, McReynolds Brothers,[5] Osborne Brothers—is indicative of the historical and musical importance of the festival even apart from its documentation of the Monroe story. And the festival was exciting for still other reasons.

Spectators witnessed the swift change that came over Benny Martin's fiddling as he had an opportunity to play with fine bluegrass musicians again after some years; and Martin's reunion with Reno (the two had started the original Tennessee Cut-Ups in 1949)[6] led to an announcement that Benny and Don would reunite on a permanent basis.[7]

The festival was the first chance for many people to hear the separate bands of Red Smiley and Reno, who amicably parted company last November. Similarly, the bands of Jimmy Martin and Larry Richardson, groups very faithful to the Monroe sound but seldom seen outside the South, got their first live hearing by many northern listeners. Lamar Grier became a permanent Blue Grass Boy on Saturday.[8]

And finally, the festival provided a fine chance for fans to compare bands; they could now easily see the contrast between the generally light and relaxed approaches of Reno and Smiley, the rich and flowing sound of the sharp-voiced Stanley Brothers, the gentle sweetness of Mac Wiseman, and the fierce and painful quality of the music of Monroe himself.

Whether you looked at bluegrass as a communal phenomenon, participated in by hundreds of musicians and thousands of listeners, or as a creative impulse stemming ultimately from Bill Monroe—and both of these visions are necessary to an understanding of the whole style—this first Bluegrass Festival was a priceless opportunity to take stock of the twenty-five years of bluegrass history. A deepened appreciation and understanding was the inevitable result.

Originally published in *Sing Out!* 15:6 (Jan. 1966): 65–69. Reprinted by permission of the publisher.

EDITOR'S COMMENTS

Bill was the central focus of the first bluegrass festival, held September 3–5, 1965, in western Virginia. Folklorist and musician Smith wrote this report on the historic event, which appeared four months later in the January 1966 issue of *Sing Out!*

Earlier in the summer of 1965, the *Journal of American Folklore* had published Smith's "An Introduction to Bluegrass," the first treatise on the music to appear in

---

5. Jim and Jesse.
6. Formed after the two had worked together as Blue Grass Boys during 1948–49.
7. The partnership of Don Reno and Benny Martin lasted until December 1966.
8. Grier had been auditioning prior to this.

the scholarly publication. When Smith arrived at the festival site on September 2, he had a copy with him. Bill read it (or someone read it to him, interpreting the "ten dollar words" that fill the piece) and later that evening, when Smith asked, Bill let the young folklorist know what he thought about it. According to Rosenberg in *Bluegrass: A History,* "Smith's statement that the music began with Monroe's post-war band, and his inclusion of Earl Scruggs–style banjo as one of the defining characteristics of the music were, Monroe told Smith angrily, 'damn lies' as far as he was concerned."[1] Hoping to set the record straight, Smith wrote the *Sing Out!* piece.

Less than three months before the first bluegrass festival, on June 30, 1965, Bill's close friend Ira Louvin died in a car accident in Missouri. Bill sang "Swing Low, Sweet Chariot" at his funeral, as Louvin had jokingly told him to do about a year earlier.

Note

1. Neil V. Rosenberg, *Bluegrass: A History* (Urbana: University of Illinois Press, 1985), 10.

The High, Lonesome Sound of Bill Monroe and His Blue Grass Boys (excerpt)

RALPH RINZLER

Ever since the mid-thirties when Bill Monroe first appeared on the country music scene, fellow performers as well as critics and fans have sought to understand and explain this terse Kentuckian and his passionate music. For more than a quarter of a century Bill spoke only through his music, but he did so with such eloquence that thousands heard and accepted this musical gospel. In recent years Bill has spoken frankly of the influences which he feels have most strongly affected his development. He has proven himself to be as articulate verbally as he is musically, yet no amount of knowledge about the man, his life, and his music can wholly clarify the mystery of Bill Monroe and his intensely personal music.

His savage, arrogant, intransigent spirit is his hallmark. The brilliant tenor and a huge catalogue of rhythms, modal tunes, and instrumental techniques are his tools. The products are musical translations of a man's soul laid bare.

This collection of songs represents a side of Bill Monroe's music and nature which is an inextricable part of blue grass music.[1] Many call it "that high, lonesome sound"— while some say "it's white blues"—"mountain blues." Most of the songs are highly personal, autobiographical pieces . . . all are lonesome and bluesy sounding.[2]

---

1. Note that three years after his *Sing Out!* article ("Bill Monroe—'The Daddy of Blue Grass Music'"), Rinzler is still spelling the name of the music with two words.
2. The album included "Letter from My Darlin'," "Memories of Mother and Dad," "On the Old Kentucky Shore," and "Memories of You."

⚬

I was going to be sure through my life I played some blues, because I always loved it that well. I was going to play the blues in my way of playing them. I use stuff that I heard from a little boy and notes that just sunk in my mind and I kept. If you'll listen to my work you'll see that there's blues in it. You know, a colored man isn't the only man that's ever had the blues, and he's not the only fellow that's ever had hardships, that went through a lot. If you're down in the dumps you like to play the blues . . . if you feel you been mistreated, why you still want to sing the blues. You don't want to tell your story to somebody, 'cause you don't want to put yourself on him, you know, but you'll sing about it; and you get enjoyment out of it.

If you get blue, why you get enjoyment out of singing the blues, and you'll write them, and you'll add them to different numbers, and you'll put them in places through numbers that you want to put them in . . . notes and things. I think you can watch people—any kind of work they do in the way of music—and tell pretty well through their life what they've gone through, if you watch it close enough.

Singing the blues, there's not everybody that can sing them. There's people that can go through them, but they don't really put in there what's really there . . . there's a lot in the blues, if you get it out of there. The notes and things will work the same as the words; they'll tell you lots of things, if you want to put yourself in there and be just thinking like the music goes.

If you study music deep enough, old-time music, why you get to learn what's good for it and what's not good for it. You just can't play it now and not pay any attention to it and do that. You've got to be thinking about it, maybe when you're working doing other things; you've got to keep your mind on that music to really get deep in it. I think I've studied old-time music deeper than anybody in the country. It all leads to where I know what was the foundation of a number in old-time music. I know what's back there and you can get it out or you can not get it out; but if it's not brought out, why I don't care nothing about really listening to it.

And it's the same thing about a song . . . just get in there and run through the words and not make them stand out. There's places in a song that some words should mean more than others and most times it's on the end of a line where they mean something. Just a voice that runs straight, that don't vary either way, why it doesn't do me any good. I like to hear up and down . . . what I mean, I like to ease up, and then, you know, pick it back up here . . . you need some volume. And that's the kind of way with a fiddle piece or any kind of number. I like to see and hear it played that way. You don't have to play a hot break on any number if you'll get down and pick out the stuff that's really in that song.

There's so many of the people that's come along today that sings like the other man sings. You take a fellow that's had money all his life, and his parents had money, and he got a good education . . . never wanted for anything. He never had anything to have the blues about much . . . had everything he wanted. You got to take a fellow that's broke a lot of times to really have the blues. Did you ever have the blues?

———————————————————————————

Originally published as liner notes for *The High, Lonesome Sound of Bill Monroe and His Blue Grass Boys,* Decca Records, DL 4780, released June 1966. Reprinted by permission of the estate of Ralph Rinzler.

EDITOR'S COMMENTS

Shortly after his 1963 *Sing Out!* article ("Bill Monroe—'The Daddy of Blue Grass Music'") was published, Rinzler became Bill's personal manager, and during the next four years he was involved in every aspect of Bill's reemergence as a major star. Early on, he convinced Decca Records to issue several albums of Bill's 1950s recordings, made all the more interesting and understandable to newer fans by Rinzler's liner notes, which included background information and listings of personnel for each recording. For *The High, Lonesome Sound of Bill Monroe and His Blue Grass Boys,* released in June 1966, Rinzler combined Bill's answers to several interview questions, permitting Bill to speak at length for the first time in print.

The first issue of *Bluegrass Unlimited* was published in July 1966, about a month after the release of this album.

"Bill Monroe: King of Blue Grass Music" (interviews)

DOUG BENSON

Program #1—Blue Grass Music Past and Present

Announcer (over Monroe instrumental): Radio McGill presents "Bill Monroe: King of Blue Grass Music," a series of programs about the man who pioneered the original blue grass[1] sound, thus introducing a new and vital element into country music. Bill Monroe is one of the most significant figures in the realm of indigenous American music because he has carved out—almost single-handed—a new style of music that has subsequently been taken up by others on a large scale. He is *the* definitive blue grass mandolinist and *the* definitive blue grass singer. Monroe's soaring tenor voice and a marked blues influence have led to the use of the phrase "high, lonesome sound" in reference to his music.

When Monroe and his Blue Grass Boys were in Montreal in November of 1966,

———————————————————————————

1. Benson, like Rinzler, spelled the name of the music with two words.

Radio McGill conducted extensive interviews with Monroe himself and with two of his sidemen—fiddler Richard Greene and lead singer–guitarist Pete Rowan—both city born and bred and both highly articulate young men. Leader and sidemen were interviewed on separate occasions so as not to inhibit the speakers in any way. When you do hear their voices juxtaposed, it is only as a result of subsequent editing of the tapes.

Bill Monroe's attitude is like that of most serious classical musicians toward his music. In conversation as well as in performance, his great respect for, and profound belief in, his music become immediately apparent. It is this conviction that has enabled Monroe to resist the trends of Nashville throughout the years. Bill Monroe stands out on the contemporary country music scene as "the man who won't sell out"!

(Music level up till end of instrumental)

This initial program we have entitled "Blue Grass Music Past and Present." And Bill Monroe is the unifying thread between past and present in blue grass music: he is the originator and has been the driving force in this field of music for more than a quarter of a century. He is still the best all-round blue grass musician today and shows no sign of letting up. In our interview with Bill, we asked him what blue grass music is and what elements have gone into its composition.

Bill: To start with, I wanted to have a music different from anybody else; I wanted to originate something. I wanted to put all of the ideas that I could come up with, that I could hear of different sounds and, of course, I've added the old Negro blues to blue grass. And we have some of the Scotch music in it—the bagpipes—and we also have hymn singing—you'll notice that down through the melodies and through blue grass. Starting with numbers like the "Mule Skinner Blues," when I first started, it had a timing to it—the beat—that just fit perfect for what I wanted to do. It's faster than most people would do "Mule Skinner" and it's in a time that you could dance by. It's good to listen to and it's good for your lead instruments like the fiddle to play the music, to play "Mule Skinner," 'cause it's got the blues in it and it just makes it perfect like that. We use the mandolin as a kind of a rhythm instrument in the group, and it sets perfect for the mandolin to keep the time the way we've got it arranged.

Benson: The rhythm of the mandolin adds a lot of drive to the music, as well.

Bill: Yeah, it works kinda like a drum would work in an orchestra.

Announcer: "Mule Skinner Blues" was written and recorded circa 1930 by the "Singing Brakeman," Jimmie Rodgers. It was number 8 in his series of Blue Yodels.[2] We asked Bill where *he* got the idea to record his own version of this song.

Bill: Why, Jimmie Rodgers, he was the first to come out with yodel numbers that I ever got to hear. He could sing 'em so good; had a wonderful voice and he played a good guitar. I always liked his singing and playing, and I guess that's how come I

---

2. "Blue Yodel No. 8" ("Mule Skinner Blues") was recorded by Rodgers on July 11, 1930, and released in Feb. 1931 by RCA Victor.

wanted to do "Mule Skinner." I wanted to put the new touch to it, and I wanted to have a different yodel from what he had. You know, I have a yodel with "Mule Skin-ner"—it's got a little laugh on the end of it—and when I seen that it would sell, that little yodel would help sell the number, why, I knew then we had something going that would be to my advantage on down through the years, with the timing of that number and everything. And with the Blue Grass Boys, it's been kinda like you going to school—you've got a good teacher over you, somebody that knows what you should do and what you shouldn't do. So we have had to kinda set a pattern with blue grass, and, of course, each year, why, I have brought out a little something dif-ferent as we've gone along. Something that's helped me and helped blue grass—I have had a lot of different people to work for me. I've been in it 27 years now . . . and I like the friendship of a man, but I don't think I would've liked to have kept the same musician for 27 years, because his ideas would run out . . . and with bring-ing in new men along to learn to play blue grass, with their ideas, why, it's helped advance blue grass along each year.

Announcer: We asked Bill how he first became interested in music as a young boy.

Bill: My mother could sing and she could play a fiddle. Of course, I really learnt to play from my uncle Pen Vandiver. I can remember hearing them play, and I would try to sing off to myself where nobody could hear me, and I knew that someday I could sing a song like the "Mule Skinner"—or any country song—because my voice would be high and could do that.

Announcer: There are two distinct influences which Bill Monroe recalls from this period of his life and both of these are clearly manifested in his unique musical style. His mother's brother—Pen Vandiver—was a fiddler of considerable talent and local renown.

Bill often talks of childhood memories of his uncle Pen fiddling "lonesome tunes," and the importance of his uncle Pen's playing—plus the blues influence of Arnold Shultz—cannot be overestimated in the subsequent development of Bill's "high, lonesome sound."

In response to a question, Bill reminisces about his uncle Pen:

Bill: He played for a lot of square dances in Kentucky. There wasn't many mu-sicians around, and back in the early days, I had to learn to play a guitar; he would let me go along with him to play guitar while he was playing the fiddle, and we'd make from from two dollars-and-a-half up to five—never over five dollars a night. So I really have to give him a lot of credit for my playing and, really, I guess, the roots of blue grass.

Announcer: At one of the dances where Bill was backing up his uncle on guitar, he met Arnold Shultz, a Negro fiddler and guitar picker whose name is almost leg-endary in that country. The young Monroe was greatly impressed with Shultz's play-ing, and although he did not sing, Bill recalls that he could "whistle the blues" bet-ter than anyone around.

Bill: It was about the last days that I spent around in Kentucky—I left there when

I was 18—and I had got acquainted with this old colored man that played a guitar, and he could play some of the prettiest blues that you ever listened to. He could also play a fiddle, and me and him has played for some dances, you know, just the fiddle and guitar. But that's where the blues come into my life, hearing old Arnold Shultz play 'em. He was the best blues player around in our part of the country there in Kentucky, and that's where most of the people that plays a guitar today—that's all come from old Arnold Shultz. It come on down through Mose Rager, from him into Merle Travis, and from him into Chet Atkins. That's where all that style of playing come from.

Benson: Now with your musical talent, you could no doubt have excelled on any number of instruments. Why did you choose the mandolin as your specialty?

Bill: Well, there was three of us brothers, to start with, that tried to play music and, of course, they was older than I was, and one of 'em—Birch—wanted to play the fiddle. Following him was another brother, Charlie Monroe, and he, of course, loved the guitar . . . and we knew that there shouldn't be two guitars and a fiddle or two fiddles and a guitar, so it left me to get some other instrument . . . and the banjo wasn't to be heard of then much—there was a few played it—and no bass fiddle at all hardly. So I got the mandolin. I wound up with that.

Announcer: I couldn't help but chuckle as Bill explained why he took up the mandolin, but it's really a sobering moment when you stop and consider that there very nearly was no mandolin in blue grass music, and that the man who literally put the mandolin on the map arrived at his choice of instrument strictly by the process of elimination.[3]

In his article on Bill Monroe in *Sing Out!* (February–March 1963), Ralph Rinzler makes it clear that Bill's unique and original mandolin style was the result of conscious effort on his part. Bill Monroe deliberately set out to pioneer a style all his own (having determined at age 13 to do so), and there can be no doubt that he has succeeded brilliantly.

Bill: Learning to play the mandolin, Doug, that's something else that I would like to tell you. In originating blue grass music I originated a different style of a mandolin. I wanted to be sure that I played a different style from other people through the country that played a mandolin. So that's worked in with blue grass too. It's been a big help to blue grass.

Benson: You've been a great innovator on the mandolin, and, of course, the instrument that a musician plays is important to him. Tell us about your mandolin—it's famous in itself. When and where did you get ahold of it?

Bill: I found that mandolin in Miami, Florida, about 25 years ago, I guess. It was in a barber shop laying in the window with a sign on it for $125.[4] I needed a mandolin and so I wound up with that one.

---

3. Earlier (ca. 1966), Bill told Rinzler in an unpublished interview, "I *had* to take the mandolin. I was put on that."

4. Bill probably found the mandolin in Miami, Florida, in 1945. See the editor's comments, third paragraph.

Benson: Why is it that on your mandolin the place where the company name appears has been scratched off?

Bill: Richard (Adams),[5] he's leading into something there! (chuckles) Well, I tell you . . . the mandolin I have is a Gibson, of course, and I had to send it back to the factory. Every time I'd need frets in the mandolin, I would get a new fingerboard put on it. And this time that I sent it back, the neck had been broke off; it needed a finger-board; it needed re-finishing; it needed keys—it needed everything, mind you. So I sent it back and they sent it back to me with just the neck put back on and that was about all. I don't know whether they just overlooked it or something and didn't do everything I said or not. But it didn't make me feel good, so I thought, well, I didn't have to have the name of Gibson. They had never done much for me. But they have done a lot for other people and I guess it's a good thing that I got this Gibson man-dolin, because I do think it's the best mandolin—especially for me—in the country.

Announcer: One of the most important things in blue grass is the singing. Bill had some remarks on the vocal aspect of his music:

Bill: I had worked with my brother till I was 27 years old, and I had never sung the lead of a number. I had always sung tenor. But starting the Blue Grass Boys, I wanted to do yodel numbers and solo numbers and still keep the tenor that I had learnt when we worked as the Monroe Brothers. So I've used duets and trios and we've always carried the Blue Grass Quartet too, because I do like to do a couple or three hymns in any concert, you know. I was the first one to ever have a quartet in a string band down south. Could have been some other parts of the country that had them, but in our part I was the first one.

Announcer: We asked Bill about the contribution his current fiddler—Richard Greene—is making to the music.

Bill: Richard is adding a lot to blue grass. It's hard to keep him from adding too much. Well, you could easy get blue grass to swinging, you know, and get it too modern . . . and I don't want it that way. The biggest job of blue grass is to keep out what don't belong in it.

Benson: When did the element of twin and triple fiddles enter into blue grass?

Richard Greene: When Bill put it in! (chuckles) Ask Bill what the first one was. I don't really know.

Bill: I was down at the Grand Ole Opry in Nashville and, of course, we rehearse a lot and this Saturday night there was a boy—Dale Potter, I believe it was—back there in our dressing room that could play a good second fiddle. So he got to fiddling with us and it sounded so good that I was gonna start on the Grand Ole Opry two weeks from that night with two fiddles—and one week from that night Hank Snow started with two fiddles. We use the same dressing room, Hank and I, and he liked it so well that he got two fiddles—Chubby Wise and Tommy Mack Vaden, I believe, was fiddling for Hank then.[6]

---

5. Sound engineer for the interviews.

6. This was probably in early 1954. Flatt and Scruggs had recorded with twin fiddles as early as 1951, and Mac Wiseman used them on his recordings beginning in 1953.

Benson: What is the important thing in a blue grass fiddle player?

Bill: Well, I think a fiddler, he should play all the old-time fiddle numbers like they was wrote and there's a lot of different notes that fiddlers today don't never learn—he skips through them, you know. And I think he should know all the shuffles and licks with the bow. I think that's one thing that makes a good fiddler. And to be a good blue grass fiddler, you're in a higher class of fiddle music than you would think about. It's not like the old-time square dance numbers that was made 30 to 40 years ago. With having the blues and everything that's been added to blue grass, if he plays a good blue grass fiddle, he's on up, you know—he's really a good fiddler. Ain't everybody that comes along can play a blue grass fiddle.

Announcer: As we pointed out earlier, Bill's fiddling uncle, Pen Vandiver, was an important influence in his development as a musician. Bill wrote a song called "Uncle Pen." It's one of his all-time classics and Bill is justifiably proud of it.

Bill: Now, take the number called "Uncle Pen," for instance. You know, everything is in that number that should be in it, because it's an old-time number and wrote about an old-time fiddler and it's a true song. You wouldn't want to go swinging on that number, you know, putting a lot of extra stuff in—because it would take away from the number, and you nearly know that that number's got everything in it that it should have.

(Play Bill's 1950 recording of "Uncle Pen.")

Announcer: Bill admires a few of the stars of commercial country music:

Bill: But there's a lot of country music—they call it country music—today that I don't like, that's just out to sell a record and they think if they sell a record that they're worth $1,000 that night and they're not, you know. I don't like that kind of musician. Some of 'em are the kind of people that if they made a little money out of it, they would still be an entertainer and make records, because they think that's wonderful, you know. A man who plays music should do his best, because if you're on radio or television, there's so many thousands watching you and listening to you that it's not something to just be played around with. I think it should be mastered.

Well, I never thought that electric instruments would work in blue grass. Of course, people like Bob Wills . . . it's got its place there, because they play for dancing and I think it's a wonderful thing for them. But I don't think it would be a bit of good for blue grass without you went all electric, you know, everything was electric.

Benson: Then it wouldn't be blue grass.

Bill: No, I don't think so. I can show you a lot of blue grass groups that has a lot of blue grass playing, but they don't have any beat to their music, and I guess that drums probably helps them.

(Hit Bill's 1955 recording of "Brown County Breakdown," hold for 12 seconds, then under.)

Bill: Doug, I have tried to keep blue grass, you know, not let it get out too far and I think that's the reason the country people really went along with the Blue Grass

Boys. And you know that blue grass has got a lot of expression in it—there's no way around it, it's got that.

(Music up for 15 seconds, then under for Announcer's extro. End of Program #1.)

Program #2—Bill Monroe: The Man And The Legend

(Hit Bill's 1954 recording of "Roanoke," then down and Announcer over music:)

Announcer: Welcome to Part 2 of the Radio McGill series "Bill Monroe: King of Blue Grass Music." This program is entitled "Bill Monroe: The Man And The Legend."

Bill: One thing about blue grass, Doug, that I don't like about it: the more you talk about it, the more it sounds like you're bragging on it. I don't want the people to think that about me, because I don't like to brag.

Greene: Bill has always gone up and he'll always go up until the end. It'll take some great physical catastrophe to stop him. (Pete Rowan: Like getting old.) No, I don't think he'll get old that way. I just can't see it.

Rowan: Take a banjo player, a guitar player, a fiddle player, and a bass player, and say they're all competent musicians, and put them with Bill and here's this driving force through all the other music in the band.

Greene: He is possibly the finest musician, the man containing the most musicianship in the entire field.

Announcer: On the first show in this series, Bill Monroe himself did most of the talking. On this program we will be hearing mainly from Richard Greene and Pete Rowan, two members of Monroe's band, the Blue Grass Boys.

(Music level up and sustain till end of "Roanoke.")

Announcer: There is definitely an aura of legend that surrounds Bill Monroe. As Richard Greene sees it, this aura is twofold:

Greene: There are two auras of legend—there's the urban and the rural.

Benson: Develop that. That's very interesting.

Greene: Due to his accomplishments and who he is and everything, Bill stands so high above all the country people that he comes in contact with and—I mean, he's not condescending or aloof—it's just that he has recorded for 30 years and in the music world of the country, he's just been the leader for so long and he's done things that to them they could never conceive of doing . . . (pause) . . . well, maybe that explains it enough.

Rowan: And he hasn't slipped either. He hasn't succumbed to things like dope or drinking or any of the things that some of the modern country musicians have.

Announcer: In the city, the Bill Monroe legend is a more recent phenomenon, since it wasn't until the folk music boom in the early sixties that Monroe received any wide exposure in the big cities of the northeastern U.S. or on the West Coast.

Greene: It had been very hard to see him in person; all you had to go on were some stories and some records. By the time you did see him, you had this fantastic thing in your mind—I even had it myself when I first met him. In fact, when I first met him (January 27, 1966, an hour or so prior to stepping on stage as fiddler for the Blue Grass Boys in concert at McGill University in Montreal.—Benson), I didn't even know it was him. I asked somebody, "Where is he?" because here was this heavy, big guy and I thought of him as a little guy because of his high voice—I know these are ridiculous associations I had—and he was dressed very casually. They had made a long road trip the previous day, and he was tired and sullen. And it was a tremendous shock to first meet him. Since I have gotten to know him, I can see from close quarters what kind of person he is and I have a great deal of respect for him, but it's not at all the kind of respect I had before I met him. It's now supported with experience.

One friend of mine in Los Angeles—when Bill played the Ash Grove[7]—interviewed him on a tape recorder backstage and this was the greatest moment of his life. At the time it was traumatic because the cord of the tape recorder tripped Bessie Lee[8] as she was walking into the place and she fell sprawling on the floor or something. This is how the thing started and he was helpless, the poor guy. Now that I know Bill, that was probably nothing but humorous to Bill. It was nothing to worry about at all. When you don't have the actual experience to relate to, all you have is hearsay and your imagination is much more free. I guess that's all it amounts to.

And there were stories going around—I'm not too good at remembering things—I just heard things about how he used to spook Chubby Wise all the time. One time he attacked him from behind as they were walking out of a restaurant, stories like this . . . or when somebody was driving a car and Bill wanted to get out for a minute and the car happened to be stopped by a cliff and Bill got out of the car and fell down the cliff . . .

Rowan: . . . got back in the car and said, "Drive on, boy."

Announcer: Is Bill Monroe a religious man?

Rowan: He chooses religious songs, or some of them anyways, for the meaning they have to him. Traveling on the bus, he'll sing hymns to himself, hymns that we sing on shows or that he's recorded.

Greene: He's not a devout churchgoer, I wouldn't say. . . .

Rowan: But he's a religious kind of man, I think. He feels a great contact with the Absolute.

(Play Bill's 1958 recording of "House of Gold")

Rowan: He works on his farm which develops incredible strength.

Greene: Yeah, we played the Black Poodle in Nashville[9] and we'd get through about 3:00 and he would go home and sleep in the field for about an hour and then,

---

7. A folk music club Bill played regularly in the 1960s.
8. Bessie Lee Mauldin, Bill's companion and bassist.
9. A nightclub in downtown Nashville's "Printer's Alley."

when dawn came up, he'd work all day till dark and then come and play the Poodle again—and this is the kind of schedule he kept.

Benson: And he'd still be in top form as a musician?

Greene: Yeah. Those were some of his best moments.

Announcer: When we asked Bill about this grueling schedule and the kind of stamina it required, he simply shrugged it off.

Bill: I don't know, Doug. . . . Back to the farming: you know, I was raised on a farm and I enjoy it so much. I like to do a lot of things on the farm that maybe down through the busy years of music, why, I missed, you know? In the spring I farm and raise cattle and hogs; and I have a pack of foxhounds that I enjoy going out a couple of nights a week, if I'm around Nashville, and listen to them run. I enjoy that kind of life. When I'm doing that, I just kind of use playing on the side. (chuckles) I work, you know, and play music on the side. But I have always been a feller, I guess, could work 24 hours if I had to do it, you know, and stand up pretty good under it.

Rowan: And another thing, Doug, that is very important in Bill's training as a musician was playing for square dances. Now there's another example of—you establish time for the dancers and then you play to the sound of their feet, just like with flamenco music—it's done to the sound of the dancers' feet. And I think that had an unquestionable effect on Bill's playing. He'll sometimes break into a fiddle rhythm on the mandolin, sort of a "Georgia shuffle," I guess you'd call it, and he says, "Now, can't you see the dancers?" or something like that. He'll talk as if he was playing for a dance. He talks about fiddle tunes all having a "time" and the time is based on the dance. He's played for the dancers and we haven't played for the dancers, so we know nothing of what he's talking about, except what comes out of him. And another time, we were in New York, driving down Fifth Avenue on a hay wagon for the New York Folk Festival,[10] and it was drawn by a horse and Bill was sitting in the back of the wagon and you could hear the horse's hooves clomping along and he was playing "Gray Eagle" and he called my attention to the fact that he was playing in time with the horse's hooves. So this recurs all through his music, you know, like playing to trains . . . sounds . . . sounds. . . .

(Hit Bill's 1958 recording of "Scotland," hold for 60 seconds, then under. . . .)

Benson: Does he do anything like these exercises you mentioned to build up his own fingers or dexterity?

Rowan: He just goes and does nine or ten hours' work on his farm. That does it.

Greene: He's not that kind of musician. That's a discipline; that's a whole other area of music. I think he said once that when he first started out, he used to practice every day, but I'm sure it wasn't scales and technique and stuff like that.

Rowan: No, but the practicing every day had the same effect as practicing every day—*as* scales. You know, he just played all the time. That's all you have to do, really. Traveling on the road with Bill, playing every night in a town or in a club—you're

---

10. June 1965.

there all the time playing, and that's the most important thing you can do to develop yourself as a musician, I think.

Adams: I get the impression that in the eyes of most blue grass people Bill Monroe is a figure to be looked up to as nothing short of a god.

Greene: That's what he is. That's the position he occupies in this field.

Benson: The "Creator and Preserver" sort of thing, if you want to throw in theological terms.

Greene: But besides that, he is possibly the finest musician, the man containing the most musicianship, the highest level of skill in music—in the entire field. The singing—there's no question about it at all. And instrumentally—to me there's no question. I mean there are great musicians in the field, but not great the way he is. Earl Scruggs was a fantastic musician and innovator, but a lot of what he did depended upon what Bill did first. And he still does it today. Every time we play, he'll just play music that's "up there." It's not just a matter of some mystical reverence. His actual deeds are more accomplished.

Benson: There is an aura of legend that surrounds him, but it's completely justified, you see, by his phenomenal genius.

Rowan: His whole creed is not to let anything slip, not to let anything fall, and while keeping his music up there, to bring out the best in other musicians and to let them bring out the best in themselves.

Announcer: Ralph Rinzler has written about "the manner in which Monroe actually breathes fire into the musicians who surround him." Does he really function as a catalyst, urging his band members on, through some intangible means?

Rowan: Yes, I'd say he does.

Benson: How? Can you express that kind of influence?

Rowan: Well, take any group of musicians and say they're all competent musicians and put them with Bill and here's this driving force through all the other music in the band, even if it's only for one show. His time is solid and perfect and he holds himself responsible for the rest of the music, if it's blue grass. Everything seems to rest on his shoulders—the time and. . . .

Benson: At his Roanoke festival, Carlton Haney was always talking about the "time" of blue grass. What is this exactly?

Rowan: Well, that's Bill's strong offbeat keeping that time, but Carlton imbues "time" with mystical meaning also.

Greene: There are lots of mandolin players in the field and they all keep time but, you see, Bill keeps it in a way—I mean, this is just the offbeat on the mandolin; there are other things that time is composed of—but, the offbeat on the mandolin, he does it so exactly right. I haven't seen anyone on any instrument hit the offbeat as precisely as he does. It's just so solid and perfect.

Rowan: Just chords . . . and, of course, the chords on that mandolin come out as a . . . I don't know how to describe it, except that instead of hearing a single note, or hearing the single notes in a chord, the chord seems to come out as a cluster of notes all at once, strong and sharp.

Announcer: Bill Monroe is such a phenomenal mandolin virtuoso that you don't ask if anyone is comparable to him as a performer on that instrument. You ask if anyone ever had a chance of coming close.

Greene: There is one person who plays the mandolin who at one time could have.

Benson: Bobby Osborne?

Greene: No, I'd say Frank Wakefield.

Benson: Tell us about that.

Greene: Now he's not deeply involved in music as he was before, a while ago. But he was after that style—he was after that picking style and the notes and everything—and he was like a child to Monroe—you know, his music—but it was the closest anyone came.

Benson: Was there a conscious attempt on his part?

Greene: Yeah, he listened to the records, got every note, every little thing, and he went after playing that kind of style. But he's let it slide; he hasn't been playing that kind of music, really, where you can do that all the time.

Benson: Playing with a city-oriented group like the Greenbriar Boys[11] would take the edge off that?

Greene: Yeah, they don't do Bill's songs. You see, you have to have those songs and that time, those changes . . . .

Benson: You have to play with Bill Monroe.

Greene: To play his style. His style is not only composed of what he does, but it's composed of everything else too—what he sings, what all the other instruments are doing. Now, the Greenbriar Boys don't play strictly blue grass, you know. They admit it. It's not a sin; that's just their choice.

Benson: How much longer do you think Bill will be an active performer?

Rowan: I think as long as he's able.

Greene: He keeps talking about ten years, which means . . . I mean, when anyone says they're going to do something for ten years and they've already done it for over thirty, it means that there's no point where he's going to stop. I think as long as he's alive—he's the type of individual that is not going to decay by natural processes; he's almost superhuman in a lot of ways, and I think as long as he breathes, he'll be on top of the field. There won't ever be a lapse. Like, well, you might say that Lester Flatt has gone down since some point. But Bill has always gone up and he'll always go up until the end.

Rowan: Until he stops playing?

Greene: Until he stops breathing. It'll take some great physical catastrophe to stop him.

Rowan: Like getting old.

Greene: I don't think he'll get old that way. I just can't see it. He's got too much fire in him.

Rowan: Well, it happens.

---

11. Wakefield had replaced Rinzler with the Greenbriar Boys by this time.

Greene: Sure it happens. It happens to everybody else, but there are always examples of people who—I've seen it—some people have enough fire that they just don't get old. Their hair gets grey, but they fight it and they stay on top. And I think he's one of the few people I've met who is going to do that—and who is *doing* it. He's already old in years,[12] but certainly not in other ways.

Benson: It would certainly be hard to imagine the extent of inner conflict that he would face if he felt that he was losing something and yet, a man like Monroe who, as you say, never wants to . . .

Greene: He just won't allow it to happen. He just . . .

Rowan: That would be the tragedy of Bill Monroe, if that happened.

Greene: Yeah, because he wouldn't allow it to happen and if it happened anyway, then . . .

Rowan: Well, one way or another, I don't think he'd let it happen. I think he'd stop before he hurt his own music.

Benson: He's been heard to say that if any of these other guys get as good as him, he'll quit. Now, whether that's facetious or just . . .

Rowan: I think he'll eventually stop traveling on the road, and he's talked about settling down to his place and teaching—actually teaching music—the way he does now, except instead of traveling, because the traveling is exhausting.

Benson: He would what—stay on the Opry and . . . ?

Rowan: Yeah, maybe do that.

Greene: The Opry will always be there.

Announcer: From the Decca album "The High, Lonesome Sound of Bill Monroe and his Blue Grass Boys," here is one of the many songs based on Bill's own life and experience—the 1952 recording of "Memories of Mother and Dad," preceded and followed by comments from Pete and Richard.

Rowan: What would you call that dissonance that they're singing there, because musically and poetically it's a beautiful thing.

Greene: That's a sustained 7th.

Rowan: O.K.

(Play "Memories of Mother and Dad.")

Benson: What comment would you make on that recording?

Rowan: Well, it's a good example of one of Bill's songs, because it relates to something from his own life, the death of his mother and father. The images in it are real images, like the tombstones and what's carved on them. And it has religious overtones. And musically, it makes use of—what did you call it—distended 7th—perverted . . .

Greene: You see, Bill doesn't think of it like that at all. What he did is: the chord line goes from G to C and so does the lead singer, but what Bill does, he just dropped down from G to the 7th note. He went (demonstrates with his voice), which is like

---

12. Bill was fifty-five years old at the time.

a blues line. But behind that, the rest of the band was going to another chord; that's what creates that sound.

Announcer: So much for the technical explanation. If you were to ask Bill himself why he sang it like that, he would probably answer something to the effect that "We just had to do it that way to make it right." He feels it should be done a certain way, so he does it a certain way. Bill Monroe has a black-and-white approach to his music: some things belong in it and some things don't. This attitude was manifested several times in our conversation. Bill would say things like: "Being a Blue Grass Boy is like going to school. You have a good teacher over you who knows what you should do and what you shouldn't do." . . . "The biggest job in blue grass is keeping out what doesn't belong in it." . . . or . . . "Take such-and-such a number. You know everything is in that number that should be in it." Bill's single-mindedness and deep conviction about what is right and what is wrong for his music is one of the factors that makes him great.

Bill: That's wonderful, for a musician to believe in himself, if he really knows that what he's doing is right. I have had some musicians with me that thought they was better than anybody that I'd ever had, you know, and they wasn't—they was about a tenth-rater, and they never would make a man as good as Brad Keith[13] or Rudy Lyle or Earl Scruggs. But they was fooled in their playing, you see? Now there's some people that know when they can play and how good they are, and they don't ever brag about it. And it's good for a man to know how good he really is.

(Hit Bill's 1953 recording of "Get Up John," hold, then under for Announcer's extro. End of Program #2.)

Originally published in *Bluegrass Unlimited* 2:5 (Nov. 1967): 4–6; 2:5 (Dec. 1967): 3–5; 2:8 (Feb. 1968): 11–12; and 2:11 (May 1968): 2–5. Reprinted by permission of the author.

EDITOR'S COMMENTS

Benson, a Canadian bluegrass enthusiast, interviewed Bill and Blue Grass Boys Greene and Rowan on November 8 and 9, 1966, and produced a series of four radio programs that aired shortly thereafter on the student-run station at McGill University in Montreal. Programs #1 and #2 (reprinted here) and the first half of program #3 were transcribed and published in five parts in the then-new *Bluegrass Unlimited* magazine, beginning in November 1967. (This selection differs from the original mainly in that the song cues have been simplified, with recording dates added.)

In program #1, which included the first verbatim interview with Bill to appear in print, it may be noticed that Benson "borrowed" a few memorable sentences from Rinzler's *Sing Out!* article, "Bill Monroe—'The Daddy of Blue Grass Music.'"

13. Banjoist William Bradford "Bill" Keith was called "Brad" by Bill Monroe because, as the oft-told story goes, Bill said there could be only one Bill in the band.

Bill's estimation of the number of years since he found his first Gibson F-5 mandolin appears to have influenced his often-stated belief that the year was 1941. However, that date is suspect because Bill said that he started using the instrument as soon as he found it, but several observers have noticed that the mandolin did not appear in publicity photos until 1945. A check of the carefully annotated receipts for posters ordered from Nashville's Hatch Show Print Company confirms that Bill did not perform in Miami until January 10–11, 1945, and it was probably then that he found the instrument. (Also, Bill would later say that he paid $150 for it.)

Rowan and Greene, featured in program #2, both left the Blue Grass Boys in the first week of March 1967, four months after the interviews.

Bill's first bluegrass festival at Bean Blossom, Indiana, was held in June 1967, about five months before the publication of the first installment of "Bill Monroe: King of Blue Grass Music."

"Growing Up in Rosine, Kentucky: An Interview with Bill Monroe"

EDITED BY ALICE (FOSTER) GERRARD

"At ten years old when some of your people dies it's not as hard on you as it is after you get on up, I don't think, to where you really understand a little bit better. And to know that was the last one of them there, that really hurt too. It's kind of like being put out on your own then, to look out for yourself. Brothers and sisters will help each other but they can't take the place of a father or mother.

"I felt lonesome . . . well, I guess, most of my life, a lot of days I'd feel like that. . . . I can see that through some of my music . . . I feel it down through the music, about lonely or lonesome, you know. If you was raised in a city you probably don't know so much about it, but being from the country, there wasn't much going on there and you have so much time to think and remember things, you know, that happened when you was a kid, and I can see that touch of the way that I feel down through my songs and through blues and that kind of stuff.

"In a way, at times, a lonesome feeling is a good feeling. If you're really moody, why, it seems like everything works together and you really get lonesome. . . . I think blues is awful bad to have. I think blues and being lonesome are two different things. You want to think things out, and you want to think about things that happened back years ago, and so many things that did happen, I've never forgotten about them and they cross my mind a lot of times. . . .

"Everybody in the country just called him 'Uncle Pen.' I can remember him, you know, when I was real small. I guess I can remember him on back when I was eight, nine years old. Back in them days you kept quiet and listened to what other older people talked about. If you didn't, you was run out of the room. Of a night, the older ones of the family would always ask him to play . . . if there was just a fiddle, why, he would play, and we'd set around him and we'd listen at him and watch him.

"I can remember Uncle Pen coming around to visit us on Sunday, bringing his family along and driving up with a team of mules. Either that or they would have a buggy—more so it was a wagon. I can remember them coming and spending a Sunday, or coming Saturday night and staying Saturday night and a while Sunday and then going back home. And we got to visit them once in a while like that, and I thought it was great to get to go to one of my aunts on the Vandiver's side and stay a weekend.

"Seemed like the Vandivers were gifted in music, just in their family. They could all play, they could all sing some, and they could fiddle the old-time breakdown numbers. And they played just to listen to and they liked it themselves. And I believe today that you have really got to like music . . . you've got to see something in your own playing to make it good for the people. You have to feel it in your heart and you've got to love to hear the melody and words and everything.

"My mother could play a fiddle too, but she didn't play it like Uncle Pen could play. She had a good high, clear voice—I could hear her singing around home, you know. She could dance the old-time backstep and that kind of stuff, and Uncle Pen could do the old-time Kentucky backstep and I learned how to do it from him. My father was a buck and wing dancer. I guess years ago they didn't have much to do— nothing to go to, and they danced, you know. They got enjoyment out of it; there's enjoyment, you know, to dance to music—to hear music and keep time with it, and, of course, the more steps you have, the more you enjoy it. It's just like kind of learning more about music.

"I have a wonderful picture of my father. When I was real small, you know, I was too small to go with him. He worked hard and he had men that worked for him and I wanted to go and when I couldn't go, maybe I would say something about it. I remember my mother would really get me. But later on, I got to seeing what kind of a man he really was, the kind of man I really wanted to follow. He was a truthful man, and honest, and would do you a favor. And I'm this much like him, if I do you a favor, I might ask you for one. That was the kind of man he was and I have tried to grow up under what kind of a man I thought he was like. I know I have an awful soft heart and I've often wondered about him—I imagine he did too.

"He had a much better education than I've got. He just went through the eighth grade, but back in them days, eighth grade was a good education. He kept his own books . . . don't matter what he bought, you'll find it in a book. If it was a plug of tobacco, sugar, anything—don't matter if it was a nickel, it was put in that book. I can see places in his bookkeeping where a man would work for thirty-five cents a day, or fifty cents, and I can remember before he passed away he was paying two and a half a day, so you can see that times changed.

"I was brought up the best way I could be brought up with what we had to do with. I could've had a better education and I could've had better clothes to wear to school, and I could've had better shoes to wear; the way it was I had one pair of shoes a year. I could've had a better chance, you know, but when your parents has got old and when your mother has died when you were ten, and when you're sixteen and your father is seventy, I don't guess they would do as much for you as they would if they was younger. Seems like they think that the older children should look after the little ones. If my folks would have had money, I could've had a better chance, but it leads back—if I'd had the best education in the world I might have not played music. So I guess things turned out better this way . . . I know what I'm here to do and what I've done all the way.

"One thing that did stay in my mind, and I can remember most of them, you know, is the fiddle numbers that Uncle Pen played. Now, that really stuck to me. I can play ninety-five percent of every tune that he played, and can still remember them. I must've listened to him awful close when he was playing.

"Uncle Pen used to play with a man by the name of Clarence Wilson—he played a five-string banjo. It's not the clawhammer style—that rapping style. It's a little different than that—with a thumb and finger. And my uncle Birch, he'd sit down and play the bass (it was smaller than a bass fiddle), and play it with a bow.

"I had some good uncles on the Monroe side, but they was working people and they didn't take time with us like Uncle Pen would have taken. Of course, my Uncle Birch Monroe, he was kind of like Uncle Pen; he would talk to all of us boys and girls, but they was a little different type of people from the Vandivers, seemed like. Uncle Pen treated me right—he treated me good. Back in the Depression days we'd set snares and traps for foxes and rabbits. And I would set them in the evening and the next morning he would go around on the trail where I had them set and he would bring in what I had caught. And I've seen him bring in as high as eight rabbits of a morning; now that's something. He really meant a lot to me; he was a wonderful uncle. He would tell me things that he thought I should do, and if he never told me anything, I knew I was doing pretty well right. You know, I don't think an uncle in this day and time means near as much as people like that meant to me back when I was young. I don't think you respect them like you did back then.

"He was a farmer, and then later on in life he done a lot of trading. Like, if he stayed the weekend with us, he'd start out on Monday morning and he'd go from one friend's house, or, on through to whoever he could run into. If he started out with a mule or a horse a-riding; if he had a pocketknife or something, he would keep trading, and maybe he'd come back at the end of that week with the same horse and a cow . . . so he must've been a good trader. I guess he enjoyed doing it and made a little something out of it. He was the kind of man that never spent any money . . . what he made, why, he kept. And I don't guess he ever banked any money. What he had, you know, was in his pocketbook.

"Learning his numbers gave me something to start on. One thing that he learnt me how to do was to keep time, and the shuffle that he had on the bow was the most perfect time that you ever heard. I give him credit for all of my timing.

"We did play for square dances when I was around twelve, thirteen years old. We used to ride mule and go play for square dances around the country. Any place that would want us, why, they'd send us word to come and we'd make a little money out of it; never over five dollars a night and most of the time a couple of dollars a night. He was a crippled man . . . he got throwed by a mule and was on crutches. He would still get on that mule with his crutches and I'd get on up behind him and we'd go play for square dances. Used to be they'd have them in Rosine, Kentucky, every Saturday night. When the weather got hot they'd have them at somebody's house that wanted to clear out a room or something, and just have a social square dance. They generally would start at 8:00 and go on up till midnight. Sometimes we'd have to go a mile and a half, two miles, three miles . . . of course, that was right back through dirt roads, you know, that was the kind of roads we was on.

"Uncle Pen's wife left and took the girl with her. The boy, Cecil, stayed with Uncle Pen. Later on, the boy died. I can remember him being buried there in Rosine. He must've been around twenty-two years old . . . I can remember them singing at his funeral[1] . . . And then my aunt, she passed away, and the daughter, she didn't live long either, and so Uncle Pen came on and stayed at our house because our father had died. There wasn't nobody left but just me and my two sisters, and Uncle Pen would stay with us. Then later on, why, Maude and Bertha moved with some of my other uncles and I stayed on with Uncle Pen.

"He done a lot of good things for me. A man that old, and crippled, that would cook for you and see that you had a bed and a place to stay and something for breakfast and dinner and supper, and you know it come hard for him to get it. . . . You eat sorghum molasses, and that's what we had sweet, and he'd fix bacon for breakfast, and maybe it was fried corn cakes, and then he might make it flour and make it three little cakes and put it in the skillet and fry it. So we might have eggs for breakfast and fried potatoes—that's a great dish in Kentucky, fried potatoes—and that's my favorite dish of all. And then at dinner he would have black-eyed peas and fat back meat in it and corn bread, and then he'd have us something for supper.

"But you know, just like that song . . . 'late in the evening, about sundown, high on the hill above the town' . . . I could hear him playing many evenings after I'd get through work. I would put my teams up downtown where I had a barn there and I could hear him playing out on the back porch with that fiddling. There wasn't no radios—there wasn't no other music in that town going but that. You know, I've heard him set out there and play them old-timers a lot of the years, and that fiddle would come down across town . . . and I guess it was three quarters of a mile up there.

"I was in Indiana (when he died in 1932) and that's the worst part of all of my life that I didn't get to go to his funeral. You know, people in a little town, they don't have telephones like they do today and that many years ago I guess it would have been hard to get in touch with us, and they probably thought that we couldn't get

---

1. Bill recorded one of the songs they sang, "Take Courage Un' Tomorrow," in 1988, released on *Southern Flavor*, MCA Records, MCA-42133.

off work, or it would take no telling how much money to have got us back, but that was the wrong way to look at it.

"I have started recording numbers, you know, that I learnt from Uncle Pen. I haven't done them down through the years, I've saved them ever since I've been in the business, but I've started now to recording them—the numbers that was played by Uncle Pen. He played numbers like 'Methodist Preacher,' 'Jenny Lynn,' and some you couldn't use the title now, like 'White Folks Ain't Treating Me Right,' and 'Going Up Caney,' 'Pretty Betty Martin,' 'The Lost Girl,' 'Boston Boy.' We recorded 'Methodist Preacher' and we recorded a number called 'The Death March.' They used this number no telling how many hundred years ago. I know there was an old gentleman in Kentucky that requested this to be played at his funeral and this man stood at the head of the grave and played this number with just the fiddle alone. Anyway . . . I've got about twenty-four, twenty-five of Uncle Pen's numbers that's never been used. I knew I was going to do them sometime and I want to do them now because if I don't do them nobody will ever know of them and they'll just be thrown away and lost.[2]

"Maybe if I hadn't heard him, I'd have never learned anything about music at all."

Originally published in *Sing Out!* 19:2 (July–Aug. 1969): 6–7, 10–11. Reprinted by permission of the publisher.

EDITOR'S COMMENTS

Gerrard (then Foster), of the well-known duo Hazel and Alice, interviewed Bill on May 16, 1969. She then extended the technique Rinzler used for his liner notes to *The High, Lonesome Sound of Bill Monroe and His Blue Grass Boys* to create an entire article for the July–August 1969 issue of *Sing Out!*

As Bill said, two of his uncle Pen's tunes had already been recorded at the time of the interview. Ten more would be recorded during the next two years, culminating in the release of the album *Bill Monroe's Uncle Pen*[1] in 1972. Five of the eight tunes mentioned in the article were included in the album (with "White Folks Ain't Treating Me Right" retitled "Poor White Folks" and "The Death March" becoming "The Dead March"). "Boston Boy" was recorded in 1994 and released that year on the MCA compilation *The Music of Bill Monroe: From 1936 to 1994*.[2] Unfortunately, "Pretty Betty Martin" and "The Lost Girl" were never recorded by Bill.

Notes

1. *Bill Monroe's Uncle Pen*, Decca Records, DL 75348, released June 1972.
2. *The Music of Bill Monroe: From 1936 to 1994*, MCA Records, MCAC/MCAD4-11048, released 1994.

---

2. Six of the eight tunes mentioned here were recorded. See the editor's comments, second paragraph.

Cover photo from *The Monroe Brothers: Their Life, Their Songs,* ca. 1937. (Courtesy of the Country Music Hall of Fame)

Bill and the original Blue Grass Boys, ca. 1939–40: Art Wooten, Bill, Cleo Davis, Amos Garren. By December 1939, they were regulars on NBC's weekly half-hour broadcasts of the Grand Ole Opry. (Courtesy of the Country Music Hall of Fame)

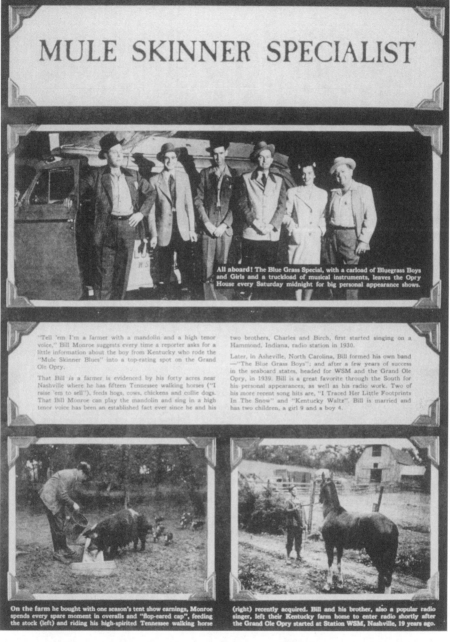

MULE SKINNER SPECIALIST

All aboard! The Blue Grass Special, with a carload of Bluegrass Boys and Girls and a truckload of musical instruments, leaves the Opry House every Saturday midnight for big personal appearance shows.

"Tell 'em I'm a farmer with a mandolin and a high tenor voice," Bill Monroe suggests every time a reporter asks for a little information about the boy from Kentucky who rode the "Mule Skinner Blues" into a top-rating spot on the Grand Ole Opry.

That Bill is a farmer is evidenced by his forty acres near Nashville where he has fifteen Tennessee walking horses ("I raise 'em to sell"), feeds hogs, cows, chickens and collie dogs. That Bill Monroe can play the mandolin and sing in a high tenor voice has been an established fact ever since he and his

two brothers, Charles and Birch, first started singing on a Hammond, Indiana, radio station in 1930.

Later, in Asheville, North Carolina, Bill formed his own band —"The Blue Grass Boys"; and after a few years of success in the seaboard states, headed for WSM and the Grand Ole Opry, in 1939. Bill is a great favorite through the South for his personal appearances, as well as his radio work. Two of his more recent song hits are, "I Traced Her Little Footprints In The Snow" and "Kentucky Waltz". Bill is married and has two children, a girl 9 and a boy 4.

On the farm he bought with one season's tent show earnings, Monroe spends every spare moment in overalls and "flop-eared cap", feeding the stock (left) and riding his high-spirited Tennessee walking horse

(right) recently acquired. Bill and his brother, also a popular radio singer, left their Kentucky farm home to enter radio shortly after the Grand Ole Opry started at Station WSM, Nashville, 19 years ago.

This page from *Purina's Grand Ole Opry and Checkerboard Fun-Fest Souvenir Album*, published in 1946, contains the first direct quote from Bill to appear in print. The band photo was taken in 1945: Bill, Jim Shumate, David "Stringbean" Akeman, Lester Flatt, Wilene "Sally Ann" Forrester, bassist Andy Boyette. (Courtesy of Tom Ewing)

The "original bluegrass band" onstage at the Opry, ca. 1947, observed at close range by Lloyd George (left), the original "Lonzo" of the Lonzo and Oscar comedy team: George, "Chubby" Wise, unknown (behind Wise), Bill, Birch Monroe (hidden behind Bill, filling in on bass), Lester Flatt, Earl Scruggs. (Courtesy of the Country Music Hall of Fame)

Bill and the Blue Grass Boys onstage at the Opry, ca. 1950: Vassar Clements, Joel Price, Bill, Jimmy Martin, Rudy Lyle. (Courtesy of Tom Ewing)

The Greenbriar Boys, ca. 1963: Bob Yellin, Ralph Rinzler, John Herald. (Photo by John Cohen)

Neil Rosenberg picking banjo with the Stoney Lonesome Boys at the Brown County Jamboree, Bean Blossom, Indiana, October 13, 1963: Jim Bessire, Roger Smith, Gary Hedrick (hidden, playing mandolin), Rosenberg, Vernon McQueen, David Hedrick. (Photo by Jim Peva)

Bill and the Blue Grass Boys with Bill's daughter Melissa Monroe at the Brown County Jamboree, Bean Blossom, Indiana, on "Monroe Family Day," October 13, 1963: Bessie Lee Mauldin, Bill, Melissa, Joe Stuart, Bill Keith, Del McCoury. (Photo by Jim Peva)

Peter Rowan and Bill picking and singing on a parade float promoting the New York Folk Festival, New York City, June 1965: Rowan, banjoist Don Lineberger, Bill, James Monroe, folksinger Carolyn Hester. Rowan mentioned this moment in Doug Benson's "Bill Monroe: King of Blue Grass Music." (Courtesy of R. A. Andreas, Bear Family Records)

Bill and the Blue Grass Boys onstage at the Opry, ca. 1966: Richard Greene, Lamar Grier, Roy Acuff, Opry staff band drummer Harold Weakley, Bill, Peter Rowan, James Monroe. (Courtesy of *Bluegrass Unlimited*)

Bill and the Blue Grass Boys at the Bean Blossom bluegrass festival, June 1970: emcee Grant Turner (in doorway), Kenny Baker, Rual Yarbrough, Bill, James Monroe, Skip Payne. At the beginning of the set, Baker had momentarily forgotten his hat. (Photo by Tom Ewing)

Charles Wolfe and Bill following the interview at WMOT radio, Murfreesboro, Tennessee, fall 1974. (Photo by Dennis Adamson; courtesy of Charles Wolfe)

"Pickin' and Singin'"

THE STAFF OF *NEWSWEEK*

Mountain soul music is what people call bluegrass. It conjures up visions of hazy mountains, ramshackle log cabins, unyielding, dirt-poor farms, whisky stills, and valleys wounded by abandoned coal mines. Or it's called simply, "old-time pickin' and singin'." Sometimes, because of its breakneck pace, it's referred to as "folk music in overdrive."[1]

There are some who just call it "Bill Monroe's music." Monroe refers to it as his music. "My music started in 1939, when I got my first band together," says the 59-year-old tenor and mandolin virtuoso. "I wanted to represent my home state of Kentucky so I took the name 'Blue Grass Boys'."

Last week Monroe held his fourth annual Bluegrass Festival on his 90-acre park in Bean Blossom, Ind. By Sunday the crowds at the five-day festival were expected to reach 12,000. What was surprising was the cross-section of America represented, some of whom came east from California and south from Canada to the hamlet lying 45 miles south of Indianapolis.

There was a good fellowship among leather-faced men in Western garb, teenage groupies posturing around the musicians, long-haired hippies with their no-bra chicks, and redneck farmers with their wives sprawled in lawn chairs and print dresses. "The people bring me to Bean Blossom," a 24-year-old jazz pianist from Chicago named Bob Hoban told *Newsweek*'s Bernice Buresh. "It's so relaxing that you can carry yourself home in a bucket when you leave here."

In the heat of sunny days, impromptu groups played, attended workshops, sipped Cokes, ate watermelon, and bought buttons that said: "Stop Air Pollution—Play Bluegrass." On Thursday a banjo-picking contest was won by 23-year-old Roger Bland, from Wheeling, W.Va. He jumped for joy at the $100 prize. "Bluegrass," he says, "it flows like a stream. The banjo is the ripples."

Intense: On Saturday, amid beech, walnut, and hickory trees, the crowd crammed themselves on plank benches to hear 25 big-name bands such as Jimmy Martin and the Sunny Mountain Boys, the great banjoist Earl Scruggs,[2] Ralph Stanley and the Clinch Mountain Boys, and the star of stars, Bill Monroe and the Blue Grass Boys. This was the band that gave the music its name. Hardly was a chord struck when the crowd erupted at the expectation of "Mule Skinner Blues," "Molly and Ten-

---

1. From "Bluegrass Background: Folk Music with Overdrive," by Alan Lomax.
2. Scruggs was making his first appearance at Bean Blossom, accompanied by the newly-formed Earl Scruggs Revue.

brooks," or Monroe's "Blue Moon of Kentucky," the first song Elvis Presley ever recorded.[3]

This intense, passionate music came out of Appalachia in the '20s and '30s. It spawned, with the introduction of electronic instruments, the commercial Nashville sound. But at the bottom of it was a pure strain, rural but not ruralized, restricted to an acoustical string band with a guitar and bass for the driving rhythm, a five-string banjo, mandolin, and fiddle for melody, and sometimes the addition of a dobro guitar, played Hawaiian style, to reinforce the twang and "the high, lonesome sound" of the fiddle.

Bluegrass is like chamber music in the intricate demands it makes upon the precision of an ensemble. And it's like jazz in the quick reflexes necessary to respond to spontaneous ideas from hot licks on banjo and fiddle. Bluegrass men[4] are masterly musicians. Says Jimmy Martin, "If a country music band loses a musician, he can be replaced tomorrow. It takes me a year to replace someone."

Sparks: Bill Monroe is "the father of bluegrass."[5] Into the music, Monroe has let flow blues, gospel, ragtime, Dixieland, and the old mountain fiddle tunes. "I knew what I was adding at each step," says Monroe. Most of the key bluegrass musicians served their apprenticeships with Monroe. Jimmy Martin did, and so did the Stanley Brothers,[6] Don Reno, Mac Wiseman, and, above all, Lester Flatt and Earl Scruggs. After Scruggs joined, making sparks fly with his revolutionary three-fingered banjo picking, bluegrass was never the same.

These days even bluegrass finds it hard to resist change. Jimmy Martin tolerates a drum during recording sessions[7] and Sonny Osborne has gone so far as to electrify his banjo. Having to compete with Nashville groups, it was better than going hungry. Most of Monroe's disciples play hard 'grass. But some of the groups such as the Country Gentlemen play "progressive," underplaying the country twang in favor of an urban sophistication.

Monroe himself is unperturbed. "It wouldn't do for me to electrify," he says. "But there's room in bluegrass for differences.[8] You know, I intended this music for country people but it's growed and gone all over. The mountain people have been with me 30 years. But my hippie fans know when the music is played right. And the

3. This was the first mention in an article about Bill that Presley had recorded his song. See the editor's comments, second paragraph.

4. These days: persons.

5. This was the first time any publication said this without reservation. See the editor's comments, third paragraph.

6. Only Carter Stanley was formally a Blue Grass Boy.

7. Except for Bill and the Blue Grass Boys, all of the major Nashville-based bluegrass bands had used drums on sessions regularly since 1965.

8. Bill's comment was prophetic. Radical differences would appear in the music in the 1970s, testing his open-mindedness to the limit.

college kids are my biggest audience. People have learned that bluegrass has a wonderful feeling. If you play it right, people know you got your heart in it."

EDITOR'S COMMENTS

This article appeared in the June 29, 1970, issue of *Newsweek.* In its third year, Bill's Bean Blossom festival was beginning to attract massive crowds and, after the Woodstock Music and Art Fair of 1969 (attended by over three hundred thousand), the news media were on the lookout for such events.

As far as I have been able to determine, this was the first article relating to Bill to mention the fact that Elvis Presley had recorded his "Blue Moon of Kentucky." It was not the first song Presley recorded, but it *was* one of the songs on his first record (Sun 209, with "That's All Right" on the A side), released by Sun Records in 1954. (The song was also recorded in 1965 by the rhythm and blues great Ray Charles.)[1]

With this article, *Newsweek* became the first publication to say without reservation that "Bill Monroe is 'the father of bluegrass.'" He would be formally recognized as such when he was inducted into the Country Music Association's Country Music Hall of Fame four months later, on October 14, 1970.

Note

1. Ray Charles, *Country and Western Meets Rhythm and Blues,* ABC-Paramount, 520, released Aug. 1965.

"Bill Monroe (from a Farm Boy to a Legend)"

JAMES MONROE

Part 1

Where do you begin? Especially when your subject is a legend in his time and practically every bluegrass and country music magazine has, at one time or another, attempted to put down on paper some of the miraculous accomplishments of this great man.

Throughout this article we will relate some incidents which have not been published previously. Since the logical place to begin would be with Bill's childhood, we'll start with the year 1911, the month of September, on the 13th day, when William Smith Monroe first saw the light of day. He was the youngest child of James Buchanan Monroe and Malissa Monroe who had seven other children—five boys, namely John, Birch, Speed, Charlie, and Harry, and two girls—Maude and Bertha.[1]

They lived on a 650-acre farm a mile and a half from Rosine, Kentucky, where his father raised his game chickens,[2] cattle, and horses. At one time, his father had thirty-two foxhounds, five or six teams of horses, and three yokes of oxen which he used for hauling. Being the son of a farmer, Bill had his chores to do which included carrying wood, gathering eggs, getting water into the house, and many other jobs which are routine for a boy living on a farm.

Bill has a fantastic memory and he recalls when his niece was born, even though he was only four years old at the time. He remembers that he and his brothers and sisters were taken to a corn crib 30' x 12' to spend the night while his sister-in-law gave birth to her child. When they went to the house the next morning, they learned they had a new niece. He also recalls that his father was an excellent accountant and kept receipts on everything—even if the money he spent was only a nickel. However, we must realize that, at that time, a nickel was a fair amount of money. He kept a set of books that would probably compare with any accountant's records today.

As a youngster, Bill followed his father around wherever he went and watched every move he made very closely. He wanted to learn to do all the things his father did and he thought by watching him closely, when he grew up, he could do the work around the farm as well as his father. He listened intently to everything his father told him and obeyed him without question. Bill never got a whipping from his father and thought his father was the greatest man in the world.

When Bill was growing up he got two pair of overalls a year. One pair he wore during the week and the other pair was for Sunday. Also, he had one pair of shoes a year. He was very careful and tried not to let anything happen to them. He went barefooted in the summertime and wore his shoes during the winter. He lived one and one half miles from school, located in Horton, Kentucky, to which he walked every day.

At the tender age of ten, Bill started breaking ground for his father. He and another boy each had a team of mules and a plow. The team he had was gentle and could be trusted and was easy to handle.

At the time it seemed hard for him to understand why he could do the plowing but couldn't drive the team of horses when they went to town. What he didn't realize at the time was that it was easier to follow the mules because they stayed right in the furrow, whereas he would have to guide the horses in the right direction. Every Saturday evening,[3] he and his father went to town to get the weekly supplies such as salt, coffee, flour, sugar, coal oil for the lamps, and whatever else they needed to get them through the week. Also, Bill got a nickel for candy each week and he made

---

1. The Monroe children in the order of their birth: Harry (1893), Speed (1895), John (1897), Maude (1898), Birch (1901), Charles (1903), Bertha (1908), and Bill (1911).

2. Like father, like son.

3. Evening, particularly in the South, is anytime between noon and twilight.

it last as long as he possibly could. Bill stayed on the wagon while his father was in the store. Even though the team was tied to a post in front of the store, Bill decided he would get some driving in while his father was inside. He pulled them up two or three steps and then backed them up, pulled them ahead and backed them up . . . sometimes he would continue this for an hour or more, depending on how long it took his father to get the shopping done.

Bill worked on the farm in the spring and summer. There was a coal mine on his father's property, but since he was too young to work in the mine, he watched his older brothers work there. Sometimes, his older brother John would let him go back into the mine with him, and he thought it was scary going back and it was cold. They got to go back about 300 to 400 feet and it was real "spooky." During the winter, he helped work in the timber, and he yarded timber with a mule when he was about thirteen years old.

When Bill was about eleven or twelve, he went hunting with his father and brothers. They didn't have to go too far because there was plenty of good hunting right on their farm. He would get so tired of walking, and when he leaned up against a post, he nearly fell asleep. He also remembers that his father and he would stay home on Saturday nights because his father thought he was too young to go to town. His father derived much pleasure out of listening to the foxhounds run.

His uncle Pen was a tradesman in his later years. When he was young, he made his living at farming, but after his family passed away, he made his living through trading. He would leave on Monday morning with not much of anything, and on Friday evening, when he came home, he would be leading a cow, or have something of much greater value than when he left at the beginning of the week.

Uncle Pen was also a good old-time fiddle player. As a child, Bill would listen to his uncle play and with his keen mind, he memorized all the tunes his uncle played, many of which he plays today exactly as Uncle Pen played them when Bill was a child. At that time, Bill didn't know if he wanted to play music for a living or what he wanted to do. However, he studied music from the time he was a little boy, listening and getting it all down to perfection in his mind. At times, he would go out into the field where he thought nobody could hear or see him and he would practice his singing. Some folks around did hear him and said he could sing higher than anyone in the country. It was not until he had reached the age of about twenty-one that he really made his decision to go and make his living in the music world. He had sung in a young class at a Methodist church when he was about twelve or thirteen. He wanted to be a bass singer because they seemed to have the much easier part. He sang with the choir for about six months, and, during that time, attended one singing convention which included about five or six classes.

Part 2

Bill's job was to water the four work horses at noon at a creek about a quarter of a mile from his house. He and three friends, the sons of a family who worked for Bill's parents, would race bareback every time they went to the creek. Bill recalls one time in particular when racing each other, his horse jumped sideways across a bad place in the road; Bill lost his balance and was thrown into some brush and logs. The boys rushed to help him and got him home. This was his last horse race, as he walked with a limp to favor his leg. To keep his folks from getting after him about racing the horses, he wouldn't say what was causing him to limp. His parents thought he had been playing around big stacks of lumber which had been left to "season" and had fallen. After a while, his father called the doctor, who just took hold of Bill's leg and jerked it out straight.

When Bill was growing up, some of the games he played were hide-and-seek, marbles, and the game Thirteen,[4] but the most fun was swinging from grapevines.

When Bill's brother Speed and the other soldiers from Rosine came home after World War I, Bill could hear them singing in the distance as they walked to their homes—"By-and-by, when the morning comes, all the saints of God shall gather home."[5] They were so glad to be back home.

The family always had time for music and, in the evenings, they always played and sang. Bill's mother played the fiddle and he remembers her always picking it up and playing a few tunes during the day. When his mother, who had spinal meningitis, passed away, it was a sad household. Bill's two sisters, Maude and Bertha, took over the work. At this time, his uncle Pen Vandiver stayed with them for a while. Later on, Bill and his uncle played for dances at people's homes. They would ride horseback to these events, Uncle Pen with his fiddle and Bill with the guitar (although he played mandolin also). They would get between $2.50 or $3.00 each. Bill also played with Arnold Shultz, a colored man, who everyone thought was the best on guitar anywhere.

When Bill was sixteen his father died, and he recalls his father being taken to the graveyard on a horse-drawn wagon. It was a family tradition that each member of the family, on their 21st birthday, should receive either $100.00 or a horse, whichever they preferred. They could either go out on their own or stay and work for their father. After the death of his father, a sale was held on the homeplace, and even though Bill was only sixteen, he was given a white horse named Pat, so he went out on his own and farmed five acres of corn and two and one-half acres of cane. When the cane was milled into syrup, Bill received 55 gallons. He kept some of it and sold the rest for $1.00 per gallon.

When seventeen, Bill yarded tie timber for his uncle Andrew Monroe and hauled mining timber a distance of ten miles—one load a day. He also farmed for his uncle Jack Monroe, using his horse Pat along with his uncle's three horses. He was paid $1.50 each day, plus his dinner. This was from early spring till the crop was in.

When Bill lived with his uncle Pen, he had various jobs, such as hauling telephone poles and crossties. The horses were kept at a barn in Rosine, and after he

4. A form of solitaire. See the editor's comments, second paragraph.
5. Bill recorded this song, "We'll Understand It Better," in 1962.

had fed and watered them at the end of the day, Bill would stay around town and he could hear his uncle Pen play his fiddle at his home, high on the hill above the town.

At the age of eighteen, Bill left Kentucky to go to Whiting, Indiana, to work for the Sinclair Refinery. His job consisted of washing, loading, and stacking oil drums. He stayed with the company four years during which time he supported two brothers and two sisters.[6] From Whiting, Bill and Charlie went to Gary, Indiana, and formed the Monroe Brothers, which later became famous all over the United States. They were sponsored by a company known as the Texas Crystals Company.

From Gary, they went to Shenandoah, Iowa, where they worked for radio station KFNF and were sponsored by the Henry Field's Store. While working at the barn dance[7] in Shenandoah, Bill met Carolyn Brown, who later became Mrs. Bill Monroe. They worked in Shenandoah for approximately one year.[8] They went to Omaha, Nebraska, where once again they worked for the Texas Crystals Company.

After leaving Omaha, they went to Columbia, South Carolina—still with the same company. They worked there for three months. This man[9] had about four or five groups across the country and one day he decided to fire all of the groups in one day. They then went to WBT[10] in Charlotte, which was a 50,000 watt station, and worked for both WBT and WFBC in Greenville for about three months. While in Charlotte, Bill's first child was born—a girl, named Melissa.

They later went to Greenville and did two programs a day—one early in the morning and another at noon.[11]

From Greenville, they went to Raleigh and worked there for one and one-half years. This was where Bill and Charlie split the team known as the Monroe Brothers.

Part 3

After the Monroe Brothers split, Bill moved his family to Little Rock, Arkansas, and joined radio station KARK. He stayed there for about three months, working with his newly-formed band, the Kentuckians, which consisted of Cousin Wilbur[12] on bass, Handy Jamison on fiddle, and Handy's cousin on guitar. He disbanded after four months and went down through Mississippi and spent approximately one month just enjoying life. From there he went to Birmingham, Alabama, to see if he could get on a station. He couldn't find what he wanted, so he went to Atlanta, Georgia, where he advertised in the local newspapers for entertainers. He tried out

---

6. Birch, Charlie, Maude, Bertha, and Bill were all living together in Whiting at the time, ca. 1930.

7. The Henry Field's Store (now Henry Field's Seed and Nursery Company) is mentioned in James Rooney's *Bossmen* as the sponsor of this radio barn dance on Saturday nights.

8. Actually, about three months.

9. Presumably the president of Texas Crystals.

10. They were working at WBT when "fired" by Texas Crystals.

11. The early morning program was at WBT in Charlotte and the noon program was at WFBC in Greenville.

12. Willie Egbert Wesbrooks. See the editor's comments, third paragraph.

several people and came up with Cleo Davis. When Cleo came by for his audition, he was not aware of the fact that he was trying out for Bill Monroe's band and when he heard Bill sing, he commented that he sounded like Bill Monroe, to which Bill answered, "I *am* Bill Monroe." This completely unnerved him and he couldn't finish his audition. Bill trained Cleo for an hour each day for a month,[13] after which they went to Asheville, North Carolina. Here Bill hired two additional band members and picked the name "The Blue Grass Boys," naming them after his home state of Kentucky. This was the year 1939, and while in Asheville, they worked at radio station WWNC.

They left Asheville and went back to Greenville, South Carolina, and stayed there about three or four months. Bill decided he would go to Nashville and try out for the Grand Ole Opry. He arrived on Monday, but they held auditions on Wednesdays. WSM was then located on the fifth floor of the National Life Building and as Bill got off the elevator he met Harry Stone, the manager of the station, and two of the announcers—David Stone and "the Solemn Ole Judge," George D. Hay. They told him since he was in town they would listen to him after lunch and to come back ready to sing about three or four songs. After they heard him they told him he and his music would be perfect for the Grand Ole Opry. He was signed as a regular member of the Opry in October of 1939. The Blue Grass Boys consisted of Cleo Davis, Art Wooten, and Amos Garrett.

In March of 1941, Bill's second child, James, was born in Nashville.

In 1942, Bill started working tent shows with Jamup and Honey, a comedy act from the Grand Ole Opry, playing mostly one-night stands. Bill worked with Jamup and Honey for about a year, and in 1943, started his own tent show, which he carried all over the southern and eastern states.

In the late forties, Bill started two baseball clubs. One was named the Blue Grass All-Stars and the other, the Blue Grass Ball Club. One club stayed in Nashville and played, and the other travelled on the road with Bill's show. After the performances, Bill and the boys would play a ballgame.

During the forties, the Bill Monroe show was on the road almost constantly, working three and four shows a day, six and seven days a week, until the fifties. In January of 1953,[14] upon his return from a fox hunt, he was critically injured in a car wreck. A truck[15] hit his car head-on and how he survived the crash is a miracle. He was in a body cast in the hospital for ninety days recuperating from nineteen broken bones. He was off the road from January through July and resumed his road work in the middle of August.[16]

In 1955,[17] Bill purchased a 90-acre amusement park[18] in Bean Blossom, Indiana,

---

13. The "training period" was longer. See "Cleo Davis: The Original Blue Grass Boy," by Wayne Erbsen.

14. January 16, 1953.

15. A newspaper account of the time described the other vehicle as a car (possibly a pickup truck).

16. Other sources have put him back on the road as early as May.

17. 1951.

18. The same description used in the *Official WSM Grand Ole Opry History-Picture Book.*

which consists of a three-acre lake, a jamboree barn, and an amphitheatre.[19] There is also a beautiful wooded area. This has become the headquarters for his world-famous bluegrass festival, the first of which was held in 1967. Attendance has increased yearly and the festival has become the largest in the United States. Every spring since 1968, Bill and the Blue Grass Boys head for Bean Blossom to make improvements on the grounds and clear out wooded areas, making room for additional parking which is vitally needed to take care of the thousands of cars and campers that converge upon the park the third week in June. Bean Blossom has become a part of many bluegrass followers' vacation schedule. It includes one week of solid entertainment. Festival time is not the only time there is action at Bill Monroe's Brown County Jamboree Park. There are shows every Sunday during the summer months, beginning in April and running through the middle of November. Both bluegrass and country music acts are featured at the park. Bill's brother Birch manages the park while Bill takes care of his many personal appearance dates.

Bill owns a 280-acre farm outside of Nashville, Tennessee, where he makes his home.[20] Here he farms, hunts, and raises his Black Angus cattle, foxhounds, and game chickens. He still farms the old-time way, using mules and horses for plowing, hauling, and cutting hay.

Originally published in *The Bluegrass Star* 1:1 (Oct. 1971): 4–6; 1:2 (Nov. 1971): 6–7; and 1:3 (Dec. 1971): 4–5. Reprinted by permission of the author and *Bluegrass Unlimited*.

EDITOR'S COMMENTS

Jim Rooney's excellent but brief biography, *Bossmen: Bill Monroe and Muddy Waters* (New York: Dial Press), was published in 1971. Later that year, when Bill's son James founded *The Bluegrass Star* magazine, he added a great deal more detail to the story of his father's early days with this homegrown report. It appeared without a byline in the first three issues of the magazine (October–December 1971). (This selection differs from the original mainly in matters of punctuation and in that one sentence has been deleted and only the first eight paragraphs of part 3 are reprinted here.)

Thirteen, one of Bill's childhood pastimes, is a variation of the card game solitaire. In the 1980s and 1990s, while traveling the country in a tour bus, one of Bill's favorite activities was playing solitaire.

The "Cousin Wilbur" mentioned here was Willie Egbert Wesbrooks, who worked and recorded with Bill again in the early forties. Wesbrooks, however, did not mention this episode in his rambling autobiography, *Everybody's Cousin*, in which he seems to have discussed every event, major and minor, in his career.

---

19. A natural amphitheater in a wooded area of the park.
20. Possibly the first specific mention in print of the (approximate) size of Bill's second farm.

In June 1971, four months before the first issue of *The Bluegrass Star* was published, Lester Flatt and Bill were reunited at the Fifth Annual Bean Blossom Bluegrass Festival.

The publication of the first issue of *The Bluegrass Star* in October 1971 coincided with the annual disc jockey convention in Nashville, which included the first "Early Bird Bluegrass Concert" that year. The February 1973 issue was the last, and the magazine was sold shortly thereafter to *Bluegrass Unlimited*.

"Mellowing Father of Bluegrass"

JACK HURST

In the beginning there was a fiddler named Pen Vandiver.

He lived on a hill overlooking the backwoods Kentucky town of Rosine and in the evenings, after the incredibly hard work that farmers did, he would waft a high, lonesome music down surrounding valleys.

One of those valleys contained the 650-acre farm tilled by Pen's sister Malissa and her husband James Monroe. Their marriage had been promoted by Pen in a way, because many an evening before it occurred, Pen had squired his sister to the banks of the Green River, to a spot where Monroe would swim across and court her.

Perhaps that was the reason Pen took the youngest of their eight children to finish raising when James and Malissa died of hard work before their time. In those days the beginning of the Great Depression was reducing western Kentucky almost to a land of famine, and four decades later the nephew would recall that he and his bachelor uncle had lived mostly on fatback and corn pone. But more than anything else, he would remember how they had worked hard in the heat of the days and how Pen had played music in the cool of the evenings.

Working in Indiana

Pen Vandiver died a year or so after the nephew reached his 18th birthday. The younger man had been working at a cash-paying industrial job for more than a year in East Chicago, Indiana, when Pen, an old man who had been seriously crippled in an accident with a mule, passed on to the hereafter.

Pen died not knowing what he had given the world, or even that he had done it a favor. The fact that Bill, the youngest of the Monroe children, had gotten to love Pen's fiddle music could not have seemed to have any national significance in 1931.[1]

---

1. Pendleton Vandiver died in 1932. Bill was twenty or twenty-one years old.

✍

Although his famed hauteur is mellowing a little as he begins his seventh decade, Bill Monroe still rarely smiles onstage—and never when he sings.

When he sings, he holds the pear-shaped mandolin close to his chest the way a careful bird-hunter totes a .410 shotgun. The smoky eyes look almost angry—stoic, at best—under the wide-brimmed white hat, staring out upon audiences as if his mind is concentrating not upon them but, rather, upon the lyric and sound of his high, cold-chill music:

> Blue moon of
> Ken-tuck-ee,
> Keep on shinin'.
> Shine on
> The one that's gone
> And proved untrue . . . .

Bill Monroe, fanatically and justly venerated by bluegrass music fans, is almost a mystery figure to his colleagues at the Grand Ole Opry. Writer of 75 percent of the music he sings, including more than 100 religious hymns, he is the leader of a whole cult of musicians who—compared to their country colleagues—seem thriftier, shrewder, sometimes less prosperous, and usually less communicative about their private lives.

Monroe, their leader, lives on a Goodlettsville farm miles away from the Nashville residence of the mother of his children. Although they were separated[2] a few years ago, however, his former wife continues to handle his business affairs, and to get in touch with Monroe, one calls Mrs. Monroe. Their daughter lives with her mother and also works in the furthering of her father's career.

Answering questions from a stranger, Monroe's manner is nearly as austere as it is onstage.

He is cooperative and direct, and his eyes back up his answers resolutely, but when the short answers are concluded, the eyes are quickly averted, and the realization comes that venerable Bill Monroe, insistently self-proclaimed "founder" of bluegrass music, is gruff partly because he is very shy.

"We worked hard back in that country," he was saying of his birthplace one recent evening.

"We farmed, worked in timber, drove crossties to the railroad, and hauled coal from a coal mine we had on our farm. You worked from Monday mornin' 'til Saturday afternoon, then you had Saturday evenin' off. There might be a ballgame or somethin' on Saturday, but there wasn't hardly nothin' goin' on back in that country. 'Course, there was church on Sundays, and prayer meetin' on Wednesday nights."

---

2. Bill and Carolyn Monroe were divorced in 1960.

Mostly Instrumental

Most of the music he heard in his youth was instrumental, and the best of it came from the artistic fiddle of Pen Vandiver. Monroe remembers that most of the pieces with words were nondescript.

"Things like 'May I Sleep in Your Barn Tonight, Mister,'" he said.

Bill Monroe began "fooling," as he puts it, with an old mandolin about the time he moved in with Pen Vandiver.[3] His father had just died, six years after the death of his mother, and loneliness may have had something to do with the gravity with which he turned to music.

The instrument he took up was a predecessor of the modern, flat-backed one he uses now. Resembling the ancient lute, its backside was full and rounded, and that is probably why Monroe refers to it now as a "potato bug" mandolin.

He took his hobby with him to East Chicago, where he worked for the next five years in a Sinclair refinery. He journeyed to the industrial suburbs with two older brothers, Charlie and Birch, who also were highly interested in music. Working at industrial jobs, they played their music in their spare time and looked for a chance to make it profitable.

"The first performing we did was with WLS in Chicago on the National Barn Dance in 1932," Bill Monroe recalled.[4] "We did old-time square-dancing."

In 1934, he began his first series of professional performances, along with Charlie, who played guitar, and Birch, a bass player.[5] They were on radio station KFNF in Shenandoah, Iowa. Working for a sponsor which used the Monroe brothers to popularize its products in one area and then another, Bill Monroe began to see some American countryside.

"I think we worked our first show for $25 a week in Shenandoah," he said. "Later on we did get up to $45 a week in Omaha, and then went to Columbia, South Carolina. Then we lost our job with that company and went to WBT in Charlotte, North Carolina.[6] We went to work for another sponsor and after a little while the same thing happened again."

Monroe said that he does not recall that the loss of the jobs was any reflection on the Monroes' talent. In fact, it may have been a testimonial to it.

Advertised Enough

"The companies had about five or six different groups working for them across the country at the same time, and we all lost our jobs at the same time," he said. "I guess they just figured they had advertised enough in those particular parts of the country."

---

3. In 1928, when his father died, Bill had already been playing mandolin for several years.

4. Even Bill could stretch the truth on this subject.

5. Birch, a fiddler, had decided to not become a professional musician at this point. Later, he did play bass occasionally with the Blue Grass Boys.

6. This occurred while they were at WBT.

By 1936, Bill Monroe says, he was making enough money off his music that he no longer had to worry about starving. What he earned, he managed well.

"I believe in eating three meals a day, and I pretty much had them, because ever since I was 18 I knew how to handle money. I'm not a miser. I mean, I'd a lot rather buy you a meal than have you buy me one. That's the way I am about that."

By the time he formed the Blue Grass Boys band in 1939, he and Charlie and Birch had split up.[7] In the months preceding his hiring by the Grand Ole Opry in late October 1939, he formed the group which gave its Kentucky name to a whole new brand of music.

"The first Blue Grass Boys were Cleo Davis on guitar, Amos Garren on bass, and 'Fiddlin' Art' Wooten on fiddle," Monroe said. "I picked up Cleo in Atlanta and Art in Asheville, and Amos in Greenville, South Carolina."

Not long before he joined the Opry, his wife Carolyn had borne him a daughter, and soon afterward she bore him a son. They named the children Melissa and James.

James Monroe is a strikingly handsome, dark, 31-year-old proprietor of his own bluegrass festival which begins its second annual run this weekend in mountainous Cosby, Tennessee. It is an obvious Tennessee model of his father's famous Bean Blossom, Indiana, festival, which was founded in 1966[8] and which drew an estimated 30,000 persons to its latest performances two weeks ago.

James probably would not be singing today if it had not been for his father.

"He shoved me out there," James said with a grin one hot afternoon at Bean Blossom.

"I didn't start playing until I was about 20 years old, and the first show I ever worked, he put me on the stage with him with a bass when I didn't even know what a chord change was. I started out just trying to keep time." He grinned again. "But I learned in some of the finest places you could learn—Carnegie Hall, the Newport Folk Festival, Albert Hall in London. . . ."

James said his early disinclination to become a musician was not a reflection of any dislike for his father's profession.

"I like all kinds of music—soul music and blues and other kinds—but I love his music," James Monroe said.

"My sister and I used to listen to him on the radio when he was on the Opry when we were just little. A lot of singers will just sing a song, but he gets everything out of a song that's in it. The reason I waited so long to get into music was just that I was bashful. I couldn't see getting up in front of people like that."

The Father of Bluegrass Music admits he saw bluegrass as the logical career for his son.

---

7. He and Charlie had split up.
8. The first Bean Blossom festival was held in June 1967.

"I want him to do what he wants to do, but I think he'd do best in bluegrass music because I think that's where people expect him to be," Bill Monroe said.

"I don't want his music to be exactly like mine, but if I had my way, I guess I'd want him to play it pretty much the way bluegrass has always been done—pure, you know. He's got a Monroe voice. It's up high and clear enough, and it carries good."

James' voice is about two keys lower than his father's—but that is still high.

Without prompting, the elder Monroe answered a question that would have been difficult to put into words.

"I guess it's been hard for him," he said, in a rare generalization of cold facts. "It's hard for any boy to come up under his father. But I've tried every way to help him, and I'd a lot rather help him than myself."

Sitting in an old barn at Bean Blossom that had been converted into a dusty auditorium,[9] James Monroe barely nodded when told of the generalization his father had made about fathers and sons. He said neither yes nor no when asked if the generalization had been true in this instance.

"I've had a lot of people come up to me after I've come off the stage somewhere and tell me that I was good, but that I'll never be as good as my daddy," he said.

"Hank Williams, Jr. and Roy Acuff, Jr. have had a hard way to go, too. The name will get you up there sometimes, all right, but it also makes people expect more of you than they might somebody else."

But he also talked of his personal relationship with his father.

"I've worked on the farm for him, cut hay and shucked corn," James Monroe said. "He was a hard man to work for. He expected the most out of you. He learned me to hitch a team when I was 11, and he only showed me once. We had 44 acres then, on Dickerson Road.

"He's got 280 acres out in Goodlettsville now, and he works it the old-time way. He plows right today with a horse and plow, and he can make you a rough-hewn log house today just the way they used to. He knows every kind of tree there is, just by looking at it, and I guess he knows how to make just about anything you need."

From a stage on a hill not too far from the empty barn in which James Monroe was talking, he and the interviewer could hear the high, chilling voice of his father as it wailed such Bill Monroe classics as "Blue Moon of Kentucky," "Mule Skinner Blues," and "Uncle Pen."

The interviewer asked James how a 60-year-old man could still sing in that throat-punishing style.

"He's always taken care of himself well," the son said. "He's never smoked or drank, and he's almost always taken care to get three meals a day even when he was on the road. He can do it because he's taken care of himself."

The gravity of Monroe's manner inspires his followers to treat him like a min-

---

9. The "barn" at Bean Blossom was always a place for shows.

ister. At Bean Blossom, one worshipper came up to ask him a question, then realized in mid-sentence that he was holding a can of beer in his hand. He put it behind his back like a child and profusely excused himself.

Bill Monroe said nothing.

✒

In the last two or three years, some of his associates at the Grand Ole Opry have observed that Bill Monroe is mellowing. He occasionally will make a joke, even, and he speaks to and obviously has genuine affection for some of the musicians he sometimes spurned after they left his Blue Grass Boys to form their own bands.

One of the reasons he is called the Father of Bluegrass Music is that he taught many of its other well-known exponents some of their most profitable lessons. Former Blue Grass Boys include such performers as Lester Flatt, Earl Scruggs, Ralph Stanley,[10] Don Reno, and Jimmy Martin, in addition to several others.

He has made extensive efforts to help some of the younger groups find places to play in recent years, inviting them to perform on his annual festival and recommending them to the operators of other festivals.

Perhaps some of the mellowing is due to the fact that he is 60 now. He admits, at least, that reaching that milestone has caused him to do some things he had always meant to do and never got around to until now.

There are several of these things, but one of the ones he is proudest of is an instrumental album, recently recorded, which contains a dozen old-time fiddle tunes.[11]

"They're numbers from my Uncle Pen that I've kept all these years and have never been played in this country (meaning everywhere outside Rosine, Kentucky) before," he said.

"I don't think he wrote any of them. I think they were just tunes that he played. But I've kept about 30 of them in my head since then, and he died when I was 19 or 20. I been meaning to record them for a long time, and I've finally got around to it.[12] I'm 60 years old now, and you don't ever know what will happen."

On the new Decca album, the listener can hear the echo of the fiddle crippled Pen Vandiver used to play on that hill above Rosine. His nephew consciously tried his best to retain on the album what he calls the "old-time" sound, and he dedicated the recording to Uncle Pen.

In an album liner which is as direct and straightforward as the nephew himself, Bill Monroe wrote a note. Addressed to "a wonderful uncle," it briefly explained their relationship for the listener. Its tone suggests a patriarch at peace:

---

10. Ralph Stanley filled in, but was not formally a Blue Grass Boy.

11. *Bill Monroe's Uncle Pen,* Decca Records, DL 75348, released June 1972, contained eleven of Uncle Pen's fiddle tunes.

12. The recording of *Bill Monroe's Uncle Pen* had begun three years earlier. See the editor's comments, second paragraph.

He was one of Kentucky's finest old-time fiddlers. And he had the best shuffle with the bow that I'd ever seen, and he kept the best time, that's one reason people asked him to play for the dances around Rosine, Kentucky.

His later years in life he was a crippled man, he had been thrown by a mule, therefore he had to use crutches the rest of his life.

My last years in Kentucky were spent with him, he done the cooking for the two of us, we had fat back, sorghum molasses and hoe cakes for breakfast, followed up with black-eyed peas with fat back, and cornbread and sorghum for dinner and supper.

I can remember those days so very well, there were the hard times, and money was scarce, but also there were the good times. If it was to do over, I'd live them again.

Rest in peace, will see you later.

Your nephew, Bill Monroe.

Originally published in *The Tennessean*, June 25, 1972, 35–36. © 1972 by *The Tennessean*. Reprinted by permission.

EDITOR'S COMMENTS

This article appeared in the Sunday Showcase section of the June 25, 1972, edition of *The Tennessean*, then Nashville's morning newspaper, now its only daily newspaper. Located among ads for the latest movies and television listings for the week, it publicized the recent release of the *Bill Monroe's Uncle Pen* album.

The recording of the album began three years earlier, in 1969, when "The Dead March" was recorded on March 26. Coincidentally, it was the first recording session on which James Monroe played guitar with Bill and the Blue Grass Boys.

Bill Monroe's Uncle Pen was the last of Bill's albums released on the Music Corporation of America's Decca Records label. In March 1973 the label was renamed MCA Records, and Bill's next album, *Bill Monroe & James Monroe: Father & Son* (MCA-310), was one of the new label's first releases.

"Bill Monroe" (interview)

STEVE RATHE

"Every field has its 'Bossman'—the one who sets the style, makes the rules, and defines the field in his own terms. In the world of bluegrass and early country music the man is Bill Monroe." Jim Rooney wrote those words four or five years ago.[1] But

---

1. In *Bossmen: Bill Monroe and Muddy Waters*, published in 1971.

they could have been written twenty-five years ago, and it's a good bet that they'll be just as accurate twenty-five years from now. The interview took place December 10, 1973, in New York City.

✍

Rathe: It's 1973, sixty-two years from when Bill Monroe was born in Rosine, Kentucky. How many years have you been on the road, making your living as a musician?

Bill: Well, Steve, I started back in 19 and 34, and that was back when you played on radio stations and got a small salary. There was three of us, Birch Monroe, Charlie Monroe, and me, workin' together as the Monroe Brothers.[2] Then, later on, Charlie and me worked together. There wasn't many shows back in them days, and I done that up till, I'd say, about 1938. So, then in 1938, why, we broke up and in 1939, I formed my own group. That's when I started getting my kind of music together to come up with something of my own.

Rathe: In the time since then you certainly have had a lot of the people who are now out front in bluegrass playing with you and the Blue Grass Boys. In some sense, it must be like being a father, being responsible for the band on the road.

Bill: Well, down through the years, seem like it's growed, you know, and it's something I like to do. I like to have a man work with me and look after him, and help him out all that I can, if he'll give me a chance. And if he would not talk and try to run things, or ask for things, I would do much more for him. I've had so much to do through the years that I haven't had time to let somebody bother me in the way of asking questions, this and that. The way that it's gone along, it's been much better for me and I've tried to make it good for the men that's worked for me.

Rathe: In Jim Rooney's book, Don Reno said you'd sometimes work with somebody for a long time, just playing a tune over and over again until they got it right. Do you still work like that?

Bill: Well, I do that a lot. But it seems like now, you know, that people have studied bluegrass so close, they know pretty well the way I want it to go. They're not hard to learn like they was back in the early days. They know a lot more now.

Rathe: What do you look for in a musician? Are you looking for someone who can pick and follow your music, or is there more to it?

Bill: Well, I like to get a man that's got some kind of foundation or something he believes in, and I hope that he's a clean-minded man, you know; one who wants to help the music along and is a wonderful trouper. That means a lot. Of course, I want him to be a good musician that's heard bluegrass.

Rathe: Is it more of a problem finding musicians today than it used to be?

Bill: You have more trouble today than you ever had, I think. I don't have no trouble with the fiddler or the guitar man or the bass, right today, but the banjo pickers are gettin' maybe a little bit lazy and they want to stay home, stay nice.[3] When

---

2. Prior to 1934.

3. Bill wasn't kidding about banjo pickers. See the editor's comments, second paragraph.

someone's got wives, of course, their wives is the boss and they have to stay at home . . . 'Course, I think we can always find musicians that'll go along and be a Blue Grass Boy . . . [But] they're more lazy today than they've been in a long time. They want to sit at home and play a little in front of somebody, and maybe their wives works, you see, and keeps the musician up. And that's the way with a lot of them today. They like to play around home, or clubs, but the money's out on the road. But it's work out there, you know, and I believe in working.

Rathe: How do you react to the criticism that while you are employing young musicians and teaching them, the amount that you pay them is insufficient to allow them to stay with you, particularly if they have families dependent upon them for support?

Bill: Well, I pay 'em all right . . . you know, that I could afford to pay 'em, and I don't think that the money played that big a part. I have always paid union scale. Even before the union was worth anything, I paid more than the union did.

Rathe: What do you think of the young musicians who play on the bill with you at festivals and concerts?

Bill: Now, if they got their own group, you know, they're not lazy. They're in there to make good out of it and get that dollar when it's ready to be paid to them. But I think that all the young musicians coming along should get in there and go to work, wherever a man needs 'em, go in there and play. Because the public is the people that pays to see you and you need to give them what they want.

Rathe: That brings up an interesting question. How do you approach a show? Is there a standard "set," or does each performance depend upon how you feel that night?

Bill: Steve, when I go on stage, I am ready. I am primed up and my nerves is on edge, and I'm ready to get out there and play to 'em. If we go on stage today, and we've never been there before, we do the number "I'm on My Way Back to the Old Home." You know, I wrote that number about my old homeplace in Kentucky. We might do "Walk Softly on My Heart"[4] or some number that really touches you. Then while that number is going on, I feel the touch of the blues, and the lonesome part of the show come in on me. But then if we turn around and we play "Raw Hide," why, I'm back in the groove. Then, maybe the "Gray Eagle," you know, and I'm ready to tap my foot because it gives me that square dance kind of feeling.

Rathe: Do you ever get to play for square dances or more casual kinds of gatherings?

Bill: If we're someplace and they want a square dance, why, we don't mind doing it because we love to play the old-time fiddle numbers. That's been a great part in bluegrass music. We played at a plantation down in Louisiana awhile back for this young couple that was getting married and all they wanted to do was square-dance or waltz or something like that. It just fell right into our hands to play for them right.

---

4. The original title of a song now usually called "Walk Softly on This Heart of Mine."

Rathe: Is there a kind of performance situation, or a kind of audience that you prefer?

Bill: No, it would be bad on us if I couldn't get them all under control, and handle them the way I want to do it. We either handle 'em or we would leave the stage, you see. They got to listen to us. It's the only way we would work.

Rathe: Have you ever had any trouble with a "hippie" or rock and roll audience?

Bill: No, I don't 'cause I know if they cut their hair off and everything, they'd look just like I would look and I don't pay any attention to that. I know that they're my fans and I want to play to 'em as good as I can. I'm glad they're on my side and I think they know that, and they know my music.

Rathe: If someone with long hair auditioned to be your banjo player, and if he could get along on the road and pick out all the numbers just right, behind you, how would you feel about that?

Bill: Well, that would be fine. I would try him out and I could tell right away if he could handle the music end of it. But then, you know, he'd have to cut off some of the hair and get to lookin' like Kenny Baker or Bill Box[5] or some of the rest of us. It's not that I'm against him wearin' his hair that way, but, you know, we have our looks, the way we are going to do it, you see, and he would have to look like the rest of us.

✍

The list of musicians who have played with Monroe at one time or another is a veritable *Who's Who.* It includes such early names as Lester Flatt and Earl Scruggs, Don Reno, Chubby Wise, Howdy Forrester, and Jimmy Martin; and a second generation of pickers such as Bill Keith and Richard Greene.

Bill: They're all good and I respect everybody that picks up an instrument and tries to play bluegrass music. Some of 'em is better than others and I couldn't say that Earl Scruggs was better than Don Reno, because Don Reno can play and Earl Scruggs can play. You can do that, you see, but I can't do that. I can't say that Howdy Forrester was the greatest fiddler of bluegrass or Chubby Wise . . . they was all good in their days.

Rathe: How about making records with other musicians in addition to your band?

Bill: That would be great. I'd love to do that. Have you heard the *Bean Blossom* album?[6] Oh, you should hear it. There's twelve fiddlers fiddling up there at one time, you know; it's Kenny Baker, and "Big Howdy,"[7] and Buck Ryan, Tex Logan, Paul Warren . . . I could just keep namin' them all. They're all playing on the number "Swing Low, Sweet Chariot," sounding like a thousand people singing. When we have two or three numbers of twelve fiddlers fiddling, it's beautiful.

Rathe: It seems to me that most of the tunes that you actually record are either

---

5. Bill's lead singer and guitarist, 1973–74.
6. Released one month before this interview. See the editor's comments, third paragraph.
7. Howard Forrester, usually called "Howdy," but occasionally "Big Howdy."

your own compositions or traditional music. Are there other performers, perhaps even outside of bluegrass, whose music appeals to you?

Bill: I like their music. You know, they're a branch off bluegrass music, and I respect them and respect their music, and I like to listen to a lot of it. But, I don't like to see bluegrass get too far out and try to put too much stuff into it. I hate to see somebody do something and getting ahead of theirself. If you was goin' to play "San Antonio Rose" like Bob Wills plays it, why, that would be fine. But if you would try to play it, like, to put a lot of stuff that don't belong in it, then I wouldn't want to hear it.

Rathe: How about contemporary music, aside from bluegrass?

Bill: Well, it's all right, but I don't listen a whole lot to it.

Rathe: I know in the forties and early fifties, when country music began to develop and some of the musicians from the Grand Ole Opry began to make it big, and the music got slick, you held firmly to bluegrass. Now that the country music is becoming more popular in the big cities, do you see a larger audience for bluegrass as well?

Bill: I think bluegrass is coming along fine. The festivals have played a great part in it, and the people are more interested in it. There's more people knows about it and understands it; and today it's all over the world. It's played a great part in music for today.

Rathe: How about young songwriters? Have you run into more of them lately?

Bill: I don't believe there are so many of them. They should write more than they do. I don't think a country writer could write a bluegrass song good. But you take somebody like Boudleaux Bryant. He come out with some pretty good stuff. He had "Rocky Top" and numbers like that. Now he's got "The Daddy of Bluegrass."[8]

Rathe: Is there a particular piece of music that you have heard lately that you really like?

Bill: I hear different things in everybody's music that I like. And if I heard something in your music, and you was a jazz musician and I wanted to save it, I would save it, and you would never know it come out of your music.

Rathe: Do you ever find licks in jazz or music that's not bluegrass?

Bill: I don't take nobody's licks. I originate licks, different ideas, different notes. Then if I come up with something that I want to save, I show it to Kenny Baker or Billy Box, and have them help me remember it. It's a way that I do music.

Rathe: You've probably run into some groups doing electric bluegrass. How do you react to that?

Bill: That's all right for them. But I wouldn't want to electrify our music because it would take away from it, I think. If they want to electify theirs, and they see a future in it, I'm for them 100 percent.

---

8. Actually titled "Daddy Bluegrass," the song was recorded by Stoney Edwards. See the editor's comments, fourth paragraph.

Rathe: Do you like to listen to it?

Bill: I don't mind if they got a good song going. But if they sang "Blue Moon of Kentucky" and they had it jazzed up like Elvis Presley did it or something like that, why, I wouldn't listen to it.

Rathe: What do you say when these young musicians ask you for advice?

Bill: I try to give them just as good advice as I can, in a way of tellin' what I think they should do, if they're gonna be a banjo player or a fiddle player or whatever . . . They need to rehearse, they need to rehearse every day, and not try to copy somebody else, and get their style going, and follow it on up. I was asked one time . . . we was talkin' about bluegrass, and folk music, and rock and roll . . . which would last the longer. I said bluegrass would. I saw that folk music would never stay, and the rock and roll, 'course, died out a lot, too. They got a little stuff they call "bluegrass rock," and I know there's no such thing as bluegrass rock, because you got to be pure in bluegrass. You might come up there and say it's "bluegrass rock," but it should be kept pure, and rock should be kept pure, and jazz should be played . . . where you're born on it.[9] It comes back to jazz or old blues or pure church song. It's got to come back down there some way. It's just like a big league ball player. There's just so far he can go and really be a big leaguer. If he went out to turn hand springs, he couldn't catch that ball right. So that's the same thing about bluegrass music or any kind of music, the way I look at it. If a man's playing the fiddle, I can tell whether he's playing that number right, (even) if I have never heard that number before. I know the way it should go.

Rathe: You have really developed your own style and led the way in bluegrass music. Are you happy when you see it come out in other ways and other places?

Bill: Yes, sir, but you could take from bluegrass music same as you could take from jazz and do it in your style and it would be fine.

Rathe: How do you feel when you sit down and look around and see hundreds and hundreds of musicians playing bluegrass, and some of them don't even know who Bill Monroe is because they might have picked up a banjo and come into it from a whole other direction?

Bill: Well, I think it's great. It gives you a feeling that they really love your music, and that's what they really want to play; that they get a feeling out of it theirself. As I have said many times, bluegrass music is kind of a challenge from one entertainer to the next. The guitar player wants to play it as good as he can, because there's another guitar picker right around the corner, and he's going to be studying hard on it, working hard on it so the man doesn't get ahead of him. That's kind of the way it is with this music.

Rathe: So far, you have been able to stand out clearly in front of bluegrass, and you've been working hard at it for a long time. I'm sure that if you wanted to, you could retire comfortably in Nashville. What keeps you working on the road? What's the thing you're after now?

9. Respecting the values one was born (and raised) with; in a natural way.

Bill: What I'd like to do now is keep my health; go, if I can, as long as possible, and help people in bluegrass music. That gives me a good feeling, that I'm doing something good every day through my life, especially now, you know, I want to do something in that day if I can. I don't want to retire.

Rathe: Is there a specific goal that you think about sometime? You have played almost every hall, you've been on TV and radio and records, worked with big names and small ones. . . .

Bill: Well, there's a lot of memories down through the years. I've had the best musicians in the world, and if they wasn't the best, I made 'em the best before I got through with them. Go back to the startin' of bluegrass music, there's a lot of memories down through the years. . . . When it comes right down to it, I want to learn to live the right way. You know what I mean, in religion. That's really the final word on it. It's what I want to do and believe in. I know that it's right and that's what it's got to come down to. That was the idea of singin' hymns and havin' a Blue Grass Quartet: to let people who follow bluegrass music know that we know that there's a better side, a better part. That's a good part of bluegrass music that we try to carry all the way.

Originally published in *Pickin'* 1:1 (Feb. 1974): 4–8. Reprinted by permission of the author and the publisher.

EDITOR'S COMMENTS

Rathe, then a freelance producer and radio show host, interviewed Bill on December 10, 1973, for the premiere issue of *Pickin'* magazine (February 1974). (This selection differs from the original mainly in matters of punctuation and in that the date in the first question has been changed from the date of publication to the date of the interview.)

Bill wasn't kidding when he complained, in a joking sort of way, about banjo pickers. Between 1971 and 1973 at least eight musicians picked banjo with the Blue Grass Boys.

The *Bean Blossom* album[1] was released in November 1973, about a month before this interview. It included four tunes played by twelve fiddlers, a truly amazing sound, recorded at the 7th Annual Bean Blossom Bluegrass Festival in June of that year. Two of the tunes, "Swing Low, Sweet Chariot" (which Bill spoke glowingly of here) and "Down Yonder" were later released on a 45 rpm single (MCA, 40220).

Bill was undoubtedly proud of the song he called "The Daddy of Bluegrass" (actual title: "Daddy Bluegrass"), written by his old friends Boudleaux and Felice Bryant. Recorded by Stoney Edwards, one of the few successful black country singers other than Charley Pride, it was released as a single (P-3766) by Capitol Records in November 1973, and peaked at no. 85 (of 100) after seven weeks on the *Billboard* country singles chart.

Three months before this interview, in September 1973, Bill had dedicated a monument to his uncle Pen in the Rosine, Kentucky, cemetery during Rosine's centennial celebration.

Note

1. *Bean Blossom,* MCA Records, MCA2-8002, released Nov. 1973.

Bill Monroe and His Blue Grass Boys: An Illustrated Discography (excerpts)

NEIL V. ROSENBERG

I have a clear memory of the first time I heard a recording of Bill Monroe and his Blue Grass Boys. It was as one of a group of neophyte bluegrass fans in a college dormitory, sometime in 1958;[1] the record was a Decca 45 rpm single of "Molly and Tenbrooks." We had been excited by bluegrass records of Flatt and Scruggs and the Stanley Brothers, and had heard about the famous recording of "Molly and Tenbrooks" that Earl Scruggs had made back in the forties with Monroe. As we listened to this record we were impressed by the banjo picking and told each other that Scruggs really did a good job on that one; and we wondered if Monroe, who (we thought) had retired, was still alive.

The misconceptions which that record conjured up were slowly corrected in my mind—I learned six months later about the other Monroe recording of "Molly and Tenbrooks" on Columbia which featured Scruggs. It took me another six months to discover that the banjo player on the Decca recording was Don Stover. And only slowly did I become aware of the fact that Bill Monroe had not retired, that he was very much alive and could be heard almost any Saturday night during the winter if one stayed home and tuned to WSM ("Clear Channel 650 on your radio dial") and listened to the Grand Ole Opry from Nashville.

It was not until 1961, some three years after I first heard him on record, that I had the opportunity to see Bill Monroe in person. I had just moved to Bloomington, Indiana, and my next-door neighbor, a fan of old-timey country music, told me about a nearby country music park which Monroe owned and his brother Birch operated. On a beautiful Sunday evening in late June—the time of year that Bill now holds his festival—we drove out into the Brown County hills to Bean Blossom. No more than a half dozen cars were there at the Brown County Jamboree, even though it was 8:00, show time, and we wondered if Monroe would actually perform for such a small crowd. My neighbor and I approached a blonde woman, standing next to

1. Rosenberg was a student at Oberlin College at the time. See the editor's comments, second paragraph.

an old Oldsmobile station wagon[2] with Tennessee plates, and asked her if Bill Monroe was really there. She assured us that he was, so we paid and went in.

Later that evening we recognized the blonde lady on stage, playing bass with the Blue Grass Boys. Other members of the band along with Bessie Lee Mauldin that day were Tony Ellis on banjo, Bobby Smith on guitar, and, filling in for that date, Shorty Sheehan on fiddle. Although there were no more than twenty people in the audience, Monroe gave a fine show. Afterward I went backstage to talk with Tony Ellis and look at his fancy Paramount banjo; he let me play a tune on it. Shorty Sheehan, who, with his wife Juanita, constituted the "house band" at the Jamboree that year, invited me to drop by any Sunday and play a few numbers on stage with them. Within a few weeks I was a member of the house band.

During the next seven years I spent many Sundays at Bean Blossom, sitting in the audience, tape-recording shows, jamming backstage or out in the parking lot, playing in house bands, and, for one season, managing the Jamboree.[3] During that time I probably missed no more than three or four shows at Bean Blossom by Bill Monroe. As I became familiar with his music I learned that the membership of his band changed constantly. On any given Bill Monroe show date there was usually one member of the Blue Grass Boys who had been with him longer than the rest; the group might also contain persons with virtually no previous experience in the band. Often Monroe would fill out the roster with local musicians, such as fiddlers Roger Smith and Shorty Sheehan, both former Blue Grass Boys. Sometimes he would bring along musicians from Nashville for a specific date. On several occasions I filled in on banjo with the group, and it was after the first of these that I, embarrassed about my lack of knowledge of Monroe's repertoire, began actively purchasing his recordings.[4]

Records have never been the most important part of Monroe's musical career. I suspect that he has often been as distant from the companies he worked for as the consumers who purchased his records. The following experience illustrates this point. On October 28, 1962, I attended a show by Monroe at the Brown County Jamboree. That year the Jamboree was leased and managed by a record store owner from Terre Haute, who had a record rack with albums for sale each Sunday before and after the show. That Sunday I found a copy of a new Decca album by Monroe, *My All Time Country Favorites* (DL 4327). I bought it and after the first show took it backstage and handed it to Monroe, asking him to autograph it. It was at once obvious that he had never seen this particular album before. He put on his glasses, read the list of titles and the notes on the back of the jacket; he turned it over and looked

---

2. A 1958 Oldsmobile station wagon, only three years old at the time, but older mileage-wise by then, and even older in memory.

3. Rosenberg managed the Jamboree during the 1963 season. See the editor's comments, third paragraph.

4. Rosenberg has written further of these days in *Bluegrass: A History* (Urbana: University of Illinois Press, 1985), and in "Picking Myself Apart: A Hoosier Memoir," *Journal of American Folklore* 108 (1995): 277–86.

at the front picture, and then, shaking his head, carefully turned the cover back over and signed it so that the autograph was upside down in relation to the printing on the back.

Excerpted from *Bill Monroe and His Blue Grass Boys: An Illustrated Discography,* (Nashville: The Country Music Foundation Press, 1974), 3–4, 22. © 1974, The Country Music Foundation Press. Reprinted by permission of the Country Music Foundation, Inc.

EDITOR'S COMMENTS

Bluegrass historian Rosenberg's first book was published by the Country Music Foundation Press in 1974, eagerly awaited by those fans who knew of its coming. Initially it was available only at the foundation's Country Music Hall of Fame and Museum in Nashville (I drove all the way from Columbus, Ohio, just to buy a copy). Packed with the first accurate data on all of the recordings by Bill and the Blue Grass Boys up to that time, a carefully-researched biographical sketch, and great photographs of past bands, it also included Rosenberg's own memorable recollections of his early encounters with Bill.

When he heard his first Bill Monroe recording in 1958, Rosenberg was attending Oberlin College, near Cleveland, Ohio. Mayne Smith ("First Bluegrass Festival Honors Bill Monroe") was one of his roommates.

Rosenberg was hired by Rinzler to manage the Brown County Jamboree during the 1963 season, replacing Bill's brother Birch, who was judged to be inefficient. Bill was angered at first, but by the end of the season he asked Rosenberg to stay on the job for 1964. However, due to his heavy course load at Indiana University, Rosenberg declined.

In March 1974, prior to the publication of Rosenberg's *Discography,* the Grand Ole Opry was moved from the Ryman Auditorium to the new Grand Ole Opry House at Opryland.

As of this writing, Rosenberg and country music historian Charles Wolfe are nearing the completion of a revised edition of the discography, to include all of Bill's recordings (1936–96).

"Bluegrass Touches—An Interview with Bill Monroe"

CHARLES WOLFE

Wolfe: Bill, how do you feel when you're called "The Father of Bluegrass Music"?

Bill: Well, I don't mind that. That's really the truth, you know. I accept that, I guess, as well as any man could. I think it's a great honor to originate a music. Really something to be proud of.

Wolfe: I'd like to go back with you and explore some of the ways you developed this music. Could you tell us a little about your mandolin playing, where it came from?

Bill: Well, Charles, to start with, I wanted to have a mandolin style of my own, not play like anybody else. There wasn't many mandolin players in the country when I started. And I didn't want to copy any of them, so I taken from the old-time fiddle music of my uncle Pen Vandiver. I guess, maybe, I taken a little from the fiddlers, you know, and put with my mandolin playing. Down through the years, since I first started, my playing has changed at least three times, and you can check back, say, in the thirties, and then check it now, and it's a little different type of mandolin. But I wanted a style of my own and that's what I finally come up with. And I guess it's helped a lot of mandolin players.

Wolfe: As you said, when you started playing, there weren't many mandolin players. About the only one that comes quickly to mind is Ted Hawkins of the Skillet Lickers.[1] Did you ever listen to him? Or know him?

Bill: No, the fiddlers with the Skillet Lickers covered the mandolin up, you know. The guitar player came out pretty good, Riley Puckett, but I didn't take anything from him.

Wolfe: Did you play the fiddle yourself any?

Bill: Oh, I used to play a little bit. Never was good enough for me to hardly listen to, much less somebody else.

Wolfe: What model mandolin did you use on the early records?

Bill: It was the F-7, the Gibson F-7. And it was a good mandolin to work as a duet, you know, when we had what we called just country singing, you know. Charlie and me. Then I kept it on until around '41, and I found this F-5 that I've kept down through the years.[2] And it's been a great mandolin in a bluegrass group. If you're

---

1. Hawkins didn't record with the Skillet Lickers until 1934.
2. Bill probably found his first F-5 in 1945.

really in a tight spot, you've got a powerful crowd or a big auditorium, that mandolin will always come through for you. It's got plenty of volume and it carries good and if you want to soften up, it's got a beautiful tone. So it's just perfect for what we use it for.

Wolfe: How did you develop that high lonesome tenor part so characteristic of bluegrass vocals?

Bill: Well, Charles, from the time I was a young boy in Kentucky, seemed like . . . my brothers, they'd all left, you know, and my father and mother had passed away, and I lived on the farm a long time, and all that I heard was a foxhound or the birds or something like that. And I would sing kindly the way I felt. I'd be out in the fields, maybe, rabbit hunting or something like that, and . . . I've always liked the touch of blues, you know, and I put some of that into my singing. I like to sing the way it touches me; it makes me feel good. And I like to sing from the heart, and in singing that way, I hope it will touch the man that's listening to me, that he will get the meaning of what I'm doing, and it will touch his heart too.

Wolfe: As a boy growing up in Kentucky, do you remember listening to any other singers? For instance, Vernon Dalhart? Jimmie Rodgers? Any of the old-time singers?

Bill: Well, Vernon Dalhart had a pretty good voice, I thought, a clear voice. People like Jimmie Rodgers touched me with *some* of the songs they sang, like the "Mule Skinner Blues." Then, later on, people like Bradley Kincaid, he had a good clear tenor voice, good voice to listen to. And, you know, Charles, I didn't sing a solo until I was 27 years old. I'd always sung tenor. But with training to be a tenor singer, to get up and hit high notes, when I started singing solo, there wasn't any trouble for me to hit any note, see? I'd trained my voice and cultivated everything and my throat was in fine shape—I never smoked nor drank—and I could hit any note, didn't make any difference. And being able to do that in singing bluegrass, "Mule Skinner Blues" or "Blue Moon of Kentucky," why, it was perfect to sing those kind of songs.

Wolfe: Probably two of the most distinctive voices in country music are yours and Roy Acuff's. How would you compare your singing with Roy's?

Bill: Roy sings the mountain type of singing, I think. My singing is . . . you know, to start with, I thought bluegrass music would never get no further than the farmer; I'd designed it the way I thought he would like it, because that was where I was raised. Since then it's spread and growed and it's all over the world today. But Roy's as good a friend as I have. But, you know, talking about vocal styles, we can't leave (out) people like Ernest Tubb. He's played his part too. I think the three names, you know, they've done a lot for the Grand Ole Opry.

Wolfe: Where did you begin making your first professional appearances?

Bill: Up in the northern part of Indiana, up around East Chicago and Hammond, Gary, right in there. We went on the radio—I did—when I was 18 years old, at Hammond, then we'd play wherever we'd get to play, anybody that wanted us, they didn't have to pay us nothing, we just wanted the experience. We thought it was great for somebody to want us to play. But then around 1934, why, they went to paying us: we got $11 a week apiece, at Gary, five days a week.

Wolfe: During this time, did you consider yourselves more singers or instrumentalists?

Bill: There were three of us working together: Charlie and me had another brother, Birch Monroe, and he was an old-time fiddler, so he wanted to fiddle a lot, and so we followed him. Once in a while we'd sing a little.

Wolfe: You made your first records with Charlie in Charlotte on February 17, 1936. How did that recording session come about?

Bill: We had two programs a day on radio in Greenville, South Carolina, or rather one in Greenville about noon and we was on in Charlotte, WBT, real early in the morning. We drove about 100 miles from one place to the other; then we played schools of a night. To make these records—they kept after us—RCA had Bluebird, that was their side label—to record for 'em, so we finally went up to Charlotte. When we got there the Delmore Brothers was recording with Arthur Smith. Our time was short—we had to get back in time to play a school that night—and they made the Delmore Brothers and Arthur sit down and let us record right quick and get back to our playing the school that night.

Wolfe: According to the files, you did nearly all those records on one take. That was quite an accomplishment in those days. Another interesting thing about this first session is that about half the numbers were sacred numbers.

Bill: Yes, numbers like "What Would You Give in Exchange for Your Soul?," "This World Is Not My Home"—they were really popular in the South and in the Carolinas. "What Would You Give in Exchange for Your Soul?" was really great; it was the talk of the country. That was our first release, backed up with "This World Is Not My Home."

Wolfe: Where did you learn "What Would You Give in Exchange for Your Soul?"?

Bill: It was a song I learned in church. Where I was raised up at Rosine, Kentucky, they had a little Methodist church there, and a Baptist church to start with, and later on a Holiness church. But I learned to sing "What Would You Give" back when I was around 14–15 years old. They used to have singing conventions and each church would have a choir and they would meet at a certain church in Kentucky and have the singing convention. And "What Would You Give" was great there, "He'll Set Your Fields on Fire," "Beautiful Life"—was great songs back in them days. So Charlie and me recorded that and it was a great number for us.

Wolfe: The conditions of recording back then were quite different than today. Do you remember having any special problems recording?

Bill: We sung on the same mike, I remember. But one thing—if Charlie said one word and I said it different, why, they never did correct us. I was real young, and we let a few things like that get by that should have been corrected. I guess it was balanced pretty good, they brought the mandolin out and the guitar and it wasn't a bad setup. I guess if we had it to do over, some of the songs would be pitched higher than we had 'em back in them days.

Wolfe: Was the man who recorded you Eli Oberstein?

Bill: That's right; he come down to get us to go with RCA, on Bluebird.

Wolfe: They had a temporary studio set up in Charlotte?

Bill: That's right, it was a warehouse, where they handled their records in Charlotte. Victor Record Company. And it was just right back . . . they had two mikes set up in this place where they kept the records. Looked just like a warehouse, wasn't nothing fancy. So we went back and sung right in the middle of this warehouse and recorded there.

✍

Wolfe: How did the term "bluegrass" come about? Had you heard the term applied to your style of music before you began using it?

Bill: After Charlie and me broke up, I was searching for a name for my group. And I wanted a name from the state of Kentucky. Before I come to WSM in Nashville—I started on WWNC, Asheville—why, I'd already decided on using the name "bluegrass," because that's what they'd call Kentucky, the Blue Grass State. So I just used "Bill Monroe and the Blue Grass Boys," and that let people throughout the country know I was from Kentucky, saved a lot of people from having to ask me where I was from. Governor Ford,[3] he claims I've done more than any one man for Kentucky—every time I use the word "bluegrass" it leads back to that state.

Wolfe: What kind of word was used to describe the music back then, before it was called bluegrass? Country music? Old-time music? Hillbilly music?

Bill: Old-time music was what they used, up in Kentucky there.

Wolfe: Can you recall the first time you heard anybody use the term "country music"?

Bill: Seems like after I come to the Grand Ole Opry in '39, a little later on they went to calling it country music. Seem like to start with, though, to me, they called it old-time music. Or mountain music. But country music come later, then country and western.

Wolfe: Would you have been insulted if somebody had called the music "hillbilly music"?

Bill: Well, I never liked the name, the word "hillbilly." It seemed like maybe another state out west would call you hillbilly if they thought that you'd never been to school or anything, that you didn't know enough to get out of where you was raised at, in a mile or so. The word "hillbilly," I've never liked that, and I've never used that in my music. I think more people every day, they're discontinuing that word.

✍

Wolfe: Could we talk about fiddling for a few minutes?

Bill: I'd like to.

---

3. Wendell H. Ford, governor of Kentucky, 1971–74.

Wolfe: The first fiddler you heard was your uncle Pen. Could you tell us a little about him?

Bill: He was my real uncle on my mother's side. He was a wonderful fiddler for the old-time square dance like they used to do. If they was going to have a square dance up there around Rosine, why, Uncle Pen was the man they called for, if they could get him. And, Charles, back in them days, if you made a couple of dollars, two dollars and a half, why, it was big money at a square dance. But he played wonderful time and it was good to dance to.

Wolfe: Did you play with him on these square dances when you were young?

Bill: Yes, I did. I played the mandolin some, and then I played the guitar some behind him. When some of the other boys had left home and gone out to work in Detroit and places, Uncle Pen and me would go play for a dance, or where they would want some playing. We'd ride horseback to get there.

Wolfe: You said somewhere else, I believe, that you felt your uncle Pen was playing something kind of close to what we now call bluegrass. What did you mean?

Bill: His timing was good and I learned to keep time from him. I've used fiddle music in my music, you know, 'cause I think the fiddle is the king instrument in string music. I've used that fiddle all the way, with banjo, mandolin, guitar, and bass—it gives me what I want in the way of instruments in bluegrass. But I can still study the sound that comes from different fiddlers, especially way back in the early days, I know how they would have played it, or the way they should have played it— I think I can just keep going on back and on back and bringing out tones the average man would never have heard of, or thought about.

Wolfe: How was the fiddling of the old-timers like your uncle Pen different from fiddling today?

Bill: Bluegrass music is a music that's really polished up. You take pains with it, and if there's a G you're playing in and it needs to go in another chord, you go there today with it. Where maybe back years ago they didn't hear that, and a lot of times there was minors and they never would go to it because they never did know how to make a minor chord. Well, bluegrass has been kind of a school for the people, in a way of learning . . . what should be put in it and everything about it. And the fiddler, he's come a long way too since the old-time fiddler. The bluegrass fiddler today, well, say we'll talk about Kenny Baker, who's with me: Kenny is as good in bluegrass as Rubinoff[4] would have been in his music years ago. That's how far bluegrass music has come along, and how the fiddler has studied his music. He knew he had to come with it in order to be what should be played today. The banjo picker has done the same thing—he has come a long way.

Wolfe: The fiddler today, then, is more intelligent and sophisticated than the early fiddlers?

Bill: That's right. He has advanced a long ways from the old-time fiddler. You take an old-time number like "Sally Goodin" played by a modern fiddler; maybe

---

4. David Rubinoff, classically-trained pop violinist of the 1930s and 1940s.

back in the old days there was fiddlers that could have played it as well as he could, but maybe the guitar picker wouldn't have been the best, or the mandolin picker, he didn't hear very well—I know when I started I didn't hear the changes like they should have been made, and had to learn all that stuff. But today they've got all the chances in the world. It's kind of like you raise a child up to get to be 7, 8 years old, well, everything is in front of him, television, and he hears radio, and he's got a good chance today to advance. Well, it's the same thing in music: the music is right there in front of all the young people and in their spare time they can take a guitar or a banjo and learn to play without any trouble, because they've heard some other man that they like in the banjo or the fiddle or mandolin.

✍

Wolfe: Some of the finest fiddlers in the country today have played under you. It reads like a Who's Who: Kenny Baker, Chubby Wise, Howdy Forrester, Art Wooten, Bobby Hicks—all of these men have been part of the Bill Monroe band at one time. How about some comparisons? For instance, how would you compare Howdy Forrester to Chubby Wise?

Bill: Either one of them would have trouble with the other man. Both great. Howdy speaks of it, that he done his best playing when he was with me. Chubby Wise would have been hard to beat. And Bobby Hicks was great in the way of knowing a fiddle; he could play the best second fiddle ever you heard—he just played exactly like the first fiddler played. Of course, Art Wooten was the first fiddler with me, from Sparta, North Carolina, and I found him in Asheville, got him in my group, come to Nashville. Art was a wonderful old-time fiddler, and he played numbers like the "Mule Skinner Blues" or "Back Up and Push" or "Orange Blossom Special." The old-time fiddle numbers, he was hard to beat, man.

Wolfe: How would you compare the technique of Howdy and Chubby?

Bill: Chubby's a little bit more a lonesome type of fiddler, and he plays some blues in it. And Howdy—now, he's the first man to play with me that played double-stop,[5] and Howdy knows that neck all the way, and he knows how to get that tone out, give the fiddle a chance. Chubby might could have beat Howdy on a song, but Howdy would have beat Chubby on a fiddle piece like "Cotton-Eyed Joe" or stuff like that. So it balances pretty close out.

Wolfe: And what has Kenny Baker added to it?

Bill: Kenny is the kind of a man that has learned my music all the way, and he's learned what I want played and plays as near like as I sing it as he can. And, you know, for a man to get up against Kenny Baker today, he'd be fighting a losing battle, because Kenny knows bluegrass music—there's never been a better one.

Wolfe: What about Vassar Clements? He's a fiddler a lot of the young people today are interested in. You had him in your band back in the 1950s.

Bill: Vassar started with me when he was a young boy, 20, something like that, or

5. Playing two notes together in harmony.

21.[6] Well, Chubby, the other fiddlers, had got out of the way, and Vassar come in. We had a number called the "New Mule Skinner Blues." Well, Vassar was powerful on that. He put some new notes in it that was fine, that every fiddler went to searching for, to do it the way Vassar done it. And Vassar is the blues fiddler, you know. Now, there's fiddlers that would beat Vassar on "Sally Goodin" or the old-time fiddle numbers, but Vassar would beat 'em on a number like the "Mule Skinner"—they couldn't touch him on that. And if you wanted some blues played, Vassar could do it.

Wolfe: You knew some of the great old-time fiddlers now dead, as well. What did you think of Arthur Smith's fiddling style?

Bill: There was a day when Arthur was *the* fiddler all through this country. You couldn't beat him with his kind of music. Arthur touched his music with some blues in it too. He played a slow bow, but he noted the fiddle beautiful. Numbers like the "Sugar Tree Stomp," numbers like that, you couldn't beat Arthur on it.

Wolfe: What about Clayton McMichen? How would you evaluate him?

Bill: Back in the early days, he was the best. I've played with Clayton, and after Clayton left the Grand Ole Opry and went to Louisville, he'd come back down here and he'd always come to me and talk with me, you know, about bluegrass music. But if you check the way I would play a fiddle number like "Fire on the Mountain," and check the way Clayton plays it, you'll find it note-for-note, the same way. Separate your notes, keep your timing right, let your tone come out.

Wolfe: When Clayton came to talk to you about bluegrass music, what did he think of it?

Bill: He praised bluegrass all the way, and he praised me the same way. He was proud of our friendship. But Clayton done a lot for music. If it hadn't been for Clayton McMichen, the Skillet Lickers would have suffered for a leader in the way of fiddle music.[7]

Wolfe: Was Gid Tanner not much of a fiddler?

Bill: Well, he was a fiddler, but was a more old-time fiddler. Clayton had studied on, and he was putting in everything in there. In a contest, Clayton would win.

Wolfe: Did you ever have a chance to hear Lowe Stokes?

Bill: Lowe Stokes was a wonderful fiddler; I heard some of the recordings he made, and I thought they were great.

Wolfe: When you were growing up in Kentucky, did they use the long bow[8] or this so-called jiggy bow?[9]

Bill: Well, that jiggy bow didn't come out till the Georgia shuffle, and that's where a lot of that started from. Of course, a lot of fiddlers played a little jiggy bow, but most of them had a little shuffle.[10] Uncle Pen had the greatest shuffle you ever seen.

6. Clements was twenty-one when he first recorded with Bill in 1950.
7. The Skillet Lickers featured multiple fiddles played originally by McMichen, Gid Tanner, and Bert Layne. Layne was later replaced by Lowe Stokes.
8. Several notes are played with one movement of the bow.
9. For each note played there is a movement of the bow.
10. A repeated rhythmic bowing pattern, suggestive of a galloping horse.

He didn't note so good, like a lot of fellers, with all four fingers, but he had a shuffle that was out of this world, man. And it was good to listen to, and he got the tone; he tuned his fiddle up, what they called the "bass and counter up,"[11] a lot of times, and he played right on the note, it wasn't neither sharp nor flat, and it was good.

Wolfe: Did you ever in Kentucky listen to Burnett and Rutherford?

Bill: Don't believe I ever heard 'em.

Wolfe: You talked elsewhere about a group called the Foster String Band; was this the group from Elgin, Kentucky?

Bill: No, the Foster String Band I knew about was from Central City, McHenry, down in that part of the country. They played for square dances, old-time fiddling and guitar picking behind it.

✍

Wolfe: How much of bluegrass music can we trace back to black artists? How much has been borrowed from Negro musicians?

Bill: Charles, it would be very little, 'cause I wouldn't let enough be put in it to make it blues music. It was just very little of it in different phrases of the singing and the notes. Now, if the number was wrote, say, "The First Whippoorwill," or numbers like that, we'd put in quite a bit of a blues. Say you're coming from the church, you'd find some lonesome sounds in church songs, you know. And a lot of my sounds come from numbers like the Methodist or Baptist or Holiness singers; you'll find that in my music, to where the Negro blues couldn't overtake it, or it wouldn't overtake the Negro blues.

✍

Wolfe: You joined the Opry in the late thirties?

Bill: That's right, started there in '39, the last Saturday night in October in 1939. Roy started about a year and a half ahead of me, but Roy taken a relief of absence once, for a year or something, and my playing has gone straight on through.

Wolfe: You knew Judge Hay, then; what kind of a man was he?

Bill: He was a wonderful man; he was just a prince. He would help you in every way and talk things out with you; you knew that Judge Hay wanted to be a friend to you.

Wolfe: Judge Hay, of course, had a reputation for keeping the Opry "down to earth." He didn't like electric instruments, didn't like drums; what did he think of Bill Monroe's bluegrass music? Did he consider this something new?

Bill: Charles, I went into Nashville on a Monday morning. I'd come from Green-ville, South Carolina. I was going to move to some other radio station. I come in on Monday and I believe that they told me that Wednesday was their day to listen, but they would be back. Judge Hay and Harry Stone and David Stone was all going

---

11. For this tuning, also called "high bass and counter," the G string, or "bass," is raised in pitch to A and the D string, or "counter," is raised to E.

out to get coffee—as I got off the elevator on the fifth floor, they was going out. And they come back and I played the "Mule Skinner Blues" for them, and "Bile That Cabbage Down," "John Henry," and another one, and they said I had the music that National Life[12] needed—that the Grand Ole Opry needed. Said I had more perfect music for the station than any music they'd ever heard. One thing they told me that made me feel good: they said, "If you ever leave the station, you'll have to fire yourself." And that stuck with me all the way.

Wolfe: You've played with some of the old-time greats on the Opry: Uncle Dave Macon, DeFord Bailey, and Sam and Kirk McGee.

Bill: Yes. In fact, DeFord and Uncle Dave and Sam and Kirk all worked for me at one time. There was four great men right there. Uncle Dave was the finest showman in the world; if the crowd really wanted him and he was selling good, he could really turn on, man. He was powerful. And DeFord Bailey, there wasn't a better man in the world than DeFord to get along with. He was just a fine man, and with the harmonica, it was great. That's a kind of music I love too, you know, the way that DeFord played. And Sam and Kirk McGee—there's not two better men in the state of Tennessee. Friends to you. As musicians, wanting to take care of their fans, and be real men. You know, down through the years I had—maybe we'd be somewhere and I wouldn't really be feeling good, and Kirk McGee would be the first man there. You can't beat them kind of people.

Wolfe: How influential do you think Sam's guitar playing has been?

Bill: It's sure played its part. Sam does a wonderful job with his playing, and it don't seem like he's slipped at all; he's gettin' way up in years, but he still plays a fine guitar. And I think a lot of people copied from Sam's playing in the way of playing a guitar.

Wolfe: If you had to pick the three finest old-time guitarists, who would be on the list?

Bill: Well, I would have to pick Travis, you know; I think he's a great man with his music, and there's been many a man that's copied from Merle. You know, they say he learned from a man in Kentucky. Well, I know this Mose Rager he learned from, he learned from Arnold Shultz, the man I speak of, a colored man, in playing the blues. So I think it all leads back to this old colored man back in Kentucky.[13]

Wolfe: You went on to make records, to go on tour and make personal appearances, and to broadcast. Looking back on it all, which do you think was probably more important to you?

Bill: Well, I would say for the bluegrass fan and the musician that's followed

---

12. The National Life and Accident Insurance Company, the original owners of radio station WSM and the Grand Ole Opry.

13. Rager learned to play from another guitarist who learned from Shultz. See the editor's comments, second paragraph.

bluegrass, the Grand Ole Opry's the most important thing. At least it was in the early days. In the early days you needed advertising, needed people to know where you was coming. That was good headquarters in Nashville and it give all the entertainers the chance to know I was there. In the early days, you know, I went 11 years without missing a Saturday night. Well, anybody that was interested in the fiddle and the banjo playing, if I . . . say, Fiddling Art Wooten left me one Saturday night, another fiddler knew he'd better get busy 'cause he, if he was going to work with me, he had to get in touch quick. It's been a turnover like that. When Don Reno heard that Earl Scruggs had quit, he was in that week, searching for me to go to work. We left Nashville, went to Taylorsville, North Carolina, to put on a show and Earl was working his two weeks out, Don Reno come to the theater, ready to go to work.

Wolfe: Speaking of Earl, when he was with you in the mid-forties, did you have any indication that this man was going to revolutionize banjo picking?

Bill: Back in the early days, Stringbeans[14] was the first banjo picker with me. What I wanted was the sound of the banjo, because I'd heard it back in Kentucky, and I wanted that in with the fiddle and the rest of the instruments. So Stringbeans give us the touch of the banjo and he was a good comedian. And when "String" quit—he had to go in service—when he come out, him and Lew Childre joined up. And Earl Scruggs needed a job. I had three appointments with him, and I missed the first two ones, and the third one I went down to where he was at, and Howdy Forrester was the man that got Earl Scruggs the job with me.[15] So when I heard Earl, I knew that that banjo picking would fit my music. It all come from a man in North Carolina named Snuffy Jenkins. That's where Earl learned from, and all the pickers that played three-finger style. But he could help take lead breaks like the fiddle, and would be a great help to me. So that's why the banjo was in my music. Without bluegrass, Charles, the banjo never would have amounted to anything. It was on its way out.

Wolfe: Was Earl using the Scruggs tuner[16] when he was with you?

Bill: I don't think so. That came later.

Wolfe: How would you evaluate Stringbean as a banjo player?

Bill: Well, of course, he played clawhammer style,[17] and he was good with that. That's the same kind of style that Brother Oswald plays. But it was good, it give you

---

14. David "Stringbean" Akeman and his wife Estelle were murdered by burglars on November 10, 1973, about a year before this interview. Bill always called Akeman by his original stage name, "Stringbeans."

15. According to several sources, including Scruggs, it was fiddler Jim Shumate, who was working with the Blue Grass Boys at the time (late 1945).

16. The device Scruggs used to change the pitch of certain strings in tunes such as "Earl's Breakdown" and "Flint Hill Special."

17. Aural evidence indicates that instead of a clawhammer style, Stringbean used a two-finger style of picking, at least on Bill's 1945 recordings.

the tone of the banjo, and a lot of numbers, that fit fine with it. But in this day and time, that's kinda a thing of the past too.

Originally published in *Old Time Music* 16 (spring 1975): 142–55. Reprinted by permission of the publisher.

EDITOR'S COMMENTS

In the fall of 1974 Wolfe interviewed Bill on radio at Middle Tennessee State University's WMOT-FM in Murfreesboro. Transcribed and titled "Bluegrass Touches," the interview appeared in the spring 1975 issue of *Old Time Music,* published in London, England. Bill and the Blue Grass Boys were appearing in the British Isles at the time (Tom Wolf was in London then and tells of his encounter with Bill in "I Hear a Sweet Voice Calling").

The legendary guitar player Merle Travis of Kentucky, who Bill picked first as one of the finest old-time guitarists, credited Mose Rager and Ike Everly (father of the Everly Brothers) with teaching him what became known as "Travis picking." Rager and Everly, in turn, reported learning from Kennedy Jones, who learned directly from Arnold Shultz.

"Common-Law Wife Seeks Divorce from Bill Monroe"

VALARY MARKS

Bill Monroe's common-law wife, Bessie Lee Mauldin Monroe, has filed an unusual suit for divorce from the country music entertainer known as the *King of Bluegrass.*

The divorce, citing abandonment and cruel and inhuman treatment as grounds, was filed by Madison attorney Homer R. Ayers late Tuesday in Davidson County Chancery Court.

For many years, however—since the establishment of Judge Benton Trimble's Fourth Circuit domestic relations court in 1956—divorce cases have traditionally been filed in Circuit Court.

Circuit Court Clerk George Rucker said today he could not remember even one case that involved a marriage in common law.

John L. Murray, chief clerk under Rucker, said he did remember one case Trimble heard in the late 1950s in which Trimble ordered the couple to get legally married before granting a divorce.

Mrs. Monroe, in her suit, lists the date and place of her marriage to the singer as "1960—Georgia, Alabama, South Carolina, and various other states."

Mrs. Monroe, 54, said in her suit that in September 1941 "at the age of 17, (she) was lured by the defendant from her home and family in Norwood, North Carolina, to become part of Bill Monroe's country music band.[1]

"She and her family were initially advised by the defendant that he was an unmarried man, that he was an honorable man, and that he would take care of the complainant as would a guardian," the suit said.

The suit said Mrs. Monroe was "soon faced with sexual demands" from Monroe and "after a time submitted and was forced into a form of concubinage under the dominion and control of the defendant."

According to the suit, Mrs. Monroe later became aware of Monroe's marriage to Carolyn Brown Monroe.

Mrs. Monroe said she traveled and worked with Monroe,[2] "serving as his mistress" from 1941 to August 12, 1960, when the defendant was divorced.

She alleged Monroe "thwarted" her attempts to form relationships with other men and when she did marry Nelson C. Gann in 1948, she said they were separated in 1951 "directly as a result of various actions on the part of the defendant." She and Gann were divorced November 28, 1951.[3]

The suit said when Monroe was divorced from his first wife, he was enjoined from marrying the plaintiff during the lifetime of his first wife, according to Trimble's final decree in that divorce.

Tennessee does not recognize common-law marriage, but Mrs. Monroe said she and Monroe traveled as husband and wife in several states which do recognize common-law marriage.

In 1954, Monroe purchased a 288-acre farm in Sumner County for their home, said Mrs. Monroe. In 1964, she said Monroe asked her to stay home at the farm and, she said, at that time she became established in the area as Mrs. William S. Monroe.

She said she was registered to vote as Bessie Monroe and Monroe continued to introduce her as his wife.[4]

The divorce suit is based on Mrs. Monroe's allegation that Monroe "completely abandoned" her in September 1970. She is still living at the house purchased by Monroe, but he "refuses to provide for her needs except for a meager supply of food."

---

1. Mauldin was born in 1920, so she was closer to twenty-one years old when she left home to go with Bill.

2. Initially featured as a singer, Mauldin became the band's bassist. See the editor's comments, second paragraph.

3. Her absence during this time may have inspired several songs written by Bill. See the editor's comments, third paragraph.

4. This may have led to Rinzler's acknowledgement of "Bessie Lee and Bill Monroe" at the end of his 1963 *Sing Out!* article, "Bill Monroe—'The Daddy of Blue Grass Music.'"

She said her health has deteriorated and she is unable to properly take care of herself. She said she has no money for future needs.

EDITOR'S COMMENTS

This dose of reality appeared in the *Nashville Banner,* the city's now-defunct afternoon newspaper, on Wednesday, July 30, 1975. It was found amid the clippings files of the Country Music Foundation Library in Nashville.

Dubbed "the Carolina Songbird," Mauldin was initially featured as a singer on road shows with Bill and the Blue Grass Boys. She later played bass with the band, eventually participating in almost all of Bill's recording sessions between September 1955 and April 1964.

Mauldin's absence from 1948 to 1951 probably inspired Bill to write "Can't You Hear Me Callin'?" (in which Mauldin is mentioned by name in the second line of its chorus: "A million times I've loved you, *Bess*"), "Travellin' Down This Lonesome Road," and many other songs of lost love written and recorded during that time.

No resolution of the suit was reported. Mauldin left the farm in 1976, and lived in the Nashville suburb of Hendersonville for a while before returning to North Carolina, where she died in 1983.

Stars of Country Music (excerpt)

RALPH RINZLER

Bill Monroe

For almost thirty years,[1] Bill Monroe's music stood as the only communication of his complex creative philosophy. His musical gospel was powerful enough to establish a new genre in country music and to attract thousands of disciples. Like many charismatic but laconic artists, he was surrounded by a public unable to penetrate the body of legend which had grown up as a result of his silence. The country people from whom he came and for whom he created were honored and content to shake his hand or obtain an autograph. With him, they shared a common cultural heritage; no explanations or analyses, however interesting, were necessary. As Carlton Haney said: "For us Southerners, it's natural. . . . The people up north, I think

---

1. From 1934, when Bill became a full-time musician, to 1963, when Rinzler's *Sing Out!* article about him was published.

truly, they have a different mind. . . . They can tell you what notes you're playing in a row . . . while down south, we don't know what we're doing. We just like to hear it. . . . Down south, any musician can sing harmony. Up north they can't. They don't understand it." Haney's point is significant. Bluegrass music is profoundly meaningful to country people; they have no need to "know what they're doing" through the descriptive means of musical notation or tablature. They accept Monroe as a leader, and if, in the early days, he offered no more than his music, they enthusiastically accepted it and did not prod for biographical and philosophical data.

This was not the case with Bill's urban, northern audience, which began to grow within ten years of the Blue Grass Boys' first appearance on the Grand Ole Opry. By the late forties the audience had expanded northward, reaching institutions like Putney, the progressive Vermont boarding school, as well as Harvard, Radcliffe, and Swarthmore by the early fifties. The 1954 mimeographed edition of Pete Seeger's manual *How to Play the Five String Banjo* included a chapter on "Scruggs style" containing the first known tablature of Scruggs's playing. Seeger's transcriptions were symbolic of the new audience's cultural distance from Monroe and his country fans. The printed page, helpful in setting forth musical techniques, aided in bridging the gap which resulted from the fact that the urban northerners did not share cultural traditions with Monroe and his southern following. There were many questions. No record notes, popular or scholarly articles, or even Grand Ole Opry song and history books had the answers. No one had the answers, nor would an attempt be made to get them for almost another decade. What were Monroe's early musical influences? What traditions did he draw on when shaping his music? What sort of man was this who stood in the capital of the new-emerging commercial country music world and bucked the tide or simply ignored it by playing with nonelectrified instruments a repertoire which included more archaic instrumental and vocal material than was played by all his peers on the Opry combined? The answers lay in the unwritten story of Bill Monroe. No country people asked; no city people could ask. Monroe related to the public only through his music.

Isolated by circumstances as a child, he remained so by choice or by habit as a man. He was conscious of the effect his indifference had on others:

> Minnie Pearl said she went five years and she wouldn't even talk to me. She said she was afraid of me. Now she laughs and talks with me. A lot of fans were that way. . . .
>
> I didn't talk much, Ralph, and I guess 'cause I didn't talk much, that the people thought, "Well, I guess he doesn't want to be bothered." But it wasn't really that. I just had a lot to do, and I worked hard. I would talk short to a lot of people. . . . I had all my life ahead of me then, you see. And I did respect the fans and my friends, but I think of them more (now) than I did back then.

One had only to watch a Monroe stage performance at a country music park, as Mike Seeger[2] and I did for eight years before speaking to Bill, and it was clear that

---

2. Seeger took Rinzler to see Bill for the first time. See the editor's comments, second paragraph.

he put up with nothing. "All right, I've got some solo numbers we're gonna do for you . . . and the first one's called 'My Little Georgia Rose,'" he would say to the audience, following this with an audible aside to the band: "In the key of B there, boys, and let's go with it." Not wishing to drop the pace of the performance, he would start beating time on his mandolin as banjo and guitar pickers scrambled for capos while the fiddlers started the tune quickly, trying to remember the subtle difference between that song and "Rose of Old Kentucky." After the performance, a few older country people who seemed to know Bill slightly did gather and talk with him. We did not know him and were young and less than courageous.

At each performance Mike and I were observing Bill's interaction with his band, focusing on his vocal and instrumental improvisations. It was clear that he was a unique synthesizer, a cultural figure of signal importance in our time. Having grown up listening to Library of Congress field recordings, we were aware of the degree to which Bill integrated elements of varied secular and sacred folk music traditions and styles. We shared observations and speculated about the figure who we knew was the originator and shaper of "bluegrass music," as disc jockeys had called it since about 1950. In 1962, a *Sing Out!* cover story naively, but enthusiastically, asserted: "Scruggs has become the undisputed master of Bluegrass music."[3] There was reason for dispute, and I felt confident that Earl himself would be embarrassed by the *Sing Out!* statement. Editor Irwin Silber agreed to do a cover story on Bill Monroe if I would write it.

On June 24, 1962, Bill Monroe and his Blue Grass Boys were performing at Sunset Park in West Grove, Pennsylvania, and the Stanley Brothers were at New River Ranch.[4] During an intermission, when I approached Bill about an interview, he merely said he knew Mike and me from years back and had seen us recording at the side of the stage, and then suggested: "If you want to know about bluegrass music, ask Louise Scruggs." He walked off.[5]

Through the intercession of Carter and Ralph Stanley, who came up from their nearby booking, Bill finally agreed to an interview, which took place in August. He answered my questions unenthusiastically, but accurately and precisely. That conversation provided data for the first substantive article on Bill Monroe, his heritage and music. It was only after Bill read that article and notes to a recording of the Greenbriar Boys[6] which clearly credited him as the originator and continuing force

---

3. Pete Welding, "Earl Scruggs—and the Sound of Bluegrass," *Sing Out!* (Apr.–May 1962), 4–7.

4. About fifteen miles to the southwest.

5. Rinzler neglects to mention an important event prior to his asking Bill for an interview. See the editor's comments, third paragraph.

6. Liner notes written by Rinzler for *The Greenbriar Boys,* Vanguard, VRS-9104, released ca. Mar. 1962.

in bluegrass music that our relationship became one of unquestioning confidence and trust and that I began to gather data for a biography.[7]

Excerpted from *Stars of Country Music: Uncle Dave Macon to Johnny Rodriguez*, ed. Bill C. Malone and Judith McCulloh (Urbana: University of Illinois Press, 1975), 202–5. ©1975 by Board of Trustees of the University of Illinois. Used by permission of the University of Illinois Press.

EDITOR'S COMMENTS

Rinzler discussed the events that led up to the writing of "Bill Monroe—The Daddy of Blue Grass Music" in the opening paragraphs of his monograph on Bill for *Stars of Country Music*.

It was Mike Seeger who took Rinzler to see Bill for the first time at New River Ranch in Rising Sun, Maryland, on Sunday, the Fourth of July 1954.[1] Both Bill and the Blue Grass Boys and Charlie Monroe and the Kentucky Pardners were appearing there on that day, Charlie's fifty-first birthday, a day "celebrated by millions."[2] (Coincidentally, within a day or two, Elvis Presley would record "Blue Moon of Kentucky" in Memphis, Tennessee.)

Recalling developments prior to June 24, 1962, when he asked Bill for an interview, Rinzler neglects to mention that in April he and the rest of the Greenbriar Boys had made a special guest appearance on the Grand Ole Opry, arranged for by Louise Scruggs, Earl's wife and manager of Flatt and Scruggs.[3] It is very likely, knowing Bill and his keen awareness of what went on at the Opry (his "turf"), not to mention how easily he could be slighted, that this is what he was referring to when he said, "If you want to know about bluegrass music, ask Louise Scruggs."

Rinzler's biography of Bill, which the University of Illinois Press planned to publish, was never completed. Answering a recent query about it for the Internet discussion group BGRASS-L, Judith McCulloh of the Press explained that "after talking with Monroe, [Rinzler] felt that the book should instead be an autobiography done by Bill, an 'as told to' sort of thing, for which Ralph would provide an extensive introduction." But writing was a chore for Rinzler: "Getting Ralph to write the *Stars of Country Music* article was like pulling hens' teeth. While he spoke and wrote with great eloquence, he didn't write easily, and there were many other tasks he enjoyed more." Busy with his job as assistant secretary for public service at the Smithsonian Institution, Rinzler briefly considered teaming up with another writer, but nothing came of it. Complications had arisen concerning royalties and whether the Smithsonian should publish it, causing further delay: "Time went by. Ralph took on more and heavier duties at the Smithsonian. Now and again he talked about doing the Monroe book—'Projects get delayed,' he once wrote me, 'not cancelled.'—but no manuscript materialized, at least nothing that I ever saw or heard mention of."[4]

---

7. This biography, which the University of Illinois Press had planned to publish, was never completed. See the editor's comments, fourth paragraph.

Charles Pendleton "Charlie" Monroe died on September 27, 1975, at the age of seventy-two. On October 10, in his memory, Bill sang "Weary Traveler" on the Friday Night Opry.

Notes

1. Information derived from an unfinished biography of Ralph Rinzler by Kate Rinzler.
2. Charlie and Bill Monroe, *The Monroe Brothers: Their Life, Their Songs* (Raleigh, N.C.: By the authors, 1937), 3.
3. From Kate Rinzler's unfinished biography of Ralph Rinzler.
4. Judith McCulloh, message from the Internet discussion group BGRASS-L, posted July 31, 1999. For information about this discussion group, send the command "INFO BGRASS-L" in an e-mail message to LISTSERV@LSV.UKY.EDU.

"Daddy Bluegrass and His Blues"

MARTHA HUME

The sun is beginning to set in Nashville and the big yellow and red sign that says "Hall of Fame Motor Inn" lights up, casting its neon glare into my room. My friend[1] and I are talking the time away until Bill Monroe calls to take us to dinner.

"Now, Martha, I want you to get him to tell you about when he was growing up in Rosine," says my friend. "You know he was cross-eyed and he never did talk and he would run away and hide in the barn when strangers came, and I think that's why he's so shy and why people think he's so stuck up. It's just didn't nobody look after him when he was little."

"Well," I answer, "we'll just have to see what he'll say. I mean there's lots of things he's told you that he might not tell me. You're his friend and he doesn't know me except for that one time I met him."

Actually, I'm not sure whether Bill Monroe will tell me anything. I've heard stories about him, about how hard it is to get him to talk and about how he might just take a notion to snap your head off. As a matter of fact, nobody I know, except for my friend in Nashville, has ever had anything good to say about Bill Monroe personally, although everyone respects his music and his position as "The Father of Bluegrass Music." It isn't exactly easy to interview a legend, especially if that legend turns out to be hostile.

"Let's get him to take us somewhere nice, like the Peddler," says my friend. "I've been trying to get him to take me there forever. We can have steak."

As I am wondering whether he's going to take us anywhere at all, or show up, for that matter, the phone rings. My friend picks it up, talks for a minute, face falling all the time.

---

1. Hazel Smith, a columnist for *Country Music* magazine.

"The man's out at Shoney's Big Boy, clear out on the interstate. He wants us to meet him out there now."

I knew it. He would pick the one place in town where it's practically impossible to make a decent tape, what with all those dishes rattling and Muzak playing and the food comes so fast that dinner's over in 30 minutes. Well, there's nothing to do except go. If he wants to eat at Shoney's Big Boy, then we eat at Shoney's Big Boy. We grab our coats, pull out onto the interstate and head south. I start reviewing my knowledge of Bill Monroe lore.

Born, September 13, 1911, Rosine, Kentucky. Mother died when he was 10, father died when he was 16, went to live with his fiddling uncle Pen, met black blues player Arnold Shultz, moved to Indiana to work in the oil refineries; joined brothers Birch and Charlie in a touring WLS square dance troupe; he and Charlie begin performing together as the Monroe Brothers, they move to North Carolina, record for RCA's Bluebird label, split up in 1938; Bill forms Blue Grass Boys; they join Opry in 1939, get first encore ever given at Opry;[2] start touring with Opry shows; Bill gets own tent show, then adds exhibition baseball team, becomes famous in the forties, career slows down in fifties, picks up with the beginning of bluegrass festivals in the sixties, now recognized as a musical genius and "Father of Bluegrass Music." We always call him "Daddy Bluegrass." I feel like a walking history book.

Our particular Shoney's is in a shopping center, with one of those great big parking lots where I'm sure I'll be killed someday by a hot-rodding housewife scratching out from the Kroger store. We pull up beside Bill's maroon Pontiac station wagon, and go inside.

Bill Monroe is sitting with his back to the door in a booth toward the rear of the restaurant. The place is filled with suburban families and their screaming kids and the clatter and the Muzak is as loud as I had expected.

I reintroduce myself to Mr. Monroe, start making some desultory conversation and order a Big Boy, fries, and a Coke. Maybe it will be easier if we talk about a neutral subject at first. He has a farm out near Goodlettsville.

"Do you have a tobacco base[3] out on your place?" I ask.

"Got it leased out this year."

"Oh. Well, we have a little base up in Kentucky. Just six-tenths of an acre, but it put us all through school. They go by weight[4] down here now, don't they, I mean, instead of by base?"

"Yeah, I believe they do."

"Oh. Well, how're things out at your place? I hear you been doin' a lot of work out there."

"Well, I got a bulldozer out there, makin' some new pasture for the cattle this summer."

---

2. This is not known for certain. See the editor's comments, second paragraph.

3. A percentage of a farmer's total acreage on which tobacco may be grown, set by government regulation.

4. Alternatively, the number of pounds a farmer may grow is now also regulated.

"What you gonna sow in the pasture?"

"Probably fescue[5] mostly."

"Oh. That's real good for cattle."

My hopes of getting the world's best interview with Bill Monroe are sinking slowly in the West. I get out the tape recorder anyhow, put it where the clatter seems the least serious, make lame assurances that he'll soon forget it's there, just talk like you usually do. Darn! I've forgotten my questions.

"I guess you haven't been playing much lately, I mean, in the winter and all, there aren't many festivals. . . ?"

"I played nine dates so far in January."

"I bet Bill plays more dates than anybody on the Opry, don't you Bill?" My friend is trying to come to the rescue.

"Probably so," answers Bill Monroe, staring off into the distance.

He looks distinguished sitting there, back straight, silver hair, eyes straight ahead. He drums his fingers constantly against the Formica table top as if in time with some rhythm in his head. He fidgets from side to side, looks like he's going to bolt any minute. But eventually he begins to talk. His conversation centers around the past, the past where there were no cars, no Shoney's Big Boys, no electric guitars. It all seems so out of place in this model of American fast food expertise, talking about 1911. Bill Monroe doesn't notice. Once he lets his mind drift back to the land, the past, to Rosine, he doesn't seem to notice his surroundings. And come to think of it, if Bill Monroe's been playing music since 1939, he must have eaten dinner in thousands of places like this. He's probably as at home here as he is out on his farm. He's telling us about foxhounds.

"I love foxhounds, you know. I love to hear 'em run as they give their mouth. A lot of people don't understand. There's lots of dogs that's got wonderful mouths. They got a high tenor voice or a deep sharp, or they'd be a turkey—you know, one that barked like a turkey—or some had screamin' mouth. Put 'em all together, it makes a wonderful sound. I keep about 15 dogs now. Late in the evenin' we have some races. A lot of things like that has helped me, give me ideas about things."

The little boy who listened to those hounds fifty years ago was skinny, shy, the youngest of 8. His mother died when he was 10 years old.

"I was alone a lot of my life, you know, when I was a kid. And nobody to play with. I started to work when I was 11 and there wasn't a lot of playtime for me, but going to school or somethin' like that, and maybe they (his brothers and sisters) would be out workin' someplace and the evenin' would be lonesome, you know. Well, that's in my music, that part of it. And that was where a touch of the blues went in it, the feelin' of it. How I was feelin' years and years ago. There's many times, I believe, when the blues does you good. It ain't only the colored folks has the blues;

---

5. A variety of grass commonly grown in pastures.

there's many a white man that's had 'em. I've had 'em, many, many times. And they's times that I have 'em today."

The blues must have come often to Bill Monroe. After his mother died, he was left with his father, already an old man,[6] and his older sisters and brothers who probably weren't too interested in their shy kid brother.

"They didn't nobody look after you, did they, Bill?" gently asks a friend. His answer is slow, and more is implied than is spoken.

"No," he answers. "I guess they'd see that I had clean clothes, you know, for the weekend. To go to school. But they had their own life to live and I guess that they thought that that might have come first. So they was gettin' married, some of 'em, and datin' girls, datin' boys. So I stayed home with my father. That's what leads back to where me and him would listen to the fox hounds, you know, and it'd be on a Saturday night. But he was up in the late sixties, goin' on 70 years old and that's probably all he wanted to do. My mother had gone. And he would never marry again—didn't want to. So to hear a good pack of fox hounds was what he loved. I stayed close to him and there wasn't nothin' to be scared about. 'Cause he was the most wonderful father in the world and a straight, honest man, truthful. I don't guess you could be any closer than me and him was. I had a wonderful feeling in me that he was a wonderful man and I was proud to be his son."

Bill's father died when Bill was 16.[7] The family moved in with relatives.

"Father and Mother died and all of 'em left home. Some was stayin' with one uncle and some with another. My sisters, I believe, was stayin' with my uncle that I was named after, Uncle William. And up at another uncle's they was havin' measles and things, and I couldn't stay there. Uncle Pen, he was by hisself and he was lonely and would like for me to stay there, so that's where I stayed. He was a crippled man and needed help carryin' water and wood. I stayed there probably three years.[8] I worked in the timber and hauled crossties."

Uncle Pen—Pendleton Vandiver—was an itinerant trader and fiddler of some note. It was while he was living with his uncle that Bill Monroe formed the core of what was to become his music. Uncle Pen knew lots of old-time fiddle tunes—tunes which Bill remembers to this day—and helped his nephew learn the all-important sense of timing that was to distinguish his music. It was also during this time that Bill met Arnold Shultz, a black fiddler and guitarist, who introduced him to the musical blues. By the time his uncle Pen died[9] and he went off to Indiana to work in the refineries with his brothers, Bill Monroe had learned the basic elements that he would use to form his musical style, but it took almost 10 years for that music to take shape.

Between the time he left Kentucky and made his first appearance on the Opry, Bill worked in East Chicago, Indiana, and ended up practically supporting his old-

---

6. He was sixty-three.

7. Bill's father was seventy when he died in 1928.

8. Probably less than two years, during 1928 and 1929.

9. Bill left Rosine before his uncle Pen died.

er brothers, Birch and Charlie, as well as several[10] sisters. Then the three joined one of WLS Radio's traveling road shows as square dancers. Birch returned home,[11] and in 1934, Charlie and Bill formed the Monroe Brothers. They worked their way through Iowa and Nebraska, then south to the Carolinas where they made their first recordings for RCA's Bluebird label. Although the pair was quite popular, personal differences came between them, and in 1938, they split up. Charlie formed his own act too, and was quite popular for several years, but he was never to gain the fame of his younger brother.

What happened was that in 1939, Bill Monroe, accompanied by his first band of what he called "Blue Grass Boys," joined the Grand Ole Opry. That first band was composed of Art Wooten on fiddle, Cleo Davis on guitar, Amos Garen on bass, and Bill Monroe on mandolin. An early picture of the band shows a young, almost funny-looking Monroe, dressed in jodhpurs, riding boots, white shirt, tie and hat, eyes still crossed, mouth tight, already intense, with a smiling group of young men behind a WSM microphone. Bill looks alone.

That first appearance on the Opry was historic. Few people have ever gotten the reaction that Bill Monroe and his Blue Grass Boys got that night. The number they performed was a new version of Jimmie Rodgers's "Mule Skinner Blues." But instead of the usual, mournful, atonal, monotonous rendering that the song got, this band provided a driving beat, and emotion that had not been there before. When it was over, Bill Monroe got an encore.

"When I first started, I knew that was the music I wanted. When I started on the Grand Ole Opry, I'd come up from North Carolina and South Carolina, and I knew that the blues was really getting ready down there, that they loved it, and I knew if I got a 50,000 watt station, I was pretty sure that they would accept it."

Accept it and like it they did—overwhelmingly. Bill Monroe was an overnight sensation. The only real competition he had came from Roy Acuff, but since they performed in different styles, there was no conflict between the two. Monroe and his band started touring with the Opry road shows six nights a week, returning to Nashville on Saturdays. Later, Bill got his own tent show and added an exhibition baseball team.

The number of famous musicians who did time as Blue Grass Boys is legion. Art Wooten was the first fiddler, Dave "Stringbean" Akeman the first banjoist. Then came Earl Scruggs, Lester Flatt, Chubby Wise (who composed what many feel was the best band), Cedric Rainwater,[12] Jimmy Martin, Carter Stanley, Don Reno, Mac Wiseman, Sonny Osborne, Charlie Cline, Vassar Clements, Kenny Baker, Byron Berline, Roland White, Howdy Forrester, Benny Martin—in short, enough musicians to form an orchestra; certainly enough to form a movement.

And a movement is exactly what was formed. Flatt and Scruggs had their Foggy Mountain Boys, Jimmy Martin formed the Sunny Mountain Boys, Carter Stan-

---

10. Two.
11. Birch continued to work at the oil refineries.
12. Stage name of bassist Howard Watts, also a member of "the best band."

ley went back to the Stanley Brothers and the Clinch Mountain Boys; Sonny Osborne joined brother Bob with the Osborne Brothers; Don Reno, with Red Smiley,
performed as Reno and Smiley; and, later, Berline and White formed a modern bluegrass group, the Country Gazette. In short, the Blue Grass Boys became a training
school for bluegrass musicians. The Bill Monroe style, imprinted on all of them,
became a branch of American music, separate from country, folk, or pop.

Today, Bill Monroe reigns as the king of his music, the instructor, the inspiration for a whole generation of American musicians. The years have metamorphosed
the shy, ugly kid into a master musician, respected by all, feared by many, a true father
figure. Like a father, Monroe is probably misunderstood by his "children."

Today, Bill Monroe is in a position which allows him to survey the scene he has
created with some detachment. The big question everyone asks him is "who will
carry on?" While it looks doubtful that anyone will have to carry it on for quite a
while—Monroe, who does not smoke or drink, is strong as a horse—he does think
about the question. He's looking for someone.

"I guess they's a good many people that could carry on. I think they will. I just
hope that they'll have a lot of willpower and treat their fellow man right. And never get above the people that you're playing for and never get above the way you was
raised. Stay down, like a man should stay. It takes willpower. I can be feelin' bad and
that willpower won't never give up."

Meanwhile, he is looking ahead. He has projects in mind, which he doesn't talk
about, of course. He's the sort of man who would never talk about anything publicly until he could spring it full-blown and perfect with a single stroke. And he's
beginning to think back, to look at what he's done, to decide if it's good.

"I believe that if I had an audience here, a thousand people, and it was a gospel
program, I believe that 90 percent of the people would just as soon hear me sing
'Footprints in the Snow.' And I can't believe the Lord would think I would be doin'
wrong if I did. There's a number that will touch you and there's nothin' leadin' you
the wrong way."

It is a strange comment. I don't quite understand. It's as if Monroe is trying to
justify his life before God.

"And I think that He knows that all the people need to get sung gospel to. But I
think that there's thousands and thousands here that ain't ready and I think that He
knows that 'Footprints in the Snow' would be good for 'em. Bluegrass has got a mea-
nin' to touch your heart. I think that the melodies, if there wasn't a word in 'em, I
believe the Lord would wonder if that wasn't a gospel song. I really think that. And
that's why I'm so proud of this music. You couldn't keep me from havin' willpower."

Bluegrass, to Bill Monroe, is a mission. It has a purpose. It is more than music.
I think this is what he's saying.

✍

The after-dinner coffee is getting cold and bitter. The lights at Shoney's seem
bright. But it feels comfortable now, comfortable to be with Bill Monroe. I hadn't

expected that. I had expected a hard man, maybe even a mean man; but Bill Monroe is neither. I *like* him and I respect him—there is something about Bill Monroe that seems special. He probably is a genius, but that's not it. It is, perhaps, that he seems honest, that he has come to terms with life, that he decided what he wanted to do and did it, a quality which I feel is admirable because I know so many people, myself included, who have no idea what to do with themselves. I tell him this.

"Well," he answers, "why don't you let nature kind of take its course, you know, and be a fine lady, a decent lady, a lady that can talk to a man or a woman. It's pretty near staying in the middle of the road. And you get so much out of life when you treat your fellow man right. There's no use arguing, life is just what you make out of it. I think that's what any person should do—man or woman."

Bill's life, whether he's playing his mandolin or working on his farm, seems to be made of whole cloth—there are no compartments. He treats his farm hands the same way he treats members of the Blue Grass Boys. If you work with Bill Monroe, you do things exactly the way he tells you to; if you don't want to do them that way, you can go someplace else, no hard feelings. That, simply, seems to be his rule for life.

"I don't let any man shove me faster than I want to go . . . or get me on the wrong track. But if it's going to go, my answer's right quick . . . I'm not going to go along the way they want to go. But the other man can decide his way too. I do ask people for their advice. I like to see what they would say before I make up my mind. I don't say I'll take their advice, but if it was good, I would take it. But if I didn't take it, I'd still listen to what they had to say about it. I always treat the other fella right . . . as long as he plays his part right . . . and you try to be friends.

"It's like a lot of people playing music. You know, when they get on stage, they get wrapped up and they let it run away with them. I've planned ahead in the way of . . . how I thought this man was, how to keep him under control and keep him in his place. Maybe the next man wouldn't be as hard, wouldn't be any trouble to handle him. Then, if there's another come along, why, he'd have to toe the mark too."

"Is that why they call you 'Bossman'?"

"Oh, they've called me a slave driver. And I say, well, maybe I was a slave driver, but if a man's going to work for you and you want him to play music, he'll have to do what you say."

"But doesn't that take a lot of self-confidence?"

"Yes, it does. Through my life, there's been very few that's argued with me."

"Musicians or everybody?"

"Everybody."

"Is that because you won't let them?"

"No, it's just because, in talking with them, I stayed ahead of them, or just kept them under control, you know, the way I thought it should be to get along. There's no trouble to handle people, you know, to do that, if you know what you're doing and stay ahead of them. And it ain't wrong. It's in order to keep them on the right track."

"You felt like you were doing the best for them?"

"That's right. It was best for both of us."

We are getting ready to leave, Bill Monroe to go back to his small apartment in Nashville,[13] to his music, to his work on the farm, me to go back to New York, a place separated not only by distance, but by time as well. Both places are equally isolated from modern America.

"Let me ask you a question," says Bill Monroe. "If you were in my place, would you have handled the people the way I have handled them, and kept them under control, all the way, and led them the way you thought they should go?"

A week ago, I would have answered "no." Today, when I stop and think, having seen how alone that way has made the man, and understanding, a little, the certainty and direction such a course requires, and what has been created, I'm not sure.

I am speechless.

Originally published in *Country Music* 4:8 (May 1976): 22–27. Reprinted by permission of Sussex Publishers, Inc.

EDITOR'S COMMENTS

Bill was interviewed in January 1976 by Hume, then managing editor of *Country Music* magazine, accompanied by her unnamed friend, later identified as the magazine's long-time gossip columnist Hazel Smith (see "The Bill I Loved"). By May of the bicentennial year, Bill's smiling face was on the cover of a "mainstream" magazine for the first time and this cover story was inside.

This selection contains the first and only mention I have found concerning Bill and the Blue Grass Boys getting the "first encore ever given at [the] Opry." While it's known that the band encored at its first performance there in 1939, it is not known for certain that this was the first occasion of an encore at the Grand Ole Opry.

Bill was not going "back to his small apartment in Nashville," but rather he was going back to a trailer in Nashville he shared with songwriter Virginia Stauffer ("With Body and Soul"). He hadn't lived on his farm in Goodlettsville for several years, due to his problematic relationship with Mauldin.

---

13. Bill was not living in an apartment. See the editor's comments, third paragraph.

"Bluegrass 'Father,' Monroe, Is at Home on the Farm"

JAN OTTESON

Bill Monroe climbed down from the seat of his tractor. He'd been out "bush-hog-ging"—clearing weeds and undergrowth from his pastures—in Tennessee's sum-mer heat. He was wearing a long-sleeved dress shirt, navy knit slacks, and white shoes.

"Since you're gonna take pictures, maybe I should go inside and change clothes," he suggested. He disappeared into a small, quaint house made of hand-hewn logs and mortar,[1] and reappeared a few moments later wearing faded bluejeans and muddy work boots.

Now the "Father of Bluegrass" was ready to be photographed in his most nat-ural, relaxed habitat—a 300-acre farm tucked away in the densely wooded hills outside Goodlettsville, Tennessee.

"You know, that house has been there for 130 years," he said, motioning behind him. "They built things to last in those days."

Like the house, the rest of the farm displays Monroe's preference for pure func-tionalism. The equipment and buildings are plain but practical, from the old recon-structed barn[2] to the unpainted storage sheds.

"This place is a lot of work, but sometimes the Blue Grass Boys come out to help. They like to get away from it all too," he said, as we hiked up toward the "holler." "You know, I've often told those boys that if they're gonna buy anything, they should buy land. It's a good investment."

Here, walking amidst his herd of cattle, on the property he's owned for 20 years, "Big Mon" seemed totally at ease with his piece of the world. He paused for a mo-ment to survey the area.

"It's really pretty out here in the fall," he mused. "You can come out here, think about what you did all summer, what's ahead of you this winter, how cold it's gon-na get, how you'll spend the nights around the fireplace in the house . . . you think about how you were raised, how your father and mother treated you, how little money you had when you was a kid . . . all of it goes through your mind."

Running a sizeable farm, complete with 80 cattle, four mules, two horses, one pony, two pigs, and a passel of bellering foxhound pups would be a full-time job

---

1. The house had not yet been renovated, and would not be until around 1981.
2. See "Bill Monroe," by Ronni Lundy, for more about this barn.

for most folks. But Bill Monroe keeps himself busy promoting and performing at bluegrass festivals and in concerts year-round and worldwide.

"I like to just run the farm on the side," he said casually. "You can relax here and get your mind off a lot of things. It's a good place to fox-hunt too. And I've always been interested in the cattle business, so I've been buildin' up the herd over the last few years."

As we walked back toward the house, he pointed to a clump of tall sycamores.

"When I first came out here, these were little bitty things. I let them be so that some day I'd have a restin' place in the shade when I was out here plowin'." Now, that's long-term practicality!

When we left Bill Monroe's farm it was evening . . . the crickets were chirping, the foxhounds were baying, the cattle were bawling, and the hogs were squealing for dinner. It was evident that these sounds were music to the ears of Monroe, as much so as the bluegrass music he popularized.

Originally published in *Music City News* 15:3 (Sept. 1977): 13. Reprinted by permission of the publisher.

EDITOR'S COMMENTS

After Mauldin left the Goodlettsville farm in 1976, Bill began fixing up the place, and this brief feature story captured him there. It appeared in the September 1977 issue of the now-defunct *Music City News,* then published in a newspaper format specializing in coverage of the local country music scene. Accompanying the article was a photo of Bill sitting on a swing with twenty-two-year-old Julia LaBella.

Notice that the crickets from old Kentucky (in the 1961 *Official WSM Grand Ole Opry History-Picture Book*) knew where to find Bill in Tennessee.

"Bill Monroe: From Refined Oil to Slick Music"

JACK HURST

The final apprenticeship of Bill Monroe, the musical master known as the Father of Bluegrass, was unwittingly sponsored by the oil refineries of East Chicago.[1] For five years before he began his professional career, he supported himself cleaning 55-gallon drums in a dirty Sinclair "barrel house."

Monroe recalls that after work one afternoon around 1930, alighting from a

---

1. East Chicago, Indiana, a suburb of Chicago, Illinois.

streetcar on his way to an apartment he shared with two brothers and two sisters, he learned that the much-feared murderer John Dillinger had robbed a bank and killed a man in his neighborhood minutes before.[2]

"It was just as quiet that afternoon," Monroe recalls, "over all that city, there wasn't a sound. Finally, a little later on, a police car went down the street after him—drivin' slow."

In later years, fellow musicians, writers, and observers of the bluegrass scene have approached Monroe with almost the same sort of fearful deference. An awe-inspiring figure who makes a high, fast music with extraordinarily grave dignity, he has long gone his own, sometimes lonesome, way in the music business.

Last year, in a move that surprised many, he participated in a bluegrass album by Tom T. Hall.[3] A few years earlier (in marked contrast to such other legendary figures as Roy Acuff, Earl Scruggs, and Merle Travis), he refused to take part in what has become one of the most influential albums in country music, the Nitty Gritty Dirt Band's huge, six-sided *Will the Circle Be Unbroken?*[4]

"I don't think (the Dirt Band) was playing the kind of music Tom T. was playing," Monroe explained in a recent interview.

"He was playing to a country class of people. He was making a *bluegrass* album. I don't know what the Nitty Gritty was playing. People like Roy Acuff or Earl Scruggs could have worked with them and it wouldn't have hurt them, but this music of mine, I originated it, and I couldn't play under another man, because my public wouldn't have liked it.

"I guess the Nitty Gritty have done a lot of rock 'n' roll too, and the bluegrass people wouldn't have liked me working with rock 'n' roll. I ain't got nothin' against it, but it's not bluegrass. All the way through, I've had to be careful how I done my music, and who I worked for."

Monroe, 66, was born in poverty in Rosine, Kentucky. After his parents died, he joined his older brothers Charlie and Birch in Indiana at age 18. Eventually, the three organized a square dance troupe that danced for the WLS National Barn Dance and on road tours.[5]

In 1938, after singing harmony with Charlie as one of the Monroe Brothers for a few years, Bill formed the Blue Grass Boys, a band that gave its name to the music. He led them with high solo singing and a driving mandolin style, and they became a training group for such other bluegrass giants as Scruggs, Lester Flatt, Carter Stanley, Don Reno, Jimmy Martin, and Sonny Osborne.

A mixture of stony egotism and the humility of the common man ("a lot of people think I'm really hard, but I don't mean to be"), Monroe is one of the more

---

2. Dillinger's bank-robbing spree began in May 1933. He was killed by FBI agents at the Biograph Theater in Chicago on July 22, 1934.

3. Bill's participation was minimal. See the editor's comments, second paragraph.

4. This three-record album (United Artists, UAS-9801) was recorded and released in 1972.

5. After forty years, it's still being implied that they danced on the National Barn Dance!

eccentric men in American music. His farm near Nashville has no telephone or modern machinery—because, he explains, "that's the way I was raised."

"When I come in off the road, and I've got three or four days, I like to see the land, the horses and the cattle, and a pack of foxhounds I turn loose every three or four days," he says. "It gets me away from a lot of noise and nerve-wrackin' people."

Despite this strong attachment to his rural youth, Monroe also seems to retain nostalgic affection for memories of urban, smoky East Chicago. Economically, it was superior to out-of-the-way western Kentucky.

"You got paid every two weeks, and you'd get around $65," he recalls. "But rent was cheap, and you could buy a lot of groceries for $5. I'd ride the streetcar to work. We'd come back in after work and eat supper, then, a lot of times, we'd go to a square dance in a club or old store or something in Hammond."

A strong and introverted youth, he developed a fanatical pride in hard work that has characterized him ever since.

"I got to where I could clean 36 oil drums in 15 minutes," he says. "I could roll two of 'em at one time and set one up with one hand. I got to where I could throw a drum like you'd throw a baseball, right-handed or left-handed, so it would slide right up to the next man and he could throw it on farther.

"I weighed about 165 pounds and was young then. I got kind of a kick out of doing it."

EDITOR'S COMMENTS

Hurst, formerly with *The Tennessean,* was the country music columnist for the *Chicago Tribune* when he wrote this column for its October 12, 1977, edition. Bill had described his torturous oil refinery job, which included washing the oil drums with gasoline, in Rooney's *Bossmen,*[1] but this was the first time it was discussed at length in the popular press.

Bill's participation in the recording of Tom T. Hall's newly-released bluegrass album, *The Magnificent Music Machine,*[2] was actually minimal. He played mandolin on only one song, "Molly and Tenbrooks," which Hall sang, recorded on July 16, 1976.

Notes

1. James Rooney, *Bossmen: Bill Monroe and Muddy Waters* (New York: Dial Press, 1971).
2. Tom T. Hall, *The Magnificent Music Machine,* Mercury Records, SRM-1-1111, released 1977.

"Bill Monroe Interview" (excerpts)

DAVID GRISMAN

Grisman: When did you start playing the mandolin?

Bill: I believe I was around eight years old.

Grisman: What made you choose the mandolin?

Bill: Well, it's a true story, you know. There were three of us (Bill, Charlie, and Birch Monroe) trying to play music, and, of course, I was the youngest of eight children, and they all was the boss over me. So, they wanted to play the fiddle, and they wanted to play the guitar, so the mandolin was all that was left. It was a "tater bug" mandolin . . . you ever play one?

Grisman: A round back.

Bill: Yes, sir.

Grisman: Was it in the family, or did someone buy it for you?

Bill: I think they bought it for me there. There was a man that had it, named Hubert Stringfield, so I think some of my people paid him three dollars for it.

Grisman: What gave you the idea to write "Raw Hide"?

Bill: There was a movie star workin' for me from . . . Indiana's where he was born and raised . . . but he lived in California then, and his name was Max Terhune. You remember when they had "The Three Mesquiteers"? He done the comedy part. So he was with me, and he'd made this movie called *Rawhide,* you know. And he toured a lot with us . . . played a lot of theaters. And I wanted to write a number and use the title "Raw Hide." So that was the number I come up with.[1]

Grisman: How did it become your mandolin trademark?

Bill: It really went to grow, that "Raw Hide" did, you know? They loved it and I don't think it's stopped yet . . . I think it's getting better all the time.

Grisman: It's the Mount Everest of bluegrass mandolin.

Bill: It's with the mandolin like "Orange Blossom Special" is with the fiddle. When we were in Japan, "Raw Hide" was the greatest number we had. It had "Mule Skinner" outclassed, and "Blue Moon of Kentucky" too.

Grisman: What about the tunes like "Blue Grass Ramble" and "Get Up John," that use other tunings? Did you do a lot of experimenting with different tunings?

Bill: Well, Uncle Pen tuned his fiddle different, you know, in a lot of those old tunes . . . and so I just started . . . I would see what I could do in the way of tuning the mandolin like he did and also in harmonies.

Grisman: Do you still come up with new tunings like that?

---

1. Bill may have met Terhune while they both were working for WLS. See the editor's comments, second paragraph.

Bill: Yes, sir. I've got a tuning now that I really want to do, and MCA wants me to put it on a record. It goes back . . . the sound, the tone, the tune of this number would go back 150 years, and there's nothing played today like that. You wouldn't need no fiddle in it . . . you wouldn't need a banjo . . . you would use a guitar, if he was careful and be quiet with it, and a bass. But that's all you would need . . . you wouldn't need another thing.[2] If I ever do this number and get it cut, I want you to listen to it, and I want you to play it down through the years.

Grisman: Oh, I'd love to. On the technical side, Bill, what advice would you give to young mandolin players just starting out? What do you think are the most important things to learn?

Bill: Well, I think that learning timing of music, what each number . . . the time it needs to be in . . . and I don't think they need to be too fast; I think they need to be where you can play right. I don't think any number should be too fast. I think you should follow the melody close, learn it good, and you don't need to put too much stuff in it . . . you can tell by the number about how much it needs. Take a number like "Uncle Pen." You wouldn't want to put a lot of extra stuff in it because it don't belong in it, you see? It's wrote about an old man, an uncle of mine, and if you got too jazzed up with it, or too smart with it, or a lot of stuff . . . it would hurt the number. So, any number . . . a waltz number would tell you what you should do with it, if you listen close. So I think that's the way you should look at it.

Originally published in *Mandolin World News* 2:4 (Winter 1977–78): 4, 6–7. Reprinted by permission.

EDITOR'S COMMENTS

Bill and mandolinist Grisman "talked mandolin" in this interview from October 3, 1977, published in Grisman's now-defunct *Mandolin World News,* a magazine for enthusiasts of the instrument.

Bill may have met Max Terhune in the 1930s when Terhune was an announcer for the WLS National Barn Dance. "The Three Mesquiteers" were featured in over fifty movies for Republic Pictures in the thirties and early forties. The cowboy trio was played by several actors including, at one time or another, comedian Terhune and a youngster named John Wayne. The movie *Rawhide,* a western drama in which Terhune had a very small role, was released in 1951. Bill's "Raw Hide" was recorded before the movie's release, in January 1951, but for some reason it wasn't released until January 1952.

The new tuning discussed here was for a tune later titled "My Last Days on Earth," recorded with just guitar and bass accompaniment on February 19, 1981. Unlike the tunings for "Blue Grass Ramble" (in which one of the mandolin's E strings is retuned to A) or "Get Up John" (in which the G strings are retuned to F-

---

2. Later titled "My Last Days on Earth," this tune was recorded in 1981. See the editor's comments, third paragraph.

sharp and A and the E strings to A and D), this tuning requires changing the pitch in three of the four pairs of strings (or "courses") on a mandolin, as follows: both G strings up to A; D strings are unchanged; first A string up to C, the other unchanged; first E string up to F and the other down to D.

"Monroe, the Father, Monroe, the Son"

DON RHODES

The first time I ever watched the Father of Bluegrass Music perform "live" was, appropriately, on the stage of the historic Ryman Auditorium in Nashville—the same stage from which Bill Monroe, Hank Williams, and Little Jimmy Dickens once made up an impromptu trio singing "I'll Fly Away" and "I Saw the Light." Ironically, not long after that, Monroe and Dickens sang "I Saw the Light" with other entertainers at Williams' funeral in Montgomery, Alabama.

The first time I ever interviewed Monroe, however, was a couple of years ago at the annual Georgia State Bluegrass Festival, held at the Shoal Creek Music Park in Lavonia, Georgia, not far from where the movie *Deliverance* was filmed.

This past summer at Lavonia, fate again had me crossing paths with the legendary figure from Kentucky.

On Friday night of the festival's second weekend, I talked with James Monroe about his father, who was due to arrive on Saturday for two days of appearances at the festival.

The situation of James Monroe is similar to, but still quite different from, other people who are in the same business as a famous parent. In James' case, however, his father created the business he has chosen for a career. It is kind of like Henry Ford's son being in the car business. The problem lies in being able to keep your self-respect and sanity, while people expect you to be as great as your famous parent.

It doesn't take too much imagination to realize the pressures experienced by Hank Williams, Jr., Henry Ford II, or James Monroe during their growing-up years. It is no wonder the children of many celebrities turn into rebels seeking some kind of real worth to their lives.

"I don't worry about what people think now. I really don't," James Monroe said that Friday night in Lavonia. "I did when I first started in this business, but I don't now."

James Monroe will never be another Bill Monroe, because, after all, Bill was (and still is) an original. It is my guess, James doesn't want to be another Bill Monroe, anyway. My impression is he wants to be recognized for what he is: A good musician, a good singer, and a good entertainer. What more could anyone in the music business ask for?

He joined his father's group, the Blue Grass Boys, in 1964. James played bass fiddle for five years, and then switched to guitar for two more years. For the past five years, he has been out on his own with his group, the Midnight Ramblers. He has enjoyed the good times on the road, while also suffering the bad.

His worst day on the road occurred only a month earlier from our conversation, when he and his bass player, Tommy Franks, were in a camper van bound from Nashville to Bean Blossom, Indiana, the site of Bill Monroe's annual festival. Other band members had taken other transportation. Franks was driving, with Monroe sleeping in the back. The van hit the back of a semi-truck. Franks was killed, and Monroe was bruised and shaken.

"It was like a bad dream," James related. "Normally, all three of my musicians would have been in the van with me, but Alan O'Bryant was driving Kenny Baker's car up and Blaine Sprouse was driving his own car because he wanted to visit people living near Bean Blossom.[1]

"We had performed at Fan Fair in Nashville earlier that week, where Tommy had also played bass for Mac Wiseman. That week also, Alan, Blaine, and Tommy had performed several nights at the Station Inn nightclub in Nashville. I had wanted to leave at midnight for Bean Blossom, but Tommy asked me to wait until 1 A.M. to leave, so he could finish the last set."

James recalled he rode up front, with Tommy driving, until about 3:30 A.M. "I decided to go in the back of the van and get some sleep. The last thing I told Tommy was for him to wake me up if he felt sleepy."

It was north of Elizabethtown, Kentucky, on Interstate 65, when the fatal wreck happened about 4:30 A.M. "When we crashed into the back of the semi-truck, I woke up. Tommy wasn't killed on impact, because I heard him holler two times. Things went wild, with the van turning over sideways a couple of times. The van nosed into the median, went into the southbound lane, and hit the guardrail. It seemed like it took forever to stop from rolling, with the van landing on its wheels. I climbed out of the back windows, because the top and middle were crushed in. The driver of the truck helped me, since he was the only one else around. We found Tommy dead. I think he had just gone to sleep at the wheel."

James tore some muscles in his left side and bruised some ribs, but was otherwise okay. "I was lucky. If you could have seen that van, you wouldn't believe I could have made it out alive."

Ten days after the accident, the Station Inn hosted "Tom Franks Night" attended by friends, family, and more than 30 Nashville bluegrass musicians, including dobro player Josh Graves. Also, a benefit show was held in late June (two weeks after the accident) at Nashville's Hillsboro High School with performers including Bill Monroe, Lester Flatt, Wilma Lee Cooper, Hubert Davis, and, of course, James Monroe.

---

1. At the time, O'Bryant picked banjo and Sprouse fiddled with the Midnight Ramblers.

"I don't think the true emotional impact of the accident got to me until the next day," James continued. "It was then I really thought about Tommy. He had been with me about two months. Anybody who travels the road a lot should keep a shotgun rider at all times. You can't be safe enough on the road. If you're not careful, you're going to get it."

The leader of the Midnight Ramblers knows quite well the feeling of being a bass player in a band, since he did that five of the seven years (1964–71) with his father. "When I decided to go on my own, it was a hard break. Suddenly, I had to do it all: To make sure of the bookings; keeping the band together; getting the material together, and emceeing the shows."

James, of course, is very grateful for the help his father gave him. "I respect him to the hilt. We have been around each other so long, we can't fool each other. I talk like him, naturally, but his voice is more Scottish. My voice is two or three keys lower than his. I'm not that good an imitator, so I can't imitate that man. If I was doing an imitation of him, I would do 'Blue Moon of Kentucky' and more of his songs. I really don't think I can do my father's songs justice."

One would wonder why James would enter a business created by his father, knowing full well he would be compared to his father. He replied, "I like the music, and when you really like something, you're going to follow it."

He said the average bluegrass music fan is one reason he stays dedicated to performing. "It's a good life being on the stage, and the people who come to the festivals are really great. They will sit in the rain for hours to hear you."

While most bluegrass musicians and stars tend to resemble weathered farmers, James is tall, well-built, and has the looks of a movie star. He is single now after a marriage failed. "You can't travel and be married," he simply explains.

Back on the subject of his father, James talked about another father-son duet album in the works for MCA Records. "We hope to record it this fall and bring it out in the spring of 1978.[2] The last duet album we did[3] was a monster in the bluegrass music field."

When Bill Monroe's touring bus—bearing on the side writing in script which proclaimed "The Father of Bluegrass Music"—came into the Lavonia festival site the day after my interview with James Monroe, I managed to board it and obtain an interview from the man who has been a member of the Grand Ole Opry since 1939, and who has been a member of the Country Music Hall of Fame since 1970.

As we sat at a table in the front "living room" portion of the bus, Monroe drummed his fingers on the table, indicating either nervousness or impatience. I never have been able to tell which it means, even though I have experienced that restlessness during other interviews with him. In spite of this motion, Monroe seemed to enjoy our conversation, talking about his son, his farm, his career, and

---

2. *Bill & James Monroe: Together Again*, MCA Records, MCA-2367, was recorded in January and February 1978 and released in June 1978, four months after this article was published.

3. *Bill Monroe & James Monroe: Father & Son*, MCA Records, MCA-310, released in Mar. 1973.

his future. At one point, he even offered me some apple pie made by a fan. I got him to laugh, and I got him to turn serious. Looking back over the several times I've been around him, he remains an enigma.

He has extreme love for his work ("Bluegrass music will play a big part in your life if you give it a chance"); takes pride in the industry he helped to create; loves his fans ("I have never passed a man who wanted to shake hands with me"), and generously has helped many dedicated bluegrass performers get started in their careers (not just people like Earl Scruggs, Byron Berline, Chubby Wise, and Vassar Clements, but also the newer stars like the McLain Family and Betty Fisher).

Talking about the future album with James, he said, "We're going to start working on it soon. We'll be picking out the songs, with some being old and some being new." Bill described James as having "the Monroe voice, but he has a style of his own."

Almost every father wants to help his son attain success, and Bill Monroe is no exception. He quickly admits to aiding his son whenever the opportunity came up.

"I went all out to help him," Bill commented. "If I mentioned an upcoming show of mine on the Opry, and James had one too, I would mention his show also. If he asked for my advice, I gave it, and if I saw something which might help him, I would tell him. I helped him all that I could."

When Bill was asked whether the Monroe name hurt or helped James, he replied, "It helped him as far as introducing him right quick . . . who he was and where he came from. I think the fans all felt for him and pulled for him, because they knew what he was up against. On the other hand, he was up against a hard road having my name."

Then Monroe turned even more serious. He even stopped drumming his fingers on the tabletop. "No father had a better son than James Monroe. And, you know, there's no son who ever knows how much his father loves him. That love is deep. It goes on for a long time. No son should let his father down, and James has never let me down."

While entertainers have a rough life on the road today, including newcomers like James, life on the road was even harder in the days before custom-made touring buses, nice air-conditioned auditoriums, and booking agencies.

Somehow, we started talking about the old tent shows. I told Monroe a story Charlie Louvin once related about how the Louvin Brothers, in their early days with other groups, would go into a town, put up a tent themselves, go to a service station washroom to clean up, drive around promoting the show, sell the tickets, perform the show, tear down the tent, and do the same procedure all over again the next day.

Monroe said he used to do the same thing, and noted one advantage of the tent shows, saying, "After you got a lot permit for the show, there was nothing anybody could do to give you any trouble. It was like owning your house, until you left the next day. At one time, I had five trucks I traveled with, besides a long, stretched-out bus we had. One truck hauled 1,000 folding seats, another hauled the tent, another hauled the light plant (generator), another was a kitchen on wheels, and the fifth truck hauled the long tent poles. All the trucks would try to arrive at a certain place outside of a town, at a certain time. Then we would drive through the town in a procession to promote the show."

Once, when Monroe and his entourage were getting ready in a motel room near where their tent was set up, they heard a loud noise. They rushed out to find a truck turned over after dropping off a 10- to 15-foot bluff. "It seemed the driver had parked the truck on a little slope above the tent, and he went to sleep in the truck. The truck rolled backwards, and came within 50 or 60 feet of hitting our tent." The tent life for Monroe lasted "six to eight years" in the middle 1940s,[4] he recalled.

Talk of old country music and early bluegrass music got around to Roy Acuff, known as the King of Country Music. "Roy's a fine man," Monroe responded. "He has his style of mountain music. I believe in a man holding what he started with. It is all right to advance your style, but not so you can't recognize it. Ernest Tubb is the same way. He's kept his style. I think Acuff, Tubb, and myself have done more for the Opry than anyone else who has been there."

It is an understatement to say Monroe has kept true to his musical style. The music is as deeply a part of his life as his roots in the Kentucky mountains. On Monroe's *The Weary Traveler* album (MCA-2173),[5] there is an instrumental highlighting Kenny Baker's fiddle playing. The tune is called "Jerusalem Ridge," and it sends chills through me every time I listen to the brilliance of the music, in terms of both performance and composition. Since Monroe wrote the number, I asked him if it is about the same Jerusalem Ridge near his hometown of Rosine, Kentucky.

He answered, "Yes, that's where we fox-hunted when I was growing up. I have loved that area ever since I was a kid. I wanted to write a song about it, and I wanted to go back in time with the music to reflect the Scottish and Irish sounds. It has been five years since I wrote it, with the song having four parts to it. I think it is one of my best numbers."

Throughout our conversation, I had been sneaking glances at a framed poem hanging on a bus wall just over Monroe's left shoulder. He apparently noticed my interest in it, and told me, "You should read that." Monroe then left me alone with the poem, while he went to the rear of the bus. The poem was composed by Jimmie Skinner,[6] with the words in charcoal over a soft drawing in the background of Monroe singing into a microphone. The drawing was by James DeMille.

Monroe said the poem, entitled "He Knew," was given to him by Skinner earlier in the year.[7] It went like this:

---

4. From the early to middle 1940s.

5. Released in 1976.

6. Skinner is famed for his singing, songwriting, and the record store he founded. See the editor's comments, second paragraph.

7. By the time this article was published, Skinner's poem had already graced the back cover of Bill's *Bluegrass Memories* album (MCA-2315), released in Oct. 1977.

He knew the world needed music that was different,
Even back when he was a boy.
With the bluebirds he'd sing 'til the whole world would ring
And Mother Nature would shout from pure joy.

He knew that in music there was sadness too.
That the good old time-tested songs
Often told of lovers, a broken romance,
Of a friend or loved one gone on.

Oft times in the cool of the evening,
When summer was turning to fall,
A short and mellow mandolin to the song "Uncle Pen"
Would blend with the nightbirds' call.

He knew long before he became a man,
He was destined to follow a dream.
That the music he'd make, he'd change and reshape
And take it far from the town of Rosine.

He never patterned himself after anyone else.
He laid a new brand of music down.
When it won wide acclaim, it acquired quite a name.
Some called it the high lonesome sound.

Today it proudly bears a title known to all.
That's Bluegrass, wherever you go.
All started by the man from Blue Grass land,
Kentucky's own, Bill Monroe.

When Monroe came back from the rear of the bus, our discussion focused on the expanding audience of bluegrass music, and Monroe's recent concerts in Japan.[8] "I didn't want to go for several years, but after I went, I realized I could have gone 10 to 15 years before that. They are wonderful people. I was not too nervous before my first performance in Japan, but I was quiet. I knew the largest percentage wouldn't know what I was saying. After the first number, they tore the house down. We played the biggest auditorium in that country. There are only about six groups from the United States that can do that. They were sold out a month in advance of our tour. We may go back. Bluegrass music is also getting very popular in Germany. It is going to be great music there."

Monroe is 66 (born September 13, 1911), but his healthy appearance makes him look younger. "I've always been a worker. I search for work. In Sumner County, Tennessee, between Goodlettsville and Hendersonville, I have a farm of 288 acres. I have horses, cattle, and a big bull. I bought the farm in 1952,[9] mainly to have a place

8. Bill visited Japan for the first time in 1974, and returned there in 1975.
9. 1954.

to hunt and to keep hounds. I got a man with a bulldozer to clear it up, saving the old, good trees, but getting rid of a lot of brush."

There was almost a gleam in his eyes when he added, "I've always loved the country . . . the beauty of it. I like to be on the hills and mountains and see the valleys."

"That's kind of like your life, isn't it, Bill?" I found myself saying. "You are now on the mountain top of your career, after a long climb, and down in the valley you can see all that you have accomplished and the greatness of bluegrass music today, due, in large part, to your work."

He responded to that analogy with a soft tone to his voice, "That's a beautiful thing you just said."

It was getting near the time for Monroe to start dressing for his first concert that weekend at Lavonia. "Do you see yourself ever quitting the road?"

Without hesitation he answered, "I don't see myself retiring. Time will take care of everything. One day it will come to an end. But, I know it would be hard to get off the road and give up the fans. That's one great thing about playing festivals and showdates each year. We meet a lot of new friends and see a lot of old ones at various places. When we near a festival or a show site, we get to thinking about who we will probably see there. That means a lot to me."

As an afterthought, Monroe concluded, "I have no regrets. It's been a good life."

The Bill and James Monroe *Father and Son* album contains on side two a number Bill wrote called "Walls of Time."[10] One verse of the song goes:

> I hear a voice out in the darkness.
> It moans and whispers through the pines.
> I know it's my sweetheart a-calling.
> I hear her through the walls of time.

Hearing that song upon my return home from Lavonia, I thought about what Monroe said about time taking care of everything and one day "it will come to an end." Then I thought about the plaque in the lobby of the Grand Ole Opry house in Nashville, saluting Monroe as the "Father of Bluegrass Music." I thought also about his thousands of fans, who have enjoyed his personal appearances. Finally, I thought about the hundreds of recordings he has made for the RCA, Columbia, and Decca/MCA companies, and the many groups which imitate his sound.

With this great legacy, undoubtedly, long after he has departed this worldly life, we will still hear Bill Monroe's voice in the darkness . . . a-calling through the walls of time.

Originally published in *Bluegrass Unlimited* 12:8 (Feb. 1978): 12–17. Reprinted by permission of the author.

---

10. Cowritten with Peter Rowan.

EDITOR'S COMMENTS

James and Bill were interviewed by journalist Rhodes on the weekend of July 29, 1977, and were featured in this cover story seven months later in the February 1978 issue of *Bluegrass Unlimited.* By that time, the father and son's second album, *Together Again,*[1] was about to be released.

Country singer James "Jimmie" Skinner is famed for his soulful singing, the songs he wrote ("Let's Say Goodbye Like We Said Hello," "You Don't Know My Mind," "Doin' My Time"), and the mail-order record store he founded in Cincinnati, Ohio, in the early 1950s. Born in Blue Lick, Kentucky, on April 27, 1909, he died on October 27, 1979.

Note

1. *Bill Monroe & James Monroe: Together Again,* MCA Records, MCA-2367, released June 1978.

"Bill Monroe Goes about the Business of Bluegrass Music"

LEE RECTOR

It is 10 A.M. A sharp buzz snaps through the silence of an empty office. A button on the telephone is blinking. No one answers.

Getting in touch with Bill Monroe during business hours may take a while. No Code-a-phone . . . no answering service . . . no way to leave a message. If you call when they're out, you just have to call back.

But, if you chance to call when someone *is* in, you are likely as not to hear the "Father of Bluegrass Music" himself answer, "Monroe Talent."

First glance around Bill Monroe's office belies the business environment of a man of influence and prominence. The talent agency is operated from a portable two-room office building out north of Nashville somewhere on Dickerson Road. If he's in town, you will know it. A 40-foot Golden Eagle[1] will be parked out front. Along the side is painted: "Bill Monroe and the Blue Grass Boys."

The bus has seen some miles; but then, so has Bill Monroe.

Monroe is the most successful man in the business of bluegrass music. In fact, if it wasn't for Monroe, there most likely would not even be a "bluegrass" music as we know it today. He wears his "father" title literally.

At 68, Bill Monroe has seen to fruition the growth of a new musical style—most

---

1. Bill's tour bus at the time, differing from the more common "Silver Eagle" model mainly in its golden trim outside and red carpet inside. Made by the now-defunct Eagle Coach Company of Brownsville, Texas, from 1956 to 1974.

of which he directed. Bluegrass affects the lives of virtually everyone who listens to radio, goes to movies, or watches television.

Reflect a moment. When Ford wants you to buy a pickup truck and is demonstrating how rough they are, what's playing in the background? Bluegrass!

That fast-food hamburger joint showing you how quick you can rush through lunch . . . they punctuate it with bluegrass.

When they have a comic chase scene in the movies, what are they two-wheeling around corners to? Bluegrass!

Bluegrass sells! It gets people on their feet, hand clappin', toe tappin'.

It all came about because of this man.

For all the accomplishments Bill Monroe has amassed since his first recording session in 1936 with brother Charlie, he one-track-mindedly went headlong into life, thinking, eating, and breathing bluegrass.

From a meager beginning as a farm boy in Kentucky, this youth would work his way to becoming a regular member of the Grand Ole Opry. He would foster such musicians as Earl Scruggs, Lester Flatt, Vassar Clements, and a hundred more. With mild determination he would take his Appalachian-like front-porch barn dance music, refine it, define it, and carry it to soaring heights. For his accomplishments he would be recognized in the Country Music Hall of Fame. And he would perfect the bluegrass festival to make hundreds of thousands of dollars for himself and others.

But fancy offices, receptionists, and all that other stuff—phooey! That just ain't bluegrass!

It is this man, looking white-haired and dignified in his pin-striped suit, who speaks. "Monroe Talent," he says into the phone . . . "James Monroe hasn't got down here. Can you leave your number so that he can call you back? (pause) This is Bill. Yes, sir. I'm fine. I just got your album and it really sounds good. . . ."

It was a bluegrass group from up north calling—the Piper Road Spring Band. They wanted to see if they can get a booking on Monroe's famous Bean Blossom festival.

Completing their conversation, Monroe informs us with pride: "Bluegrass is turning out to be more like a school of music for people than anything else, and it's really come along in that way. It's learned a lot of people how to play.

"Bluegrass has advanced way on from the way old-time music was played years ago, you know . . . just G, C, and D is about all they played. In bluegrass, music is all up and down the neck. And it's give people in a lot of other kinds of music help too. I can see where it's been placed in other people's music, country songs, and people like that.

"It's a music that they get a lot of good out of. If you listen to it," Bill says, "you will hear many tones and feelings that you wouldn't hear in a lot of other music. The way they do the music, the way they put the notes in it, and the way they slur from one note to another, it just digs into a lot of people.

"There are a good many different ideas in bluegrass music, and different places of the numbers that touch different people. Like, if you was a Scotchman, or if you come from that country, you might like the Scotch bagpipe sound. Or if you lived in this country, you might hear a lot of old-time fiddle music in it too. And there's gospel in bluegrass music. There's old colored blues in it, you know, and some jazz. It's got a hard drive to it. A lot of people like the drive. The good banjoin' and fiddle-drive mandolin, it makes you want to dance lots of times. And there's times when it makes you want to waltz or fox-trot real slow, like they did years ago. So that's dug into people and they understand it and they want to know more about it, the more they hear it."

The influences that are what Monroe describes as bluegrass music today rubbed off from years and years of traveling thousands of miles to play dance halls, square dances, schoolhouses, and the like.

"Back in the early forties, we was drawing good crowds. Of course, the admission wasn't too much. But that give the people in this little town a chance to hear the Blue Grass Boys and that made 'em feel good. A lot of the old-timers that loved music, they'd come right out there and sit all the way through it.

"I used to work five days a week on the road and be here (Nashville) on Saturday (to play the Grand Ole Opry). I think we went 11 years the first time and never missed a Saturday night.

"If you've got a lot of willpower and you're young, it don't hurt you. Back in them days, you know, we traveled in a two-seated car and tied the bass fiddle on the top. Then, a little later, we got a station wagon. But, we didn't have as many clothes back in them days to keep clean and carry with you as you do today. If you really love show business, if you really like to play to people, you love to get on the road and go to some town where you think that they're really wanting you there. It makes you feel good."

"Buzz," the telephone interrupts.

"Monroe Talent," Bill answers. "It's at, uh, I believe, the Asheville Auditorium. Where are you calling from? (pause) Well, I don't think you'll have any trouble finding it. (pause) I believe so. (pause) You're welcome!"

Monroe cradles the phone.

"That was from Alberton, Georgia. They're coming up this Saturday night and they want to know where we're playing."

It's evident that, although Monroe sometimes might seem aloof, from making infrequent eye contact in conversation, he genuinely cares for "the people"—his audiences. Patiently, he listens on the phone to numerous left-field questions and patiently answers all, speaking with everyone who calls.

"Back when I was young," Bill confides, "I had an awful temper. Of course, back in them days, people was different from what they are today. They didn't—the language they used was much better. You know what I mean—cleaner. They didn't cuss you all the time. That's something I never believed in. I was raised never to take that stuff."

But, Monroe admits the years have mellowed his temper somewhat.

"Buzz!"

"Monroe Talent . . . Hello! James hasn't got down yet. All right. Yes, sir. Yeah, pretty good. O.K., fine. He'll be in tomorrow. Yeah, fine. O.K., do that!"

Monroe humbly admits that he presently is the only bluegrass recording artist in the country on a major record label.[2] Even though bluegrass music has proven "commercial," time after time, for sales jingles and background music, bluegrass hits are few and far between.

Monroe's stream of bluegrass hits came years ago, when such tunes as "Mule Skinner Blues," "Blue Moon of Kentucky," "Footprints in the Snow," "Uncle Pen," and others were big sellers. His current MCA albums, mostly Bean Blossom festival specials, are about the only bluegrass product that is widely distributed to record stores. Most other bluegrass records are found in specialty shops, ordered through the mail, or sold by the musicians themselves at appearances.

It concerns Monroe that more bluegrass music is not played on the radio. He thinks increased radio exposure of the music would increase public demand and, therefore, more bluegrass acts would be recording for major companies.

"Here's the way that I look at music." Monroe gazes straight ahead and frowns. "I'm by all music the same way. Let's say that you were going to church and they wouldn't let a lot of people come in if they belonged to another denomination. Well, that wouldn't be right. It should be free to anybody that wants to come there, as long as they're the right kind of people . . . as long as they're decent and they act right. The church should help anybody. I think the Lord would want all the churches to do that.

"So I think if it's a radio station, (just) because they play Top 40 all the time, they shouldn't shun a good gospel quartet. There's a percentage there that would like to hear some good gospel singing. Well, there's a percentage that would like to hear some bluegrass. So I think that if I owned a radio station, I would lean a little bit to everybody—to all kinds of music.

"I like the blues as well as any kind of music. I like gospel. I like western swing— Bob Wills' stuff. You couldn't throw that aside. I would play some bluegrass. I wouldn't play it 24 hours a day, but I would play some of it . . . let people know that I knew something about bluegrass and I respected it. The same about gospel music, Cajun music . . . I think they should be played."

"Buzz!"

"Monroe Talent. James hasn't got around. Who's speaking? Yeah, Ernie Ashworth. Ernie, I called you earlier today and I've been waiting for James to get down. I don't know. He's been tied up all day. Yes, sir. I'm sure he's going to be in the office tomorrow. You getting along all right? I was asking Howdy Forrester, have you heard anything about Ralph Sloan . . . how he's getting along? He did go home. I didn't know that. Well, that's good. Ernie, we'll call you tomorrow around two o'clock."

---

2. Bill had been the only bluegrass artist on a major label for about five years. See the editor's comments, second paragraph.

Monroe hangs up.[3]

Bill was concerned about the condition of Ralph Sloan, the leader of the Grand Ole Opry square dance team, the Tennessee Travelers. (Sloan would die the next day.) Bill expresses sadness at the fact that so many great country entertainers have died over the past few years.

"It seems like, in the last ten years, there's been a good many of them that have left," Monroe offers. "People like Jimmie Skinner and Lester Flatt. Red Smiley, he passed away, and Chubby Anthony . . . he was a fiddler, you know."

The reflection naturally took us to a time when Bill Monroe will no longer be around to carry the lead in bluegrass music.

"That's going to come, you know," Bill promises. "And I just hope there'll be some people . . . take James Monroe or a lot of these young entertainers or some of the old-timers still hanging around. I hope they will stand up for what's right and play the music as pure as they can play it for the people. There's one thing that I hope: that the people, when the time comes, that there will be somebody that will get in there and will hang on and do it right . . . someone that's got a lot of will-power and can get things done." (Monroe's daughter, Melissa, has also recorded.)[4]

Evening was coming around and Monroe began to think about getting back to his farm, a place where he says he can take off the "role" of Bill Monroe, the legend, and put on the "clothes" of Bill Monroe, the farmer.

"I love to go there and loaf around, you know," he informs. "I don't care how hard the work is, or how great it is—if it's plowing or anything like that. I do it myself. I love Mother Nature and I love the lay of the land.

"I watch every day for the sunset." Monroe smiles as the sunset reflects in his glasses. "I've always done that. I love the sunset. You know it's different every day. It always has a different set."

The image brought to mind one of Monroe's favorite moments, when, at the end of his great Bean Blossom festival, he calls all the entertainers on stage for a grand finale. Sometimes 100 or more musicians are standing there with their stringed instruments ringing like a bluegrass orchestra through the woods.[5]

"I really think the Lord would be proud of that," Bill offers. "I know that the music touches a lot of people and they love it. They know it's coming down to the closing of the festival and it's always kinda touched me, because maybe you're going one direction and maybe somebody else will go to Texas or Oklahoma, just having to go all directions to get back home. Really, you don't know whether you're going to see a lot of them or not again. It's always touched me."

As the sun dropped behind the Goodlettsville, Tennessee, hills, Bill Monroe was

---

3. Bill seldom said any goodbyes before hanging up the telephone.
4. Melissa Monroe recorded for Columbia Records in 1950–51 when she was thirteen and fourteen years old; three 78 rpm singles were released.
5. Perhaps the author was thinking of the festival's "Sunset Jam."

leaving his modest office and stepping into his pickup truck for home. Another day of business has come to an end.

Originally published in *Music City News* 17:10 (Apr. 1980): 16 Reprinted by permission of the publisher.

EDITOR'S COMMENTS

Bill was at the office on Tuesday, March 11, 1980, "taking care of business" while being interviewed by Rector, then the editor of *Music City News*. This cover story appeared a few weeks later, in the April 1980 issue. Not long after, a telephone answering machine was installed at Monroe Talent Enterprises, 3819 Dickerson Road in Nashville.

Bill had been the only bluegrass recording artist on a major record label for about five years when this article was published. Lester Flatt (RCA), Jimmy Martin (MCA), and the Osborne Brothers (MCA) had all made their last major label recordings by the end of 1974.

"Bill Monroe's Mandolin Gets an Apologetic Facelift"

LAURA (EIPPER) HILL

Bluegrass patriarch Bill Monroe is generally tight of lip and stern of demeanor, but yesterday he beamed widely and declared the day one of the greatest of his life.

The smile and the unaccustomed verbal extravagance were only fitting. Monroe had just been reunited with an old and dearly-loved friend—the battered, time-worn Gibson model F-5 mandolin on which he's played his famed bluegrass tunes for 40 years. The reunion marked the end of a nearly 20-year-old feud with the Gibson Guitar Company, which presented Monroe with the instrument yesterday at Monroe's Dickerson Road offices, after completely refurbishing it.

"This is wonderful, nothing like it," Monroe said as he cradled his trademark instrument on his lap. "There's not another mandolin in the world can touch it. It's stuck with me all the way, and all these years it's done what I wanted it to. It's wonderful to have it back. This is one of the greatest days of my life."

The instrument, which Monroe bought in a Florida barbershop in 1941,[1] spent the last few months in Kalamazoo, Michigan, at Gibson's plant. There, a team of

---

1. Probably 1945.

senior craftsmen gave it the kid glove treatment, making amends for a botched repair job—the source of a grudge Monroe held for 18 years.

"To start with, I'd bought this mandolin and it was everything I wanted. It was the one," Monroe said. "I worked hard and played it hard and, after a while—I guess about 20 years—it needed a new fingerboard, some work on the neck, and, back then, I wanted it refinished. Well, I sent it on up to Gibson in Kalamazoo and they kept it for about four months, and when they sent it back, they hadn't done what I wanted.

"All they'd done was the fingerboard and I got so aggravated that I just took the Gibson name right off it. Cut it out with a pocket knife."[2]

Over the ensuing years, the mandolin, sans its mother-of-pearl Gibson logo, became nearly as famous as its owner among bluegrass fans. The apologetic Gibson people repeatedly offered to repair it, but Monroe wasn't buying.

"Different fellows from Gibson came down from time to time, but I just couldn't see it," Monroe said. "Then, about a year ago, I was out at the Grand Ole Opry, talking backstage with Billy Grammer, who introduced me to Mr. Wall from Gibson. Grammer was pulling for me to make it up with them and be friends again. So I talked on it with Gibson and we got it settled to where the mandolin would go back to them to be repaired. I don't think it would be lying to say I saw tears in that man's eyes."

Gibson's research and development manager Rendal Wall and artists relations manager Patrick Aldworth took over from there. High-level discussions took place at the Gibson plant. Memos outlining precisely what would and would not be done flew back and forth from Michigan to Tennessee. Aldworth and Wall flew the mandolin back to the plant in its own airplane seat. Once there, it became the property of a handful of top Gibson instrument experts who replaced parts, re-glued veneer, and proudly replaced the Gibson name on the mandolin's neck,[3] next to a name plaque[4] custom-made for Monroe.

"We had a lot of pleasure doing this," Wall said as he presented Monroe with the newly-repaired mandolin, a series of color "before" pictures, the rattlesnake tail that had been inside the instrument,[5] and the nameplate[6] with the missing logo.

"I don't think there's been an instrument in the history of Gibson that has been handled with as much care. We estimated that 150 years of seniority and talent went into this work and we're delighted to have it done for Mr. Monroe."

A note signed by the Gibson employees who worked on the treasured instrument said simply: "We hope you like the repair job that we have done on your mandolin. Thank you for the pleasure of serving you."

---

2. This occurred in 1952, according to Sonny Osborne. See the editor's comments, second paragraph.

3. On that part of the neck called the "headstock."

4. A nameplate that covers the instrument's neck adjustment mechanism.

5. The rattlesnake rattle acted as a natural dehumidifier, thereby, according to tradition, improving the tone.

6. The old veneer covering the headstock.

Monroe expertly ran his fingers over the instrument, worn through in parts from years of spirited playing,[7] and allowed that this time Gibson had done the job right.

"Just listen to this," he said as he plucked out a rapid-fire "Sally Goodin." "Listen to how it rings and keeps on ringing. I've been offered $40,000 for this mandolin, but I don't think I would sell it, even if they went up to $500,000. It's meant so much to me and what I wanted to do that I wouldn't put a price on it. Everything with Gibson is 100 percent. They've done a good job and we've made up and forgiven each other, which, I guess, is the way it should be."

Originally published in *The Tennessean,* Oct. 9, 1980. © 1980 by *The Tennessean.* Reprinted by permission.

EDITOR'S COMMENTS

The end of Bill's long-standing feud with Gibson was reported in this article, originally published in *The Tennessean* on October 9, 1980, the day after Bill's reunion with his newly-spruced-up main mandolin. It was reprinted shortly thereafter in the November 1980 issue of *Bluegrass Unlimited.*

According to former Blue Grass Boy Sonny Osborne, who was working with Bill at the time, Bill's "modifications" to his mandolin (including scraping off a good bit of finish) were made in 1952, not in the 1960s, as Bill estimated here. (Osborne can be seen recalling the event in the film/video *Bill Monroe: Father of Bluegrass Music,* Original Cinema, 1993.)

"My Tribute to Monroe"

MICHELLE H. PUTNAM

The Father of Bluegrass, William Smith Monroe:
You created your music and then watched it grow.
Traveling the country, mandolin in hand,
Playing the only music I want to understand.
Doing "Mule Skinner Blues" and the great "Uncle Pen,"
I wonder if you knew where it would all end. . . .
You were born in Kentucky, a town called Rosine:
Where the grass grew so blue, instead of just green.
September the thirteenth, Nineteen hundred and eleven,

---

7. And spirited scraping.

Blessed with a talent that came straight from heaven.
Your music, your life: The two became one
And your smile warmed the world like a spring morning's sun.
You took a chance with the music you made.
You believed in yourself and were never afraid.
You've given me encouragement for the music I play
And you've helped so many artists along their way.
You and your "Boys" have a place in my heart
And I've loved them all, right from the start.
William Smith "Bill" Monroe . . .
What will we do when you finally go?
"My Last Days on Earth" made me break down and cry,
For I knew that someday you surely would die . . .
But I knew too, I'd always have your sweet memory
And no one, nor time, could take that from me:
The memory of your smile, your look, your touch,
The wise eyes I've grown to respect so much.
The music you've made down through the years
Has brought the world laughter and joy mixed with tears.
Your bluegrass that you've always played straight from your heart:
The world will have lost its Master when you finally depart . . .
But you've made your life full, you've taken the dares
And I'm writing this now so you'll know I care.
I won't want you to have gone on your way
Without me having had my chance to say
How I've loved you so, these past five years:
Father figure, my friend . . . it fills me with fears:
What will I do when you're gone from my world?
I will be such an unhappy girl.
My Master will be gone: No more "Uncle Pen,"
And the festivals will never be the same again.
I'll never hear "Raw Hide" played exactly right,
I'll never drive for hours through a long, lonely night
Just to have the opportunity to see you play. . . .
It'll be hard to cope, once you've gone away. . . .
I wonder if I'll give up my picking too?
Your passing will turn my green eyes to blue.
But I'll still have you in mind's memory—
You'll be in my heart for all the world to see.
There's never been anyone quite like you.
Without you, Bluegrass won't know what to do.
There's talent—yes, plenty in this world today,
But none that can ever stand up and say:

"I created this music, this wonderful thing.
God gave me this voice and I've let it ring!"
You've given so much, William Smith Monroe.
My love will be here long after you go.

This selection is previously unpublished. © 1981. Reprinted by permission of the author.

EDITOR'S COMMENTS

The *Master of Bluegrass* album,[1] released in the summer of 1981, included "My Last Days on Earth." After hearing the somber tune for the first time, Putnam, a guitar-playing medical lab technician, writer, and devoted fan, expressed her feelings in this poem, dated July 20, 1981. A framed copy hung in Bill's room on the last "Blue Grass Special" tour bus, and is now displayed at the Bill Monroe Museum and Bluegrass Hall of Fame in Bean Blossom, Indiana.

At the time he recorded "My Last Days on Earth" (February 19, 1981), Bill was undoubtedly aware that he had been diagnosed with colon cancer, probably influencing his choice of the title for the tune. He underwent surgery about three weeks later, on March 9, 1981.

Note

1. *Master of Bluegrass*, MCA Records, MCA-5214, released June 1981.

"Stayin' on the Right Road"

CAROLE LEDFORD

"Newgrass? How do you mean that?" A smile lights up his face. "Oh, you mean somebody that's trying to branch off on the wrong road? Tell 'em I said to get back on the right road and they'll be much better off!"

It's hard to separate the man from the legend. He's sometimes shy and sometimes opinionated, sometimes naive and oftentimes brilliant. He's Bill Monroe, keeper of the tradition.

"Well, it wouldn't matter if I had all new songs," says Monroe, "I'd still do them my way. I'd have control over the way I think they should be done and I'd keep them the way I think the people would love to hear me do them."

Perhaps it's the shyness, or maybe just his own brand of humor, that often causes Bill Monroe to speak of himself in the third person. "That boy stays right in there, don't he? I'm telling you, I've often wondered how that boy can keep his voice in such good shape and sing to people the way he does. I'm proud of him, I really am."

Suggestions that maybe he's not being serious elicit the response, "Sure, I'm serious. I mean every word of it!"

Whenever he's not on stage, a feeling of restlessness seems to surround Monroe. His mind seems to function on several levels at once, and always one has the impression that there's a tune running through his head even when he's talking about or doing something else.

"In the run of a year," Monroe commented, "I write a good many instrumental numbers. I write more for fiddlers than anything else. I've got some songs that I wrote down through '79, and I'm going to get around to recording them sometime."

Bill Monroe and the Blue Grass Boys keep a heavy schedule, on the road four days a week or more.

"The schedule is tough, it really is," Monroe, now 70, readily admits. "We're out there a lot of the time, but I like to play for the people. I like to see my friends all over the country and meet new people. I like to keep our friendship good. I travel as much as they want me. If they want me every week of the year, that's what I do."

"Of course, I love to have a little time off around Christmas time to buy a few presents, you know," he smiles. "'Cause there's a lot of people who really give me some trouble if I don't give them a present!"

Acknowledging the increased popularity of bluegrass music, Monroe says, "I think it will continue. It's going to stay here with us. It's the music that the people love and if it were taken away from them, they'd really be hurt over it."

As you may have noticed, almost every comment of Bill Monroe's centers on the people, the fans of bluegrass. He really cares how the audience reacts to his music and he loves to see a wide range of ages in the audience.

"Some of our biggest fans are college kids," he says. "It's part of what makes playing so interesting—to know the kids out there are playing the music too. A lot of them do a wonderful job."

Is there any group with the talent and staying power to take his place? "Oh, there'll be somebody," Monroe says with conviction. "There's a lot of people now that could come right in there and do a great job. They all work together a lot, try to do it right, and keep the music the way I think it should be. A lot of them know how I think it should be."

What about Bill Monroe's own continued success? "I've always had willpower. I don't believe in giving up. I like to work, play and sing. It takes a lot of money in this day and time to operate the way we do. Money hasn't been everything I've wanted down through the years. I love to play, have a good life, stay healthy, and meet my fans and friends. I try to see them at least once a year."

Monroe's own strength of character comes out in his advice to young pickers. "One thing is to work hard and never give up. Have a lot of willpower. Practice a little each day."

Personal integrity is a definite part of Monroe's strength. Smoking and drinking are not among Bill Monroe's vices. "Oh, if somebody made me mad," he admits with a rueful grin, "I might say the wrong kind of word. But I'm not going to say it until they do and I don't believe in using a filthy word. I was raised to control that. To be a real man, you've got to control it."

Appearances are often deceptive. At times, Monroe seems almost frail, an assumption that is quickly dispelled by a hearty handshake. A recent stage performance at Sunset Park in Pennsylvania had the audience spellbound. They loved it when Bill and bass player Mark Hembree treated them to a little exhibition of the Kentucky backstep.

Monroe takes an almost childlike pleasure in the knowledge that his voice is as strong and clear as ever. Even the normal audience chatter ceased when Monroe's fantastic tenor soared out over the solid quartet singing. Maybe it was simply the fact that almost every other person had a tape recorder going, but a look around at the faces in the crowd revealed more than a few awestruck expressions. They were watching the master at work and they knew it.

The opinions of two of the Blue Grass Boys reflect the feelings of the fans. Butch Robins, 32, has been with Bill Monroe almost four years. "Music is the magic of the moment," says Robins. "The music changes every day in the sense that it becomes more sophisticated in the image it presents to the world. The people never change. Monroe's music puts the accent on a clear melody line. He's always coming up with more sophisticated, more complex fiddle tunes. He writes mostly fiddle tunes; he thinks that way."

A talented banjo player, Robins has worked with some of the best-known names in bluegrass. In working for Monroe, Robins finds, "The opportunity to learn is constantly with you."

Bass player Mark Hembree, 25, agrees. "It's working for a legend," says Hembree. "There's a lot I can learn. He's a musical genius. Monroe can play sparingly and still play more music than someone else who hits a lot of notes. He's a consummate musician."

Hembree has been with the band less than two years. With a definite twinkle in his eye, Monroe tells how they got Mark in the group. "We were playing in Wisconsin and he came around, looking like he needed to shave and clean up some, you know, and he looked like he needed some money, so we just gave him a job."[1]

Bill Monroe had this final comment to offer: "I'd like to say that I have tried to treat my fans and friends right down through the years. I appreciate them being good fans and loving bluegrass music and I want us always to be friends."

---

1. Bill loved to tease this way. See the editor's comments, second paragraph.

Apparently, the fans feel the same way. The day after this interview, Bill Monroe accepted the *Music City News's* award for the Best Bluegrass Group of the Year—again.[2]

Originally published in *Blueprint* 3:6 (Dec. 1981): 11, 14. Reprinted by permission of the publisher.

EDITOR'S COMMENTS

This brief article was published in the December 1981 edition of *Blueprint*, a free bluegrass newspaper in the Washington, D.C., area. The interviews for it were done over a year earlier, during Bill's appearance at Sunset Park in West Grove, Pennsylvania, on June 10, 1980.

Bill loved to tease, and his story about Wisconsin native Mark Hembree is a classic example of his depreciative humor, usually reserved for his closest friends or musical associates, and was probably told in Hembree's presence.

Bill and his Blue Grass Boys won the fan-based *Music City News* "Bluegrass Band of the Year" award in 1980 and 1981. Prior to that, the Osborne Brothers had won the award nine years in a row (1971–79).

"Cleo Davis: The Original Blue Grass Boy"

WAYNE ERBSEN

On March 9, 1919, a doctor rode his horse-drawn buggy through the hills of northwest Georgia to the home of Ben and Effie Davis. He was summoned because Effie was about to have a baby. By the time "the Doc" had left, Effie and Ben were the proud parents of a healthy baby boy. As yet, they had no name for him. By and by, they gave him the name Cleo.

As young Cleo was growing up, he was surrounded by music. Mama played the pump organ and sang the old hymns along with her brothers and sisters who practically filled up the tiny church where they worshipped. His dad picked a five-string banjo in the old clawhammer style. Cleo remembers his father taking the banjo off the wall and holding it next to the fireplace or wood-burning oven to warm the coon skin stretched over the banjo. This, his dad told him, would tighten the head and give it the proper "thump." Cleo couldn't get near enough to that banjo. Sometimes on a Saturday night his uncle Jim Davis would come over to the house with a mouth

---

2. The band won the award two years in a row. See the editor's comments, third paragraph.

harp and they were often joined by Efrid McDowell, Mama's cousin. Efrid always brought a shiny black Stella guitar with him.

In the summer months, the men gathered on the porch to play. With the older folks looking on, the children would often join hands and dance in the light of an oil-burning lamp or the nuts that were set ablaze in the yard. When Cleo wasn't dancing, he'd often wrestle the lard bucket away from his brothers Dell[1] or Bob and beat rhythm on it like a drum.

After Mama died, Cleo went to live with his uncle Marcus,[2] who kept the boy entertained with a five-string banjo. He and another uncle,[3] who played the fiddle, made Cleo more determined than ever to learn to play string music. When he was about ten years old he heard that there was going to be a music program at the schoolhouse just down the road from where he was living. He never heard of Gid Tanner and Riley Puckett, but he knew if they were coming all the way from Atlanta to play, they must be good. On the night of the concert, Cleo walked barefoot down to the schoolhouse. When he got there he found out the admission was 15 cents more than he had, which was nothing. Not to be turned away, he slipped around the side of the building where he could listen in through the window. Since it was summertime, the windows to the auditorium were open, so young Cleo could hear everything that went on in the hall. He remembers hearing them play "Down Yonder" and "Back Up and Push," which Tanner and Puckett had made famous on Columbia records.[4]

Inspired by what he had heard, Cleo walked home determined to make himself a guitar. He searched until he found an old oil can to which he attached a sawmill strip for a neck. After punching a hole in the top of the can, he stretched a single strand of screen wire over the top of the can and his one-string guitar was complete. "I sang and yodeled and strummed that guitar until my sister chased me out of the house. There wasn't a barn, so I had to go out into the woods to play. I kept on singing and carrying on 'til I drove all the wild animals back into the river swamp."

Then the resourceful Cleo Davis caught some rabbits and traded the skins to a peddler he met on the road for a harmonica. After growing weary of blowing on the harmonica, he swapped the harmonica and a Barlow pocketknife for an old beat-up Stella guitar. Even though the guitar had come unglued around the edges, had a warped neck, and no strings, Cleo marveled at his prize. He soon set to work and with the help of some shoe tacks managed to tack the top back on the guitar. He then took a worn-out set of his uncle's banjo strings and before long, his guitar was strung up and ready to play. His sister, however, took a dim view of this and Cleo soon found himself back in the woods, happily singing and playing to himself.

When Cleo got a little older, he started working as a farm hand in Collard Val-

---

1. Leddell Davis, father of bluegrass musician David Davis, leader of the Warrior River Boys.
2. Marcus McDowell, brother of Effie McDowell Davis.
3. Possibly Jim McDowell.
4. The two tunes would be made famous by Tanner and Puckett's RCA Victor recordings of 1934.

ley, near Rome, Georgia. He'd plow cotton and corn and perform other farm duties for 35 cents a day plus room and board. After several months, he was able to save
enough to order a guitar out of the Sears and Roebuck catalog for the sum of $2.40.
This guitar was to replace the old Stella, which one of his brothers had sat on and
broken. Cleo's new guitar, along with an instruction book and a pick, finally arrived.
He learned how to tune it and could play G, C, and D. The first tune he attempted
was "It Ain't Gonna Rain No More."

Although phonograph records were rare and treasured commodities in the
north Georgia mountains where Cleo was living, he did manage to get a copy of
the Carter Family's 1928 release of "Wildwood Flower." Like many a country guitar
player, Cleo soon mastered the guitar part to "Wildwood Flower" and he also learned
guitar runs and songs from Blue Yodeler Jimmie Rodgers. He remembers plowing
with a mule while singing and yodeling his way through many of Rodgers' songs.
"It got so that the mule couldn't work unless I was singing and yodeling. I did notice that the old mule would shake his head when I'd hit a high note. I thought at
first he was just flipping off the horse flies, but I later realized he was trying to tell
me I was giving him a headache."

Cleo and that mule parted company when he moved in with another uncle[5] in
Cedartown, Georgia, near where he was born.[6] "I had a cousin there named Georgia McDowell[7] who did a better job than I did on her Kalamazoo guitar.[8] In the
evening we would sit on the porch, strum guitars, and sing 'My Old Pal of Yesterday.' That's where I learned to harmonize. It wasn't long before I could sing most
any part. We'd just switch the harmony around and play guitars right on. My uncle
played the five-string banjo and the harmonica, so we were in pretty fair demand
to play for parties. I still didn't know any more than G, C, and D, so if we couldn't
play a song in G, we didn't play it."

The year was 1938, and Cleo found himself again on the move, looking for work.
This time he crossed over into Alabama and landed a job as a farm hand for an old
gentleman named Hans Graves, who was a tenant farmer. By the time he had laid
that one-horse crop by, he had made up his mind that there must be more to life
than plowing with a mule. He collected his $18 wages for a month's work, and told
his buddies he was going to look for something better.[9] Dressed in his Sunday
clothes, he caught a ride on a truck headed for Atlanta. There he met a cousin[10] who
invited him to stay with him while he looked for a job. As luck would have it, the
next day he was hired to work an ice truck for the sum of $1 a day, which was more
money than he'd ever seen in his life.

---

5. Jim McDowell.

6. Antioch, eight or nine miles to the southeast.

7. Marcus McDowell's daughter.

8. A Gibson guitar, made in Kalamazoo, Michigan.

9. There are intriguing parallels in the early lives of Davis and Bill. See the editor's comments,
second paragraph.

10. Henry Gallamore.

"One night in late August 1938, a friend, who was a policeman named Ed Daniels, came running over to the house waving a copy of the *Atlanta Journal* in his hand. He spread open the paper and pointed to a small ad wanting someone who could play guitar and sing old-time songs. I tried to convince Ed that I barely knew how to hold the thing, and that I didn't even know an entire old-time song, but he wouldn't listen. He and my cousin fairly insisted that I check out the ad and promised a little violence if I didn't. Since I didn't even own a guitar at that time, my cousin went down to the hock shop and bought me one for about $2.40. So again dressed in my Sunday best, I picked up that guitar and a copy of that newspaper clipping and went across Atlanta to check out the ad. My cousin went with me to make sure I didn't lose my nerve.

"We got to the location in the ad and found it to be a small trailer sitting next to a service station. When we approached the trailer we heard country music coming out of that thing. I was a little hesitant to knock on the door, so I waited until the music stopped. Two or three guys came pouring out, and the man inside told them if he decided, he'd give them a call. We were then invited in, and I trailed in last. Introductions were passed around, but I never got his name. He said, 'Well, who plays the guitar?' I eventually pulled it out from behind me where I had it hid and said, 'I do, sir.' He asked, 'Well, what can you play?' 'Oh, maybe a verse or two of "This World Is Not My Home" or "What Would You Give in Exchange for Your Soul,"' not knowing at that moment who I was talking to. My mind then flashed back and I remembered how I had learned those two songs. Several years before, I had picked up the Grand Ole Opry over radio WSM. There I heard people like Arthur Smith and the Dixieliners, Clayton McMichen, and the Delmore Brothers. I thought the Delmore Brothers were out of this world. A little later, some other brother acts came on the scene such as the Callahan Brothers and the Shelton Brothers. Then I heard two brothers who had exactly what I thought I'd been looking for—the Monroe Brothers. I had no idea where they were located and had never seen them, but I had picked up one of their records of "This World Is Not My Home" and "What Would You Give in Exchange for Your Soul?"[11] and that's how I learned those songs. I was awakened out of my thoughts when the man standing before me asked, 'You can sing "What Would You Give in Exchange for Your Soul?"' I said, 'Yes, sir. I think I can sing that.' So we proceeded to tune up together, but I soon found out that my $2.40 guitar would not tune up to that beautiful mandolin he had. So he tuned down to my guitar, and we hit out. We had done about a verse and a chorus to 'What Would You Give in Exchange for Your Soul?' when I recognized the voice. I didn't recognize the name, but I recognized the voice. This had to be one of the Monroe Brothers. I got so scared that I lost my voice and had to quit playing. He asked me what was the matter and I told him I had forgot the song. So we talked for a moment and I tried to calm down. I think he knew what had really happened

---

11. This was the Monroe Brothers' first release on RCA Victor's cheaper-priced Bluebird label (B6309).

to me. I had realized that I was standing there singing with Bill Monroe and I was shocked beyond reason. So I finally recovered and he said, 'Let's try "This World Is Not My Home,"' so we tried that. I was beginning to get brave and sang nearly two verses until I got scared to death and lost my voice again. He had to laugh a little about that and kidded me and said, 'You'll get over that.' We did a better job of it the next time. His wife, whose name is Carolyn, was sitting at the end of the trailer, listening. He said, 'Carolyn, what do you think?' She said that I sounded more like Charlie than any man she ever heard not to be Charlie Monroe. I seen a grin come over Bill's face and he said, 'Let's try that number again.' I think we did it still a little better that time and he turned around and told Carolyn that 'I think I found what I been looking for.' I figured he couldn't have been looking for very much to have found it in me.

"To my amazement I found out that he was satisfied with our sound and that he and Charlie had split up in Raleigh, North Carolina, some time before and that Bill had stopped in Little Rock, Arkansas, and formed a group there called 'The Kentuckians.' He stayed there a few months and either they didn't go over too well, or he was unhappy with their sound. So he headed back to Atlanta, Georgia, where he and Charlie had worked a guest spot a few years before.

"Bill asked me if I could come back to the trailer the next morning about 8:30. I told him I would, not knowing what was in store for me. So I caught a streetcar and was right back there the next morning. We drank some coffee, and Bill asked me if I knew of any music shops downtown where we could go look at some instruments. I told him I did, so we went downtown and looked at the guitars hanging in pawn shop windows. We finally found a big orchestra-type guitar that Bill strummed approvingly. He handed it to me and asked me how I liked it. I'd never played a guitar that cost more than $2.40, so this $37.50 guitar was the most beautiful thing I'd ever seen. I nodded furiously. Bill told the man we'd take it and, at that moment, I hit the door hard and fast. This old country boy only had about a dollar in my pocket and there was no way I could buy that guitar. Bill paid the man and walked out with that guitar.

"Bill then asked me if I knew of any good men's shops. I told him there was a couple of nice ones just down the street. We went into one and Bill told the man to fix me up with a new suit of clothes. Bill said to 'Fix him up from the floor up.' So the man brought out shoes, pants, shirt, tie, and socks and I tried 'em on. Bill told the salesman he wasn't finished yet. 'Do you have any John B. Stetsons?' So the man brought me out a John B. Stetson (hat) with a wide brim and when I got through dressing, James Cagney or George Raft had nothing on me, so long as I kept that Stetson pulled down over my eyes. Then Bill told the man to fix him up in the same style. So Bill paid the man and we walked out of there looking nearly alike, except that Bill outweighed me by about 40 pounds. When we got back to his trailer I started to carry the guitar inside, but he told me to take it home with me. I still didn't know what the score was, and I didn't dare ask. Bill Monroe is a man you don't get a lot out of and sometimes it's better not to ask. He didn't talk a lot, but when he did talk, he made it count. I thought to myself that I'd play the guitar for a couple of days, and then Bill would come and pick it up, so I took it home with me.

"The next day I got a call from Bill and he wanted to know if he could come out. I said, 'Sure,' so he came out and told me then what he had in mind. He wanted to come out to my house where there was plenty of room, and no one to run off, and rehearse. So we rehearsed every afternoon for about two and a half hours 'til way up about Christmas time, when we knocked off for the holidays. He said that he wanted to teach me all the songs that he knew, all the guitar chords that he knew, and all the runs that he knew. Since Bill knew all the guitar chords and runs that his brother Charlie had played, it wasn't very long until Bill had me sounding just like Charlie Monroe. I truly think that at that moment what Bill was looking for was not a group, but the Monroe Brothers' sound. I'm not even sure Bill realized this fact. But whether he knew it or not, Bill was trying to follow the Monroe Brothers' style. Since he was back in the territory that the Monroe Brothers had worked and made their name so famous, it was natural for Bill to want to continue with a sound he knew would sell. And we did sound very much like the Monroe Brothers with our extreme high harmony and smooth sound.

"I remember that when Bill was helping me with my guitar playing, I always used a flat pick; a Nick Lucas pick. I was never able to use a thumb pick and finger picks like some fellers did. I would get those things tangled in the strings like a bull caught in a barbed wire fence. And I never did use a capo when I was with Monroe, not even in the key of A. I had long fingers, so I could make the long A chord. With my fingers being so long, I could make all the runs without using a capo. In fact, I can't recall seeing any capos in the early days.

"Charlie Monroe used to have a run that he'd do in the key of G, and Bill taught me how to make it. As the weeks went by, it seemed like Bill and I kept picking up speed until we were playing faster and faster. But we were as good on the slow numbers as we were on the fast ones. I found out quick that you don't make mistakes when playing with Bill, so we practiced never making mistakes. In order to stay up with Bill, I used the old Charlie Monroe G run until it got to a point where I could no longer make it and keep up with Bill . So I had to find something I could do and keep up with the fast pace that we had set. So, with the help of Bill, I modified the old Charlie Monroe G run. I made it into what is now known as the 'famous Lester Flatt G run.' I not only could make it in G, but also in the keys of C, D, and even in A.

"When the Christmas holidays were over, we went down to WSB in Atlanta for an audition. The Crossroads Follies were very popular over WSB at that time, but after we auditioned, the manager told us that they only used groups, not duets. He told Bill to go out and pick up a few other guys and that he'd make a place for him on the Crossroads Follies. Bill chose a few choice words and told the manager that that wasn't what he had in mind and we walked out. We then went down to WGST radio in Atlanta and got an audition with them. They told us they liked us very much but that they couldn't use us because they already had a fine duet team working with them at that time by the name of the Blue Sky Boys, which was Bill and Earl Bolick. Bill was rather disgusted, so we went back home. He then asked me if I could be gone for a few days and I told him that I could. He told me to pack a few things and tell my people I'd be gone for two or three days, and to be at his trailer in the morning.

"When I got there, Bill had his 1938 Hudson Terraplane loaded up and ready to go. So we got in and headed out, although I had no idea where we were going. After we got out on the open road, I asked Bill where we were going. He said we were headed for Asheville, North Carolina. I thought, 'Where in the world is Asheville, North Carolina?' This country boy had never been anywhere, so Asheville could have been in Europe, as far as I was concerned. He said it's up in the Blue Ridge Mountains, but I didn't know where that was at either. I had heard of the Blue Ridge Mountains, but I sure didn't know where they were. We rolled on to Greenville, South Carolina, where we spent the night. In the morning we checked with WFBC radio in Greenville, but the Delmore Brothers had just started at that station, so they didn't need another duet. We rolled on to Asheville,[12] where the Delmores had just left. In Asheville, we auditioned at a small station named WWNC. They asked us if we could come back and take over a fifteen minute program called 'Mountain Music Time,' which was broadcast at 1:30 in the afternoon. Bill answered that we could, so we piled into Bill's Hudson and headed back to Greenville to pick up the trailer. At last we had found a home base from which to start building our reputation.

"On the way back to Asheville, with Bill's trailer in tow behind, I had a need to know what Bill was going to call us. I really didn't know his intentions about a band, because Bill doesn't talk much. Bill said, 'Bill Monroe and the Blue Grass Boys.' I questioned 'Blue Grass Boys,' being from the hills of Georgia, and not knowing anything about bluegrass. So I asked him about it, and he said, 'I'm from Kentucky, you know, where the bluegrass grows, and it's just got a good ring to it. I like that.' We used to get a lot of kidding about that name in the early days. You could hear all sorts of little remarks when we'd play schoolhouses, like 'Bill Monroe and the Glue Brass Boys.' As the years pass by, of course, I'm real proud that I was an original member of the Blue Grass Boys.

"When we got to Asheville, Bill parked his trailer next to an old service station and I got a room across the street for a dollar and a half a week, plus a meal ticket to the Asheville lunch room and boy, we were set! I thought Asheville was the coldest place on the face of the earth. It froze your thoughts before you could think 'em. We walked up to the radio station each day and played our fifteen minute program. I believe the announcer referred to us as Bill Monroe and Cleo Davis, although quite often our mail was addressed to the Monroe Brothers. Apparently, that's who many people thought they were listening to. Of course, we did sound very much like the Monroe Brothers, and featured many of the songs that Bill and Charlie had made popular. I think that Bill was trying to stay close to the Monroe Brothers' style. He was back in the area where the Monroe Brothers had once worked, so he was trying to stay with that sound to regain his popularity over the airwaves as he was building his own group.

"As the days went by, Bill and I spent a lot of time rehearsing. We had to get

---

12. Apparently leaving the trailer in Greenville.

each note exactly right before it went on the air. It was almost as if 'you don't make a mistake on one of Bill Monroe's shows, especially on the road.' That's bending the truth a little, but that's how Bill was, and probably still is. You must be nearly perfect. We weren't, but we thought we were."

As Bill Monroe and Cleo Davis kept rehearsing, they continuously added new songs to their repertoire. "We picked up numbers that other people were using. We learned the Delmore Brothers' old tunes like 'Southern Moon,' 'The Nashville Blues,' 'Gonna Lay Down My Old Guitar,' and 'When It's Time for the Whippoorwill to Sing.' We also learned some of the Callahan Brothers' songs. They were very popular and had a beautiful sound. They sang the blues type of songs, the tear-jerkers. The Callahans were especially known for their duet yodeling. The Monroe Brothers also featured the duet yodel, but we turned the blue yodel, with the duet yodel, into our theme song on the air. That's what we always came on the air with and what we'd use to sign off. As we went off the air it sounded like two foghorns moving out into a deep fog."

It wasn't long after Monroe and Cleo started their radio program over WWNC in Asheville, North Carolina, that Monroe started advertising over the air for other musicians to join their band. As the hopeful musicians would show up for an audition, Monroe and Cleo usually auditioned them together, with guitar and mandolin. Among the first musicians to show up for an audition was fiddler Art Wooten, from nearby Marion, North Carolina. In addition to his fiddle, Wooten brought with him a contraption he called a "one man band." Cleo remembers that "it was like half an organ, with Art sitting with his knees under the thing. He also had a 5-string banjo and a guitar built into it. He picked it with one foot and chorded with the other while, at the same time, playing the fiddle. He also had a harmonica rack around his neck and played the fiddle and the harmonica at the same time. We used that act on stage with the Blue Grass Boys many times."

Although Wooten had a smooth fiddle style and was known to have played some beautiful harmony on the fiddle, his style was not quite what Monroe was looking for. But Monroe took his mandolin and worked with Wooten until he had the fiddler playing in the style that he wanted.

Another hopeful musician showed up at radio Station WWNC by the name of Tommy Millard, from Canton, North Carolina.[13] Millard was a blackface comedian and Cleo fondly remembers him being extremely good at playing the role of the blackface rube comedian. "He would always break me up with his act when he'd go out on stage. As a matter of fact, I couldn't even play straight with him, 'cause I'd get so tickled. Bill would have to take my part and play straight with him while I stood off in the wings and laughed. He didn't sing or play an instrument, though he did have two big tablespoons that he'd play back-to-back. He would beat those spoons on his knees, between his hands, on his shoulders, under his arms, and up and down his legs. He was real good at it. I also believe that he had a couple of bones in his suitcase that he'd use from time to time on our shows."

---

13. This was the first mention in print of former Blue Grass Boy Millard.

In addition to using their fifteen-minute radio show to advertise for other musicians, Monroe used the program to advertise shows they were playing in the area. People would write in to the radio station to arrange for the Blue Grass Boys to play a show, and it was Monroe's wife, Carolyn, who took care of most of the correspondence at that time. Monroe made sure the handbills were printed to promote the shows in little schoolhouses around Asheville. Many times, Cleo and Carolyn would make the rounds of the schoolhouses, making arrangements for the shows. After the handbills were printed, they'd go back and distribute them and maybe play that night, or possibly the next night.

Cleo remembers that "we charged 15 and 25 cents admission and would often play to fifty or seventy people. One of our earliest shows was held at the Franklin County Courthouse.[14] We played right in the courtroom. Those kind of shows were sponsored by the PTA or some church. Sometimes, we'd have to play two shows. We generally played an hour and a half program. At that courthouse, I remember we opened with a fast fiddle tune, like 'Fire on the Mountain,' had two or three fast duets like 'Roll in My Sweet Baby's Arms,' maybe an old blues number, a duet yodel, and a skit of ten or fifteen minutes. We had a skit that was mighty popular called 'The Pickpocket Game.' I always came up short on that deal.

"I recall one show we played at the city auditorium in Knoxville, Tennessee. I had to wear a dress, so I rolled my trousers up to my knees and put on a long dress, so I looked like a young girl. Bill was supposed to be my sister and had 'herself' a hot date (Art Wooten). I got jealous and was on stage fussing real big about how 'she' was able to get a date, and I wasn't. Tommy Millard was supposed to come out on stage to quiet me down. He had a *True Story* magazine that he was going to show me to quiet me down, but I wouldn't pipe down, so he hauls off and whops me upside the head with it. That old floor had just been oiled and was slippery, so I slipped and both feet went straight up in the air. The audience went wild, thinking it was part of the act, but I can assure you, it wasn't!

"The very first schoolhouse I played was at the Cashe Valley School auditorium, near Brevard, North Carolina.[15] We started with 'Katy Hill,' and then hit 'em with 'Foggy Mountain Top' with a fast yodel, and then some of the old blues numbers similar to the Callahans. We came back with the Delmore Brothers' 'Southern Moon' and then did one of our skits. For a gospel song we did 'What Would You Give in Exchange for Your Soul.' That always brought the house down. That night we were going to do this gospel number 'When the World's on Fire.' We sang a verse and a chorus and Bill played the chorus on the mandolin. When he finished, I could not for the life of me think of the first words of the next verse. It just simply wouldn't come to me. Bill quickly picked it up and played it through again. By this time I'd turned every color of the rainbow and he saw that I was scared to death. He looked over at me and grinned and I came up with something, some verse. Possibly the

---

14. Franklin County, North Carolina, is in the eastern part of the state, about 250 miles from Asheville.

15. About twenty-five miles south of Asheville.

people didn't even notice what was going on. That song was the last number before Tommy did a comedy skit. I was off in the wings and I told Bill I didn't think I
could go back out there and face those people again. At that point, Bill made one of
the greatest moves that he ever made for me. He assured me that I *had* to go back
out there. He said that, not because of *him,* but because of *me.* He said you must go
back out. He said if I'd let that stop me, I'd never be able to go back out again. He
said I had to go back out there to prove to myself I could do it. He assured me that
I could do the job and said I was going to do just fine. He said I just got scared and
that it wouldn't happen again. So I went back out there like a veteran and I never
did forget my lines from that time on."

In spite of the fact that the Blue Grass Boys were quite busy playing small schools
around western North Carolina, Monroe was not happy with the setup. He was
searching for a sound, and would not be satisfied until he found it. He knew he
wanted a bass in the band, and he wanted to move to a more powerful radio station. After three months in Asheville, the opportunity came. The Delmore Brothers had left station WFBC in Greenville, South Carolina. So Monroe made contact,
and the Blue Grass Boys were immediately hired to fill the spot vacated by the Delmores. Shortly after the move to Greenville, Millard departed and was replaced by
a young man named Amos Garren. Garren was a talented bass player who also sang
and did comedy. Finally, Monroe had the sound he was looking for. He had a tightly-
knit group that was willing to put in the long hours of practice it took to weld itself
into a cohesive unit. But musicians cannot live on music alone, and money was
indeed scarce in those lean times. As Cleo put it, "We were about to starve to death.
Those were bad times and we were not making much money. Sometimes, we'd take
in $25 or $30 a night in the little shows and we'd play most every night. Bill paid me
$15 a week, when we were working. When we weren't working, he couldn't pay me
anything, though he did pay for my haircuts and my laundry. Back in those days,
Bill was more like my older brother, though he wasn't that much older than me.[16]
But he'd been around a lot more than I ever had."

While in Greenville, South Carolina, Monroe, as usual, kept his trailer parked
next to a service station. Needing a place to rehearse, the owner of the station, Gene
Rampy, suggested they were free to use an old grease house in back of the station if
they cleaned it up. So Monroe and the Blue Grass Boys pitched in and cleaned up
that old grease house and even added a few seats. Their practice room was complete.
Cleo remembers that during the practice sessions they'd hold every afternoon, sometimes they'd draw bigger crowds than at some of their shows. "Out of that grease
house came the now-famous 'Mule Skinner Blues,' 'Footprints in the Snow,' and
'No Letter in the Mail.' Songs that are now considered American standards like 'Roll
in My Sweet Baby's Arms' and 'Foggy Mountain Top' had their birth in bluegrass
style in that old grease house. It really takes me back to think of the practice sessions we held there. We had so many good times, so many laughs in there. Bill started
working on 'Footprints in the Snow,' a song I'd heard my mother singing when I

---

16. Bill was about eight years older, similar to the age difference between Charlie and Bill.

was a little boy. Bill started singing it, and I didn't think he was singing it the way it was supposed to go. He changed it around to suit himself, and it worked. People really loved it. Also in the grease house, Bill started working on 'Mule Skinner Blues.' I thought he'd written it. I'd never heard Jimmie Rodgers do it until later. So Bill worked it out with that yodel, and almost brought the house down with it. I remember how we worked up 'No Letter in the Mail.' The writer of that song was Bill Carlisle. The Carlisle Brothers had recorded it pretty fast. I copied the words off the record and tried to remember the tune. I worked it out at my house with the guitar, with the help of Art Wooten on the fiddle. I slowed it way down, as it's sung today. After I got so I could sing it pretty good, I sang it for Bill and we made a powerful duet out of it. Later on, it went over good on the Opry."

The Blue Grass Boys stayed in Greenville for about six months. Though the band maintained a busy schedule of rehearsals and performing, pickings were rather slim. But even though the band was not financially rewarded during its stay in Greenville, they could plainly see that this period was a valuable one for honing down their sound to polished perfection. It was in Greenville that Monroe established the basic sound that would carry the Blue Grass Boys to the Grand Ole Opry. While in Greenville, the first Blue Grass Boys quartet was formed. Cleo remembers how this happened. "People don't realize it now, but I sometimes harmonized with Bill. In the early years I was very capable of harmonizing with him. I had a real high-pitched voice, so I would harmonize with him in many instances. It may seem strange to say, but Bill Monroe and I used to do 'He Will Set Your Fields on Fire' as a duet. I would lead it and Bill would sing the tenor. And then Bill would pick up the bass lead, and I would follow him with the second part. On the tail end of the bass I would come in and Bill would jump up to tenor.[17] Later on, when the Blue Grass Boys came into being, I sang bass all the way through. My good friend, Amos Garren, did the lead, Bill sang tenor, and 'Fiddling Art' Wooten did the baritone. On 'Life's Railway to Heaven,' Bill would lead it and we all came in on the chorus. I always sang bass on the quartets, and lead on the trios."

In addition to the trios, duets, and quartets, Monroe often sang solos. Cleo remembers one of the first solos he heard Bill do was "Blue Eyes."[18] "We used it in a comedy skit. Tommy Millard came out in blackface while Bill was singing that song. Millard would be crying as Bill was singing 'Blue Eyes' so sad and lonesome. Millard would lean on Bill's shoulder, almost going into convulsions. Not only did Bill sing 'Blue Eyes' as a solo, but also numbers like 'Mules Skinner Blues,' 'Footprints in the Snow,' and 'Blue Yodel Number 9.'[19] Bill did them as specials and put them over with such style that he was continuously searching for new ones."

When Monroe finally recorded with this version of the Blue Grass Boys[20] for

---

17. The Monroe Brothers had recorded the song using this arrangement in 1937.

18. Full title: "I'm Thinking Tonight of My Blue Eyes." See the editor's comments, third paragraph.

19. Davis may have been thinking of "Blue Yodel No. 7," which Bill recorded in 1941.

20. Bill did not record with this version of the Blue Grass Boys. See the editor's comments, fourth paragraph.

Victor on October 7, 1940, he chose "Mule Skinner Blues" for his first recording. Much importance has been placed on the fact that Monroe himself played guitar on that first recording. Some writers have explained it by saying that Monroe played the guitar to give that special "bluegrass time" that only he could give. It is more probable that Monroe simply felt more comfortable playing the guitar rather than the mandolin when he went to the microphone to sing solos. After all, when playing with what must be considered the original Blue Grass Boys, composed of Cleo Davis, Art Wooten, and Amos Garren, Monroe nearly *always* accompanied himself on guitar when he sang solos. He would trade his mandolin for Cleo's guitar and sing solos like "Mule Skinner Blues," "Blue Eyes," or "Footprints in the Snow." Later, apparently, Monroe grew more accustomed to singing solos while playing the mandolin, and never again recorded playing guitar.[21]

After working out of Greenville, South Carolina, for about six months, Monroe was growing restless. As Cleo explained it, "It was a struggle to get the group up and off the ground. It took a lot of patience and determination, and I think Bill was loaded with that. In the six months we were in Greenville, we had done about all we could do. Things just weren't that good. We were making progress, but not as fast as Bill wanted.

"One day, Bill called me up to the house and asked me what I thought about going to the Grand Ole Opry. I foolishly said, 'Do you think we're good enough?' He laughed and said we're as good as the best over there, and right now, we're better than most of the rest. I thought that if Bill Monroe thought we were good enough, we were good enough. I said, 'Man, I'm for it.' 'Course the Grand Ole Opry is, in my estimation, the ultimate dream a country musician can have. He told me to go back and tell the other boys to get their toothbrushes ready; we were going to Nashville. We arrived in Nashville and got an audition and it was with none other than the Solemn Old Judge, George D. Hay, and David Stone, who listened in.[22] They put us in one of the studios and we really put on the dog. We started out with 'Foggy Mountain Top,' then Bill and I did a duet tune with a duet yodel, fast as white lightning. We came back with the 'Mule Skinner Blues' and 'Fire on the Mountain,' and I think that really sewed it up. The Solemn Old Judge, George Hay, and David Stone came walking in and asked Bill if he could be here to take over the first spot on the Grand Ole Opry on Saturday night. Bill said, 'Yes, sir.' As we left the studio, Bill told us we had a job to do. We had to travel back to Greenville and get that trailer and be back in Nashville in time to open the curtain Saturday night. We were for it. You ought to have seen those country boys move. We moved across those mountains like they weren't there. We were back in Nashville way ahead of time. We were wild and rough and ready. And I think that first Saturday night, we pulled off a few firsts. We were the first ever to walk out on the stage of the Grand Ole Opry dressed in white

---

21. Based on aural evidence, it's believed that Bill also played guitar on "Dog House Blues," the fifth of eight items recorded at the October 7, 1940, session.

22. Also present was David Stone's older brother, Harry, who had replaced Hay as station manager of WSM.

shirts with neckties on. I also think we were the first country music quartet to ever hit the Grand Ole Opry. When we hit the stage, such performers as Roy Acuff, Pee Wee King, Uncle Dave Macon, and Sam and Kirk McGee, who were standing in the wings watching the Blue Grass Boys when they pulled the curtain on us, could not believe when we took off so fast and furious. Those people couldn't even think as fast as we played, I believe. In fact, there was absolutely nobody living who had ever played with the speed that we had. I believe we opened up with 'Foggy Mountain Top' with that wild duet yodel that we had and came right back with 'Mule Skinner Blues,' some fast tune like 'Fire on the Mountain' or 'Katy Hill,' and 'Roll in My Sweet Baby's Arms.' Those people like to played us to death that night. I don't think there was any other act that got to play more than one tune that night. To say the least, the show was really on the road. We had done exactly what we started out to do."

After Bill Monroe and the Blue Grass Boys joined the Opry, requests to play came flooding into the band. One tour took the band to Staunton, Virginia. Cleo remembers that "We were in Staunton, Virginia, with a great fiddler friend of mine, Tommy Magness, who was fiddling with us at that time. He came up with a fiddle tune called the 'Orange Blossom Special.' We were doing a two-day stand at the Visulite Theater, and Tommy and me were rooming together. I had my guitar in the room, and he had his fiddle, and he played me the 'Orange Blossom Special,' and, man, I thought I'd never heard such a train tune. 'Train 45' wasn't that good, and neither was 'Lee Highway Blues.' The 'Orange Blossom Special' took it all, and Tommy knew the words. We went over the words and learned the song. And we went downstairs and got a portable recorder at a music shop, and tried to record it in the lobby. We couldn't get a true sound in the lobby, so the man took us in the public rest room and locked the door. We set the recorder on the john, and me and Tommy Magness recorded the 'Orange Blossom Special.' I sang tenor in the duet. While in the bathroom, we also recorded 'Peach Picking Time in Georgia' and 'The Hills of Roane County.' When we got back to Nashville, we called Bill over to listen to it. He liked it. Tommy had picked up an old record by the Rouse Brothers, who were good friends of Chubby Wise, an old Florida boy. Chubby and the Rouse Brothers wrote it, and Chubby gave it to the Rouse Brothers. They copyrighted it and recorded it, but Tommy Magness and me took it to Nashville. Bill, he let Tommy Magness and me do the 'Orange Blossom Special' on the Grand Ole Opry the next Saturday night. The following Saturday night, me and Bill did it, and from then on, me and Bill did it.[23]

"I stayed at the Grand Ole Opry until late 1940 when I left the Blue Grass Boys and came to Lakeland, Florida, and took on a brand new show of my own over radio WLAK."

Originally published in *Bluegrass Unlimited* 16:8 (Feb. 1982): 28–30; 16:9 (Mar. 1982): 59–64. Reprinted by permission of the author.

23. "Orange Blossom Special," introduced to the band by Magness and Davis, was recorded at Bill's second RCA Victor session on October 2, 1941, with Wooten fiddling.

EDITOR'S COMMENTS

The first in-depth look at any of the original Blue Grass Boys, this article by musician Erbsen provided a fascinating look at Bill and the beginnings of bluegrass music in 1938–39. It originally appeared in two parts, in the February and March 1982 issues of *Bluegrass Unlimited.* (This selection differs from the original mainly in matters of punctuation and in that one paragraph has been divided into three paragraphs and four paragraphs detailing Davis's later career have been omitted.)

There are intriguing parallels in the early lives of Cleo Davis and Bill Monroe: both of their musically talented mothers died when the two men were young, both later lived with their mothers' brothers, who inspired them to play music, and both worked hard on others' farms before their musical careers began.

"Blue Eyes," one of the first solos Davis remembered Bill singing, was undoubtedly "I'm Thinking Tonight of My Blue Eyes." As "Blue Eyes," it was recorded by several performers in the 1930s, including Fisher Hendley and His Aristocratic Pigs in 1938, with "vocal and bawling" credited to "Baby Ray."[1] Bill, however, never recorded the song.

When Bill and the Blue Grass Boys made their first recordings for RCA Victor in Atlanta on October 7, 1940, the band included Clyde Moody (guitar), Tommy Magness (fiddle), and Willie Egbert "Cousin Wilbur" Wesbrooks (bass). Art Wooten, the only one of the original Blue Grass Boys who ever recorded with Bill, fiddled at the band's second session on October 2, 1941. (A live recording of Bill and the original Blue Grass Boys doing "Mule Skinner Blues" on the Opry in 1939 is included in the MCA compilation *The Music of Bill Monroe: From 1936 to 1994.*[2])

Notes

1. Fisher Hendley and His Aristocratic Pigs, "Blue Eyes," Vocalion 04718, released May 1939.

2. *The Music of Bill Monroe: From 1936 to 1994,* MCA Records, MCAC/MCAD4-11048, released Aug. 1994.

"Bill Monroe—The Master Speaks" (interview)

RAY EDLUND

Edlund: We're at the San Mateo Center for the Performing Arts, October 8, 1981, and Bill Monroe is here—and welcome, Bill, back to California.

Bill: Thanks, Ray. It's always a pleasure to come back out here.

Edlund: You started playing professionally with your brother Charlie about what time, Bill?

Bill: Well, Ray, we started trying to get on the radio stations back in 19 and 30.

Nineteen thirty was the first time I ever got on a radio station in Hammond, Indiana. We worked as the Monroe Brothers, back in the early days. There were three of us together, and we had other jobs on the side, you know, 'cause there wasn't a whole lot of money in music back in them days.

Edlund: You worked in an oil refinery, didn't you?

Bill: Worked at Sinclair refinery for 5 years.

Edlund: And then you and your brother Charlie got a record contract with Victor.

Bill: Started out with, we left Indiana and went into Iowa, and from there to Nebraska, and we was workin' for a company out through that part on radio, you know, had radio programs. Then we moved on to South Carolina, North Carolina, and down in that part of the country. I guess in 19 and 36 we made our first record for RCA there at Charlotte.

Edlund: And what was that? Do you remember?

Bill: I believe, "What Would You Give in Exchange for Your Soul?" and "This World Is Not My Home."

Edlund: Those were pretty big hits back in those days, weren't they?

Bill: Down there they really loved them.

Edlund: They sure did. What was your audience mostly like back then?

Bill: They were just good country people, just down-to-earth, good people. They were hungry for music and singing. They loved it.

Edlund: There were a lot of brother duets at the time, the Bolick Brothers, the Callahan Brothers. But you guys seemed to have an intensity about your music, a real drive, something that the other groups didn't seem to have. Can you get into that a little bit, why you were so different from the other groups?

Bill: Well, I wanted to play instrumentals, you know. Some of the songs I wanted to speed them up so they wouldn't all be the same. So it kindly worked that way. It seemed like a lot of the duets, the brother acts, they was really good. The Callahan Brothers—I really liked their singing—and the Delmore Brothers, people like that. They had good duets.

Edlund: People were just kind of amazed, by your mandolin picking especially, and Charlie's . . . they hadn't heard guitar runs like that and mandolin runs like that and the high tenor. Did you guys work on that a lot or did it just come naturally? Did you actually feel that that's what you wanted to do?

Bill: To start out with, I tried to learn to play the mandolin, you know, and that's what I came up with. I liked the old-time fiddle music—the way people would play numbers on the fiddle, and so I played a lot of those numbers, like "Soldier's Joy" and numbers like that. Played it like you'd play it on the fiddle, you know, that kind of style. But like you said a while ago, a lot of the duets, they just sung. They didn't do any playing. It was all slow.

Edlund: That's right. You guys sure led the way into what later became known as bluegrass music. You left your brother Charlie in 1939 or so, and formed your own group.

Bill: I guess it was in 1938 when me and Charlie broke up. When I worked with Charlie I had one style of tenor, and when we broke up I changed my style of tenor singing altogether. People like Brother Oswald[1] taken that style of tenor and they carried it on. My style of tenor now is altogether different from what I sung with Charlie. Bluegrass is different from the way me and Charlie sung. We sung the old country way of singing string music, playing string music and singing, back in the hills of Kentucky. It come from years ago—the way they would have probably sung it. Bluegrass was a different type of music, different timing to it and everything. Different style from what Charlie and me done.

Edlund: You added a banjo, it was "Stringbean," or Dave Akeman, who was your first banjo picker, and why did you decide to put a banjo in your band?

Bill: To start with, when I originated the Blue Grass Boys, I taken the guitar and the fiddle. I had to have a fiddler in it and bass. And then I got started doing tent shows and the bass man was a comedian, Cousin Wilbur. Then I got to thinking I wanted two comedians and I needed the sound of the banjo in the bluegrass. So Stringbeans was a good comedian and played a good banjo and was a good singer, so I hired him. He was the first banjo player for me.

Edlund: Then, later on, you hired a young banjo picker named Earl Scruggs and things started happening, especially over WSM's Grand Ole Opry. Could you reminisce a little bit about your reactions during those years when Earl was with you on banjo and the new sound of banjo was happening, and the new sound of bluegrass music?

Bill: Well, the bluegrass music had already taken hold when I started there in 1939, before Earl Scruggs ever come in the picture. Right in '42 and 3 was my greatest years in bluegrass, in the early days, and they was hungry for it and there was a demand for it and we had big crowds back there in the wartime there. So, Stringbeans he had to go in service. Don Reno would have got the first chance, but he had to go in service, so that gave Earl Scruggs the chance to come in and be a Blue Grass Boy. He was 19 years old.[2] Earl Scruggs was the kind of a banjo picker that learned from Snuffy Jenkins, that's where Earl's style come from.

Edlund: But you knew what you wanted. You wanted that particular style of picking, didn't you?

Bill: I knew that it would be all right with my music. Without bluegrass, the five-string banjo would have never survived. No way! And the fiddlers would have been mighty scarce without bluegrass, because about that time the electric instruments come in and they didn't need a fiddler. They didn't need nothin' but somebody to play the guitar and take breaks, and the steel guitar. . . . So, if it hadn't been for bluegrass, the fiddlers would be hurting and the banjo pickers—there wouldn't have been any.

Edlund: You had some mighty fine fiddlers with you and also, well, anybody in

---

1. Beecher "Pete" Kirby, dubbed "Bashful Brother Oswald" by Roy Acuff.
2. Scruggs was twenty-one in December 1945 when he joined the Blue Grass Boys.

bluegrass who's gone on has played with the Blue Grass Boys at some time or another, Bill. How do you pick the guys that work with you?

Bill: Well, if I think they're good enough for me to let 'em work with me, I can learn them a lot after they come along, and make them play the way I think it should be played. Keep out everything that don't belong in bluegrass. That's the way I done it all down through the years with different people. Like Chubby Wise, on the fiddle, he wanted to play swing and jazz and I wouldn't let him, 'cause he was in bluegrass then and he needed to play my style. That was the way it was with a lot of different people, in their music. They had to play bluegrass. When they would play it like I wanted it played, why, they would learn how to play bluegrass right, and then they could go on out on their own and people would hear about them and know they had been on the Grand Ole Opry, and . . . (It) give them a name. I tried to feature them every Saturday night, like Earl Scruggs or Lester Flatt, I gave them a chance to do a number where a lot of people would never let them do it. It would have been a group and not nobody's name would have been called. I wanted to help them and I knew that if I would build them up, people all over the country would like to hear them, and to give them a chance to help on the front gate too.

Edlund: What sort of times were those, back in the forties? Was it hard to get jobs in those days? Was it pretty rough for the musicians playing bluegrass music?

Bill: Well, there wasn't a whole lot of bluegrass, you see. When I started with this music, I guess the Stanley Brothers was the first to follow behind me in my way of playing it. Then people like Jim and Jesse was coming along and the Osborne Brothers and Lester and Earl. I guess they worked with me three and a half or four years[3] and then they went out on their own. Lester had been working with Charlie Monroe and he was a tenor singer and played a mandolin. So they didn't know nothing about Lester until he come to me on the Grand Ole Opry. And Earl Scruggs had never been heard of either; Stringbeans had never been heard of either; and Chubby Wise. But to be on the Grand Ole Opry, it helped me a hundred percent because the people would listen to it all over the whole country, and back in the early days, it would reach out a long ways. So it was good for the bluegrass music and the people that played bluegrass. It helped all the way around. And when I went to the Grand Ole Opry and tried out and they accepted me, they said if I ever left, I would have to fire myself. So, the last Saturday in this month, it will be 42 years at the Grand Ole Opry.

Edlund: Congratulations!

Bill: Thank you. Thank you a lot.

Edlund: That's amazing! There was a time when, well, competition got pretty fierce in the 1950s, or so, when people started listening to other kinds of music and it wasn't so easy to get a job. Could you tell us a little about those years with you and the Blue Grass Boys?

Bill: Well, back when the music began to come into the picture, like rock 'n'

---

3. Lester: a few months less than three years; Earl: a little over two years.

roll. . . . Bluegrass, you know, was, I don't know how many years ahead of rock 'n' roll, and if you listen to rock 'n' roll, they play the same timing as we play. Their timing was taken from bluegrass. 'Course, they would write their songs and put a lot of swing in it, or however they wanted to do it. Bluegrass, I think . . . well, we could still have crowds, you know, and had work, because back in them days we had tent shows that we booked ourselves all over the country. But rock 'n' roll really got big there, you know? It really hurt a lot of the country singers, is what rock 'n' roll hurt—the old-time country singers that had been on the Grand Ole Opry for years—it tore them plumb down to where they couldn't have no crowds any place they would go hardly. But bluegrass was a new music too, so it survived, and went through the hard days, and now it's a great music.

Edlund: It sure is. Let's jump up a few years, Bill, to right now, where you are recognized as being the creator of this style of music, and it wasn't always that easy, I am sure. What do you feel now when you know that people recognize you for the genius that you are as far as creating this style of music, and that so many people are so devoted to this type of music? How does that make you feel?

Bill: Well, it makes me feel good to know that I done something with what I set out to do with the music I that originated and started. To know that it will grow down through the years, and so it's on up to where it's at today. It lets me know that I have done something that will be here, so I am proud of that. I really think . . . if you think back over it, bluegrass has made more friends than any music in the world. Now you . . . if you went to a country show or a rock 'n' roll show, you might never see the people there again, but bluegrass is a music that's festivals all over the country. They have festivals and you will meet people there and you will plan on going back the next year and meet them again and hear the music.

Edlund: And it's a family-type music too.

Bill: It really is, and, Ray, it's a clean music. It's a decent music. There's no smut in it, nothing like that—no sex in it. So if you get right down to where it's at, it's a great music and, just like I said, it's respectable and I'm really proud of that. Bluegrass gospel, you'll never beat it today, man. The gospel quartets all over the whole world will never beat bluegrass gospel singing. A lot of (gospel) singing has gone with the drums and all this and that in it, but bluegrass is still right down to earth with the fiddle, mandolin, banjo, and guitar. So, I think it's really wonderful—gospel singing.

Edlund: What do you see as sort of the trend of bluegrass over the next, say, 20 or 30 years or so? Do you think it will just keep gaining in popularity and etcetera?

Bill: Well, now you know yourself that the bluegrass is different people playing it. They're going to play it their own way, the way they think should be. If they want to put blues in it or jazz it up like that, or however they want to go, people will still know that it is a copy off of bluegrass music. That's them for it. Now, out in this country here, I've been coming out here for I don't know how many years and a lot of people out in this country plays the pure bluegrass music and sings it.

Edlund: Butch (Waller) for one.

Bill: Yes, sir. On up through Oregon, Washington, and up through that country there, they're staying pure with a lot of it. A lot of people are still staying that way. That is really wonderful. It ain't a thing to be ashamed of. It's the way you want to hear it. You get good out of bluegrass music when you play it. You're not just playing it for the crowd out there. You get something good out of it yourself. It pays you, down through the years, to hear yourself play bluegrass music and to know that you're trying to play it the way the people would like it.

Edlund: Bill, how many songs have you written? Do you have any idea? It must be hundreds!

Bill: Ray, I'd say I've hit around better than a hundred instrumental numbers and right around a hundred or better in gospel songs. And numbers like "Uncle Pen" and "Blue Moon of Kentucky," I don't know how many numbers I have put together and wrote. I'd say that I'd get up close to five hundred, something like that.

Edlund: (Of) all the tunes you've written, which are the ones that you are really proud of, that you think will last for generations, and that you yourself like to sing over and over—tunes that you really like?

Bill: Well, numbers like "Uncle Pen," it tells the story about my uncle, you know, that I learned to play from, the first fiddler I ever heard, and "Blue Moon of Kentucky" is a really great number to me. A lot of instrumental numbers I love, like "My Last Days on Earth." It's really done awful good.

Edlund: That's on your new album.[4]

Bill: That's right . . . and it really tells a story and you can think back over it, say, when you get on up in years, way on up there, and you're not able to work much and you know you don't have a lot of time left. You think about what I'm telling you and listen to that number there and it will really tell you. It's got a story about it. But it's really sold good and I'm proud of that number. And the mandolin album I have, that's the first one I've ever made. I'm glad I did because it's really done fine. And a lot of the numbers in there, like "Old Ebenezer Scrooge"—I love that kind of number—or "Come Hither to Go Yonder," numbers like that. It's just like I told you. You get a lot of good out of playing your notes, your melody, the way you want it to go, the sound you put in it.

Edlund: So you really have a feeling for the songs you write—that's obvious to me. You mentioned to me a couple of years ago about "Crossing the Cumberlands"—I got that feeling of the pioneers and the hardships they had. It's true your songwriting is wonderful. I don't think a lot of people are really aware of what a fine songwriter you are—they love you for your mandolin picking, your singing, but I guess they don't know that you write most of your songs.

Bill: I really get a lot of good out of writing. I really love to write. I like to put a song together and I like to write a true song. I've wrote a good many of them, like "My Little Georgia Rose" is a true song, "Uncle Pen" is a true song—numbers like that. I love 'em. I search for sounds and tones that goes way on back hundreds of

---

4. *Master of Bluegrass*, MCA Records, MCA-5214, released June 1981.

years ago, in the way of the sound. I know they'd be back there, when people was learning to play fiddles, and that's the way that they would've loved to have heard that kind of sound years ago. And I know that the fiddlers today don't do that. They play a number that has already been wrote, and they write a few, but they write the way they think it should be today. I search for sounds and tones to put in my numbers and I love to do it that way. I like numbers like that.

Waller: On "My Last Days on Earth," a lot of people would say that strings don't belong in bluegrass music. Could you speak to that?

Bill: They was so far back in the background that they didn't hurt anything. The mandolin was up front, and so I won't have let them take it over, you see. That's being in . . . controlling it, keeping it like it should be. They brought in the sounds of Mother Nature: the wind, the ocean, the birds—the sea gulls, you know—and the sound of the harmony, the sound of the fiddles. And, Butch, the symphony there in Nashville—they was in on that too. They would do their part. I was down there when they was . . . fillin' in, you know . . . and they'd go through that, then they'd come out there and sit down and cry. It was so sad, the number was to them.

Waller: You laid your part down first and then they overdubbed theirs?

Bill: Yes, sir. Yes, sir. They wrote their parts. They play by notes, by music, is the way they do, so they didn't have any trouble following the notes and everything.[5]

Edlund: Bill, do you think you are going to start taking it a little easier now? You have been on the road for 50 years and people know your music now all over the country. Of course, they want to see you, but do you think you are going to kick back and not travel so much, not work so hard?

Bill: Ray, I have that in my mind to do that, you know, but seems like now they want to book me more, you know? Somebody's wanting me to come and play for them all the time, till where I don't have a lot of time off. We're with this Buddy Lee Attractions, you know, and dates are coming in from all over the country, and I love to travel and love to work. I don't like to let any day get by if I don't do something. Of course, the time will come when you are going to have to stop, slow down, and that'll be it. Right now, I would hate to stay in Nashville, knowing that Butch Waller was wanting to see me out here, and Ray was wanting to see me. And I wouldn't come to California, this country? That would really hurt me. 'Cause I love to come out here and see my friends and fans. So, I don't want to stop now.

Edlund: You work your boys pretty hard. What do you ask of them when they're up there on stage, when they're Blue Grass Boys and they're playing for you?

Bill: I ask them to get up there and play it the best they can, to work hard. If we're up there for 45 minutes, to give the people the best they got. I want them to get up there and be sober. I want them to get up there and respect the people. And that's what I expect out of them and they know that they have to do that. I don't like to make it rough on anybody, any musicians. If you're paying the man to do it,

---

5. Following the recording of Bill's part, first the vocals and then strings were added. See the editor's comments, second paragraph.

you want the best out of him you can get out of him. So that's the way I am. It will help them in the long run. If Kenny Baker's fiddling, he better give them the best he's got because if he don't, people will say, "Oh, Kenny Baker ain't as good as he used to be." So he's goin' to have to get in there and do it like I said and really work hard at it. The banjo players and all of them needs to do that. That's the way they've done it all down through the years, so there's nothing wrong with that.

Edlund: Say, Bill, who is your favorite lead singer, if you can narrow it down to one or two guys, throughout the years of the Blue Grass Boys? Who's your favorite guitar picker?

Bill: Well, Ray, they all was good men. They was in different years, you know? The year they would be in working with me, it would be hard for anybody to beat them. Just like when Lester was with me, you couldn't have beat Lester. When Jimmy Martin come along with me, Lester couldn't have beat Jimmy Martin. When Edd Mayfield was with me, neither one could have beat Edd Mayfield, because with the bluegrass music and our way of doing it, if you got a good lead singer that can sing high enough now, and he's in there and he's being backed by the Blue Grass Boys and all that, he's hard to beat. And Carter Stanley was a fine man with me. Pete Rowan was fine. You couldn't have beat Pete when he was with me. And I think when James, my son, was with me, we done some fine singing together. He played a great part. And so, they all had their years and it would be hard to say there was just one good man, because there was more than one good man.

Edlund: A lot of times when you're singing, Bill, you actually sing the lead with your tenor and the others follow behind you. That's a little bit unusual in the music.

Bill: My oldest brother[6] said that I done that, but to keep it right up where it belongs, it might sound like the tenor was strong, or carrying it, but it was to pull on the lead singer and make him come on.

Waller: You would lead the song, but not sing the lead part. You would be leading the phrasing.

Bill: That's right. Yes, sir.

Edlund: What are your plans for the future? Are you going to do any fox hunting over the winter, Bill?

Bill: Ray, my hounds is ready, and I have ten foxhounds, and when I work in Nashville at the Grand Ole Opry on Friday and Saturday, around Monday night or Tuesday night, I turn them out, and then again around Thursday or Friday—turn them loose a couple of times a week. Of course, in the fall the land is damp and they can scent that fox all over the country, so there will be a lot of fine running this fall and this winter.

Edlund: Bill, I certainly want to thank you for taking time out and talking with us, and it's always a pleasure to have you here in California. I sure am glad that you came this time.

---

6. Bill may have been referring to Harry Monroe (Sept. 8, 1893–Aug. 20, 1954), who was reputed to have been a good fiddler in his youth.

Bill: Well, Ray, I am glad to talk with you. It's pretty hard to get me started, but after you get me started, why, it's. . . .

Edlund: I don't want to quit, really.

Bill: I'm glad to do it with you, and I'm proud of all you folks out here for helping me with bluegrass and telling the folks about it and letting them know about it.

Edlund: We couldn't have done it without you.

Bill: And I would like to say hello to all of my friends and fans out here, and I wish 'em all the best.

Originally published in *Bluegrass Breakdown* 8:2 (Mar.–Apr. 1982): 6–8; 8:3 (May–June 1982): 10. Reprinted by permission of the interviewer and publisher.

EDITOR'S COMMENTS

Bill had recovered from his cancer surgery and was on tour in California in October 1981 when he was interviewed by Edlund, one of the hosts of "Pig in a Pen," a bluegrass and old-time music radio show in Berkeley (KPFA-FM). Near the end of the interview, Edlund was joined in the questioning by Butch Waller, leader of the bluegrass band High Country and then-president of the California Bluegrass Association (CBA). The interview was published in two parts, in the March–April and May–June 1982 issues of the CBA's *Bluegrass Breakdown* magazine. (This selection is based on a review of the interview tape and differs from the originally published text.)

Bill recorded "My Last Days on Earth" originally with the backing of only guitar (Norman Blake) and bass (Mark Hembree) on February 19, 1981. At the suggestion of producer Walter Haynes, background vocals were added on April 7 and strings were overdubbed on April 28, 1981.

Bill's brother Birch Monroe, born on May 16, 1901, died on May 15, 1982, one day before his eighty-first birthday.

"Happy Birthday, Bill Monroe!"

MARTY GODBEY

On September 11, 1982, more than twenty-five thousand people gathered in Louisville, Kentucky, to help Bill Monroe celebrate his seventy-first birthday.

The occasion was the tenth annual Kentucky Fried Chicken Bluegrass Festival, and although the celebration was two days early, that didn't matter to those present, or to the hundreds of people who had cooperated to make the day a very special one.

Among the gifts which were presented were a custom-made beaver hat, a hand-crafted, handtooled leather mandolin case, and an inlaid rosewood birthday "card" containing the good wishes of the more than seventy current and former Blue Grass Boys who contributed to the gifts.

"A lot of other people wanted to help," said former Blue Grass Boy Doug Hutchens, who thought up the presentation and made all the arrangements, "but it seemed more appropriate if it came just from people who had played with Bill down through the years."

The idea occurred to Doug as recently as June 25th, at the Jellico Creek Bluegrass Festival in Williamsburg, Kentucky, when Bill Monroe, with the help of fiddler/deejay Paul Mullins, surprised Kenny Baker on *his* birthday.[1]

At Bill's request, Paul came up with a disreputable old fiddle. "It had been hanging up in the barn for a couple of years," Paul said, "and even had a hornet's nest in it!"

Kenny was suitably impressed with the gift, and everyone at the festival enjoyed the joke—especially Bill Monroe.

"He got such a big kick out of planning that stuff for Baker," said Doug. "I got the idea right then. I got a whole lot from Bill, back when I was working for him. He wouldn't ask us to do anything he wouldn't do himself, and I wanted to do something for him."

Engaged in compiling a record of all the people who have ever played with Bill Monroe, Doug had the addresses of many Blue Grass Boys who, like himself, wanted to "do something for Bill." He sent each of them a sheet of special stationary on which they could write notes and special messages, and built a handsome rosewood cover, inlaid in ivory and trimmed in herringbone, in which to bind them.

"It was just some old guitar backs," Doug said with his usual humor, "that I ordered from Martin." Completed in advance, the cover was not assembled until the day before the presentation.

"Bill Keith's page came in by Federal Express just before I left, all the way from Woodstock, New York, to Pippa Passes, Kentucky. It cost him nine dollars to send it, but it got here in time."

After the idea for a leather-covered mandolin case came to him, Doug wasted no time. He got in touch with John Paganoni, who built the rough case and shipped it to Louisville, where the leatherwork was done by Nick Boone of The Leatherhead.

"It's English stitching," Doug explained, "which is very painstaking and doesn't show. He worked until midnight several nights—there wasn't much time."

The case, with its leather cover, was then sent back to Paganoni, who assembled it and did the finish work. "He took a day off from work to finish it," Doug said appreciatively, "but I was afraid for a while we were going to have to buy it a seat on a plane to get it here in time."[2]

---

1. His fifty-sixth birthday.
2. Paganoni lived near Manassas, Virginia, close to Washington, D.C.

Meanwhile, contributions were coming in at such a rate and with such enthusiasm that Doug thought a hat might make a good second gift. "I saw on the CBS news that a man named Randy Priest in Eagle, Idaho, made custom hats, so I called him up. It turned out that he was a Monroe fan, and was really pleased to have the chance to make a hat for Bill. It is 4-X beaver, the best you can buy, in silver gray."

Kentucky Fried Chicken officials had already planned recognition of Bill Monroe's birthday as part of their festival, but additional time was generously allowed for the Blue Grass Boys, several of whom were planning to attend.

"I didn't know who was going to be here until I saw them," Doug said. "If they came, they came on their own."

The "first Blue Grass Boy," Cleo Davis, was the first musician Bill Monroe hired after he and brother Charlie separated. Hired in Atlanta in 1939,[3] Cleo has fond memories of his work with Bill, and tells marvelous stories about "the old days." He and his son and grandson drove all the way from Highland City, Florida.

Merle "Red" Taylor drove from his home in Tupelo, Mississippi, to spend the night with Gordon Terry in Nashville, and then the two of them drove up to Louisville. Outstanding fiddle players who toured[4] with Monroe in the 1950s, Red and Gordon both played with the band which included Jimmy Martin, Rudy Lyle, and Joel Price. "I took Red's place in the band," Gordon said. "I wouldn't have missed this for the world."

Tex Logan and his daughter Jody flew in from New Jersey. "It's a legend that I was a Blue Grass Boy," Tex said. "I never was, but I've played so much with him, and have filled in and so on, and people think I was. I guess I'm an *honorary* Blue Grass Boy!"

Byron Berline, scheduled to appear on the festival with "Berline, Crary, & Hickman," was present for the occasion. "I hope I'm in the shape you're in when I'm seventy-one!" he said to Bill on stage. Byron played with the band for seven months, from March until September of 1968,[5] "And I wouldn't have left if I hadn't had to go in the service!" he added.[6]

And, of course, Doug Hutchens, who played bass during the summer of 1971, was on hand to enjoy something he had worked toward nearly all summer.

At the start of the birthday portion of the festival, Bill received a framed festival poster, featuring his own portrait against the Louisville skyline, from Claudia Sanders, widow of Colonel Harland Sanders.[7]

Bill quoted Colonel Sanders as having said, "Bill Monroe and Colonel Sanders have done more for Kentucky than any two men." Mrs. Sanders and Bill paused to

---

3. 1938.

4. And recorded.

5. 1967.

6. Before leaving, Berline recorded two Monroe originals, "The Gold Rush" and "Virginia Darlin'" (named for Virginia Stauffer), and the traditional "Sally Goodin" on Aug. 23, 1967.

7. Kentucky Colonel Harland Sanders died in 1980. See the editor's comments, second paragraph.

admire a huge cake in the shape of Kentucky, and the crowd sang "Happy Birthday" to both of them, Mrs. Sanders having recently celebrated her 80th birthday.

Then his Blue Grass Boys filed on stage, one by one, Bill greeting each with a big hug and an expression of friendship.

The wrapped package containing the hat was presented by Wayne Lewis, another with the mandolin case[8] by Gordon Terry, and a portion of the birthday "card" was read by Cleo Davis.

Later, during his performance, Bill called each of the visitors up to play or sing with him, as he has done with guest artists in the past.

While Byron Berline was playing "Sally Goodin," Bill beckoned to Wanda Hill, of Snow Hill, North Carolina, one of the Green Grass Cloggers standing beside the stage, and danced a spirited (and expert) clog until the end of the tune, when they finished with a flourish and a deep bow.[9]

The sky was blue, the sun shone, and a good time was had by all—Happy Birthday, Bill Monroe!

Originally published in *Bluegrass Unlimited* 17:5 (Nov. 1982): 14–16. Reprinted by permission of the author.

EDITOR'S COMMENTS

Bill's birthday was usually observed in some way at the annual free Kentucky Fried Chicken Bluegrass Festival in downtown Louisville, but nothing like the celebration of his seventy-first, held on September 11, 1982. This report on the event by Godbey, a writer and wife of Frank Godbey, founder of the Internet discussion list BGRASS-L, appeared in the November 1982 issue of *Bluegrass Unlimited.*

Kentucky Colonel Harland Sanders, founder of Kentucky Fried Chicken, was born in Indiana on September 9, 1890. He bought a service station in Corbin, Kentucky, in 1930, and opened his first restaurant in one of its storage rooms. He died on December 16, 1980.

Amazingly, in August 1982, one month before he "danced a spirited (and expert) clog" at the Louisville festival, Bill had endured two more operations, one to drain his kidneys and the other for an enlarged prostate. Brief mention of "emergency surgery"[1] was made in the September 1982 *Bluegrass Unlimited,* but no further details appeared in print until 1985 (see Richard D. Smith, "Bill Monroe—His Best Days on Earth").

Note

1. "General Store," *Bluegrass Unlimited* 17:3 (Sept. 1982): 14.

8. The same case in which Bill carried his main mandolin throughout the rest of his career.

9. Bill had undergone two more operations just prior to this birthday celebration. See the editor's comments, third paragraph.

"Bill Monroe"

RONNI LUNDY

The house Bill Monroe lives in is 140 years old. The 288 acres it sits on are just north of Nashville, Tennessee, but the land looks like the hilly farms around Rosine, Kentucky, where Monroe was born on September 13, 1911.

There's a stream coursing through the Tennessee farm, with a spacious dog pen built along part of it for the hunting hounds. There's an abundance of blackberry bushes clinging to the hills.

There's enough bottom land to stand a mess of sweet corn and beans, enough ridges and hollers to make a Kentucky-born man feel secure.

The house itself is made of logs with wide, plank porches and a big wooden swing in front. The path through the yard is lined with big rocks, one from each of the 50 states.

Inside, the house is dark and cool, even in the heat of summer. The living room has a huge stone fireplace, a heavy desk, and a large television set. It also has a cheap, dusty hi-fi with a few albums flung casually next to it.

At first glance, that hi-fi makes no sense.

This is, after all, the home of a working musician—a man who, with his brother, Charlie, was one of America's first great recording stars—a man who has recorded 37 albums[1] himself and is credited with creating an entire musical genre: bluegrass.

Virtually every bluegrass musician in the last 20 years—from Ralph Stanley, Earl Scruggs, and Jimmy Martin to young modernists like Ricky Skaggs and J. D. Crowe— have said they first heard the music on radio and then learned to play by piecing together the basics from the precious records they were able to buy and play at home.

But here in Bill Monroe's home, the record player looks like an afterthought— something left behind by a grandchild or one of the tenant hands. "No, I don't listen to records much," the father of bluegrass says.

Why should he?

When Bill Monroe first heard the music that became bluegrass, he wasn't listening to another musician on record or radio. He was listening to something in his head—a mix of sounds and feelings that had caught his ear and heart and that he wanted to bring together in a music that would be uniquely his own.

He was listening to the blues of the black musicians where he grew up, particularly a brilliant guitar man named Arnold Shultz who befriended and taught him. And he was listening to the high, calling cry of the field hands he worked and sang with.

---

1. Thirty-two Bill Monroe albums had been released at this time. See the editor's comments, second paragraph.

He was listening to the longing and lamentation of the voices singing out in the Methodist and Pentecostal churches near his home. And he was listening to the sound of fiddles: the lonesome whine echoing the bagpipes of Scotland, the Monroe family's homeland, coupled with the lively dance step of the fiddle played by Uncle Pen, his mother's brother and an itinerant trader/musician who took young Bill under his wing when his parents died early on.

But, perhaps most importantly, Monroe was listening to an unrelenting rhythm of his own.

It was a driving and impatient force in him that demanded that this music he was trying to form be played faster than the actual beat, more emphatically than country or gospel or blues had ever been played before.

In time, he pieced together the sound he heard—from his own music and the music made by the hot, young hillbilly musicians he found eager to join his band. He trusted only his own ear to tell him what parts he should keep (the five-string banjo) and what did not belong (the accordion he used briefly), until he came to the sound that satisfied him.

It's no wonder, then, that the house in which Bill Monroe lives has no expensive sound equipment, no thousand-dollar stereo. Because even now, some 40 years after the sound took its first form on a 1939 broadcast at the Grand Ole Opry,[2] the music that matters most to Bill Monroe is still the music he hears himself.

That music has become Monroe's voice, a means of communicating with the world for a man who, by his own admission, is not very comfortable with words.

Like many Kentuckians, Bill Monroe loves a good story as much as the next man. He sees the world revealed in anecdotal glimpses. He, in turn, chooses to reveal himself the same way.

Songs have been the safe but telling vehicles for letting the world know who he is and what he is about. The loneliness of lost love is in "It's Mighty Dark (for Me) to Travel." The father letting go of his daughter speaks in "The Little Girl and the Dreadful Snake." And then there is the wordless melancholy dance with death in his recent instrumental "My Last Days on Earth."

The story of his early life and the history of bluegrass music also have been his way of telling the world, particularly interviewers and historians, about himself. The story hardly changes in repeated tellings.

But the cadences of Monroe's voice, the quaint words, the archaic structure of the sentences, give the story fresh life no matter how many times it's told. And the rapid rush of Monroe speaking in that fast-beat timing that is his trademark gives the story the intensity it deserves.

"It was kindly a lonely life," he often begins. Or, "We didn't have much money, down on the farm. . . ."

2. Shortly before this article was published, the Grand Ole Opry was sold to the Gaylord Broadcasting Company. See the editor's comments, third paragraph.

Between the lines is the loneliness of being born the last and eighth child, born with lousy eyesight but also a yearning to be a baseball player. There's the pain of losing parents at an early age, and the comfort of the friendship of an uncle who was both a crafty trader and remarkable fiddle man.

He will talk about the fear of a country boy who had to travel north to the city to compete in the heaving economics of a changing world and the sharp bitterness that grew from the scorn he felt in the city, where his only valuable commodity was the width and strength of his back, loading barrels at a warehouse.

And underlying it all is the unspoken bitterness of the littlest brother who always got the leftovers—right down to the mandolin, the instrument no one wanted in the family band.

And there is the pride.

Sometimes it's tender and glowing, as he describes the unexpected joy of being chosen to play guitar with Shultz and playing straight through until dawn at an all-night country dance.

Sometimes it's fierce, as he points out that he has always made a living, a good living, playing bluegrass—while other country musicians have risen and then foundered on the changing trends of the decades.

That pride is the single most important element in Monroe's music. That pride is legendary.

"That's what makes a man: that, if a tree is in the road, he ain't gonna stand there and try to push it out of the way with his car," said Butch Robins, Monroe's banjo player from 1978 to 1981.[3] "He's gonna walk over there, pick the damn thing up, and push it out of the road and eliminate it. That's what a strong man does.

"I seen Monroe put a bridge timber on his back and walk with it. The man gets out, he picks up the tree, throws it out of his way, and then he goes on. And it's done with posture, with presence.

"A proud man walks with definition. He walks with very sure, confident steps that come down smack on the beat. And Monroe is the one who somehow brought that force into his music. And the music has such focus that, even in its weakest moments, it can chill the fiber of a human."

It was this chilling pride that spoke to the mountain people who heard his piercing voice over the radio and who responded by becoming staunch fans.

It was this pride that made him cling to his sound when rock 'n' roll knocked the underpinnings out of the country music industry in the 1950s, when other country stars began to change over to a smoother sound.

Some people even say that it is the enormous strength of Monroe's pride that put him back on the stage, back on the road after surgery for cancer looked as if it would end his career in the spring of 1981.

But if the pride has sustained him, it also has cost him. And his single-minded devotion to the music has cost him, as well.

---

3. 1977 to 1981.

He and his wife, Carolyn, divorced in 1953.[4] He'll allow as how life on the road is hard on a marriage, but won't elaborate. His companion of several years, Julia LaBella, left him to marry a young musician closer to her own age last fall.[5]

He has little contact with his daughter, Melissa; and his relationship with his son, bluegrass and country performer James, has been marbled with the stress that comes when a powerful father dominates the field of endeavor pursued with far less success by his child.

He has paid a price in friendships, too. His career has been marred with bad feelings and rumored feuds. Carlton Haney, the promoter credited with giving bluegrass new life when he organized the first major outdoor festival in 1965, says he has not spoken with his former friend Monroe since a disagreement over bookings a dozen years ago.

But Monroe is not a man without affection. Most of that affection comes from and is given to his fans.

✍

It's noon in a motel cafe where Monroe eats in Goodlettsville,[6] and it's as if all the customers in the place are at a party for him.

One elderly couple brings him a newspaper clipping about bluegrass. A burly man in overalls calls out his name. A minister and his family at the next table come over to say goodbye because they are moving to Memphis. The waitress delivers iced tea to Monroe as soon as he sits down. The jukebox is spiked with Bill Monroe songs. Before leaving, Monroe moves quickly through the room, picking up and paying for the checks for everyone who has spoken to him.

He also can be a patient and giving teacher. When Robins left the band in 1981, Monroe started looking for a new banjo man.

"They came to the office every day when he was in town," said Betty McInturff, his personal secretary since 1981. "There was this one boy who could play so well, and Bill said, 'I'd surely like to have him in the band.'

"But the boy couldn't sing, wouldn't sing, and Bill had to have a baritone. They must have sat in that office for an hour, Bill singing all the parts and then saying to the boy, 'Won't you just try? You can learn as you go along.' But the boy said, no, he just wasn't a singer.

"And Bill finally had to let him go because, you know, he had to have that baritone part in the band for the harmonies. But when he did, he told the boy, 'Now, you go back and try to learn like I showed you because I just might need me another banjo player someday, and I'd really like to hire you.'

"And I was really struck by how much time he spent with that boy—how hard it was for him to let him go."[7]

---

4. 1960.

5. Julia LaBella and Bill met in 1976. See the editor's comments, fourth paragraph.

6. Mason's Motel and Restaurant, 901 South Dickerson Road, north of Nashville.

7. The banjo player who auditioned for Bill is Rodney Carter of Eva, Alabama. He's still picking and not singing.

Monroe seems most comfortable in relationships, like these, that maintain a distance—teacher to student, host to his guests, performer to his fans, father of bluegrass to his sons.

Kenny Baker has played fiddle with Monroe for two dozen years, the longest any musician has been a Blue Grass Boy. He lived in a tenant house on Monroe's farm in 1958 and 1959, and the two men share an interest in cattle and game cocks as well as their love of music.

Baker says that when Bill quits, he'll hang it up, too. Baker talks about Monroe's fairness, his skill at writing a song, his strengths as a bandleader and a musician. But Baker doesn't characterize their 24-year association as particularly intimate.

"You might say it's a friendship," he said. And when asked if the sorrowful themes in the music reflect the realities of Monroe's life, Baker said, "I haven't the faintest idea. I think he lives a pretty full life."

Who does know him well, then? Who might have a deep understanding of him? Monroe first brushes the question aside with a joke ("You don't believe what I've been telling you?"), then turns solemn.

"There's no one," he says, looking off into space. A few moments later, he ends that afternoon's interview.

✍

Interviews with Monroe can end abruptly, particularly if they stray too far from upbeat discussions of the music or his already well-documented past.

He is not comfortable answering direct questions about who he is and why, who he might have liked to have been, and who he might like to become. He is not likely to open the door to himself to anyone who walks straight up and knocks. But he does, from time to time and in comfortable surroundings, allow glimpses of the man behind the legend.

"I want to be your friend," he says to Pat McDonogh[8] and me when we arrive at his annual summer festival in Bean Blossom, Indiana, in June. "That's what my life is, to be friends with you and you. I'll tell you something else my life is. I like to see the sun shine. I like to see the sun set because every time it sets, it's in a different place."

He gravitates toward the sunset each of the two evenings we are there, talking about when and where it will go down. The first evening, at Pat's request, he poses in the shadows of the tall trees at Bean Blossom, his ruddy cheeks glowing in the fading sunlight. The next night, it is he who seeks out Pat for more pictures just before dusk.

He is exuberant in Bean Blossom. He has just bought a horse, a blue roan. He shows us how he trims her tail, her mane, and forelock in a strange, short crop with just a few strands hanging from the tail.

---

8. A photographer for *The Louisville Times*.

"That's the way we did it down in the country where I'm from. I don't know why. That's just the way we did it there," he says.

All of his horses, brought up to Indiana from the farm in Goodlettsville so his fans at Bean Blossom can see them, have their hair cut the same way.

The second day we are there, he hitches up some of the horses and his mules (Bill and Jim, named after him and his son) to three wagons loaded with hay. They parade through the festival grounds, a strange and moving sight. They make their way through the trees like ghosts of another era, and then stomp and whinny down the road flanked by garish concession stands.

The red, blue, and yellow lights of the food stalls flash and beckon, but Monroe, standing in the center wagon, the reins held firmly in his hands, stares straight ahead. Nothing in the carnival atmosphere around him seems of importance to him. He is only intent on showing the fans how it used to be.

On stage he is vibrant—clogging with the Koskela sisters who play as the Wildwood Pickers, spinning stories between songs, making jokes about the band and himself, his legendary stinginess, his strict demeanor.

"These strings must have been on here for three or four months," he says when his mandolin pops one. "I broke two a couple of days ago and one right now. I've got five to go. It's cheaper to buy strings in a set. Boy, you know, I sure do believe in saving that money.

"Everbody's been decent people here," he says later to the crowd. "They might have drinked some, but I didn't see them. They must have got under their tent and done it."

While the particular numbers he plays in a performance are chosen spontaneously (most of his shows now include a long period of requests), the type of number he plays follows a set structure.

He opens with something upbeat, then usually follows with a song that features the banjo.[9] These days he does a medley of some of his best-known songs, including "Blue Moon of Kentucky" and "Molly and Tenbrooks." Interspersed among the other numbers are a couple of gospel tunes and a lot of his jazzy blues.

"When I started this music, I was going to make sure I put some blues sound into it," he had explained during an earlier interview. "It makes me feel good to hear it. And then, it makes me sad lots of times. When we do a sad number, the next number we do might be different from that. And so it works out all right.

"A lot of my life has been lonely, it sure has. The music's made me think about things and what was going on through life, what was on up ahead of me, and when I got up in years, what was past and behind me.

"But everything is working out all right."

---

9. The lead singer was usually featured after the opening number, followed by a banjo tune.

⁄⁊

The last two years have been back-to-back sorrow and light for Monroe. His brother, Birch, died in July of 1982,[10] leaving only his sister, Bertha, and himself alive of the Monroe family clan. His companion, Julia, left him that summer and, during 1982, he was hospitalized twice.

But this May he was invited to lunch at the White House in recognition of his unique contribution to American music.

This spring and summer he met with civic and business leaders in Nashville, Louisville, and his home county of Hartford[11]—all interested in beginning some form of museum/archive that would honor him and bluegrass music.

This July he made his first trip to the Holy Land, performing twice in Israel and being baptized in the River of Jordan. ("It meant so much to me. I've sung about that river all my life.") For Monroe, a Methodist, it was his first baptism by immersion.

He is currently working on a project that delights him, a record of duets with several of the big names in country music.[12] And his personal management through the Buddy Lee Agency in Nashville has been taken over by a young man, Tony Conway, who seems to be sympathetic to Monroe's moods and needs.

He is writing songs again, too, he said. After he wrote "My Last Days on Earth" in 1980,[13] he didn't write anything for a while. But on a ride from his farm to the diner in Goodlettsville in July, he suddenly handed me the folded-over copy of the *Nashville Banner* that had been lying on the seat of his Cadillac between us. There, scrawled in ink above the newsprint, were these words:

> The day time sunshine,
> The night time light—
> What would we do without them both?

"What do you think about that?" he asks. "That seems like it might make a pretty good number?"

⁄⁊

Retirement? More performing? These are questions that naturally swirl around Monroe as his Tuesday birthday approaches. He'll be 72, and says he's still unsure of the choices that remain open to him.

He walks around his farm, moving at that brisk clip, proudly pointing out that the land is plowed with a mule team, exactly as it was in Rosine when he was a boy.

There is the barn that he and James hauled over and reassembled piece by piece

---

10. Birch Monroe, born on May 16, 1901, died on May 15, 1982.
11. Bill's home county is Ohio County; Hartford is its county seat.
12. *Bill Monroe and Friends,* MCA Records, MCA-5435, released before the end of 1983.
13. 1977.

from the property a few miles away on Dickerson Road,[14] where Monroe lived until his divorce.

There is a beautiful, two-story tenant house currently occupied by a family that helps him work the land.

And there is his own house, lovingly restored to its original log-cabin beauty with a tin roof for listening to the rain. ("There is nothing I love more," he says, "than to listen to the sound of the rain at night on a good old tin roof. And there is nothing I hate more than to hear a man cuss the rain or the snow.")

"Yes," he says, "this place is where I come to rest. I don't know what I would do without it. And now I want to ask you something. What would you do if you was me? Would you go on playing music? Or would you come here and retire and work this land?"

Standing in all the comforting beauty of the old-timey farm, it's a hard question to answer. The desire in him must be strong to be here where the past he so prizes has been re-created. But it can't be stronger than the desire to tell the world about the past, can it? To keep on singing about the pain and joy in his heart?

I wait for him to say.

He doesn't until much later in the day, when he offers that he doesn't think he could retire. "The music, it's kindly my life; and the people, the fans, they are in a way like family."

But maybe the better answer was something he had said earlier in the day, when he grabbed my elbow and trotted me over to a portico just built on the outside of a dairy barn.

"Now I'm going to show you something here that some people might not believe. See these two posts here?" he said, pointing to the thick logs of locust wood holding up the roof.

"Well, I cut these logs last year and put them up here. This wood's dead. But look at these," he said, reaching out to touch several green and heavy branches that had sprung alive from the logs' drying sides.

"Now, that tree has got these branches coming from it, but I cut it a good two feet from the ground. Isn't that something? And the locust, it's a good, strong wood that gets harder and better the older it gets."

Originally published in *The Louisville Times*, "Scene" magazine, Sept. 10, 1983, 17–23. © 1983, Courier-Journal and Louisville Times Co. Reprinted by permission.

EDITOR'S COMMENTS

The Louisville Times published Lundy's probing feature story on Bill in the now-defunct newspaper's "Scene" magazine section on Saturday, September 10, 1983, the weekend before Bill's seventy-second birthday.

---

14. The "old reconstructed barn" mentioned by Jan Otteson in "Bluegrass 'Father,' Monroe, Is at Home on the Farm."

At that point in time, thirty-two Bill Monroe albums had been released; twenty-seven by Decca-MCA, three by Columbia's Harmony label, and one each by Decca's Vocalion and RCA's Camden labels. By 1996, four more albums and two cassette/CD recordings would be released by MCA.

Two months before this article was published, in July 1983, the Dallas, Texas–based Gaylord Broadcasting Company (later the Gaylord Entertainment Company), a subsidiary of the Oklahoma Publishing Company, purchased WSM radio (including the Grand Ole Opry), the Opryland Hotel, and the entire Opryland entertainment complex for an estimated $300 million. The properties were bought from the American General Insurance Company, which had acquired all of the Opry-founding National Life Insurance Company's holdings in 1982 for $1.5 billion.

Julia LaBella (mentioned previously in the comments for Jan Otteson, "Bluegrass 'Father,' Monroe, Is at Home on the Farm") was born in Lubbock, Texas, on August 4, 1955. She and Bill met at the first Berkshire Mountains Bluegrass Festival in Hillsdale, New York, on August 1, 1976. A talented singer, she married dobro player Alan Phelps on September 1, 1982, and the two worked briefly as a duo. The union was short-lived, however, and she returned to Nashville in the 1990s to be reunited with Bill.

"Bill Monroe's Birthday Party"

SANDY ROTHMAN

In the words of organizer Doug Hutchens, we came to celebrate "the day it all began."

A birthday party is a very personal thing. But then, bluegrass is a very personal thing—the music originated by Bill Monroe.

That's why, on the evening of September 13, 1983, some 180 of his closest friends, neighbors, fans, and musicians met at Mason's Restaurant in Goodlettsville, Tennessee, for the second annual surprise birthday party for Bill. (The mayor of Nashville also proclaimed the day as Bill Monroe Day in Nashville.) Begun last year in Louisville by Hutchens, the tradition is too well established now to ever again be a surprise to Monroe. But this time, he was clearly surprised.

"I thought they were planning a dinner. And I expected a present or something, nothing like this. They told me there was to be a wedding—to throw me off, I guess."

"They" are David and Jenny Graff, proprietors of Mason's Motel and Restaurant on Dickerson Road, not too far from Monroe's office and home. "I just love that man," Jenny said, "and do you know, he comes to eat with us every day that he's in town. My husband said he could die today, now that we've been able to host this party for Mr. Monroe."

By the time Bill arrived at Mason's and saw the large gathering, he had it all figured out. Hutchens had worked with the agreeable Graffs to arrange media coverage (including the Nashville Network), as well as emcee work by WSM's Grant Turner and gift presentations by former Blue Grass Boys.

The first gift was a white Stetson from the Graffs. Next, a custom-made brown and cream hat ordered by Hutchens from Randy Priest of Eagle, Idaho. "I'm set for the winter now," declared Bill. Then he shouted, "Oh boy, oh boy!" as he viewed a specially-made saddle by master leather craftsman Nick Boone of Louisville, who was present.[1] Beaming, Nick said his labor of love had taken between 60 and 80 hours of work. This had been planned all year by Hutchens and was purchased by him with the help of contributions from friends and musicians he contacted by mail.

Bill has 29 horses and still rides, and he described the horse he would place the saddle on—his name, where he was from, how many hands tall he is, his weight and color. He would look fine in the new silver-trimmed saddle.

Bill's former manager, Ralph Rinzler, presented the annual "birthday card," another Hutchens brainchild, which is a volume of personally-written notes to Bill on design letterhead circulated and collected by Hutchens. This year the card was bound in a hardwood cover edged in ivory, inlaid with a pearl[2] flowerpot as found on Monroe's mandolin headstock. Where *"The Gibson"* would appear, David Nichols of Waddington, New York, had inlaid *"Happy Birthday"* in pearl Gibson-script. Over 60 heartfelt messages from close friends and musicians filled the card.

Other personal gifts were opened later, making Mason's seem like Christmas in September. Punch, ham biscuits, and appetizers were served, along with slices of the hat-shaped birthday cake Bill had received a couple of days earlier at the Kentucky Fried Chicken Bluegrass Festival in Louisville. Larger than the size of a restaurant table, the huge hat-cake rode from Kentucky to Nashville untouched, a guest of honor in Monroe's bus.

Bill asked for a second piece.

One current and thirteen former Blue Grass Boys were present: Frank Buchanan, Bob Fowler, Doug Hutchens, Dan Jones, Ralph Lewis, Wayne Lewis,[3] Benny Martin, Curtis McPeake, James Monroe, Clyde Moody, Sandy Rothman, Bobby Smith, Joe Stuart, and Roland White.

Also in attendance were Clarence Greene, John Kaparakis, Rev. Ray Flatt, John Hartford, Bill Carlisle, Marty and Charmaine Lanham, Lance LeRoy, and Jim Rooney—along with Bill's grandson, James William ("Jimbo") Monroe II; his personal secretary, Betty McInturff; Dee Dee Prestige;[4] many other well-wishers; and even Bill's favorite waitress at Mason's.[5] A photographer snapped them together. Bill calls the young waitress "the old woman," and she insists he is her favorite customer.

Jenny Graff announces that tomorrow's dinner will be corned beef and cabbage.

---

1. Boone helped build the mandolin case given to Bill in 1982.
2. Short for mother-of-pearl.
3. The then-current Blue Grass Boy present.
4. Toured with Bill in 1989–90 as "Diana Christian."
5. Thelma Henderson, who, as of this writing, is still working at Mason's.

The camera crews are packed and gone, and everyone drifts outside to leave. One of Bill's farm hands hefts the new saddle into a car. Farewells are said all around and faith is once again affirmed that bluegrass is more than a music: it is a community, a caring family, with the ability to create lasting friendships.

A few days earlier, in a Louisville hotel near the festival, Bill stepped into a crowded elevator. He spotted Doug Hutchens in a sport coat and cowboy hat.

"Are you a Blue Grass Boy?" quipped Monroe.

Hutchens could only nod yes, sir.

"Do you know the old man that leads 'em?"

On his birthday night, Bill Monroe is a young 72 and he is the last to leave Mason's Restaurant. Much of the bottom layer of the tall cake—the hat's brim—remains inside Mason's.

"You keep it here," Bill says to the Graffs.

"This night has sure put Goodlettsville on the map," muses Jenny. "I'll serve a piece of this cake tomorrow to everyone who comes in, at no charge, and I'll say it's from Bill Monroe."

"Fine," says the Father of Bluegrass Music.

Outside the air has become refreshingly cool. It has been a hot day in the relentless Tennessee summer; we went to Mason's for the party, we had a good time, and when we came outside it had turned towards fall, as if in honor of Bill Monroe's birthday.

Heading for his car and the farm, Bill looked happy, relaxed, and healthy. "It sure is a wonderful breeze tonight."

We came to celebrate this day, the day it all began, and the breeze was welcome and wonderful.

Originally published in *Bluegrass Unlimited* 18:6 (Dec. 1983): 32–33. Reprinted by permission of the author.

EDITOR'S COMMENTS

Mason's Restaurant was the scene of the second surprise birthday party for Bill, actually held on his birthday in 1983. This party was a little more intimate than the first, attended by only "some 180 of his closest friends, neighbors, fans, and musicians," including former Blue Grass Boy Rothman, who played guitar and banjo with Bill in 1964. His coverage of this special gathering appeared in the December 1983 issue of *Bluegrass Unlimited*.

Bluegrass Breakdown: The Making of the
Old Southern Sound (excerpts)

ROBERT CANTWELL

Whoever has seen Bill Monroe up close, on stage, especially in these late years of his career, will remember that he carries himself with a kind of austere majesty, as if time had already chiselled him, like his presidential ancestor, from a block of marble; by whatever art it is that a man conveys his character and sense of himself to the world, Monroe seems to continue a lineage that reaches back almost to Lexington, the heart of the Blue Grass and the Athens of the West. He is a striking figure, dashing and patrician, presenting that peculiar vividness and clarity we associate with statesmen or movie stars. Even now Monroe is an extraordinarily handsome man, whose face, with jutting jaw and aquiline nose, is delicately constructed and whose expression, enigmatically compounded of arrogance, sorrow, and humor, is perilously easy to misinterpret. His mouth, with its pouting lower lip and faint sneer at the corner, the corner that opens slightly with the effort of playing the mandolin, is drawn tight with a kind of vigilant mistrust, the mouth of a Scots ancestor; the eyes are a pioneer's. Whatever may be hidden in the recesses of Monroe's personality, this public image shows not a trace of vanity, pomposity, vulgarity, or corruption, though in a man less reserved each of these traits might easily blossom out to destroy the subtly theatrical poise Monroe's image demands.

Monroe has the rugged dignity one sees, for instance, in the stark daguerreotypes of Lincoln; and when this impressive figure descends from the stage, in a western-cut, cream-colored, tailored suit and a Stetson hat, he is predictably an object of veneration. Autograph seekers flock around him, and if the concert has been held in the South it becomes apparent that Monroe's audience constitutes one of the last genuinely rural classes in America, with traits that recall now largely forgotten stereotypes that used to distinguish the rube from the city slicker. What precisely characterizes this audience, or why it is so distinctively itself, why it is, in a word, so vividly Appalachian, I am at a loss to explain. Perhaps it is the effect of poverty, whose marks are everywhere—poverty of the endemic kind, I mean, that over a generation or so has become a principle of life, in evidence even when a flimsy new prosperity of wages has diverted its course. Good nutrition and dental care are apparently among the casualties of mountain folklife. Overweight in varying degrees is a general blight. Faces are sharp, sometimes coarse or picturesque, often interesting, seldom beautiful. Gestures are large, unprepossessing, at times childlike, voices warm and animated, relations among people convivial and enthusiastic. There is pride in fashionable grooming and dress, though seldom are they the fashions that rule the day elsewhere: Appalachian dress, like other aspects of Appalachian culture, salvages the scraps of the past. Everyone's hair is done up, men and women, in sometimes lavish or foppish ways that may suggest either the antebellum ballroom or the ducktails and teases we used to see around the soda fountain during the Eisenhower era. Both men and women dress to emphasize their sex, men favoring the bulging bicep, perhaps a tattoo, some variety of western boot; women, tight-fitting blouses and pants and feminine frills, though only a few—the most sexually conspicuous—wear makeup: perhaps the old church sanction against it remains silently in force. Older men and women, more simply and conventionally groomed and dressed, represent the rural folk of a generation or so ago, Bill Monroe's generation; Monroe himself, apparently immune to these changes, has transcended the times and stands out like a lighthouse among his people.

With this audience Monroe is warm, often witty, but rarely familiar. He willingly poses with admirers for photographs and never fails to respond politely to compliments. It is astonishing how frequently a man or woman will recall to Bill having seen him at another show ten, fifteen, even *thirty* years ago: his fans are loyal, and Monroe often rewards them with some honest recollection of the time and place, and sometimes with some mutually familiar name. I have never seen him ignore a person soliciting his attention, though he may behave coolly towards one or another of whom he disapproves—particularly those who seem to have no pride or self-respect: for Monroe, certain counterculture types fall into this class, as well as the inevitable thug or drunk.

Bill Monroe is no teenage idol, but something far more durable—a patriarch, whose dedication to his sprawling, incoherent family is never more apparent than when he has occasion to lead them in song at one of his bluegrass festivals or pays them tribute to writers and reporters. Asked recently if he had thought of retiring, having dashed back to the Opry stage after major surgery,[1] he answered—honestly, I think—that he didn't want to let his fans down. His leadership in fact has the character of spiritual guidance, with special attention given to the young and to the solidarity of the bluegrass community; his public pronouncements are implicitly or explicitly affirmations of the wholesomeness, honesty, and decency of bluegrass music. Though not an eloquent man, Monroe is thoughtful, with the habit of reflection upon matters of principle deeply established in him; it seems there is virtually nothing in the way of music or conduct that has escaped his consideration.

Monroe's personal life has not been free of the ordinary human failures and distress: a long and mysterious estrangement from his brother Charlie, which persisted through Charlie's last illness and about which many lurid stories have grown up;[2] a

---

1. Probably prostate enlargement surgery, August 1982.

2. Up to and even after Charlie's death in 1975 it was *rumored* that Bill and he were "estranged," but, as Ralph Rinzler indicates (in *Bill Monroe and the Blue Grass Boys: Live Recordings,* vol. 1: *Off the Record*), this was not the case in the sixties.

disabled but not entirely dissolved first marriage[3] and a child who suffered crippling emotional difficulties;[4] a love affair which ended in a lawsuit after twenty years,[5] as Monroe entered late middle age; in this private dimension, Monroe is simply a man like other men, neither better nor worse, whose weaknesses may stand out more vividly, and perhaps have more devastating effect, in the general amplitude of his character. "I guess if I hadn't left Rosine and gone up North," he told a reporter, "I'd probably be just like the other folks who live here now, farming and raising a family. I probably wouldn't have gone through seven, ten, fifteen women."

One side of Monroe quite probably is the issue of childhood privations. All who know him, as we've already noted, recall his many years of isolation, when his intense concentration on his work seemed to exclude most ordinary social intercourse. Even now there are periods when he will sink into a taciturnity so profound—almost a kind of trance—which the most urgent business cannot draw him out of; yet he is also, at times, highly animated and voluble. He shows little eagerness to fraternize with other musicians, though old friends and young admirers constantly seek him out. Among these he is passive and may seem remote or forgetful, though he never forgets a request made of him, a favor owed or favor granted, an insult or injury, real or imagined, done. Until the influences of the folk revival began to work upon him, his fierce competitiveness at least partially blinded him to the achievements of other bluegrass musicians and, more importantly, to his own immense contribution to others' achievements. Against some people he has harbored resentments of a most durable and intransigent kind; his readiness to believe he has been deliberately slighted or wounded is probably connected to his tempestuous love life, which for some people contrasts sharply with the rigorous standards of decency he holds up to others. What Rinzler calls his "savage, arrogant, intransigent spirit," so impressive in his music, cannot but trespass somewhat upon the laws that govern ordinary personal conduct, from which as an artist Monroe has won a certain limited immunity. He lives, like a poet, in a moral universe of his own making which, though it may not touch ours at every point, has the integrity and wholeness that is the heart of morality.

Among his friends Monroe is relaxed and affable, and though his authority, especially over band members, is always implicit, he never exercises it in a wanton or arbitrary way. He inspires allegiance, and his friends take it upon themselves to protect and defend him. For there is something infinitely delicate and terribly vulnerable in Monroe. One hears it in his speech, which is quaint, lilting, sometimes so musical that he seems more to sing than to speak; delicately articulated words fall from his lips with a quickness and liquidity which suggests he has formed them from light. Sometimes he walks delicately, too, as if he were afraid of falling—perhaps because his vision is poor—and will unconsciously extend his hand for aid.

---

3. I presume the author is referring to the professional relationship that existed between Bill and Carolyn after their divorce in 1960.

4. Bill's daughter, Melissa.

5. Actually, over thirty years.

In some of his habits, too, there is a boy-like charm. He reads with high scrutiny, moving his lips whisperingly as he goes, sometimes annotating the text—I have heard of a copy of Woody Guthrie's *Bound for Glory* whose margins are black with Bill's comments. He is excessively fond of sweets, rarely failing to order the chocolate sundae or wedge of cake[6] at roadside cafes along his route, his love of sugar being his only obvious vice, one he shares with other conservative rural people such as the Amish. His life on the farm in Goodlettsville, Tennessee, where he raises cattle, quarter horses, foxhounds, and game hens, is like theirs, deliberately conservative and antiquarian in spirit. Most of the work on the farm is done by draught horses and mules, for Bill believes that tractors are too dangerous.

Kentucky planter, then, and Tennessee farmer—but what identity has Bill Monroe adopted for his *offstage* public role, the one which has come upon him in the final quarter of his career, as the "Father of Bluegrass Music"? Monroe's speech and gestures, his oblique and steady grace that is almost womanly, his alert and agile hands massively framed, his careful dress and finger rings, the silver hair that curls behind his ears—I see in Monroe the dandified rural evangelist, the man risen out of his station in response to a call compounded equally of spirit and flesh, who perhaps has won fame for himself, as they did in the old days, "in proportion to the carrying power of their voices in the open air."[7]

Bluegrass music, particularly the summertime outdoor bluegrass festival, with its potluck supper, jam session, gospel sings, and the like, has swept into the social and psychic space occupied a century ago by religious revivals and camp meetings. Thus it is a kind of religious leadership that Monroe exercises, appropriately paternal, mannerly, reverent, and, when he is in his musical pulpit, fired by the Holy Spirit.

EDITOR'S COMMENTS

Cantwell's examination of bluegrass was published by the University of Illinois Press in 1984. These excerpts from its first chapter include some of his most perceptive impressions of Bill in the early 1980s.

---

6. Usually pie, not cake.

7. Maud Karpeles, *Cecil Sharp: His Life and Work* (Chicago: University of Chicago Press, 1967), 151.

"The Bill Monroe Museum and Bluegrass Hall of Fame: The Dream Comes True"

DOUG HUTCHENS

A Bluegrass Museum and Hall of Fame has been the dream of bluegrass entertainers and fans for many years. It seems that every few years various efforts have been made to organize the bluegrass community for a museum and/or "Hall of Fame" effort. During the summer and fall of 1983, Bill and James Monroe took positive steps to bring about the realization of this dream. Bill stated recently, "The Hall of Fame, I guess, should have been started 20 years ago. It's been a lot of work, but it should have been done a long time ago . . . I know that more people are going to come down every week. I think it's good for the bluegrass entertainers and for their fans. A lot of people take vacations in Nashville and it'll be a good place for them to visit and it will be a real help to bluegrass music."

Work began in the late fall of 1983 and continued throughout the winter and spring of 1984. The existing building was completely renovated and an addition was added to the front, doubling the amount of floor space. In May 1984, the doors were opened. Fans were finally able to visit the Bill Monroe Museum and Bluegrass Hall of Fame. On June 4th, 1984, the Grand Opening was held. Bill said, "A lot of things went on that day in the way of taking pictures, looking at the place, different people playing music. They'd brought their music,[1] several different groups."

The Museum itself sits on a four-acre site in Music Valley, off Briley Parkway, near the Cumberland River in Nashville. Its location is close enough to the Opryland complex for convenience (less than a mile), but in a less congested area bordered by a family campground, where a relaxed atmosphere prevails.

Upon entering, visitors first find themselves in the souvenir and record shop. Within this area a large array of gifts and recordings are for sale. T-shirts, mugs, hats, and belt buckles are sold for remembrances of the trip to Nashville. In the record shop, many hard-to-find bluegrass recordings are available, just the place to complete that record collection of one's favorite bluegrass artist.

The Museum area is a work of art. As you enter the double doors, you pass by a large, lifelike portrait of Bill Monroe with his famous F-5 mandolin. Directly over the main door hangs a painting of a scenic farm with log cabin, farm animals, and a working gentleman with an ax. One can readily see that the artist captured the essence of life for the Father of Bluegrass. Bill commented: "That was done by Hope Randolph of the Lost Kentuckians. The cabin, I guess, is supposed to be Uncle Pen's

---

1. Meaning they'd brought their instruments.

cabin. She put Stringbeans back there in the blacksmith's shop. I doubt if String-beans could ever shoe a horse, but they've got him in the blacksmith's shop any-way. Now, String could plow though. He could plow corn and stuff like that (with a mule or horse). He's come out and would work with me and plow. Me and him plowed a lot of times."

Once in the Museum, you are witness to displays of many influential bluegrass and country music entertainers of today and of years past. Displays of belongings of Stringbean, Earl Scruggs, Jim and Jesse, Lester Flatt, James Monroe, the Osborne Brothers, the Whites, Wilma Lee and Stoney Cooper, Larry Sparks, Clyde Moody, and the list goes on. . . . The cases that line the walls are filled with many items donated by other artists: one of Red Taylor's fiddles, Jim Eanes' gold record of "Little Brown Hand," priceless, rare photographs, songbooks of years ago, and a 78 rpm record collection which includes a copy of the very first Bluebird recording of the Monroe Brothers. The cases are literally stuffed with interesting memorabilia.

The Museum also has an area for the stars of country music. Roy Acuff, Ernest Tubb, Johnny Cash, Barbara Mandrell, Dolly Parton, and over fifteen other artists have personal belongings on display. Bill commented on the Country Room: "Well, I have so many good friends in country music, people like Johnny Cash, Waylon Jennings. I know they appreciate the Country Room so they can display some of their things."

The Hall of Fame Room has a special meaning for all who visit there. James Monroe commented on how the members have been and will be chosen: "Bill Monroe picks them. It's hand-picked. It's people who he thinks have contributed to the business. He knows what every band can do, he knows what every picker is putting down, and he knows who should go in this Hall of Fame. Naturally, every-body can't go in the first year. It's going to take some years to do all that."

Ten individual artists or teams were inducted into the first group to enter Bill Monroe's Bluegrass Music Hall of Fame. Each member is displayed in a familiar full-color photograph. On a stand below each photograph, an appropriate acknowledge-ment of their achievements and highlights of their careers has been capably penned by Lance LeRoy. The 1984 inductees include Bill Monroe, Lester Flatt, Mac Wise-man, Earl Scruggs, Carl Story, Don Reno and Red Smiley, Ralph and Carter Stan-ley, Bobby and Sonny Osborne, Jim and Jesse McReynolds, and the Country Gen-tlemen.[2] Bill talked about the ten initial members: "I guess, really, the Stanley Brothers were really first when it came to people following me. They'd been follow-ing me before Lester and Earl started with me, you see. Lester had been with Char-lie Monroe, you know, and Charlie didn't play bluegrass. So, the Stanley Brothers really would be the first, I think, when it came right down to it, who was the first bluegrass group. Of course, a lot of people are fooled in that. Flatt and Scruggs start-ed with me, got the publicity, and was featured a lot, and their names growed fast-

---

2. Conspicuously absent from this list is Jimmy Martin, who would not be inducted into the Bluegrass Hall of Fame until 1998, after Bill's death.

er. Mac Wiseman is a good bluegrass singer. He didn't work with me too long, but Mac has done a lot for bluegrass. I guess Carl Story also followed bluegrass a long time too, and sang a lot of gospel. He was a Blue Grass Boy early on. He played a fiddle with me. Now, Lester Flatt, he was a powerful man in bluegrass music. We all miss him. Earl Scruggs really did a lot when he came in there with me. Reno and Smiley had a good bluegrass group for a long time and I think they should be in the Hall of Fame. Their friendship lasted on up until the end. I think that if there's anyone who deserves to be in the Hall of Fame it's the Osborne Brothers, Jim and Jesse, and the Country Gentlemen. They've all had wonderful bluegrass groups and they've stayed close together through the years."

The displays in the various rooms are superb, the Hall of Fame Room is inspiring, but when one walks into the Bill Monroe Room, you are able to witness the master himself. Large photographs fill the walls with familiar Bill Monroe poses. The display cases lining the walls are filled with bluegrass history. Awards, precious photographs of days past, brother Birch Monroe's fiddles, an F-5-style mandolin built especially for Bill by Randy Wood, a model wagon train given to Bill by Gary Thurmond, each item with its own very special meaning to Bill. I asked him about the Bill Monroe Room: "Well, there is so many things in there that I've saved down through the years. I didn't know I had that many things. We put a mandolin in there, plus, I believe, the band fiddle that a lot of different fiddlers played, you know, like Red Taylor and men like that. There's a fiddle in there that belonged to Birch too."

One might think that once the Museum is open, all the work is over. This is not true. There are several ideas presently under consideration for expansion, as well as a constant striving to improve the existing areas.

The Blue Grass Boys wall isn't quite complete yet. Bill explains: "The Blue Grass Boys Wall will be pictures of every man that's ever worked with me."

Avenues are being explored to erect a bronze statue of Bill, either beside the Museum or on the hill which overlooks the Museum and the Music Valley area. Bill commented: "That's where we were going to put the statue, but I don't know now. A lot of old people would have to climb that hill, and we haven't really decided where it is going to go. I think the statue would really be good on the hill though."

A possible extension of the showroom is also being considered. James explained, "We'd like to add on to the back, maybe another 30 to 60 feet. The cars he's (Bill's) had through the years could go in there. Like the Chrysler Imperial he had the wreck in, in 1953. The old Hudson Hornet. I can't remember what year on that. I think it was in the forties. That old 1946 Chevrolet stretched-out bus could also go in there.[3] And it could be an addition to what we already have."[4]

The building of a concert area on the grounds is also a future possibility and there is hope of a live, late-night broadcast similar to Ernest Tubb's Midnight Jamboree.

3. 1941 Chevrolet airport limousine.
4. These vehicles were not actually in the Monroes' possession at the time.

Jim Bessire,[5] who manages the Bill Monroe Museum and Bluegrass Hall of Fame, commented on the favorite areas and some of the well-known visitors to the museum and Hall of Fame: "I would say the Bill Monroe Room and the Hall of Fame Room are the most popular, along with the display with the old pictures of Jim Eanes, Clyde Moody, and, particularly, that picture that was taken down in Linebaugh's Restaurant, where they are all crowded around the table with Judge Hay. Almost all the artists have been by: Johnny Cash . . . Larry Sparks . . . Jim and Jesse . . . Mac Wiseman and Ralph Stanley have been by, and you'll see Bill Monroe in at least a couple of times each week. They'll stop by for coffee and sign some autographs."

James comments, "People are steadily bringing things in. Bill Harrell brought in a banjo and guitar, and they're coming in from different places. One of the main things is pictures. It's hard to get your hands on old pictures."

James also has hopes of a future Bluegrass Music Week, possibly beginning in 1985. "I'll tell you what we'd like to do here: He (Bill) and I have talked about it. On his birthday, September 13th, we'd like to have a Bluegrass Music Week here in Nashville. It would be for musicians, deejays that do play bluegrass music, bluegrass promoters, and magazines. It would be a start and it would give you something to start from. We could also put the new members in the Hall of Fame then. The main thing to me now, though, is to show this museum for what it really is: It's Bill Monroe's way of showing bluegrass music off and honoring the Hall of Fame members."

After spending time looking over and over the displays of the Museum and Hall of Fame and hearing of the future plans,[6] one must ask oneself, "Is this real, or am I in a wonderful dream?" Then you need only to walk back through the Hall of Fame Room once again, through the Bill Monroe Room, and then you can say to yourself, "It's been a long time coming, but, yep, it's real!"

Originally published in *Bluegrass Unlimited* 19:4 (Oct. 1984): 1–11, 31–34. Reprinted by permission of the author.

EDITOR'S COMMENTS

The Monroes had high hopes for this expensive new venture and, as reported by Hutchens in this *Bluegrass Unlimited* cover story of October 1984, they already had big plans for the future shortly after its grand opening on June 4, 1984. (This selection differs from the original mainly in matters of punctuation and in that one paragraph has been condensed.)

The big plans were not to be, however, as the museum and hall of fame failed to attract tourists to its off-the-beaten-path location at 2620 Music Valley Drive. In 1986 its displays were moved to a building in the even further out-of-the-way Twit-

5. Later Bill's road manager (1991–96).
6. The future plans were not to be. See the editor's comments, second paragraph.

ty City complex in Hendersonville. Eventually, in 1992 it was relocated to a new building at Monroe's Festival Campground in Bean Blossom, Indiana, where it remains today.

The building that originally housed the museum and hall of fame was converted, at considerable additional expense, into a supper club. Opened in 1987, Bill Monroe's Bluegrass Country closed in 1989.

Carolyn Minnie (Brown) Monroe, born on May 15, 1913, died about eight weeks after the Grand Opening of the Bill Monroe Museum and Bluegrass Hall of Fame, on July 31, 1984.

"Bill Monroe—His Best Days on Earth"

RICHARD D. SMITH

The stories I had heard about Bill Monroe over the past few years had not been happy ones.

About four years back, he had undergone major surgery, said to be for colon cancer. Although the operation was successful and he resumed touring, I watched him mount a stage slowly and with some difficulty at a show thereafter. He performed well, but looked thin and a bit haggard.

Then came his instrumental album, *Master of Bluegrass,* featuring a melancholy masterpiece with the ominous title "My Last Days on Earth." Was Monroe telling us that he had resigned himself to an imminent end? Friends who had seen him last spring told me he had had trouble hitting his trademark high notes and had apologized to the audience for this.

Then, as the summer progressed, came the rumors—that MCA Records was dropping Monroe, that touring was getting to be too much for the near-seventy-three-year-old patriarch of bluegrass, that he was retiring.

That such rumors were not widespread gave me hope they were, in fact, mere rumors. But there were other causes for hope. Why would MCA drop an artist who has been a consistently strong seller since signing with its Decca predecessor three decades ago? And, of course, there's the man himself, known for his determination, dedication to his beloved music, and his clean, healthy, strenuous lifestyle.

"Bill's the iron man," New England mandolinist/tenor Joe Val once confided to me. "You'll never know how strong he is until you stand at a microphone and sing with him." Joe doesn't have such a weak voice himself.[1] And this strength runs in Bill's family. I well recalled Bill's older brother, Charlie, who once nearly pitched

---

1. Joe Val (born Joseph Valiante on June 26, 1926, in Everett, Mass.) died about a month after this article was published, on June 11, 1985.

me on my face with a friendly, but exuberant, clap on the back. He was nearly seventy-two at the time and had just recovered from a heart attack.

So how could a man from such solid stock ever give up the music that has been his whole life, body and soul?

As it turned out, I was scheduled to play in a band at a festival that Bill Monroe was headlining at the end of the summer, the Waterloo Village Bluegrass Festival, Stanhope, New Jersey. It's an opportunity, I decided, to put down my mandolin, pick up my journalist's pad, and find out about the state of Bill Monroe today—which is, in large part, of course, the state of bluegrass music.

Monroe is scheduled to arrive Sunday and play two shows, first at a small gazebo at one end of the grounds, and then closing the festival with a long set at the main stage. But Sunday wears on, and Monroe doesn't arrive.

An omen of what I'll find? Festival promoter Charlie Catalano doesn't seem concerned. His calmness in the face of a situation that would be giving most promoters a stroke on top of a nervous breakdown, has a lot to do with Monroe's reputation.

"He'll show up," says Catalano simply. "He always does."

The Foot and Fiddle Dance Company fills in at the gazebo with a high-steppin' show that highly entertains the gathering crowd. Then a fine, young newgrass band, the Mainline Ramblers, is playing a tightly-arranged, hot instrumental when a cheer goes up from the back of the audience. Sounds like Nantucket sailors sighting a huge whale, but, instead, it's the whale-like shape of the Blue Grass Special bus. Bill Monroe and His Blue Grass Boys have arrived.

Monroe and company are soon hurrying over to the gazebo stage. Bill mounts the back steps briskly. He gets out his famous Gibson Lloyd Loar F-5 and quickly tunes up. He looks good, solid, with healthy weight on his large frame. His ears perk up at some of the jazzy riffs his young colleague is playing. When the Mainline Ramblers come off the mikes, their mandolinist is surprised and pleased to have Monroe offer compliments.

Needless to say, the very large crowd now in front of the stage is fairly buzzing with excitement. You can tell how widespread Monroe's popularity is just by how his fans dress—they're wearing everything from conservative blouses, shorts, and summer dresses to bluejeans (new and patched), granny gowns, Harley-Davidson t-shirts, or no shirts at all.

Professional musicians, too, have gathered to hear Bill. One is offered some precious sitting space up front, with apologies that the dirt might soil his stage clothes.

"Heck, I think I'd sit in cow manure to listen to this man," is the reply.

Everyone else is about equally psyched up at the chance to see the Father of Bluegrass, but I try not to be psyched out. My pick is down, my pen is in hand. No matter how much I love this music, no matter how many of his records I've ground down to 16⅔ rpm to learn the notes, no matter how deeply I've studied his singing and his style, if Bill Monroe is going into decline, I want to be objective and truthful about it.

The band cuts into "Sweet Blue-Eyed Darling" and a fast-paced set. Monroe's playing is rhythmically solid, and has those little surprises at the end of each solo that catch you off guard, just when you think you've heard it before. I'm constantly shaking my head in pleasure and admiration at the man's musical powers. Although his lead singing work is fine and his falsetto clear, he does, in truth, have some initial difficulties in his upper range. But these quickly prove to be the result of having to hurry off the bus and on stage without any warm-up (it turns out that a private plane crash on the interstate highway has been responsible for Monroe's delay, and he apologizes to the understanding audience).

Later in his set, and then at the main stage, fully warmed up and using his power, Bill's singing is its usual awesome, in number after number. The Blue Grass Quartet is back and singing "Working on a Building." Bill goes from a high lead, with scary blues notes in the upper range, to an even higher tenor harmony demanding quick shifts to falsetto. He doesn't just sing it correctly, he turns the song into a true tour de force.

As he ends his first set, I hurry to the back of the stage, hoping to say a few words before the inundation of fans that I know is just a few steps behind me. I introduce myself as a writer for *Bluegrass Unlimited* (of course, I've spoken to Monroe on a dozen previous occasions, but how would he remember me out of a million questions, autographs, and handshakes?), express the interest of the magazine and its readership in what he's doing right now in his career, and ask if I might have an interview, if he can fit it into what has been already a difficult day.

Monroe looks up and looks at me. His eyes peer out behind thick reading glasses[2] as he prepares to sign the first of a couple score of autographs. But the eyes are clear and steady as they take me in.

So is the voice that answers me in the familiar direct style. "We'll see if we can set it up."

I have to make my way out of a gathering of Bill's admirers. But soon, back at the Blue Grass Special, he graciously allows me some time for questions. My first one is, simply, What are his future plans?

"Well, I have a lot of good fans," he replies, "and I want to come around and visit them at least one time every year and play to them."

"So you plan to keep on touring, your same schedule, and recording?"

"Yes, sir."

Indeed, Bill Monroe will keep on, as Tony Conway confirms. Conway, of Buddy Lee Attractions, Inc., in Nashville, has been Monroe's booking agent for the past several years.

"We're keeping Bill busy," said Conway as I spoke to him a few weeks later, "as busy as he's ever been and maybe more. He's fully recovered from his operation,[3] he gets a lot of exercise working on his farm, his health is excellent.

---

2. The lenses in Bill's glasses were thick, but not only for reading.
3. His prostate enlargement operation in early August 1982.

"The direction we've taken over the past few years," Conway continues, "is to put him into events that give him the most exposure. We've had a lot of talks about this. In October 1984, he took on his busiest month ever. Besides nine festivals in the United States, he appeared on several TV shows. Then he toured Japan and Hawaii and came back for several West Coast dates."

Monroe's current popularity is measured today, not just in terms of its longevity, but in its actual upswing as well. This would be enough to make him a booking agent's dream, but there's more. In a time when major entertainment stars, country singers included, have become increasingly temperamental and unreliable, where concert no-shows have gone from being an accepted eccentricity to being a true insult to fans and a liability to promoters, Bill Monroe is valued and admired for his consistency.

"He's a pleasure to work with," Conway declares with evident appreciation. "He's a gentleman. He's loyal, honest. If he says he'll do something, he will."

Such professionalism has been carried by Bill to amazing heights, as Tony reveals. "Prior to his operation, Bill was taken seriously ill while at a festival in Canada. I tried to stop his tour, but he wouldn't stop.

"He was taken to the hospital in an ambulance. He was in great pain. But while he was being treated in the emergency room, he kept telling the doctors and hospital personnel, 'I've got to be back at 3 P.M. I've got a show to do.'

"Then—on his own initiative and completely against my wishes—he had himself put back in a wheelchair and taken in an ambulance back to the festival. He had himself put up on stage and he did his afternoon show.[4]

"His fans mean the most to him," concludes Conway. "It tears him up if he can't play for them."

"To get to a place like we are here today," says Monroe as he looks around the festival grounds, "to see my friends and fans, to play requests if they want me to, to stand with them and talk with them, and have pictures made—it means a lot to me."

To have pictures made—as a photographer, the phrase seems to me more accurate, and certainly more charming, than "taking" a picture. One woman at the Waterloo festival wants to have a picture made with her standing by Monroe. She gives her camera to her husband and catches Bill as he emerges from the back of the main tent. They pose together, but, wait, the camera doesn't seem to be working.

She steps forward to fix it and then turns around. Bill Monroe is gone.

Obviously, she has taken up just too much of the great man's time. She's bored him and he's walked off. With a quick cry of surprise and despair, she rushes forward, desperately hoping to persuade him to give just five more seconds.

Those of us standing at right angles to the scene see what's really happened. Monroe has mischievously ducked into the performers' entry and is hiding there with a wink and a grin. As the woman runs back, he jumps out and gives her a big

4. The events discussed here occurred in early August 1982. See the editor's comments, second paragraph.

hug. They turn to the lens with broad smiles on their faces, the picture is made, and I wish I had a print of that one.

I also realize I'm doing this story in an election year and that hundreds of candidates would grit their teeth in envy at Monroe's popularity.

But Bill Monroe has not mellowed into a glad-hander or the musical equivalent of a baby-kissing office seeker. Indeed, he is still (as Ralph Rinzler once so well phrased it) "a man of princely bearing and precious few words." He can be as intimidating as ever, in his own way. The fan who tries to sidle up to Monroe and impress him with knowledge or accomplishments will still be quickly sized up and treated to a polite, but painfully obvious, silence.

But, his musical accomplishments aside, just why is Bill Monroe such an awe-inspiring figure? The question is worth delving into, because it has much to do with what bluegrass music is and why.

Of course, one is always impressed by Monroe's confidence and the sureness with which he discusses his art. "I wanted a style of music of my own," he says. "I was going to play a different style of mandolin from other people. I was going to sing different. I was going to train my voice to sing tenor with any man."

Standing next to Monroe, it is easy to appreciate that this big, large-framed fellow is the descendant of the hefty Scotsmen who grew strong from labor in fields and foundries, and then tossed hammers and tree trunks around for sport. But there's more. Bill may not be gregarious, but his body language speaks volumes about the man. In a world of nervous people who fold and unfold their arms, put their hands in and out of pockets and on and off hips, shift their weight from one foot to another, cross and uncross their legs, here we have a gentleman who stands calmly, quietly, hands at his sides and weight evenly balanced over two firmly-planted feet. Even a judo expert might struggle unsuccessfully to throw such a man, and, surely, little in life has thrown Monroe down. No wonder this man inspires awe. He also exhibits a type of personal style and elegance that seems the hallmark of another era.

So it is hardly surprising that bluegrass music is a style with dignity, balance, strength, and elegance. Even when playing a brief solo offstage on an F-5 copy, at the request of its maker, these qualities are evident. Also evident are the aspiring mandolinists peering over Bill's right shoulder, trying to drink in every note and nuance of the master's distinctive playing and timing, as he serves up "Paddy on the Turnpike."

"This will be a good mandolin when it's played in," says Monroe, handing it back.

"I've got Gibson Mona-Steel strings on it now," says the luthier, "but I guess I ought to use the bronze."

"Yes, Gibson Bronze are the best."

Bill advises young players coming up to "practice every day from 30 minutes to 45 minutes a day, and let one day help the next. It's like going to school—you learn from one day to the next. Don't ever give up on it.

"And bluegrass really is a school of music for a lot of young people today," he observes. "Bluegrass will put you into another class of music, if you want to go there."

I broach the subject of traditional bluegrass vs. newgrass, jazzgrass, etc., by asking Monroe about the young player of hot licks he had complimented earlier at the gazebo.

"But he plays a lot of good bluegrass, too," observes Monroe. "He's got some good bluegrass notes in there, too.

"Everybody's got their right to have their style," he continues. "A lot of the young people, you know, they want to put more into it, you see. A lot of people see where they can take it or what they can do with it.

"They'll come with some new notes or different ideas about it."

At first, this idea of "notes"—bluegrass or newgrass or whatever—may not seem important. After all, a musical note is a musical note, isn't it? Not as Monroe uses the term. A famous composer and music theorist once said that music is the space between the notes. The effects of music occur between each note and are largely determined by how each note is held and how the next one is played.

Thus, for Monroe, a "note" is more than a simple frequency, pitch, or place on a scale. When he refers to playing "a good note," he is encompassing the entire process of selecting a note, deciding what amount of emphasis or attack it should have, how long it is held, and just how it is cut off or left to sound before the next note. The possibilities for subtle stylizations in such spaces between notes are about endless. And Monroe, of course, is a master at getting them—so much so that his timing and phrasing are absolutely unique, immediately recognizable, even when he's playing a borrowed mandolin.

Many of the "hot" mandolin pickers who used to scorn Monroe's selection of notes as being limited and simplistic now rather frequently admit that knowing what Monroe plays is still a league away from how he plays it, and, probably, nobody is in that league.

Despite his tolerance for those who "want to put more into it," Monroe remains true to the philosophy that the melody of each number contains the material and possibilities for beautiful performance, and that's what his public wants.

"The people who really come to see you love to hear the melody played right, with good timing to it. That's the way they like to hear it." Monroe also agrees strongly with those who say that people may come to bluegrass for its exciting picking, but they stay for its distinctive singing.

There are some lovers of bluegrass who, quite unwittingly, might turn bluegrass into a museum piece by performing or requesting the same numbers again and again. It is disappointing to see talented bandleaders and seasoned sidemen playing only the familiar songs at a festival in a predictable, didactic event. It is significant, then, even ironic, that the man who started this tradition is not content to rest on his laurels, although he certainly could. He knows that through the years, this philosophy has led to the emergence of great new tunes and talents.

"I feature all of my people that play with me," he declares. "Give them a chance to sing a solo, or play the fiddle or play the banjo. I give them a chance too, you see.

"I believe in coming up with some new material. I don't believe in singing the old all the time. Get a new gospel song or a duet or a good trio, a new instrumental. And see what the people would like about it.

"Like 'Jerusalem Ridge'—it's a fine fiddle number and it's a shame for people not to hear it."[5]

The creative process is unceasing for the founder of bluegrass music. Sometimes, he seems to visualize a scene as he composes. Other compositions seem to spring up from sounds deep inside.

"Like 'Old Dangerfield,' it goes back a long time, how the people would have danced and listened to the music.

"On 'My Last Days on Earth,' I couldn't sleep, I got up. It was way on down below zero, and I thought, 'I'm going to just take my mandolin and see what I come up with, just start tuning a different style of tuning.'

"So I came up with this tuning, C-sharp minor,[6] and went to trying to put some notes into it and this number about wrote itself. When I'd make a note, it'd just fill in and go on and make another note with the melody."

The recorded version of "My Last Days on Earth" might have come as a real shock to traditionalists. Here was the unmistakable timbre and timing of Bill Monroe's mandolin surrounded by sea gulls and eerie wind sound effects, a full vocal chorus, violins and cellos. One can almost picture chairs falling over, cars driving off the road all over bluegrassland as the song is broadcast for the first time.

"They wanted to put that in it," explains Monroe, "like it would have been a long time ago, maybe two hundred years back in time . . . the sea gulls and that, that would have gone back in time too, you know. It would have been years and years ago with that sound.

"And they fit in those instruments, the violins and cellos, and the voices. They had some fine singers who could sing high. I got to thinking on it. I liked it. And it was going to be in the background."

"Bill came to me with this number," says Walter Haynes, his record producer, "and I thought it was a masterpiece, something I hope will be a standard for him and for other bluegrass mandolinists in the years to come.

"We used just three pieces at first, mandolin, guitar, and bass. I got to hearing some things I wanted to try with it. I took them around to Bill and suggested them. He liked them. He liked them so much that he kept them."

Haynes is a former Grand Ole Opry back-up musician[7] who, like many others,

---

5. Ironically, this tune was involved in a dispute over new material less than two months later. See the editor's comments, third paragraph.

6. The tuning was actually a D minor tuning, but with all of the strings tuned down one-half of a step (to avoid excess stress on the mandolin's top), it became what Bill called a "C-sharp minor" tuning.

7. A steel guitarist.

was intrigued by hearing Monroe at close hand. Later, Haynes went to MCA Records as a protégé of Bill's longtime producer Owen Bradley, eventually becoming a vice-president of A&R before going independent. Those years led to a mutual trust and appreciation that have continued between Haynes and Monroe for over a decade of recording.

"You have to earn that trust," acknowledges Haynes. "Bill's very sensitive about his playing and the band's sound. He has a particular sound in mind, one he knows his fans expect, and he doesn't want to disappoint them."

Booking agent Tony Conway adds, "That may be why he has avoided a lot of TV appearances. He's very concerned with his band's sound, and he may have been concerned it didn't come out right on TV. But he's had a chance to listen to his appearances on the Nashville Network and the 'Austin City Limits' show and others, and he seems more comfortable with it now."

Bill performed on Ricky Skaggs' *Country Boy* LP, playing mandolin. They played Bill's "Wheel Hoss." The tune won a Grammy for "Country Instrumental," awarded in February of this year.[8]

Monroe accepted an invitation to have a featured role in the music video for Skaggs' "Country Boy," shot on location in New York City. The film opens in a fashionable office. Monroe[9] confronts Skaggs and asks Ricky if, despite his success, he's still a country boy.

The high point of the piece comes when Bill meets some young New York break dancers. He goes them one better by doing the Kentucky backstep. Bluegrass and country music fans have responded to the video with amazement and delight.

Bill's fans can be assured that whatever he records, any new ideas or directions will only be undertaken with his approval and that he maintains artistic control over his work.

"You might say I get a lot of direction from him," comments Haynes. "He knows what he likes. If I have an idea to add, I'll suggest it. If he likes it, we go with it. If not, I won't push him. Whatever we do, we have to make it to Bill's timing and sound."

A great challenge in this regard came during the recording of the *Bill Monroe and Friends* album.[10] "They kept on wanting me to do it, MCA, you know," says Bill. "I didn't know whether to do it or not, whether the country people would like it or the bluegrass people would like it. So I finally agreed to do it, and it's worked out fine."

It was an album that presented tremendous difficulties for its producer, along with its rewards. Haynes readily acknowledges the problems of trying to blend and record so many different voices and performance styles with Monroe's. There were added problems of scheduling sessions for many busy people, some performers

8. 1985.
9. As "Uncle Pen."
10. Bill's latest release at the time.

coming into the studio with rough voices after weeks on tour, and so on. But there were also the lighter moments.

"We recorded the album at Burns Station Sound, in Burns, Tennessee, outside Nashville. It's a modern recording studio in an out-of-the-way location. Bill loves a place like that.

"I don't think the people in Burns knew there were so many famous country performers in town, right in their midst. Then Barbara Mandrell showed up. You see, she flew in, in her helicopter. People thought maybe there was a plane crash out in the field, so they came up to see what was going on.

"When they found out what was happening, we had to get two policemen, one to guard the helicopter and one to guard the studio!"

When the *Bill Monroe and Friends* album was limited to a single record (instead of a proposed two-LP set), a lot of prominent Nashville artists actively seeking to be included had to be turned down. Why such a rush among an industry that just a short time ago was merely tolerant of its acoustic "poor cousin" of bluegrass?

"Well," says Haynes, "Bill's a living legend and there's not many of those around today. There's his wonderful music, which everyone, just about, loves. But, I guess, too, he commands tremendous admiration in the country music industry today for what he's done and stands for.

"People admire him for staying with his vision. He's always upheld what bluegrass means to him. And he's always a clean show. He's never been involved with the drinking and drugs that some people get caught up in. He won't permit those things around him."

"I've never smoked or drank," acknowledges Monroe, "and that's been a big help to me. I've kept drinking out of my music, you see. Whiskey and beer, there's a few who loves it, but I'm hard on them people."

It would be inaccurate and untruthful to state that Bill Monroe has no critics or detractors. Due to the man's tremendous stature, they merely are less outspoken. Some former Monroe sidemen have complained privately of personality conflicts with their bandleader, of long hours and low pay, and, in a few cases, some have expressed the feeling that they contributed so much to a new song as to have deserved co-authorship credit.

Yet other former Blue Grass Boys have publicly stated just the opposite—references are constantly made of Bill as being "like a father to me" or "like a brother." Musicians have spoken warmly of the rewards of working with Monroe on the road, or of writing a song with him for which they received proper credit.

There are numerous expectations that must be sorted out for a bandleader and sideman to work well together. The point here is not to sort these out. In all fairness, too, it must be noted that Bill has dealt patiently with having been treated by many musicians as an educational and professional stepping stone.

"Some players would work for me about two or three years, learn to play and sing. Lots of them would go on out there, get their own band. And it was time for me to have a new man to come in and sing."

Kenny Baker, prior to recently branching out on his own, had been Monroe's fiddler and instrumental right-hand man for the past decade and a half. Guitarist/lead singer Wayne Lewis has now served a longer hitch than many in his position. This stable core to the Blue Grass Boys is allowing current shows to be exceptionally polished. This has been a great aid to Bill in recording, too, since most of what he does in the studio differs little from its live version.

"When Bill hits the studio, he's ready to go," says Walter Haynes. "It's 'Let's go, boys!' He'll bring a song in, he'll have his arrangement worked out, and that's it. He rarely needs more than two or three takes.

"And he does it all at the same time, vocals and instrumentals. We rarely have to do any overdubbing. That's another reason his sound is so good."

Walter Haynes' experience with recording bluegrass music right at the source has been so positive that he's looking forward not only to his next projects with Monroe,[11] but also to recording other bluegrass bands arriving in Nashville for sessions. He plans to offer his services to professional and semi-professional bands looking for experienced production in their first albums.

With his eclectic musical background and constant creativity, I've often wondered if Bill Monroe could have created, say, another distinctive type of music besides bluegrass.

"Well," he reflects, "if I wanted to, I could have come up with other kinds of music, too. But I've been busy, and I've held right on to bluegrass music. I don't let anything interfere with it."

But what might those other musics sound like?

Bill smiles, looking the very smallest bit embarrassed, then replies with a twinkle in his eye, "I wouldn't want to mention them!"[12]

Looking back over some of the well-known chapters of this man's life in light of his current success, I note some very happy ironies. As a boy living along the main road by Jerusalem Ridge near Rosine, Kentucky, he frequently hid in the barn to avoid being teased by passing strangers because his eyes were slightly crossed. Today, other strangers will be unhappy if they can't publicly meet him and be photographed with him. As the youngest boy, he was left with the mandolin as a third choice after the family fiddle and guitar were taken by his elder brothers. Even then, he was forced to play with four strings so he "wouldn't make too much noise." Today, people build mandolins like his and gather round to learn every note of his playing. His music was assumed to have been left behind in the fifties and sixties by an electric, glittery Nashville. Today, the superstars of country and western have clamored to record with the Father of Bluegrass Music.

Far from being the twilight of a musical god, these times represent, perhaps, Bill Monroe's best years on earth. He's healthy, prospering, and so is bluegrass. He has

---

11. *Bill Monroe and Friends* was the last Monroe album produced by Haynes. See the editor's comments, fourth paragraph.

12. Ralph Rinzler asked Bill about this in the sixties. See the editor's comments, fifth paragraph.

a Bluegrass Hall of Fame now on Music Valley Drive in Nashville, a mile from Opryland. It's a project he takes evident pleasure in. But bluegrass itself need not end up a museum piece. Indeed, the months and years ahead hold new ideas, new songs, new experiments, and even artistic risks for the founder of bluegrass.

And there will always be the name for his music.

"To know I was getting my music put together, that was fine," he reflects, "but, later on, it came into being bluegrass, being called that. That meant a lot."

I cannot imagine a time when Bill Monroe will ever retire. Before taking my leave, I express this to him.

"No, sir," he agrees, adding quickly, "but you know it'll come. Just like you, it'll be your last days on earth. So you'll have to tell the people goodbye, because that'll be the end of it."

But not the end of bluegrass. Who can say but that this powerful music may go on for centuries? And as long as bluegrass is played, heard, and loved, Mr. Bill Monroe will never have a last day on earth.

Originally published in *Bluegrass Unlimited* 19:11 (May 1985): 14–22. Reprinted by permission of the author.

EDITOR'S COMMENTS

Smith, author of the Monroe biography *Can't You Hear Me Callin'*, interviewed Bill at the end of August 1984 for this cover story in the May 1985 issue of *Bluegrass Unlimited*. (This selection differs from the original in that sentences regarding Walter Haynes's recording business have been deleted.)

The events discussed by Tony Conway occurred in early August 1982. On the way to a festival in Nova Scotia, Bill complained of pain and was taken to a hospital in Halifax, where emergency surgery was performed to drain his kidneys. Afterward, he insisted on going to the festival, which was nearby, and he played one song in a wheelchair that day, and returned each day for the next two days to play one song. He was then flown back to Nashville in WSM's corporate jet where he underwent an operation for an enlarged prostate. A week later he was back on the road, and a month later he was dancing at his birthday celebration in Louisville.

It's ironic that Bill should mention "Jerusalem Ridge" in connection with performing new material. Less than two months after Smith's interview, on October 12, 1984, fiddler Kenny Baker quit after an onstage dispute over whether or not he would play the tune. At that point, he had played it often at shows for over ten years.

Bill Monroe and Friends,[1] released in 1983, was the last Bill Monroe album produced by Walter Haynes. He produced or co-produced seven other albums for Bill, beginning with the *Bean Blossom* album, released in 1973.

In a 1960s interview (a tape of which Smith had possibly heard), Rinzler asked Bill about "the other music" he'd said he could create, to which he replied, "I can picture it now, you know, vision it, and see it, and hear it. I would be tied up to where

I couldn't do it without making myself out, you know, not true to bluegrass, not believin' anything I ever said for 25 years in it, you know—just throwin' that much of a life away. . . . I could make it the biggest thing in the country today if I would do it, you know."[2]

Shortly before this article was published, on April 24, 1985, Bill, seventy-three, married Della Streeter, forty-four.

Notes

1. *Bill Monroe and Friends,* MCA Records, MCA-5435, released 1984.
2. Ralph Rinzler, unpublished interview with Bill Monroe, ca. 1966.

"Worst-Case Repair"

ROGER SIMINOFF

Without warning, one day in 1972, a lunatic with a hammer threw himself on Michelangelo's 473-year-old sculpture *La Pietà* at St. Peter's basilica in Rome. Before horrified guards could pull him away, he had done terrible damage to one of the world's most venerated works of art.

There was no one to stop the vandal, or vandals, who broke into Bill Monroe's home in Goodlettsville, Tennessee, last November 13.[1] While Monroe and his wife[2] were away for the afternoon, someone took an iron fireplace poker and battered Monroe's historic 1923 Gibson F-5, his trademark instrument.

For the world of acoustic string music, the wanton act was just as shocking as the *Pietà*'s defacement had been to the world of art. Here in the *Frets* offices people talked in hushed tones, shaking their heads in disbelief. Worse yet, we learned, a companion 1923 F-5 owned by Monroe had been even more brutally damaged.

I couldn't escape a feeling of devastation. Knowing the instruments' construction as well as I did, knowing what Bill's trademark mandolin represented, I felt almost personally injured.

But just as work had begun immediately to restore the *Pietà*, preparations were already underway to put bluegrass' most famous instrument back together. The restoration, I knew, would be no easy task. It is difficult enough to build a mandolin out of new wood. It is something else again to try to piece one together out of splinters.

When I placed a call to my friend, Bruce Bolen, Gibson's Artist Relations department head, he told me the company had already phoned Monroe to offer its

1. 1985.
2. Bill and Della Streeter Monroe were married on April 24, 1985.

aid. Bruce had been personally involved in the much-publicized restoration of the mandolin four years ago, which ended a 30-year rift between Monroe and Gibson. He was as firm in wanting to maintain that good relationship as he was in his desire to see the irreplaceable instruments saved.

The ticklish restoration assignment soon went to Charlie Derrington, a luthier in Gibson's Research and Development department, who is responsible for a lot of sophisticated custom and prototype work. Charlie is a mandolinist himself, and owns a 1925 F-5 (which he promptly offered to let Monroe use while the two F-5s were being rebuilt).

Any luthier tackling the job would face several serious problems. First, the pressure of working on a priceless historic instrument—with the world watching. Second, Monroe's "mindset" regarding the tonal properties of the instrument, and his reliance upon that exact tone for his distinctive music. Third, the need to use as many original pieces as possible in rebuilding the mandolin. Fourth, the requirement that the mandolin emerge from the shop with its original finish. Fifth—there would be no second chance!

Not content just to rely on his own considerable skill, Charlie also consulted William Moennig, one of the country's leading violin restorers. As of press time for this issue, work on Monroe's famous first-line instrument, serial no. 73987,[3] was progressing very well. Charlie reported that it took "about a week and a half to catalog most of the pieces of the top. Gluing it together," he said, "was a tweezers-and-magnifying-glass job."

Charlie actually began with the back, gluing the lower bout[4] back together "while everything was still in its original configuration." That done, he was able to remove the back so he could operate on the inside of the instrument.

"Where there is an original piece, I will definitely reuse it," Charlie said. "I am a stickler for originality, and I want this mandolin to come through with as many original pieces as possible."

Some small fragments of the original binding[5] were missing, however, and these will have to be replaced. In checking the binding, Charlie made an interesting discovery. "Apparently, the back had been pulled off once before," Charlie said.[6] "The back binding is not original. I have some binding here at Gibson that is even closer to the original than what is on the mandolin now, so I do plan to replace that. But with the exception of finishing and coloring directly over the repair lines, neither F-5 will be refinished."

An old lutherie standby, Franklin Titebond cement, was used to rejoin the rim to the blocks.[7] "The rim went back together easily," Charlie said. "That piece of

---

3. Dated July 9, 1923.
4. A section between the two "points" decorating one side of the body of an F-5 mandolin.
5. Inlaid plastic strips that protect and decorate the edges of an instrument's body and neck.
6. Derrington guesses this happened in the early seventies.
7. The "rim," in this case, is the side of the mandolin. The "blocks" are actual blocks of wood glued to the inside of the rim to create a "platform" onto which the top is glued.

maple had been like that for so many years, it was like putting a hand in a glove. No problem."

The biggest difficulty Charlie has encountered? "The neck angle on the mandolin is incorrect," he said. "When the back was removed before, it wasn't refitted properly and the neck angle slipped. So I'm going to have to pull the neck back a bit to reset the angle and get the correct bridge height. I'm a little worried about the increased bridge load[8] on the top; but I think it will be all right."

Another problem area involves the egg-sized oval of worn-away wood just to the treble side of the fretboard extension—worn thin by years of scratching from Monroe's fingernails. "It was so thin there that, when the instrument was damaged, the tone bar[9] underneath it was cracked," Charlie said. "I'm going to have to put an overlay [a thin veneer-like piece of wood] in to reinforce that area."[10]

Charlie warned Monroe that, in spite of all the care going into the restoration, it would be too much to hope that the rebuilt mandolin would sound exactly the same. "I let him know right up front," Charlie explained, "that any time something like this happens to an instrument that has been stressed a certain way for so many years, and alters those stresses, something is going to change."

If the restored mandolins aren't almost as good as they were before the vandalism, it won't be because Gibson and Charlie Derrington didn't do everything humanly possible. "We have a commitment to getting them right," Bruce Bolen told me. "We're willing to do whatever it takes."

Originally published in *Frets* 8:2 (Feb. 1986): 40, 45. Reprinted by permission of the author and the Miller Freeman, Inc., Music Group.

EDITOR'S COMMENTS

Bill was plagued by vandals and thieves in the fall and winter of 1985, beginning with the defacing of his car with spray paint in September and ending with the burglarizing of his tour bus in December. But the worst of it, by far, occurred on Wednesday, November 13. After finding the carnage, Bill called Blake Williams, his banjo player at the time, who advised Bill to gather up every piece he could find into a bag.

Siminoff, founding editor of *Frets* magazine, wrote this brief but detailed report not long after repair work by Charlie Derrington had begun. By the time it appeared in the February 1986 issue, Bill's main mandolin was only a few weeks away from being returned to him.

---

8. With increased neck angle, a higher bridge is required, and higher strings exert more pressure on the top.

9. A piece of spruce glued to the inside of the top, under the bridge, which transmits tone throughout the instrument.

10. Later it was found that the tone bar was not cracked, only dislodged.

Bill relaxes on a swing at his farm with horse trainer Sandy Jackson and her son Jack (left), and Julia LaBella (right), September 1977. (Photo by Jan Otteson; courtesy of *Music City News*)

Mentioned in "Bill Monroe Goes about the Business of Bluegrass Music," this was the main office of Monroe Talent Enterprises (3819 Dickerson Road, Nashville, TN) throughout the 1980s. (Photo by Tom Ewing)

Bill, holding his birthday "card," with former and then-current Blue Grass Boys at the Kentucky Fried Chicken Bluegrass Festival, Louisville, Kentucky, September 11, 1982: Kenny Baker, Byron Berline (hidden), Doug Hutchens, Wayne Lewis (hidden), Bill, Tex Logan, "Red" Taylor, Blake Williams (hidden), Gordon Terry, Mark Hembree (hidden), Cleo Davis. (Photo by Marty Godbey; courtesy of *Bluegrass Unlimited*)

Bill dancing with Wanda Hill of the Green Grass Cloggers while the Blue Grass Boys play "Sally Goodin," at the Kentucky Fried Chicken Bluegrass Festival, Louisville, Kentucky, September 11, 1982: Wayne Lewis, Hill, Bill, Byron Berline (behind Bill, guesting on fiddle), Blake Williams, Mark Hembree. (Courtesy of *Music City News*)

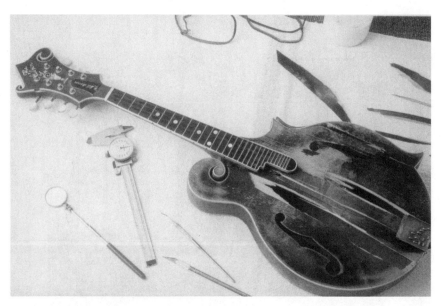

Bill's damaged mandolin, November 1985. (Photo by Jim Devault)

Bill playing his restored mandolin, with repairman Charlie Derrington (center) and guitarist Chet Atkins, February 25, 1986. Derrington is telling Atkins the chords to "Wheel Hoss." (Photo by
Charmaine Lanham; courtesy of *Bluegrass Unlimited*)

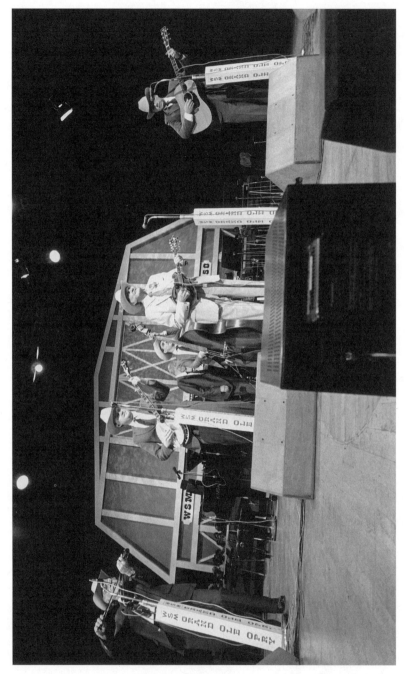

Bill and the Blue Grass Boys onstage at the Opry on October 28, 1989, Bill's fiftieth anniversary on the show: Clarence "Tater" Tate, Blake Williams, announcer Grant Turner, Billy Rose, Bill, Tom Ewing. (Photo by Les Leverett)

Bill on the farm, April 9, 1992. In the background is his log cabin home. (Photo by Sandy Rothman)

Auction advertisement for Bill's farm from *The Tennessean*, April 10, 1994. (Courtesy of Tom Ewing)

Bill singing an impromptu "Blue Moon of Kentucky" to the delight of President Clinton at a White House reception following the National Medal of Arts presentation, October 5, 1995. U.S. Marine Master Gunnery Sergeant Charlie Corrado, at the piano, was asked to accompany Bill but didn't know the song. (Photo by Doug Mills, courtesy of AP/Wide World Photos)

Bill's tombstone in the Rosine Cemetery, Rosine, Kentucky. (Photo by Sandy Rothman)

WILLIAM SMITH "BILL" MONROE WAS THE YOUNGEST OF EIGHT CHILDREN BORN TO JAMES BUCHANAN MONROE AND MELISSA ANN VANDIVER MONROE AT THE MONROE HOMEPLACE ON JERUSALEM RIDGE NEAR ROSINE, KENTUCKY.

AS A YOUNGSTER, BILL WORKED ON THE FAMILY FARM AND ATTENDED HORTON GRADE SCHOOL THROUGH THE SEVENTH GRADE. IN HIS SPARE TIME HE WENT FOX HUNTING WITH HIS DAD AND LEARNED TO MAKE MUSIC FROM HIS MOTHER AND HIS UNCLE PEN VANDIVER.

BILL LOST HIS MOTHER WHEN HE WAS NINE YEARS OLD AND HIS FATHER WHEN HE WAS JUST SIXTEEN. AFTER LIVING WITH HIS UNCLE PEN, BILL LEFT HIS HOME IN KENTUCKY AND BEGAN THE JOURNEY WHICH LED HIM TO THE CREATION OF "BLUEGRASS MUSIC" AND TO BECOMING ONE OF THE TRUE LEGENDS IN THE AMERICAN MUSIC INDUSTRY.

IN 1935, BILL MONROE MARRIED CAROLYN MINNIE BROWN. THEY HAD TWO CHILDREN MELISSA KATHLEEN MONROE, BORN SEPT. 17, 1936, AND JAMES WILLIAM MONROE, BORN MARCH 15, 1941.

BILL MONROE BECAME A MEMBER OF THE GRAND OLE OPRY IN NASHVILLE, TENNESSEE, IN 1939. DURING HIS CAREER HE WOULD SELL MILLIONS OF RECORDS, WIN MANY NATIONAL AWARDS FOR HIS MUSIC AND PERFORM AT THE REQUEST OF FOUR UNITED STATES PRESIDENTS.

GOD BLESSED BILL WITH A RARE MUSICAL GENIUS AND THE WILLPOWER AND DETERMINATION NECESSARY TO BRING HIS MUSIC TO MILLIONS OF FANS AROUND THE WORLD. FOR MANY OF THOSE FANS AND FOR ALL OF US WHO ARE MEMBERS OF HIS FAMILY,

BILL MONROE IS "BLUEGRASS MUSIC!"

WALK SOFTLY AROUND THIS GRAVE FOR MY FATHER BILL MONROE RESTS HERE AS THE BLUE MOON OF KENTUCKY SHINES ON.

SON: JAMES WILLIAM MONROE
1997

The inscription on Bill's grave marker. (Photo by Sandy Rothman)

"Bill Monroe's Mandolin Is Restored"

CHARMAINE LANHAM

Gibson employees and management joined newsmen, photographers, and television cameramen around a veiled case at the Gibson Guitar Company's Nashville headquarters. February 25, 1986, was the day that the company would return Bill Monroe's Gibson "Lloyd Loar" F-5,[1] completely restored, to him. For this major restoration job they would charge him nothing. And they would be returning to him his most precious possession.

Excitement ran through the crowd as Gibson President Henry Juszckiewicz stood by, and acoustic engineer Charlie Derrington handed Monroe's mandolin back to him, whole. The joy on Bill's face was unmistakable. After inspecting and strumming the mandolin, Bill turned to us with his arms wrapped around the instrument in a "big bear hug." He was a happy man; a musician reunited with his instrument.

The most frequent question had been whether the mandolin would sound the same after the repair of the extremely serious damage. It was evident that Bill was pleased with the sound and several remarks were made that the mandolin still had that special depth and punch that distinguishes this most rare of mandolins.

Bill remarked that "it still sounds tight. It needs to be played, broken in again." The next few weeks or months will tell.

"I'm so glad to get this back. As long as I live we want to stay together and I want to play it. People all over the world will be happy to know this mandolin has been put back together. I'm going to play it on the Grand Ole Opry this weekend."[2]

Someone called for a tune and Bill, always one to oblige with his music, waited while a guitar was found for Chet Atkins, who had dropped by for the ceremonies. Bill and Chet broke into a lively rendition of "Wheel Hoss," then Bill turned to Chet and asked, "Can we play some blues in the key of E?" Chet reckoned they could, and we were treated to a blues duet on mandolin and guitar.

This was the happy ending to a drama that had started quite tragically months before. Although Bill was rarely separated from his instruments, he was not at home November 13, 1985, when an unknown person or persons laid his two priceless Gibson F-5 mandolins side by side on the fireplace hearth and pierced them both with a fire poker. Although it is still a mystery who could have done such harm to these

---

1. Named for the musician and acoustical engineer who helped design and test the mandolin in the 1920s.

2. In honor of the occasion, Bill wrote a mandolin tune he called "The Lloyd Loar." He played it several times on Opry broadcasts, but never recorded it.

rare treasures, one thing was all too clear: the resulting damage was extreme. There were even some fears that the instruments might not be repairable, that they might never again be played, or might become museum pieces or "wall-hangers."

The mandolins were brought to craftsman Charlie Derrington, with the slivers of wood from both instruments in a paper bag.[3] Separating, identifying, and cataloging these slivers would become one of the most time-consuming and difficult jobs involved in the painstaking reconstruction. The word soon came out, the mandolins would be made playable. The job on the first mandolin alone would consume three months of 40-hour weeks for Derrington. The work was to be paid for by Gibson.

"Gibson never did a better job than for this mandolin," remarked Bill with a smile.

For Charlie Derrington, this was an event he would never forget. He spent three grueling months working on just one mandolin, putting aside all other projects. The pressure on him was great, with the bluegrass world patiently waiting for the results: "Would it be playable?" "Would it sound like it used to?" And the inevitable, "When will it be finished?"

Charlie says he's glad it's finally over. It turned out well and the pressure is off. He is going to move more slowly on the restoration of the second damaged F-5. It was used less than Bill's main one, and suffered less top and back damage overall. However, it has a more serious problem in some ways, because the tone bar is broken. Tone bars have to be tuned perfectly to achieve the sound of the Loar models, and Charlie says it will be tricky, but not impossible, to replace the tone bar successfully. He is confident all will go well.

Henry Juszckiewcz, president and part-owner of the Gibson Guitar Company, explained that one of the things that attracted him to Gibson was its heritage. Although in recent years Gibson was known more widely for its line of electric instruments, their history begins with acoustic instruments.

"If you go back further, you find the roots of the company are in acoustic instruments: banjos, mandolins, and guitars," he explains. He anticipates a growth year with some new developments mixing with the more traditional instruments. Gibson now has a pickup built into the bridge of their acoustic Dove and Hummingbird guitars. The pickup has been formulated to preserve the non-electric sound of the instruments.

Juszckiewicz explains that "acoustic instruments are much more difficult to build than electric. Of course, there will always be parts of the building process which will be done on the production line instead of by individual craftsmen."

The new owners have plans to "upgrade and expand Gibson service" by increasing emphasis on authorized regional service centers, so that Gibson customers can get repair work done closer to their homes and not have to send their instrument to the factory if it needs service or repair. "It is difficult to deal with people on a one-to-one basis at the factory," he adds.

---

3. Actually a plastic garbage bag.

As for major repair on Bill Monroe's second mandolin, Charlie is putting it on no time schedule. "I told Bill I had some other projects I would need to work on now. He understands. I put so much time all at once into the other one. All I can say is, I'm glad it's over. The pressure is off, and I can take my time on the second one."[4]

And so a new lease on life has been offered two rare and wonderful old mandolins.

Originally published in *Bluegrass Unlimited* 20:10 (Apr. 1986): 40–41. Reprinted by permission of the author.

EDITOR'S COMMENTS

Bill displayed his now-classic hugging-the-mandolin pose for the first time on February 25, 1986, when he was reunited with his main mandolin. Lanham, a photographer and wife of Nashville luthier Marty Lanham, told of the happy reunion in the April 1986 *Bluegrass Unlimited.*

"Bio: Bill Monroe"

ROGER WOLMUTH

Charlie Derrington had seen lost-cause instruments before—even "guitars that had been run over by trucks." Yet nothing had prepared the master restorer of the Gibson Guitar Company for what he saw in Bill Monroe's Nashville offices last November. Vandals had broken into Monroe's country cabin in the Tennessee hills and taken a fireplace poker to his famed 1923 Gibson mandolin. Now it lay in a garbage bag on Monroe's desk, its punctured body surrounded by nearly 200 pieces of what could pass for barbecue kindling. As a candidate for restoration, "it was definitely a worst case," says Derrington. "I was kind of shocked."

So were Monroe's fans. He was, after all, an American music patriarch, the man who in the forties had forged country gospel, blues, and quickstep mountain fiddle tunes into a new form of folk art. Just as bluegrass music could claim Monroe, now 74, as its father, its kinship to the old mandolin he had bought for $150 back in 1941[1] was just as certain. For more than four decades, its bright, distinctive sound had endured—along with Monroe's high, plaintive tenor—as the music's most recognizable voice. One music writer likened its destruction to the defacement of Michel-

---

4. Derrington returned Bill's other F-5 to him three months later, in May 1986. This mandolin, serial no. 72214, is the older of the two, dated February 26, 1923.

---

1. Probably 1945.

angelo's *Pietà,* and for a while "mandolin players and bluegrass people from all over the country were calling me, crying," says Derrington, who set to work repairing the damage as best he could.

Monroe, meanwhile, clung to the hope that he could put the instrument back into use, not just a showcase. Looking ahead to 1986, in the midst of his eighth decade, he would once again be hitting the road for more than 150 appearances. To mark his 50th year as a recording artist, he was scheduled to go into the studio in late summer, and in June there would be the 20th anniversary of his annual outdoor bluegrass festival in Bean Blossom, Indiana.

Derrington toiled for three solid months, much of it with "tweezers and a magnifying glass." In February he finished, and miraculously the mandolin's old sound seemed remarkably intact. Although years ago the flinty Monroe had taken a knife and angrily carved the Gibson name out of his instrument following a dispute over repairs, he and the company had made their peace, and this time Gibson offered their work as a gift. At his Nashville workshop, Derrington returned the mandolin to its owner, then watched as Monroe gave it its first test. Says Derrington: "He had tears in his eyes."

Five months later, Monroe has finished the day's first set at Bean Blossom and has come offstage to mingle with the fans at his outdoor festival. His appearance the previous night at the Grand Ole Opry didn't end until after midnight, and he has traveled here directly for the festival's first weekend. Others have traveled, too—from Oregon and Ohio, New York and Maryland—to attend this 10-day fete, and Monroe is a gracious host, faithful to the simple civilities learned from his rural upbringing.

Many of those now greeting him have camped overnight on the festival grounds, and Monroe, dressed in an off-white suit, shoes, and western hat, looks like a courtly country preacher in their midst. A potbellied guy in shorts is at his side holding a dog-eared snapshot from an earlier festival. "That was me and you in Florida when you played with Ricky Skaggs!" he proclaims.

"Good to see you again," Monroe answers politely.

"Could I have my picture taken with you?" asks a woman. "You sure could," says Monroe, slipping off his glasses and staring amiably at a camera-toting husband.

Moments later he meets a young mother holding a photo of "little Jessica back at home: She dances to your music all the time." As Monroe looks at the picture, Mom hands over an opened autograph book for little Jessica's hero to sign.

"I'll tell you something," confides another admirer as Monroe continues. "He goes around giving babies and little kids quarters. All the time."

Monroe can show a sterner side as well, and often there is more of the country preacher than appearances alone. The next day, he and his Blue Grass Boys come on stage early to start the traditional Sunday morning gospel set. There's a hitch, though: For some reason the microphones have been set up wrong. Jim Deckard, the festival's 27-year-old sound man from Indianapolis, runs up from his control board under the trees and starts making adjustments. He is a rock tour veteran who has worked for Springsteen, the Cars, and other big acts, and in a few minutes he has the problem solved. As he prepares to leave, Monroe looks at the T-shirt and cutoffs he's wearing, leans away from the microphone and says softly, "You need to get yourself a suit of clothes, son, if you're going to work up here with us."

For his band members, such proprieties are nonnegotiable. Monroe's son James, 45, played with the Blue Grass Boys for several years and remembers the night he forgot to wear his hat for an appearance at the Grand Ole Opry. That evening he watched the show from the wings. Worse lapses can mean a one-way ticket to the woodshed for the people Monroe employs. "They got to do what I say to do," he says evenly. "I don't want nobody comin' around workin' drunk. And a filthy mouth, I wouldn't put up with that. Bluegrass music is respectable."

Monroe's hardwood notions of respectability were shaped in the farm country of western Kentucky where he grew up the youngest of eight children. The family cut timber from their 655 acres of land, mined its coal in the fall, and in the springtime planted corn and tobacco. Privately, Monroe will tell how he and his father shared a pick-me-up "dram of bourbon" before their chores every day. That habit didn't stick. The family's work ethic did. So, too, did the sounds of gospel sung at the local churches, the blues played by a black family friend, and especially the fiddle music of his uncle Pendleton Vandiver, that Monroe heard as a child.

In Uncle Pen, the young Monroe found his spiritual and musical mooring. In later life he would celebrate the fiddler in song, record a bluegrass album of his dance tunes, and cite his hotfoot hoedown tempos as the spark to his own later style. "He was a wonderful uncle," says Monroe, "and I could always remember how he sounded—what kind of timin' he had to his music. And that's something I learned when I was young, to keep the timin' straightened out right."

It is one of country music's ironies, surely, that Monroe never followed his uncle as a fiddle player. Older brother Birch had done so already, and with brother Charlie playing guitar, Bill was left holding the mandolin as the logical alternative in a family band. Worse yet, he was told to remove half of the instrument's eight strings because "they didn't want me to play too loud."

By the time Monroe was 16, his parents had died and, after a short stint with Uncle Pen, he followed his brothers to Indiana in search of work. The Great Depression was ready to roll, and Monroe traveled light, packing a sixth-grade education, a farm boy's muscle, and a mandolin. For the next five years he worked at a Sinclair Oil refinery, cleaning, stacking, and beating dented oil drums back into shape. "I enjoyed it," he says of the hard labor, "because I could handle it good." On the side, he and his brothers played their music at private parties and went on tours as exhibition square dancers. Then in 1934 Birch dropped out of the family trio, and Bill and Charlie teamed up as a duet. With sponsorship from a Texas laxative company, they found steady work on radio; two years later, they signed their first recording contract.

The Monroe Brothers cut 60 songs in all, but their harmony on records never carried into real life. After two years of sibling squabbles,[2] they broke up, and in 1939, Monroe formed his first band of Blue Grass Boys. While the new group's mix of instruments—fiddle, bass, and guitar, plus Monroe's mandolin—came straight out of the old country string band tradition, Monroe began adding his own brand of octane. What he wanted, he says, was "to give the people a new timin' to the music that they wasn't acquainted with." He succeeded. That fall the group made its Grand Ole Opry debut with a rendition of "Mule Skinner Blues" pushed into overdrive, and its effect was startling. "Those people couldn't even think as fast as we played," boasted one band member[3] later.

For a few years Monroe experimented with the group's personnel and with the sound. He tried adding a jug player,[4] an accordion,[5] even a harmonica.[6] "We was workin' on it, workin' on it all the time, addin' to it and keepin' out things that didn't belong," he says. When labor troubles and wartime rationing limited production of 78-rpm recordings, he went on the road, leading seven truckloads of equipment[7] and his own traveling tent show. To boost attendance, he put his band members into baseball uniforms and challenged local teams before the performances.

In 1945 Monroe hired a Tennessee guitarist named Lester Flatt and a North Carolina banjo player named Earl Scruggs, and finally lit the fuse to the music he wanted. During the next three years, together with bassist Howard Watts and fiddler Chubby Wise, they established the prototype for a generation of bands to come. Even today, many consider that short-lived postwar group the most remarkable ever in bluegrass.

Soon, Monroe's sidemen would leave to become competitors, and his once-personal style of music would become public domain. Its reach, at times, was surprising. In 1954, a young Memphis truck driver took a Monroe-written waltz titled "Blue Moon of Kentucky," changed its beat and put it on his first-ever 45. Elvis Presley later apologized to the composer for taking such liberties, but other early rockers would borrow as well. "Buddy Holly was one of the biggest Bill Monroe fans that ever lived," says country star Ricky Skaggs, a longtime friend and admirer of the bluegrass architect.[8] "If you listen to Buddy's singing, a lot of his high-pitched stuff, he would put a little yodel kind of thing on the end because it sounded like Monroe."

Even Skaggs, Monroe's junior by more than four decades, could find much to learn from the master. For a while, "everybody who was playing mandolin was learning from Bill Monroe," he says. "His style is a mixture of Mississippi Delta blues,

---

2. Bill and Charlie worked together as a duo for four years.

3. Cleo Davis in Wayne Erbsen, "Cleo Davis: The Original Blue Grass Boy."

4. John Miller, mentioned for the first time in Rinzler's monograph in *Stars of Country Music*, played jug with the band for about three months, in Asheville, North Carolina.

5. Played by Howdy Forrester's wife, Wilene, who used the stage name "Sally Ann," ca. 1945.

6. Played by "Curly" Bradshaw, ca. 1945.

7. Bill mentioned *five* trucks in Don Rhodes, "Monroe, the Father, Monroe, the Son."

8. Holly is reputed to have liked bluegrass, but it is an exaggeration to say that he was "one of the biggest Bill Monroe fans that ever lived."

jazz, old-time country, and a very, very lonesome Appalachian sound. I think Bill's music will go down in history as being one of the most pure, traditional, rare forms of American music. In fact, I think it really does epitomize American music."

A few months after Elvis,[9] Monroe re-recorded "Blue Moon of Kentucky" himself, this time adding a 4/4 rockabilly beat of his own. It was a rare concession. He found little to use in the newer music, and as rock's popularity picked up speed, he stuck firmly to his notions of what bluegrass should be. He spurned electric instruments and percussion, remained intolerant of band members who freewheeled with the form ("They need to get out on their own if they're going to do that") and refused to bend to an increasingly commercial Nashville sound. There were difficult times, and his struggles were often more than musical. A car accident in the fifties left him with 19 fractured bones and a long hospitalization; a life away from home left him with a broken marriage.

Eventually, with the folk revival of the sixties, Monroe's stubbornness turned to advantage. Discovered by a new generation of fans, many of them young urban musicians, he came to be seen as the one unchanging standard by which bluegrass could be judged. It is a tough standard, to be sure. Newer bands can cut their cloth to newer tastes and fashions, but not Monroe. His, after all, is a special music. "I want to keep it set," he says. "I want to keep it right."

Just right is how things are on Monroe's 288-acre farm in Goodlettsville, north of Nashville. Hard rains had shotgunned down earlier in the week, but now sunshine is filtering through the huckleberry and gum trees. Times are busy. Four mares have foaled in the past few days—the latest just 14 hours ago—and on Monday the cattle will be wormed. Monroe has been up since 6:30 this morning working on fences.

Despite surgery for colon cancer in 1980,[10] and for gallbladder problems two years later,[11] Monroe is no front porch farmer. He can still plow with his favorite 10-year-old mule, chop his own wood, and put in a summer's day of work. Living on the land, he says, "brings you back to the way you was raised." It's a sentiment understood by son James who, like his older sister, Melissa, 49, lives nearby. "Goin' on his farm is almost like goin' back in time," James says. "There's a feelin' you get when you go out there. . . ."

Monroe's home on the farm is a 140-year-old tin-roofed, two-story cabin. A porch wraps around two sides, with an old-fashioned swing and a high-backed church pew for seating on summer evenings. He shares the quarters with his second wife, Della, 45, a striking Minnesotan and the daughter of one of his former booking agents. The couple married last year, and Della confides that she has "temporarily" quit her job as an accountant because "Bill doesn't want me to work."[12]

9. Two months after Elvis.
10. 1981.
11. Prostate problems one year later.
12. Bill and Della had been married about a year and a half. See the editor's comments, second paragraph.

Monroe has no such notions for himself, of course, and by nightfall he and Della have made the 30-minute drive down I-65 to the Grand Ole Opry. He's been a regular on its stage for 46 years and can boast that he's only missed his starting time on three occasions: twice because of car failure and once after a bridge washout. In 1971,[13] he was honored as the Father of Bluegrass when the Country Music Association inducted him into its Hall of Fame, and he will perform at the Opry at least 20 times this year.

In his dressing room Monroe unpacks the old mandolin and runs through a few licks. "It seems like the sound is comin' back more to it all the time," he says, obviously satisfied with the instrument's recovery. Then, one by one, his band members enter the room. First is banjo player Blake Williams, 29, so clean-cut he might have stepped out of a seminary yearbook. Next is Tater Tate, the group's 55-year-old fiddler (and part-time bus driver), followed by guitarist Tom Ewing, 40, who joined the Blue Grass Boys only one month earlier. Last to arrive is bass player Johnny Montgomery, 58, who's quickly reminded by Monroe that he hasn't yet put on his tie.

While the musicians tune, Monroe quick-fingers a new song he's written. Asked what it is, he replies simply, "The Lloyd Loar," and says no more. Monroe is a man of basic virtues, one who remembers favors given and received, and this is for the latter. Loar was the concert mandolinist who helped design the special instrument that Monroe is playing—the one that Charlie Derrington saved—and the song is a simple thanks for both.

When Monroe finishes the tune, he and the band gather in a circle and start their pre-performance warm-up. Other musicians from out in the hallway begin to drift in quietly, wanting to hear this show before the show. Suddenly the room, carpeted, mirrored, and modern, is filled with echoes of old Appalachia and country churches, of black men's blues and barn-dance fiddle tunes. The kaleidoscope of sound is the old-time music that Bill Monroe made new again more than 40 years ago—and will again tonight.

Originally published in *People Weekly,* Sept. 1, 1986, 48–50, 53–54. © 1986 by Time Inc.

EDITOR'S COMMENTS

Wolmuth, then a senior writer for *People Weekly,* visited Bill and Della at the farm in June 1986, came to the Opry with them, and followed Bill to the Bean Blossom festival that weekend. This "Bio" was featured prominently in the magazine's September 1, 1986 issue. (Wolmuth, formerly with *Time,* is quoted in Jack Flippin, "Nobody Does It Like Bill.")

Bill and Della Monroe had been married about a year and half when this arti-

13. 1970.

cle was published. They would divorce about a year and a half later, in January 1988, while Bill was recording his *Southern Flavor*[1] album.

Note

1. *Southern Flavor,* MCA Records, MCA-42133, released 1988.

"Bill Monroe's Mandolin"

JIM HATLO

Which of Antonio Stradivari's violins is the greatest? Which is the most celebrated guitar ever to carry the name of José Ramirez, or of C. F. Martin? Throw those questions out to a panel of instrument historians, and you'll probably have a lively discussion on your hands. But if you ask, "What is the most famous mandolin in the world?" there is no contest. Hands down, the superstar of the whole mandolin family is Bill Monroe's 1923 Gibson F-5.

The mandolin—serial number 73987—officially came into being on July 9, 1923, when its label got the approving signature of Gibson acoustic engineer Lloyd Loar. The "5" designation showed it was one of Gibson's "Master Model" instruments, a series that included the L-5 archtop guitar, the H-5 mandola, the TB-5 banjo, and a small number of K-5 mandocellos. Loar was a prominent classical performer, hired by Gibson in 1919, both as a resident endorsing artist and as a manager/consultant. Besides being an internationally renowned mandolinist, Loar was an avid builder and musical acoustics researcher.

Popular history tends to give Loar all the credit for Gibson's Master Model line, but the Model 5s actually were the brainchildren of Lewis A. Williams, a founder and major stockholder of the original Gibson company; and Gibson designers Andrew Jay Reams, Jr., and George D. Laurian. Williams, Reams, and Laurian have been forgotten, however, because Loar was the man who personally tested and certified—or rejected—each Model 5 instrument the factory produced.[1]

Through innovative marketing and promotion, Gibson had created and sustained a nationwide boom in mandolin orchestras, beginning in 1909. In the process, their flatback, carved-top mandolins displaced the Neapolitan bowl-back mandolin[2] as the standard for the instrument. But by 1920, postwar public tastes were turning to Dixieland, and the brash new resonator banjo was taking over.

Nobody knows exactly what happened to no. 73987 during the 18 years between the day Loar signed it in 1923 and the day Monroe found it in 1941.[3] According to

1. From 1922 to 1924.
2. The kind of "tater bug" mandolin that Bill originally learned to play on.
3. Probably 1945, thus twenty-three years.

Monroe, it was in excellent condition when he spotted it in the window of a Miami barbershop, while touring in Florida. Previously he had been playing a Gibson F-7, but he wanted something better. He tried the F-5, was delighted with it, and bought it for $150. Not a bad deal considering that, in 1923, new F-5s had listed at $100 more.

On that $150 transaction has turned hundreds of thousands of dollars in mandolin sales over the last 45 years. In Monroe's hands the F-5 became *the* mandolin for bluegrass and its associated styles. Today, dozens of makers, both large and small, in America and abroad, produce F-5 replicas, imitations, and variations of their own; and vintage Loar F-5s bring prices as high as $9,000.[4]

Lloyd Loar never lived to see his name become a household word among American string musicians. He died in September 1943, the day after Monroe turned 32. Bluegrass was still a new phenomenon in country music; and Loar didn't follow country music. It's questionable whether the classical virtuoso would have been flattered to learn that his Master Model mandolins were destined for their greatest glory in what was then called "hillbilly music."

Ten years after Monroe bought no. 73987, it returned to the Gibson factory in Kalamazoo, Michigan. Monroe shipped the instrument back to undergo some repairs. The neck had been broken in an accident,[5] and the F-5 also need refretting, refinishing, and a new set of tuning keys. Monroe was without the mandolin for four long months; and when it finally arrived from Gibson, he was furious to discover that only the neck replacement[6] had been done.

Angrily he took a penknife and scraped the inlaid "Gibson" logo from the headstock. (Some accounts say that Gibson did refinish the instrument, but not to Monroe's satisfaction, so he scraped the new finish off as well).[7] For nearly 30 years after that incident, the country's most prominent mandolinist turned a cold shoulder toward Gibson.

Around 1954, the headstock picked up another battle scar. A fall broke off the ornamental scroll at its tip.[8] Monroe kept the broken piece, intending to have it glued back in place, but eventually it was lost. Missing its logo and its peghead scroll, the trailworn F-5 came to be virtually a bluegrass totem.

Such craftsmen as Randy Wood, owner of the onetime Nashville Pickin' Parlor, helped keep no. 73987 in playing order during the sixties and seventies. As much as Monroe loved the instrument, he worked it long and hard; it got little rest. Though he acquired other mandolins, no. 73987 remained his main performing and recording instrument.

---

4. Loar F-5 prices are currently as high as $50,000.

5. As Bill told Doug Benson (in "Bill Monroe, King of Blue Grass Music"), "the neck had been broke off."

6. Meaning the neck was placed back into the body of the mandolin, not that it was replaced with another neck.

7. This occurred in 1952.

8. The headstock scroll was broken off as early as 1947, judging by photographs of the band taken during that time.

In 1980, Gibson (well aware that Monroe was the best advertisement the company's mandolins ever had) made a peace offering. It presented Monroe with a new F-5L, the carefully-researched replica edition of the original Loar F-5. Along with the presentation, Gibson made an offer: It would undertake any and all repairs Monroe wanted done to no. 73987, free of charge.

Monroe accepted both the new mandolin and the offer. His old F-5 came home to its birthplace once more, this time as a guest of honor. A team of luthiers headed by Gibson mandolin expert Richard Doan went to work on giving the famous instrument a scroll transplant and a face-lift.

Doan made a new scroll from matching curly maple, and a new veneer was shaped to fit the restored peghead face. Then the veneer went to Kalamazoo inlay specialist Maude Moore, who duplicated the original pearl-work. Finally, the new facing was carefully mated to the original binding. The Gibson crew installed new tuning machines and a new fretboard, and in early October (the turnaround period was only a little over a month, this time), the company gave the mandolin back to Monroe at a Nashville press conference.

Five years later the instrument was in the news again; but the news was grim. On November 13, 1985, a vandal broke into Monroe's home and took a fireplace poker to the historic mandolin and another 1923 Loar that Monroe owned, one he kept cross-tuned[9] for performing his 1981 instrumental hit "My Last Days on Earth." The instruments were left cracked and splintered, with gaping holes in their bodies. Nearby, some framed pictures were smashed. Nothing else was touched.

To the bluegrass community, the wanton destruction of the mandolins was more than vandalism; it was sheer sacrilege. Few doubted that the world's most famous mandolin had played its last concert. But again, enter Gibson. The company volunteered to see if—at its own expense—it could restore the broken instruments. Luthier Charlie Derrington of Gibson's Research and Development department was put to work full-time on the formidable job. This time, however, the work was done in Nashville. Two years earlier Gibson had shut down its historic Kalamazoo plant for good.

Derrington began with no. 73987, which had escaped with slightly less damage. After days of painstakingly cataloging the pieces of the ravaged top, some no bigger than splinters, he mapped out a plan of attack and—with tweezers and a magnifying glass—started putting the instrument back together. Wherever possible, he used original material. For three months he toiled over the mandolin, consulting with violin restoration expert William Moennig along the way. Finally, on February 25 of this year, Gibson invited Monroe to its Nashville factory and called another press conference.

The reconstruction of no. 73987 was finished. Monroe would again take possession of his favorite mandolin. But would he take it back to play—or was it now fit only for display, as a famous relic, in his Bluegrass Hall of Fame?

---

9. Any variation of standard tuning which produces an open chord.

Monroe was as surprised as anyone at the press conference when he tried out the mandolin on "Wheel Hoss," a tune he first recorded with the instrument in 1954. "It sounds good!" he exclaimed. "It's awful close to the old sound! Time will take it back to what it was."

In a recent interview with *Frets* columnist George Gruhn, Monroe said that the "aging" of the mandolin was proceeding as he'd hoped.

"It's settled down a lot now," he said. "It's just going to take a little bit longer. I sure appreciate what Gibson and Charlie Derrington have done. This mandolin's played a big part in my music. It's always been ready to go. It's had a lot of volume to it, and you could play the notes good, and it rang. It's been a good mandolin down through the years."

And so a bluegrass tradition continues. This month, as Bill Monroe celebrates his 75th birthday, the master mandolinist and his 63-year-old mandolin go on making music, and making history, together.

Originally published in *Frets* 8:9 (Sept. 1986): 32, 37. Reprinted by permission of the Miller Freeman, Inc., Music Group.

EDITOR'S COMMENTS

Frets magazine saluted Bill on his seventy-fifth birthday with its September 1986 issue. It included, among several articles relating to him, this feature on his mandolin by special editions editor Hatlo.

"Bill Monroe" (interview)

GEORGE GRUHN

Gruhn: You're the foremost teacher in bluegrass; a lot of people have come to work for you, almost like going to school, and, later, gone on to form bands of their own. How do you go about teaching your music?

Bill: It's not so hard. They listen to my music and they can tell right there what I want. If they go the wrong way with it, then I tell them, and I tell them how to keep it right. Bluegrass people learn pretty fast.

Gruhn: It's never bothered you that your band frequently is a stepping stone in younger players' careers?

Bill: It's built people's names up. If you were a Blue Grass Boy, you knew your name would be called on the Grand Old Opry, and that helped you, whoever you were. So if you worked for me a year and a half, up to three years, then you were ready to get out on your own. And that was all right with me, because, by that time, I needed somebody else in the music. That's the way it's worked. I think it's been better that way than it would've been if I'd kept four of the same players all the way through, you see. It's given people a chance to hear all kinds of banjo playing, and singing, and fiddle players.

Gruhn: Some Blue Grass Boys have started very young, haven't they? Vassar Clements was less than 16 when he began fiddling with you.[1]

Bill: Well, Sonny Osborne was 14 when he started playing banjo with me; so you see, I've worked with some pretty young kids. But now, you take Bill Keith: He was a powerful player with the Blue Grass Boys. He had a style of his own when he came, another style to put in bluegrass, and it fit right in.[2]

Gruhn: Your own playing has changed over the years. Do you feel you play better now than you ever did?

Bill: Well, it seems that I know more about it now than I did when I was young. I keep learning, so it's kind of worked out that way. I like to write on the mandolin, and that all works in there together—hearing the notes, and figuring out how to get them the way you want to hear them played.

Gruhn: I'm sure that nobody could define bluegrass better than you can. What really makes it different from old-time music, or jazz, or some of the new acoustic styles?

Bill: Bluegrass is a pure music. You follow the melody right, and you don't put in no hot, know-it-all fiddle that don't belong in there. If you're just trying to show off, that ain't going to get it; it sure won't get it with me. It's the same thing with the mandolin. I play enough notes on the mandolin to take care of Bill Monroe and the Blue Grass Boys, but I also play the rhythm, and help keep the time straightened out. Now, old-time mountain music and fiddle playing is a different kind of music altogether. Those old-time fiddlers like Arthur Smith and Clayton McMichen, they could play a fiddle number, but they couldn't play a song right in bluegrass because it was a faster time (tempo) than they ever played. It was bluegrass that got the drive. And that music in the early days was just in keys like G, C, and D, while bluegrass would take you on up the neck to A, or B natural.[3] Nobody ever sung in B natural that I know of, then,[4] but my voice was high and G was too low for it, so it had to move on up.

Gruhn: Does bluegrass have much in the way of blues influences?

Bill: Yes, sir. You can hear the blues in there on a lot of songs; and gospel. And in some of the music, you'll hear just a wee bit of jazz, or a little bit of swing, with the fiddle or the mandolin or the banjo. Back in the early days they didn't know how to do that.

1. Clements was twenty-one when he joined the Blue Grass Boys in 1949, but filled in with the band in the early forties when he was a teenager.

2. Keith was twenty-three when he joined the Blue Grass Boys.

3. Bill's way of referring to the key of B major.

4. In old-time country music.

Gruhn: Where do you draw the line? Is there a point where it isn't bluegrass anymore, with music like progressive bluegrass or newgrass?

Bill: It's not grass then; it's another kind of music. We are not going to call it "grass." There's a lot of swing and jazz, but people tend to run wild with it, and I don't believe any music should be handled that way. When they get out like that, I don't even want to hear it. They should take it into another field and play another kind of music.

Gruhn: What kinds of music do you listen to when you're not performing, besides bluegrass?

Bill: I hear a lot of music on the radio as we travel, and I like a lot of the young country singers today who are coming on. I like to hear the way they sing; they're learning a lot about how to handle their voices. Back in the old days, they didn't know these things. I've always liked Bob Wills' style of music; he played in sort of an old-time way, but people could dance to it. There are some guitar pickers that I like to hear, like Merle Travis; of course, he's passed on. Chet Atkins is a fine guitar player. I've always loved his playing.

Gruhn: You've mentioned some people and styles that use electric instruments. You're not prejudiced against electric instruments?

Bill: No, sir. You could even play electric fiddle and I'd like listening to it. But, you know, if you're going to, I think you should have it all electric or no electric. I think they should all be the same. You can work an electric bass in, because it's a deep sound. But it was years and years before there ever were electric instruments in bluegrass,[5] and for my music, I want to keep it that way.

Gruhn: You've had ideas for music outside of bluegrass, haven't you? I recall you jamming once with Sonny Osborne at the Grand Ole Opry, with a tune you'd written that was supposed to include a trombone part.

Bill: Yes, I wrote one like that. It's called "Trombolin," for mandolin and trombone. I've got to get that to Danny Davis.[6] That's who it needs.

Gruhn: When you're jamming with people like Sonny, it seems that often you're not doing the kind of music you play with your band. Sometimes it's old tunes you did 50 years ago.

Bill: We like to see how far we can take the sound back, the way they did it back then. You don't want to forget about where you come from, you see. Now, me and the Monroe Brothers used to play the old square dance music, and the old-time style, the mountain-type of singing. Of course, my uncle Pen was a wonderful fiddle player—he was one of the first men I ever heard play the fiddle. And I still like the old-time fiddle music.

Gruhn: Since those days playing square dances, life on the road has changed a lot, hasn't it?

Bill: Well, you take when I started with the Grand Ole Opry: between Nashville

---

5. Jim and Jesse, in the mid-fifties, were probably the first major bluegrass act to use an electric bass.

6. Leader of the Nashville Brass.

and Knoxville there were just a lot of gravel roads. And all of us would pile in a little old car, you know, and haul the bass on top. There wasn't much room, but we made it all right. You can do a lot of things when you're young, looking to tomorrow with your music, and what's going to come up for you. But now the roads are wonderful, and to travel in a bus is good for me. I have a room of my own in it, where I can sleep. I like to lay down and sleep for a couple or three hours, then get up and ride and see the country. And I have got to see every sunset that I can! That means so much to me. I like to see the sunrise, too, but with traveling all night a lot of times, I'm not up early enough. But I love the sunsets.

Gruhn: At 75, you're maintaining a touring schedule that might drive some younger musicians into the ground.

Bill: Well, I would say this year we'll put in 250 dates. We're playing all 50 states.[7] I want to do all I can, and I think it's turning out to be a wonderful year.

Gruhn: With all the festivals you play, including your own, do you think that bluegrass is bigger than it's ever been?

Bill: Yes, I really do believe it is. I think the festivals have done a lot for people all over the country. They spend a lot of money for the entertainers, and that's been a big help for the bluegrass artists.

Gruhn: Did the festivals help keep bluegrass alive in the late fifties or early sixties,[8] when it was suffering because of the popularity of rock 'n' roll?

Bill: I think the festivals helped a lot. They let a lot of people all over the world know about bluegrass. Of course, bluegrass people don't ever give up. They hang right in there, and they like to hear the music themselves, but they like to play for other folks too. So the people kept it going. Back then, a lot of people didn't even know how to promote bluegrass, or even start and handle a festival. There were just a few around the country who could. But a lot of folks have learned, and so, festivals have been really great for bluegrass.

Gruhn: Today, I imagine even the small festivals can find quite a few bands.

Bill: There are a lot of young bluegrass groups coming along now that are out of this world, boy. They can really sing the harmony and play the music. Every time we travel around the country, they're playing bluegrass music. They're all over the country, and I like to hear them play.

Gruhn: Just as there are a lot of bands that have been influenced by you, there are a lot of mandolinists you've inspired—even though their styles may be quite different.

Bill: Yes, everybody has the right to come up with their own styles. And like you say, it's different from my style of playing. You take Jesse McReynolds, he's one of the most powerful mandolin players in the world. And Bobby Osborne, the same way; he really gets a good tone out of the mandolin. Everybody's got a right to play it the way they want to play it.

---

7. Only a shortage of bookings prevented him from reaching his goal. See the editor's comments, second paragraph.

8. The first bluegrass festival was held in 1965.

Gruhn: So there is room in bluegrass for individual styles. There are bluegrass bands that don't sound anything like the Blue Grass Boys, but they're still real bluegrass—is that a fair statement?

Bill: That's right. They're playing the songs their own way, the way they want to hear them played. There are a lot of them who have been on it a long time, and I'm for them 100 percent.

Gruhn: Though you've had an enormous impact as a mandolinist, you used to play the guitar quite a bit, didn't you?

Bill: Yes, sir, but it got where it was kind of bothering my mandolin playing, with my wrist. You don't play the guitar the same way you would play the mandolin. So I eased down on it.

Gruhn: Have you played any other instruments besides mandolin and guitar?

Bill: I can play some tunes on the fiddle, but they're not very good. I'd be ashamed for people to hear them. I think I could take the time to learn the bass. I don't know but very little about the banjo.

Gruhn: Looking beyond the mandolin to your whole career, what do you feel are your greatest accomplishments?

Bill: Well, I'm glad to be in the Country Music Hall of Fame. But I'm really glad that now we've got the Bluegrass Hall of Fame for the bluegrass people. We're going to do some great things there. But like I said, I like to write. I like to write numbers for the mandolin, or the fiddle, or the banjo—taking some new notes, you know, and seeing how I would fit them into this tune or that tune, and make it work the way I hear it. Maybe do it like the old-time music, the way they would have played it years and years ago. That pays off a lot; it just does a lot of good for me. I sure don't want to quit!

Originally published in *Frets* 8:9 (Sept. 1986): 38–41. Reprinted by permission of the Miller Freeman, Inc., Music Group.

EDITOR'S COMMENTS

Frets magazine's salute to Bill included this interview by instrument dealer and *Frets* columnist Gruhn. (The published interview is a condensed version of a much longer one conducted in July 1986.)

Bill's goal for 1986 was to play all fifty states, and only a shortage of bookings prevented him from reaching it. By year's end, however, he had performed in over half (twenty-eight) of the United States and in the District of Columbia. He also traveled to England, Ireland, Germany, and Switzerland in March, and the Bahamas (on the first "bluegrass cruise") in October.

"Recording the Grammy Winner: Bill Monroe in the Studio"

THOMAS GOLDSMITH

Bluegrass music as played by Bill Monroe is like no other sound on earth—and getting it on tape is like no other recording session.

The sounds of bagpipes, blues, mountain churches, and running brooks are echoed in Monroe's tunes—it's not necessarily music composed with the studio in mind.

"I write for the music and for the sound," Monroe said during sessions for his *Southern Flavor* LP.[1] "I write all the time when I'm on the road. I can write an instrumental in just a minute."

Singer-mandolinist Monroe may come up with his tunes spontaneously, but the often startling contours of his music required all the attention of the players gathered for the session at Sound Stage Studios. Joining Bill for the recording were Tom Ewing, guitar; Blake Williams, banjo; Tater Tate, bass; Mike Feagan, fiddle; as well as ace fiddlers Buddy Spicher and Bobby Hicks.

"People don't realize it, but bluegrass is hard," Hicks said while rehearsing a complicated tune. "There's nothing to hide behind, there's no drums." No electric instruments, synthesizers, or drums make appearances at Monroe sessions. However, his latest efforts in tradition-based music are captured by the latest in digital technology.[2]

"It's more microphone placement than knob twisting, but that's the way all recording should be," engineer Steve Tillisch said about recording Monroe. "You want to get as natural a sound as possible on each instrument."

In the small room where the musicians were playing, bluegrass sounded like chamber music. Every note played by each instrument was clear and distinct, not strident, yet the whole had great rhythmic drive and pulse.

The players heard each other directly, not through the earphones almost universally used in studio sessions.

"As close as we are in here, we don't need headphones," said Blue Grass Boys bassist Tater Tate. "I don't hear good, but I can hear in here."

The first tune on the agenda was an instrumental called "Stone Coal." "I put that together up in the eastern part of Kentucky," Monroe said. "Ricky Skaggs and his father were there and his father came up with that name, 'Stone Coal.'"

---

1. *Southern Flavor*, MCA Records, MCA-42133, released in 1988.

2. This method of recording is completely different from the old technique. See the editor's comments, second paragraph.

In the first full run-through of the song, Monroe played the fast-rambling theme, patting his foot all the while, then merely looked at the trio of fiddlers. They erupted into a triple-fiddle version of the tune, just as Monroe had harmonized on a specially-tuned mandolin.

"It's something I came up with myself," he said of the cross-tuning. "It's something like what I used on 'My Last Days on Earth,' but it's different."[3]

Next, the ball was handed back to Monroe, who got appreciative grins from the other players with a solo consisting mostly of syncopated rhythmic strums across all eight strings of the mandolin. That performance didn't make it on the record, but it woke everybody up.

After the first take, or recorded version, everyone filed into the studio's control room, which looked like the command center of the Starship Enterprise. "That's a different style of mandolin, isn't it?" a smiling Monroe said as he came back into the control room.

The informal musicians, clad almost without exception in plaid flannel shirts, were in contrast to Monroe, who wore a western banker's three-piece suit and hat. They all gathered behind the massive, futuristic mixing console to listen to the take, Monroe patting his feet as if to dance.

Then they took a minute to iron out the fine points of the arrangement. "O.K., let's see if I can remember," said producer Emory Gordy. "It starts off with chimes on the mandolin and then Bill does one chorus, then the fiddles, then Bill, then the banjo, then the fiddles come back, and he does it again with no bridge."

Everyone nodded and appeared to take this in. No one made any notes—there wasn't a written piece of music in sight.

"Right now, you're all playing kind of tentatively—probably because you're not comfortable," Gordy said. "Also, I've got a request for the bridge section."

"We don't take requests," Hicks joked, to general amusement.

After the musicians went back in the recording room, Gordy said he typically has Monroe and the band play a song several times over to get the best performance, rather than building a recording piecemeal—"overdubbing" each instrument separately.

"They need to hear each other when they are playing," the producer said. "When you overdub, the first guy doesn't get the benefit of what the second guy does."

Through speakers in the recording room he said, "All right, we're going to go for four or five takes in a row."

As Monroe and his musicians played his tune over and over, the piece began to take definite shape. All the solos tightened up, as did the rhythm instruments, and the ensemble sound of the fiddles.

"Once they get locked in, the tempo's always the same," Gordy said. Monroe, accenting his phrases with body English, became more aggressive in his playing, his hand bobbing up and down as he picked.

---

3. The tuning is like that used for "My Last Days on Earth" mainly in that three pairs of strings are affected. See the editor's comments, third paragraph.

"At his age, he begins to lose energy, so you've got to catch it when it's there," Gordy said.

But after what was to be the final take, Monroe said, "Was I supposed to do it one more time? Let me do it again."

Said Gordy: "That other was the last take; this will be the next-to-the-last take."

After a strong version of "Stone Coal" was committed to tape, everyone took a brief break.

"When we first started recording we just had one microphone," mused Monroe, who started making records with his brother Charlie in the 1930s. "The old days were awful good days, but we've got to move it along."

After some discussion, Gordy and Monroe decided next to record another instrumental, "Texas Lone Star." It's an intricate, three-part fiddle tune that young fiddler Mike Feagan took a little while to work out with veterans Hicks and Spicher.

Meanwhile, banjoist Blake Williams and guitarist Tom Ewing were honing their parts for the tune, recordings of which took up much of the afternoon. Like several of Monroe's compositions in recent years, "Texas Lone Star" has a skirling, flowing, minor-keyed sound that seems to recall both his Scottish ancestry and his fondness for Texas fiddle music.

"We could have been playing in Texas when I wrote that," Monroe said. "It's just a number that we could play in Texas. One that might have the sound as it might have been played years ago."

Originally published in *Bluegrass Unlimited* 23:10 (Apr. 1989): 46–48. Reprinted by permission of the author.

EDITOR'S COMMENTS

Goldsmith, a reporter for *The Tennessean,* attended the second recording session for Bill's *Southern Flavor* album, on January 5, 1988, and his observations were published more than a year later in the April 1989 issue of *Bluegrass Unlimited.* In the interim, the album had won for Bill the first Grammy award in the new Bluegrass Album category from the National Academy of Recording Arts and Sciences.

The "latest in digital technology" used to record the *Southern Flavor* album and Bill's previous release, *Bluegrass '87,*[1] is completely different from the analog recording technique. Each tune is played through and recorded several times and, later, it's possible to electronically combine the best parts of each recording to create a seamless composite. There is no final "best take" as in analog recording.

The tuning for "Stone Coal" is like the tuning for "My Last Days on Earth" mainly in that three of the four courses are affected: G strings are unchanged; D strings are tuned down to C; the first A string is tuned down to E, the other down to G; and the first E string is tuned way down to G and the other is tuned down to C.

Southern Flavor was the last of Bill's recordings to be released in "long-playing" (vinyl) album form by MCA.

Note

1. *Bluegrass '87,* MCA Records, MCA-5970, released 1987.

"'Womanizing' Led to Monroe Tussle, Ex-girlfriend Says"

CHARLIE APPLETON

GALLATIN—An ex-girlfriend says she was trying to get bluegrass music legend Bill Monroe to swear on the Bible that he was not a "womanizer" when he grabbed the book and allegedly assaulted her.

As a result, the woman says, her glasses were broken and she sustained numerous bruises and other injuries in the attack that followed.

Wanda Huff, a 51-year-old Birmingham, Alabama, dog trainer, filed assault charges against the 77-year-old "father of bluegrass music" on Monday. A preliminary hearing is set for next Wednesday in Sumner County General Sessions Court.

Monroe is free on $500 bond. He declined to comment on the incident when contacted at his home off Long Hollow Pike near Goodlettsville this morning.

The divorced mother of two sons said she was Monroe's girlfriend for 3½ years, but was trying to break off the relationship when the alleged assault occurred.

"I was leaving him, and I wanted my things back. I was just getting my things out of his house. I had some very valuable jewelry in there.

"That's when he just started tearing things up. I told him to stop, and I asked him if we couldn't just end this thing on a very peaceful note. I said, 'It's not worth this. You've got a bad heart,'" Huff continued.

"Things kept on, and finally I said, 'Bill, if you haven't been running around with these women, here's the Bible. . . .'

"I said, 'Swear on it to me that you have not been running around, because that way you'll tell me for real.'

"He said, 'I'm not going to do it.' That's when he took the Bible and—swack—right in the mouth," the 5-foot-5 woman says. "It was a big ol' Bible."

Huff, who works out with weights at a gym, says she could have hurt the elderly musician but chose to just push him away. "Bill takes nitroglycerin for his heart, and all I need is for the old man to drop dead on me and I'd be in trouble."

"He then slapped me real hard on the side of my head and broke my glasses. I grabbed for my glasses, and that's when he hit me again and then shoved me up against something, and I fell on the floor.

"While I was on the floor, he kicked me three times. I was still pleading with him to stop this.

"I just wanted out. I told him to keep everything, and I got up off the floor. That's when I started screaming just as hard as I could, but he just laughed at me.

"He put his arm up against my throat and shoved me up against an old iron stove," said Huff, who sustained a broken neck in an accident several years ago.

"About that time we noticed some love letters from his old girlfriends, and right next to them was a stick of stove wood. He grabbed it up, and I saw him coming at me with it. I put my arm up and I stopped it.

"He grabbed me and started shaking me and said, 'I'm going to break your neck.'"

Huff said she started screaming again, and Monroe's farm manager, Archie Mills, came in the house and helped her escape.

A native of Rosine, Kentucky, Monroe and his Blue Grass Boys band joined the Grand Ole Opry in 1939. He still performs about 150 show dates a year.

His best-known songs as composer include "Blue Moon of Kentucky," "Uncle Pen," "Kentucky Waltz," and "Footprints in the Snow."[1]

He recently won the first Grammy award presented for the bluegrass-style music he founded.

Originally published in the *Nashville Banner,* May 3, 1989, A-1, A-8. © 1989 by the *Nashville Banner* and *The Tennessean.*

EDITOR'S COMMENTS

On Monday, May 1, 1989, Bill's log cabin home on the farm was the scene of an event that would soon make headlines around the country as the "Bible Belt" incident. First reported by the Nashville newspapers on May 3, with Bill declining to comment, *Nashville Banner* reporter Appleton gave Huff an opportunity to tell her side of the story in lurid detail.

---

1. Although one of his best-known songs, "Footprints in the Snow" was not written by Bill.

"Charges against Monroe Dropped"

CATHERINE THOMPSON

GALLATIN—Grand Ole Opry star Bill Monroe was exonerated in court here yesterday when an assault and battery charge filed against him 10 days ago by an Alabama woman was dismissed.

Monroe, 77, listened calmly as Sumner County Assistant District Attorney General Dee Gay told the court that he doubted the veracity of Wanda Huff, 50, a Birmingham dog trainer who charged Monroe with hitting her in the face with a Bible and kicking her at his Sumner County farm on May 1.

"In my opinion, the state of Tennessee cannot carry the burden of proof and we ask that this case be dismissed," Gay said.

Gay told General Sessions Court Judge Jane Wheatcraft that Huff had harassed and threatened the life of Monroe. He also said sheriff's officers confiscated a loaded .25-caliber automatic pistol from her truck yesterday before the proceedings began.

"I am happy that it's over with and that I can go home and enjoy life," Monroe said after the case was dismissed.

The performer told reporters he "didn't like" the public attention generated by the case, "but I think my fans and friends knew it was wrong."

Huff left the courthouse in tears, insisting she never threatened or harassed Monroe. She claimed Monroe had paid witnesses to discredit her charges.

"The rich win again," Huff said, adding that she felt betrayed. "I don't have the money to buy witnesses, and wouldn't have tried it if I did. I did not ever threaten to kill him. If I wanted to kill him, I had a million chances."

Monroe's son, James, said Huff had stalked his father for almost three years, but denied that his father ever had a relationship with her.

"Do you know why we are here? Because she saw my father on television being baptized in the Jordan River.[1] She told him later, when she saw him being baptized, God told her that He wanted her to have him."

James Monroe said his father first met Huff backstage after a performance, when she told the entertainer she was going to kill herself.

"He talked her out of it. Can you believe that?" he said.

He said that since his father's first meeting with Huff, the woman has persistently harassed the performer, sometimes calling him up to 20 times a day and often using different aliases.

---

1. Bill was baptized in the Jordan River during a trip to Israel in July 1983.

Sumner County Sheriff Richard Sutton said the court ordered Huff searched when she arrived for court at the request of Monroe's attorney. Nothing was found on her person, but Sutton asked her if she had a weapon and she replied she had one in her truck. Officers confiscated and kept the handgun, loaded with at least six bullets.

Monroe was granted a restraining order against Huff yesterday, and Wheatcraft said Huff has agreed to comply with it.

A native of Rosine, Kentucky, Monroe started his professional career in the 1930s as a duet partner with his brother, Charlie. He brought his Blue Grass Boys band to the Grand Ole Opry in 1939.

His classic bluegrass sound came together in the mid-1940s when Lester Flatt and Earl Scruggs were members of Monroe's band.

Originally published in *The Tennessean,* May 11, 1989, 1A, 4A. © 1989 by *The Tennessean.* Reprinted by permission.

EDITOR'S COMMENTS

The case was resolved on Wednesday, May 10, 1989, and, as reported by Thompson of *The Tennessean* on May 11, Bill was exonerated after a loaded gun was removed from Huff's pickup truck. What really happened at Bill's home on that first day in May will probably never be known, but the outcome of the hearing definitely places Huff's entire account in doubt.

About a month later, following the Bean Blossom festival in June, Bill was filmed revisiting his old homeplace near Rosine for the documentary *High Lonesome: The Story of Bluegrass Music* (Northside Films, 1991). Segments with the Blue Grass Boys (Tom Ewing, Billy Rose, Tater Tate, and Blake Williams) on the last "Blue Grass Special" and at the Bell Cove club in the Nashville suburb of Hendersonville were filmed on Bill's birthday in 1989.

"50 Years on the Grand Ole Opry"

THOMAS GOLDSMITH

Bill Monroe celebrated his 50th anniversary at the Grand Ole Opry, October 28, 1989,[1] in front of a cheering, capacity Opry House crowd of more than 4,400 people. Yet those in attendance in Nashville that night make up only a small portion of

---

1. Fifty years to the day after his first appearance on October 28, 1939.

the folks who have reason to celebrate Monroe's Opry milestone and other achievements:

Bluegrass lovers all over the world should celebrate, because the style they love wasn't widely heard until Monroe assembled it from his far-reaching influences after joining the famed country music show in October 1939.[2]

Kentucky partisans should join in—Monroe, a native of Rosine, is such a strong booster of his home state that his Blue Grass Boys band even bears Kentucky's nickname.

The 175-plus former and present Monroe sidemen, including lots of top bluegrass names, ought to signal their appreciation for the invaluable, tough-minded music instruction Monroe parceled out along with sometimes meager pay.

Anyone who plays mandolin should take part, because Monroe's lightning-fast, hard-hitting approach raised the instrument to a new level of usefulness and influence in country music and beyond.

Songwriters and people who love good tunes ought to send good wishes, too— Monroe's decades of composition have not only produced worldwide hits such as "Blue Moon of Kentucky" and "Uncle Pen," but also such hauntingly original instrumentals as "Jerusalem Ridge," "Lonesome Moonlight Waltz," and "My Last Days on Earth."

And, in the end, people who believe that an artist should stick by what he knows to be right—through thick and thin—should cheer long and hard for Monroe. He is widely applauded now, but he played and sang with just as much conviction during the many years when most people "didn't know what it (bluegrass) was, or why it was being brought out," as he once said.

Monroe's music has been far from static during the last half-century, but its elements have basically remained the same—Scots-Irish fiddle and bagpipe music, the lonesome blues, down-home gospel singing, and a driving beat that comes straight from Monroe's heart.

Monroe turned 78 September 13, but shows no signs of slowing down professionally, although he's eased the pace of his manual labor around his farm north of Nashville. He fully enjoyed the grand old celebration of his half-decade with the Opry—he starred in a 60-minute TNN special, sang and danced with Emmylou Harris during a special Opry segment, received a handmade presentation mandolin, among other tokens of recognition, and dispensed celebratory cake backstage after the show.

"Fifty years—think about it," Monroe said during his third Opry show of the day.[3] "It's really a long time, but I've really enjoyed it. They've treated me good at the Grand Ole Opry and I'm staying right here with 'em."

The nationally-televised duets with Harris were a highlight of the celebration. The "founder of new traditionalism" and the originator of bluegrass raised their

---

2. Bill would argue that bluegrass was "assembled" *before* he joined the Opry.

3. Bill and the band played an Opry matinee (not broadcast), the televised "Opry Live" portion at 7:30 P.M., and, later that night, the 10:45 P.M. show.

voices together on "Kentucky Waltz," "My Rose of Old Kentucky," and "Blue Moon of Kentucky," creating a unique and memorable blend.

"He puts us all to shame," Harris said of Monroe.

She came away from the experience saying that Monroe's Opry anniversary should be made a national holiday. Other top country and bluegrass stars talked about Monroe in TNN video clips seen before the live segment.

"I don't think he ever realized how much his music influenced American music," Ricky Skaggs said. "Buddy Holly was a dyed-in-the-wool Bill Monroe fan—Monroe's music was a big key to rockabilly." Dolly Parton recalled recording her version of "Mule Skinner Blues" because it had been her father's favorite song. She also summed up Monroe's achievement: "He put together a new sound." Ralph Stanley called Monroe "My favorite entertainer, one of the greatest entertainers that has ever been."

"I was always nervous to play with him," veteran banjoist Doug Dillard said on videotape. "I knew if I was playing his music, I wanted to play it right. Bill Monroe's been my idol for years in bluegrass."

TNN footage also showed Monroe in performances from the sixties and seventies and—in contemporary clips—riding horses and looking after livestock on his Sumner County farm. In a pre-show interview, Monroe talked of his hiring at the Opry in October 1939, when Opry officials told him if he ever left he'd have to fire himself.

"To say we are proud of Bill Monroe is an understatement," Opry manager Hal Durham said live on the Opry that night. "When you say 'bluegrass,' only one name comes to mind—Bill Monroe."

Durham presented Monroe with a lavish token of the Opry's appreciation, a handmade Barnes and Lamb mandolin complete with a carved likeness of Monroe's face as part of the headstock. Monroe gave the sparkling new mandolin the once-over, then grinned broadly as he spotted his own face looking out from among the tuners.

"There's Bill Monroe right there!" he told the Opry crowd as he pointed out the carved head.

The F-5-shaped mandolin bears the legend "Father of Bluegrass—Bill Monroe" on its face. The back has elaborate wood inlays and Monroe song titles as decoration. Barnes and Lamb are the Baton Rouge, Louisiana, instrument makers who have crafted presentation violins for Roy Acuff, John Hartford, Frazier Moss, and others.

Nashvillian Larry Cordle, composer of the Ricky Skaggs hit "Highway 40 Blues," appeared on the TNN Opry segment to sing "Kentucky King," a Monroe tribute song he wrote with hit tunesmith Jim Rushing. And *Bluegrass Unlimited* publisher Pete Kuykendall made an onstage presentation of a plaque commemorating Monroe's long tenure and achievements in music. Backstage after the show, Monroe helped cut a huge anniversary cake provided by the Opry, making sure his current Blue Grass Boys were on hand for picture-taking. A number of former Blue Grass Boys also turned up backstage: they included James Monroe, Roland White, Vic Jordan, Doug Hutchens, Wayne Lewis, Peter Rowan, and Bill Keith.

Rowan and Keith, two of the first northern, college-boy Blue Grass Boys of the sixties, were full of tales of Monroe's Station Inn appearance the Friday night before the big anniversary show. It was actually Rowan's show at the Nashville bluegrass haven—he was backed up by dobroist Jerry Douglas, bassist Roy Huskey, Jr., and drummer Larry Atamanuik, the last-named, like Rowan, a Seatrain[4] veteran. Keith, who was headed for a banjo workshop in Alabama, had been asked to sit in, but declined until Monroe walked in around midnight and took the stage.

"The magic took place," Rowan said of the all-star jam session. "There were some big sounds going down."

Rowan and Monroe sang "Walls of Time" together for the first time in years. Keith played "Devil's Dream," which turned into "Gray Eagle," which turned into "Sally Goodin." Monroe played for more than an hour, then, reportedly, sat down and ordered a pizza. The whole incident brought to mind something Monroe told me during an interview earlier this year.

"If you were playing music and I was playing music and we were both real young and you went ahead and got to doing good and I did pretty good, we'd want to see each other and speak and talk and play a little music together," he said. "That's the way bluegrass has stood down through the years."

All the activities surrounding the Opry celebration highlighted what may be Monroe's biggest year yet. In February, he won the first bluegrass Grammy ever awarded, for his *Southern Flavor* LP. In April, he received honorary membership in the Sonneck Society, a nationwide association of music educators and scholars, which held its annual meeting in Nashville. The society's annual award, previously given to classical composer Virgil Thomson and highly-regarded academic figures, had never gone to any performer (or any star) of popular music.

"By conferring honorary membership on Bill Monroe, the Sonneck Society recognizes a living treasure of American music," the society's Judith McCulloh said upon presenting the award.

"He transformed the old-time Anglo-American vocal and string band styles into a dynamic new genre."

Monroe's year was marred briefly by a May incident in which an Alabama dog trainer accused him of hitting her in the face with a Bible at his home. Monroe was cleared of the charges during the same month.

During the summer, Monroe and the Blue Grass Boys taped a series of performances at the Opry for his new live LP.[5] *Bill Monroe and the Blue Grass Boys Live at the Grand Ole Opry*[6] presents the man and his late-eighties band in crisp current recordings, but also includes a rare treat—a 1948 Opry performance of "New Mule Skinner Blues,"[7] recorded live at the old Ryman Auditorium.

---

4. The rock band Rowan joined after working with Bill.

5. This recording was released on cassette and compact disc only. See the editor's comments, second paragraph.

6. Correct title: *Live at the Opry: Celebrating 50 Years at the Grand Ole Opry.*

7. Incorrectly titled "New Mule Skinner Blues" on the release, this recording is actually a rendition of "Mule Skinner Blues."

Monroe kept up his customary hard-driving pace of public appearances in 1989—he'll chalk up about 150 dates for the year, according to Buddy Lee Attractions, his Nashville booking agents. He suffered poor health during a trip to Japan,[8] but staged a dramatic backstage recovery to star in a country music festival that drew more than 20,000 fans.

Fall saw the release of a fabulous four-CD Monroe package from Germany's Bear Family Records. *Bluegrass: 1950–1958*[9] presents previously unreleased tracks[10] as well as classic performances from one of Monroe's truly golden periods.

Originally published in *Bluegrass Unlimited* 24:6 (Dec. 1989): 9–11. Reprinted by permission of the author.

EDITOR'S COMMENTS

Goldsmith's coverage of the celebration of Bill's fiftieth anniversary on the Grand Ole Opry on October 28, 1989, appeared in the December 1989 issue of *Bluegrass Unlimited*.

Live at the Opry: Celebrating 50 Years at the Grand Ole Opry[1] was recorded in May and June of 1989 and released just before the anniversary on cassette and compact disc only. It was nominated for a Grammy in 1990.

The "previously unreleased tracks" ("My Carolina Sunshine Girl," "Ben Dewberry's Final Run," and "Those Gambler's Blues") on the first Bear Family boxed set of Bill's recordings (*Bill Monroe—Bluegrass: 1950–1958*),[2] were previously unreleased in the United States. They had been released in Japan in 1974 on *Bill Monroe and His Blue Grass Boys, Volume II*[3] and "bootleg" copies of the album, made in Germany and titled *Blue Grass Special*,[4] were available briefly in the United States in 1975.

What would be Bill's last project for MCA Records, the all-gospel *Cryin' Holy unto the Lord*,[5] was released in 1990.

Bill's daughter, Melissa Kathleen Monroe, fifty-four, died on December 3, 1990.

Notes

1. *Live at the Opry: Celebrating 50 Years at the Grand Ole Opry,* MCA Records, MCAC/MCAD-42286, released 1989.

2. *Bill Monroe—Bluegrass: 1950–1958,* Bear Family Records, BCD 15423, released fall 1989.

3. *Bill Monroe and His Blue Grass Boys, Volume II,* MCA Records, MCA-9269/71, released in Japan, 1974.

4. *Blue Grass Special,* unauthorized German release, BS 3, 1975.

5. *Cryin' Holy unto the Lord,* MCA Records, MCAC/MCAD-10017, released in 1990.

---

8. September 20–23, 1989.

9. *Bill Monroe—Bluegrass: 1950–1958,* Bear Family Records, BCD-15423.

10. These recordings had been released previously in Japan and Germany. See the editor's comments, third paragraph.

"On September 13, William Smith Monroe Turns Eighty"

RICHARD SPOTTSWOOD

If he didn't actually invent a classical American music, it's because no one ever really has. Did he create bluegrass? Yes, certainly—with brother Charlie in the mid-1930s, with his Opry band in 1939, with the Flatt-Scruggs-Wise-Rainwater organization again in 1945, and with the music he's written and performed ever since. You'd be hard put to name many others who've managed to be as consistently creative as Bill Monroe, who still regularly travels the highways with a hardworking band and manages to produce a new record every year.

At eighty years of age, Bill Monroe remains, unarguably, the very best performer on an instrument that few took seriously before he demonstrated its potential. A handful of surviving records by Italian-American mandolinists from the 1920s reveal a comparable degree of virtuosity, but in a style which was alien to the string band settings of southeastern America. Bill's mastery of his instrument was somewhat the result of accident. As the youngest of six[1] in a musical family, his first mandolin was the only available instrument in which older brothers and sisters took no interest.

Over the years, his instrumental technique developed, not from other mandolin players, but from what he absorbed from Uncle Pen's fiddle and Arnold Shultz's guitar. By the early thirties, when Bill, Birch, and Charlie were appearing with a square dance team on the WLS Barn Dance in Chicago,[2] Bill was paying attention to the hot string bands of the Prairie Ramblers and Georgia fiddler Clayton Mc-Michen, who were also regulars on the show. The former group is of particular interest. The Ramblers, like the Monroes, were western Kentuckians; fiddler Shelby "Tex" Atchison even hailed from Rosine. More important, bassist Jack Taylor was the first to appropriate that instrument from jazz and use it in a string band. Not long afterwards, it became a staple of western swing bands, along with the drums, piano, and guitar from jazz rhythm sections. Back east, Roy Acuff worked with a bass player named "Red" Jones on the former's first records in 1936. Bassist Amos Garen joined Bill in 1939 and was present when the Blue Grass Boys made their first Opry appearance in October; since then, the instrument has rarely been absent from a bluegrass band—or country bands either, for that matter.

The 1939 band also included Art Wooten, the first of a long line of world-class

---

1. Eight.
2. The brothers danced for the WLS National Barn Dance, not on it.

fiddlers like Tommy Magness, Gordon Terry, Chubby Wise, Kenny Baker, Bobby Hicks, Charlie Cline, Howdy Forrester, Benny Martin, and Tater Tate, who've graced the Blue Grass Boys over the years. Bill Monroe thinks, composes, and voices his instrument like a fiddler. However ambivalent he's felt over the years about the role of the banjo in bluegrass, fiddling has always been close to his heart and high on his list of musical priorities.

It's surprising to remember that the 1939 band was only a quartet, with Cleo Davis taking the part of lead singer and guitarist. Davis didn't last long enough to make the band's first record date of 1940, a year after it first appeared on the Opry. Clyde Moody, a man with solid qualities of his own, took over the spot, spending most of the war years with Monroe before successfully striking out on a solo career. Moody also had a worthy list of successors, including Pete Pyle, Lester Flatt, Jimmy Martin, Edd Mayfield, Del McCoury, Wayne Lewis, Tom Ewing. . . .

As for the banjo, that may be a different story. Certainly the sound Earl Scruggs got from that instrument, which came blasting out of AM radios in the 1940s, was both overwhelming and revolutionary. It had the subsequent effect of redefining the music in its own image, a process the reticent Mr. Monroe could only have halted by leaving the music. Even today, people who should know better consider the banjo the first requirement of bluegrass, despite the fact that Bill Monroe clearly has held other ideas. He liked the old-fashioned sound of the instrument, but didn't see fit to join it to the Blue Grass Boys until Stringbean joined in 1942—as a combination comic/instrumentalist in the old minstrel tradition, whose sound, judging from the records, never quite fit in.

Earl Scruggs, on the other hand, not only fit in, he threatened to run away with the show. Surely there were uncomfortable moments as audiences wildly cheered the young man whose revolutionary approach, to an instrument which had all but been discarded, sounded as dramatic as Monroe himself had ten years earlier. Whether he wanted to or not, Earl Scruggs routinely upstaged his boss for most of the time they worked together—and it's to Bill Monroe's everlasting credit that he didn't mind. The argument continues as to whether there was bluegrass before Scruggs; I feel there was, since the sounds of the mandolin, fiddle, rhythm instruments, and vocal duets, trios, and quartets were already in place before the war. But there's no question that the banjo was the last foundation block of the bluegrass sound in its classic form. Even the dobro, for all its contributions, has never become as essential to the fabric as the first five instruments. This is surely due to Monroe's refusal to have one in his band.

It's remarkable enough that Bill Monroe has survived to begin his eighty-first year on this planet, given the amount and intensity of his work, the endless miles of highway, and endless amounts of bad food consumed over those miles. But that he survives as the world's very best performer on his chosen instrument, as a singer with at least most of his voice (and all of his gifted ear) intact, and as a bandleader whose music continues to instruct and inspire, is truly phenomenal. Pianists like Vladimir Horowitz, Artur Rubenstein, and Eubie Blake survived into their eighties and beyond, but these were seated solo performers who worked when they chose rather than under the demanding and less rewarding conditions imposed even on a veteran musician of Monroe's status.

It would be hard to find another musical figure to whom Bill Monroe's multi-faceted achievements could be compared. Bob Wills comes close: like Bill, he created a new music by synthesizing and expanding on earlier styles, creating a successful formula whose effects have lasted for generations and, thereby, created new traditions out of old ones. The comparison fails only when you consider the two as actual musicians. Wills was a congenial old-style Texas fiddler who collected a broad array of talented musicians and allowed them to develop on their own. He created an eclectic mixture of the blues, hoedowns, country songs, pop songs, western songs, big and small band jazz, though he contributed only to the more traditional pieces he could comfortably play, leaving the hot licks to the likes of Joe Holley, Jesse Ashlock, and Johnny Gimble. Monroe, on the other hand, developed a unified set of music principles, teaching each sideman exactly what was necessary to make his music work and drawing his material from a limited range of country songs and composing hundreds—even to this day—to fit the bluegrass aesthetic. Even though Bill's descendants have departed from his model in numerous ways, it's safe to say that all of them are aware of the model itself and the musical integrity for which it so firmly stands.

Bluegrass has been a major American musical achievement, not only in its development but in its persistence and worldwide spread. Bill Monroe, who at one time saw those who emulated his music as claim-jumpers and competitors, has long since accepted Ralph Rinzler's early sixties designation of him as the Father of a discrete musical style.[3] If imitation is the sincerest form of flattery, Bill's thousands of flatterers pay tribute to him each time they pick up an instrument. I think it's safe (or soon will be) to number him among this century's greatest music figures, like Igor Stravinsky, Hank Williams, and Duke Ellington.

September 13 will be here shortly, and don't be surprised to see more tributes planned than the guest of honor can possibly keep up with. But the birthday gift is really the one Bill Monroe has given us—and it's the gift that keeps on giving.

Thank you, Bill, and Happy Birthday!

Originally published in *Bluegrass Unlimited* 26:3 (Sept. 1991): 27–28. Reprinted by permission of the author.

EDITOR'S COMMENTS

This birthday salute by one of the founders of *Bluegrass Unlimited* was included in the September 1991 issue. Just a few weeks before its publication, on August 9, Bill

---

3. Rinzler was not the first to call Bill the Father of Bluegrass, but his memorable validation of the designation might make it seem so.

underwent double-bypass heart surgery at Baptist Hospital in Nashville. By September 12, the day before his eightieth birthday, he willed himself able to play a few songs at his four-day Autumn Bluegrass Festival at Bean Blossom, and by the end of the weekend he was "jamming" onstage with the Kentucky Headhunters and Marty Stuart. It was an inspiring demonstration of the willpower Bill had often spoken of.

"Bill Monroe"

CHARLES WOLFE

It was a cold February day in 1950, and at two o'clock that afternoon Grand Ole Opry star Bill Monroe was driving down to the Tulane Hotel, on Church Street, in downtown Nashville. He was on his way to the Castle studios, a remodelled dining room in the hotel that had become Nashville's first real recording studio; there he would meet Paul Cohen, the A&R man for his new record label, Decca. In fact, Monroe's very first session for Decca was set for 2:30 that afternoon, with a second three-hour session scheduled for 7:30 that night. Monroe had seven songs ready, but even then he knew it would be a long day: He had a new, young band, most of whom had never recorded before, and a new producer to break in as well. And to top it all off, Monroe was in a crisis of sorts in his own career: Though his distinctive music was starting to take off, it was also threatening to get away from him, as young bands around the South began copying the "high lonesome sound." His new bosses at Decca seemed nervous about Monroe tying himself too much to this sound, and had been making noises about a more mainstream style.

On that day Monroe was 39 years old, and he had been recording for some 14 years—first with his brother Charlie on the old Bluebird label before World War II, then with his own bands for Bluebird and, since 1945, for Columbia. Each label had brought him major successes: "What Would You Give in Exchange for Your Soul?" with his brother on Bluebird; "Orange Blossom Special" and "In the Pines" with his pre-war band for Bluebird; and "Kentucky Waltz," "Footprints in the Snow," and "Little Community Church" for Columbia. Since September 1946 his recordings had included the singing and guitar of Lester Flatt and the revolutionary banjo sounds of Earl Scruggs. He had won national fame in the early 1940s by landing himself and his Blue Grass Boys a spot on the NBC network portion of the Grand Ole Opry, and the incredible popularity and influence of bandmembers Flatt and Scruggs had caused crowds at the old Ryman to shake the place with their screams and whistles. Monroe was popular enough to get his own tent show when he went on Opry tours, and for a time he even carried with him an amateur baseball team.

By the end of the decade, though, things were taking a different turn. For various reasons—some personal, some professional—both Flatt and Scruggs decided to leave the band in early 1948, and afterward decided to form their own band. "Bill might have always had the feeling that we planned it," Flatt explained years later, "but actually we hadn't." Monroe felt he had helped mold the two into the stars they were, and did not take kindly to their departure; he told them there was no way they could make it on their own. The bitterness was strong, and remained for years; it even extended to Monroe's trying to keep them off the Opry in the early 1950s.[1] As they started their new career in east Tennessee, Flatt and Scruggs were careful not to use the word "bluegrass" to describe their music—since the word was part of the actual band name used by Monroe—The Blue Grass (written as two words) Boys.[2] But inadvertently their fans conspired against them; not wanting to anger Lester and Earl by mentioning Monroe by name, fans started asking for the "old Blue Grass songs" they had done in the 1940s. The name stuck, and soon other people were using the name of Monroe's band as a generic term to describe the music played in that style.

Monroe was also finding out that fame bred imitation. Over in Bristol—the same place Flatt and Scruggs would go—in the late 1940s was another band called the Stanley Brothers who were becoming adept at copying Monroe's sound. Mac Wiseman, who had worked with Monroe in 1949, recalled: "When the Stanley Brothers first started, whatever Bill did Saturday night on the Opry, they did next on the Bristol program that they were on . . . . Well, Bill used to see red. He used to hate the word Stanley Brothers." The Stanley Brothers weren't really trying to rip off Monroe—they simply loved his music, and the way he did it. "It wasn't that they were out to steal corn out of his corn crib," says Wiseman. But things came to a head in September 1948, when the Stanleys did their cover of Monroe's famous race horse song, "Molly and Tenbrooks," and released it on the small independent label called Rich-R-Tone. The problem was that Monroe had not yet released his own record of the song—Columbia had held it back during the 1948 recording ban. To make matters worse, Monroe then learned that his own record company, Columbia, had signed the upstart Stanleys to a contract in March 1949, and had rushed them into the studios before scheduling any sessions with him. And worse yet, one of the first Columbia releases by the Stanleys (June 1949) was a song called "Let Me Be Your Friend" which bore a close resemblance to Monroe's most recent Columbia release, "It's a Dark Road to Travel"[3]—though it had composer credits to Carter Stanley. Monroe was understandably furious, and that fall decided to sever ties with Columbia. (He was even angrier with them the following fall, when they signed up his old sidemen, Flatt and Scruggs.)

---

1. Actually, there were few ill feelings between Bill and Flatt and Scruggs before 1953. See the editor's comments, second paragraph.

2. It's doubtful that Flatt and Scruggs would have even considered using the word "bluegrass" to describe their music at that point.

3. More correctly, it was *one of* Bill's most recent *releases.* "It's Mighty Dark to Travel" (actual title) was released in December 1948, and there were two other releases by Bill prior to June 1949.

But Monroe was far from feeling washed up on that February day as he walked into the Tulane Hotel. He had always responded well to challenge, and a couple of upstart bands trying to make it by playing what he considered "his" music weren't about to intimidate him. Two of his new musicians were singer-guitarist Jimmy Martin and fiddler Vassar Clements. Martin, who would later win fame on his own with songs like "Widow Maker," was from Sneedville, Tennessee, and was working as a painter when Monroe found him. "He had a wonderful voice that would really fit with mine," Monroe recalled later, in a memorable understatement. Young Vassar Clements was also destined for bigger things—the 1974 album *Hillbilly Jazz* would redefine the role of fiddle in country and bluegrass music. Like Chubby Wise, Vassar was from Florida, and in fact had met Monroe through Chubby; after auditioning with "Orange Blossom Special," Vassar was hired by Monroe to replace Chubby. "We had a number called 'The New Mule Skinner Blues,'" recalls Monroe. "Well, Vassar was powerful on that. He put some new notes in it that was fine, that every fiddler went searching for." Monroe especially liked Vassar's ability to play the blues; "there's fiddlers that could beat Vassar on 'Sally Goodin' or old-time fiddle numbers, but Vassar would beat 'em on a number like the 'Mule Skinner'—they wouldn't touch him on that."

In fact, "New Mule Skinner Blues" was one of the songs cut that February afternoon, and one that would become one of Monroe's best-known Decca sides. It was a remake of the old Jimmie Rodgers song Monroe had first cut back in 1940 for Victor—and the first song he had sung on the Opry.[4] "We don't do it the way Jimmie Rodgers sung it," Monroe notes. "It's speeded up." Monroe also brought to the session three new original songs, "My Little Georgia Rose," "Memories of You," and "I'm on My Way Back to the Old Home." All three were autobiographical—almost confessional—in nature; in "I'm on My Way Back to the Old Home" he was especially evocative at calling up the scenes of his youth in Rosine, with the echoes of the foxhounds running at night. Monroe's mother had died in 1921, when he was ten; his father (who had been 54 when Bill was born[5]) had died in 1927,[6] when Bill was 16. Now, as he entered his 40s himself, Monroe found himself thinking more about his childhood and his old homeplace.

That night, when the band reassembled for the second session, Monroe brought out two songs associated with his fellow Opry singer, Hank Williams. Banjoist Rudy Lyle recalled that during this time "Hank Williams used to prank with us a lot, especially at the Friday Night Frolic up at old WSM on 7th Avenue. . . . He used to always kid Bill about where he got his banjo players."

A few weeks before, Williams had given Monroe a song he had written called "Alabama Waltz." It was designed to take advantage of the fad for state-named waltzes—Monroe had done the "Kentucky Waltz," and everyone was cutting the

---

4. More likely, the first song he had sung *solo* on the Opry.

5. J. B. Monroe, born October 28, 1857, was almost fifty-four when Bill was born.

6. He died on January 14, 1928.

"Tennessee Waltz." Monroe also brought out "I'm Blue, I'm Lonesome," which, though credited on the label to "James B. Smith," was really the joint production of Monroe and Hank Williams. On tour with Williams, Monroe had been fooling around with the melody on his mandolin backstage, and Williams overheard him; he liked the tune and set words to it. For months the pair had sung the song backstage for their own amusement, and Monroe thought it was worth preserving on disc—even though Williams' MGM contract forbade him to sing on the session. Cohen agreed. By 10:30 that night, the session was over, and Paul Cohen declared that the new Decca artist was on his way. Monroe hoped so, too.

Unlike Monroe's A&R man at Columbia—the veteran Art Satherly, who tended to let Monroe go his own way—Paul Cohen was younger, more aggressive, and was determined to make Nashville into Decca's country and western center. He was also interested in creating sales, and was disappointed when Monroe's first Decca release, "New Mule Skinner Blues" and "My Little Georgia Rose," rushed out in March, fell with a thud; it failed to dent the charts, and was not even noted in *Billboard*. Cohen decided to find more commercial material. One number was suggested to him by Eli Oberstein, the former Bluebird executive who had been A&R man for the Monroe Brothers back in the 1930s. Oberstein had released it on his own independent Hit label: a song called "The Old Fiddler," written and sung by an Arkansas composer and singer named Hugh Ashley. Ashley had written the song to an old fiddle tune[7] played by a local character named Frank Watkins (though the old fiddler referred to in the lyric is called "Uncle Ben"). Cohen got the song to Monroe, persuaded him to record it at his very next session (April 8, 1950), and rushed it into release as his second single. Though *Billboard* noticed this one in its new release, it too sank like a stone—even with Williams' "Alabama Waltz" on the flip side.

"The Old Fiddler" did have an unexpected effect, though. Six months later, at the very next session, Monroe presented Cohen with his own version of a song about an old-time fiddler—not Uncle Ben, but "Uncle Pen." As Monroe explained it years later: "My uncle, Pen Vandiver, was one of Kentucky's old-time fiddlers, and he had the best shuffle with a bow that I'd ever seen, and kept the best time. That's one reason people asked him to play for the dances around Rosine. . . . My last years in Kentucky were spent with him." Monroe had gone to live with Pen Vandiver when his father died, and the teenager spent countless hours travelling with him to square dances and learning the rudiments of his music. Vandiver died in 1932, and during this "confessional" period, Monroe began to write a song about him.

Hugh Ashley always assumed that "The Old Fiddler" had inspired Monroe to write his own song about a fiddler, and this seems still likely, though Monroe himself has denied it. Rudy Lyle recalled that Monroe wrote the song "in the back seat of the car up on the Pennsylvania Turnpike on the way to Rising Sun, Maryland." Fiddler Merle "Red" Taylor, who later worked with Monroe, felt that he had come up with the fiddle part to the song after Monroe had sung some of the lyrics to him

7. The melody more closely resembles that of an old folk song, "Wreck of Old 97."

one night in a hotel room. Singer-guitarist Jimmy Martin, in his 20s at the time, also recalls helping Monroe work on the song "while riding on the bus and in little schoolhouse rooms." (Taylor played the fiddle on the original record of the piece, done in October 1950, and Martin and banjoist Lyle were also on the session.)

Cohen saw at once that this was a much better song than "The Old Fiddler," and rushed it out by Christmas, 1950. Though it never reached the charts, it sold well, was played everywhere, and was soon on its way to becoming a country standard (Porter Wagoner and Ricky Skaggs would later each do remakes of it).

Even so, Cohen and Decca remained dubious about the "old-time" sound of Monroe's all-acoustic Blue Grass Boys band, and decided to try with Monroe what they had done with most of their other Nashville singers: have them record not with their own bands, but with a special team of crack studio men. An opportunity to try the plan came sooner than they expected. In March 1951, Cohen got wind of the fact that Eddy Arnold had recorded a version of Monroe's old 1946 hit, "Kentucky Waltz," and decided to rush Monroe back into the studio to do a new cover of his own song. The trouble was that Monroe was on tour, and to fly the whole band back to Nashville was more than the company would pay. Finally, Monroe himself was flown back and put in the studio with some of Nashville's best session men: electric guitar player Grady Martin, fiddler Tommy Jackson, even Farris Coursey on drums. On "Kentucky Waltz," Owen Bradley even played a skating-rink organ— on others a romping honky-tonk piano. One song from the session, a souped-up version of "The Prisoner's Song," featured Grady Martin's electric guitar to the point where the arrangement approached rockabilly. The session marked the first time Monroe had recorded with electric instruments and drums; not wanting to make waves with his new producer, he cooperated.

Cohen liked the sound, and in April scheduled more sessions under the new format. This time he let Monroe use his regular banjo player, Rudy Lyle, but once again added a drummer, an electric guitarist, and bass player Ernie Newton. Oddly, most of the cuts were versions of Jimmie Rodgers' songs, cut to cover Columbia's set of Rodgers' songs done by Lefty Frizzell. This time, Decca realized the experiment wasn't working. Owen Bradley, who was now Cohen's assistant and actually overseeing many of the sessions, recalled how much Monroe himself disliked these arrangements; many of the cuts were not even issued at the time. Decca's marketing people had even tried advertising some of the sides—such as "Lonesome Truck Driver's Blues," a shameless cover of Bob Newman's King hit—in *Billboard* with no reference at all to "The Blue Grass Boys." But trying to separate Monroe from his "sound" or band merely irritated his old fans, and won no new ones. By the end of 1951, Decca had given up, and Monroe himself had seen the danger of trying to modernize his style.

A story Owen Bradley tells reflects just how much Decca gave in. At one session later that year, scheduled for 8:30 in the morning—an ungodly hour for most, but one that didn't bother Monroe in the slightest—Bradley assigned an assistant just down from New York to oversee things. About noon, Bradley got a call from the new man; he'd been in the studio an hour with Monroe, and had only finished one song. "And I can't understand a word he says," he concluded. Bradley told him not to worry—let Monroe do what he wants, and when he feels the take is right, go on to the next one. In other words, let Monroe be Monroe.

The New Yorker finally agreed, and the session concluded. With it came a production style that would endure for the next four decades and beyond—that would see both Decca (now MCA) and Monroe through one of the longest artist-company relationships in country music history. For Monroe, it was an important victory, as well as a vital watershed in his own career. He had weathered a serious crisis, but now was ready to embark on the most productive decade of his career.

Originally published in *The Journal of the American Academy for the Preservation of Old-Time Country Music* 16 (Aug. 1993): 8–11. Reprinted by permission of Sussex Publishers, Inc.

EDITOR'S COMMENTS

Wolfe recreated some of the important events in Bill's career in the early 1950s for the August 1993 issue of *The Journal of the American Academy for the Preservation of Old-Time Country Music,* a publication of *Country Music* magazine. This article was based on his research in the writing of the informative booklet for the first Bear Family boxed set of Bill's Decca recordings.

Contrary to popular belief (which is restated here), there were few, if any, ill feelings between Bill and Flatt and Scruggs before 1953. There's no doubt that Bill was unhappy when these two great performers left the Blue Grass Boys. But after Flatt and Scruggs teamed up, Bill reportedly guested on their radio shows throughout the South, to advertise his appearances, and their relationship wasn't unfriendly. In the summer of 1953, however, the twosome's new sponsor, Martha White Mills, brought them to Nashville, gave them an early morning radio show on WSM, and began to seek Grand Ole Opry membership for them. At that point, in Bill's eyes, Flatt and Scruggs became his competitors.[1]

Note

1. Conclusions drawn here are based on conversations with Earl Scruggs (1995) and Mac Wiseman (1996–98).

Bill Monroe and the Blue Grass Boys:
Live Recordings, 1956–1969, vol. 1:
Off the Record (booklet excerpts)

RALPH RINZLER

A Visit to Rosine and Other Observations

In late July 1963, Bill Monroe asked Del McCoury[1] and me to accompany him on a trip from Nashville to Rosine, Kentucky. As agreed, we met Bill in the parking lot at Goodlettsville. We had difficulty finding him because, though he was standing near-by clad in baggy bib overalls and a baseball cap, he looked nothing like the dapper Bill Monroe we were used to as a performer. In the back of his pickup truck were two hound dogs destined for his brother Charlie and two piglets for his brother Speed.[2] On arriving in Rosine, we delivered the animals, and Charlie immediately insisted that they try out the dogs' ability to speak, taking us into the woods for a sojourn which lasted until the wee hours of the morning. There was no trace of the often overemphasized animosity between them. Del and I were regaled with jokes and stories about the old days.

After about three hours of sleep, Bill awakened Del and me, and following a quick breakfast with Charlie, Bill led us up the hill to his childhood home. As we approached it, he recounted the story of his returning to Rosine in his late teens for the first time after his initial departure and the pain he felt at seeing no light in the window of his old home. He stressed that this was the first time that he understood fully how alone he felt in the world and noted that this experience was the impetus for his writing the song "I'm on My Way to the Old Home." Monroe's mandolin solo on the magnificent February 3, 1950, Decca studio recording of this song cries out of the wrenching pain of this experience.

On reaching the top of the hill where the house stood, Bill further explained that the path on which we were now standing was formerly the main road between Rosine and the next town.[3] He recounted his practice of running and hiding in the barn when he saw strangers coming down the road, because he did not want to put up with the derision of those who found his crossed eyes an opportunity for ridi-cule. He then took us down to the barn where we discovered that a trunk full of his father's papers, correspondence, and farm transaction logs had been scattered out

---

1. McCoury had joined the Blue Grass Boys about four months earlier, in March 1963.
2. Speed Monroe, then sixty-eight and Bill's oldest living brother, died in 1967.
3. Possibly Hartford, the Ohio County seat, about five miles to the west.

across the floor. He expressed a combination of rage and despair at his brothers' lack of respect for their father's documents. We spent an hour gathering all the papers and replacing them in the trunk, which we then took back to Nashville. At my request, Bill gave me two of the numerous log books his father so meticulously kept. He described his pride at the care and precision of his father's documentation and noted his sense of satisfaction that his family was both literate and highly competent in basic mathematics. The message that I derived from that experience with Bill was that his music was only one aspect of the deep commitment he felt to his family and regional culture.

✍

If you were driving him a long distance at night and he was concerned about the driver staying awake, he would draw on his extensive body of philosophical thought and historical incident, recounting stories that he knew would keep you from falling asleep at the wheel. In contrast, on many occasions when the Blue Grass Boys were on the road with Bill and Bessie, the 1958 station wagon,[4] which had already travelled about 250,000 miles, was loaded with string bass, all the other instruments, six people, and their luggage. Under these conditions, Bill could withdraw into a pensive silence that might last two or more days. He was never unpleasant or glum, one never knew if he was composing tunes or studying on the past or planning some aspect of his musical development, but not a word was spoken by Bill and consequently anyone else in the car.[5] Occasionally Bill or Bessie would instruct the driver to pull into a gas station or restaurant. On entering the restaurant the band would take a table, Bill would either go to the telephone booth or the washroom and, on emerging, would sit alone at a table at the opposite end of the room.[6] The days of silence did create mild tension under the circumstances . . . particularly when days of travel were sparsely dotted with performances but the long distances required that we drive all night and never sleep in a bed for as many as three days at a stretch. Sometimes after a few days of silence, Bill would come up with a melody which he'd either sing or pick out on the mandolin. Sometimes he might have a refrain to go with it, or would ask the group in the car to help him set words to the refrain.[7] He would then teach the vocal lead to his singer and they would rehearse the song without any verses as a means of honing it and establishing it in

---

4. That same old Oldsmobile that Neil V. Rosenberg saw at Bean Blossom (see excerpts from *Bill Monroe and His Blue Grass Boys: An Illustrated Discography*).

5. In later years, Bill would still "withdraw into a pensive silence." See the editor's comments, second paragraph.

6. Traveling in a roomier tour bus in the eighties and nineties, Bill would almost never seek this kind of privacy.

7. It was common for Bill to ask for help in writing a song. See the editor's comments, third paragraph.

memory. Thus, life on the road was fascinating, exhausting, and worth everything it took out of you.

Originally published in the booklet for *Bill Monroe and the Blue Grass Boys: Live Recordings, 1955–1959,* vol. 1: *Off the Record,* Smithsonian/Folkways, SF CD 40063. © 1993. Reprinted by permission of Smithsonian/Folkways Records.

EDITOR'S COMMENTS

Rinzler's recollections of his travels with Bill in the early 1960s were included among his notes for this 1993 Smithsonian/Folkways CD release.

In later years Bill would still "withdraw into a pensive silence," but never for as long as Rinzler observed in the sixties. Most noticeable after performances, his silences had the same effect on others, however, and the bus was usually a very quiet place after shows. For Bill, those times seemed to be a respite from the clamor and noise of the day, a much-needed time out for this basically quiet and introspective person.

As Rinzler described here, it was common in the early years for Bill to ask band members for help in writing a song. In a recent interview, Mac Wiseman recalled writing the last verse of "I'm on My Way Back to the Old Home," for which he never claimed credit.[1]

Note

1. Interview with Mac Wiseman, May 6, 1997.

"Bill Monroe Has Lots to Sing but Little to Say"

JASON DePARLE

GOODLETTSVILLE, Tennessee—The Father of Bluegrass Music was walking slowly and nursing a bruised bottom.

He had risen at dawn in the century-old cabin where he has lived for 40 years[1] and stalked across a buttercup field on his way to feed the hens. He fell and landed on a rock.

"Boy, you really have to watch when you get older," he said later, less to his visitors than to his own, disbelieving self.

A half-century ago, Bill Monroe melded a mandolin and a yodel into an art form

---

1. Not continuously.

called bluegrass, and traveled so relentlessly that his stamina was nearly as renowned as his music. But at 82, he is suffering from more than bruises.

He injured his arm over the winter, fractured his hip in March, and all but broke his heart in April, when debts forced him to put his 288-acre homestead here on the auction block.

While Mr. Monroe was too proud to seek money from his scores of musical protégés, the blow of the sale was cushioned by the owner of the Grand Ole Opry, where he has performed for nearly 55 years. The owner, Gaylord Entertainment Company, bought the property for $300,000, agreeing to let him use the cabin and the surrounding 14 acres for the rest of his life.

"It's a shame," Mr. Monroe said, speaking of the sale. "You hate to lose anything like that."

Legendary Stubbornness

A visit with Mr. Monroe on his rustic porch is largely a nonverbal affair. About one question in four moves him to an answer, often a monosyllabic one. He responds to an inquiry about songwriting by asking the cost of a visitor's shoes.

His stubbornness is part of his legend. After Lester Flatt and Earl Scruggs left his band in 1948 to find their own niche in the maturing genre, he refused to speak to them for 23 years.[2]

While Mr. Monroe's friends say he has mellowed, this was not apparent when he told a visitor that his walkway contained a stone from every state. "Really?" the visitor asked.

"Why would I lie?" he snapped, his fierce blue eyes bracketed by white mutton chops. "I ain't a Yankee."

His losses are large, but so too is the air of reverence that surrounds him. Ricky Skaggs, John Hartford, and other disciples come to collect songs and stories on his porch. A doting young housekeeper prepares his meals, and a church friend ferries him in a white Cadillac to his weekend appearances at the Opry.

A definitive compact disc collection is due out from MCA within a month, featuring 98 of his more than 500 recordings and an engaging text by John Rumble, a historian at the Country Music Foundation in Nashville.[3] And on June 16, Mr. Monroe will be the host at his 26th annual music festival in Bean Blossom, Indiana.

Making peace with Mr. Monroe after a long estrangement, his former banjo player, Butch Robins,[4] was stunned at his mentor's physical and financial worries. "He's just an old man who needs some friends right now," Mr. Robins said, tears in his eyes.

---

2. Probably closer to seventeen years, from 1953 until 1970, when Scruggs appeared at Bean Blossom.

3. *The Music of Bill Monroe: From 1935 to 1994*, MCA Records, MCAC/MCAD4-11048, released in Aug. 1994.

4. 1977–81.

But when Mr. Monroe was asked to sum up his own circumstances, his voice grew soft and grateful.

"It's great to be the Father of Bluegrass Music," he said. "I have my friends and my fans all over the world. And I want to thank the Lord for being with me all the way."

Learning from His Uncle

He grew up the youngest of eight farm children in Rosine, Kentucky, about 30 miles north of Bowling Green. Plagued by a crossed eye and ashamed of his appearance, he would hide behind the barn when strangers came to visit.

His mother fiddled and sang, and his uncle, Pendleton Vandiver, was an accomplished fiddler who helped impart Bill's sense of timing. But when his older brothers commandeered the more popular instruments, fiddle and guitar, Bill was left to hone his talent on a $3 mandolin. His parents had died by the time he turned 16,[5] and his aloneness was virtually complete.

"It was a hard life, to come up with no money," he said. "You'd sing a lot of sad songs. It'd really touch you back then, the old-time songs like that."

Mr. Monroe's brothers coaxed him out of Kentucky during the Depression for a job outside Chicago. He formed a band there with his brother Charlie, and they hit the road, sponsored by a laxative company. The quarrelsome duo split in 1938, and a year later, Mr. Monroe landed a job at the Opry.

He named his band "the Blue Grass Boys" after his home state, and an entire branch of American music then named itself after his band. In describing Mr. Monroe's precision and speed, one critic argued that he was "less playing the mandolin than piloting it."[6]

Three crucial years began in 1945, with the addition of Mr. Flatt on guitar and Mr. Scruggs on banjo. Mr. Scruggs' banjo style, with its revolutionary three-finger roll, supplied the final, essential ingredient to the sound Mr. Monroe was creating, one characterized by his high tenor and syncopated rhythm and his band's competitive, driving solos.

But his two disciples left him after three years of low pay and long travel.

The folk movement of the early 1960s brought Mr. Monroe a new surge of popularity, after rock 'n' roll had pushed him aside.

While the new generation celebrated him as an embodiment of a noncommercial past, Mr. Rumble noted they were forgetting the showman's roots in the tent shows and vaudeville acts typical of early country music past. Mr. Monroe's early comic skits not only featured blackface routines, but also had him sometimes performing female roles in a dress.[7]

---

5. Bill's father died after Bill had turned sixteen.

6. Robert Cantwell, in *Bluegrass Breakdown,* describing Bill's playing on the original recording of "Blue Grass Breakdown."

7. In these cases, Bill was not unlike most country music entertainers of the day.

Handshake Still Strong

In latter decades, Mr. Monroe has carefully cultivated the image of the churchgoing patriarch.[8] When the Nitty Gritty Dirt Band assembled a group of his peers for the recording session that produced the 1972 album *Will the Circle Be Unbroken,* he refused to attend. He said the band members wore their hair too long.[9]

Mr. Monroe's own white hair is shaggy these days, stretching toward the collar of his blue flannel shirt. The rhinestones on his lapel shimmer: "Jesus." His legs are weak, but he shakes hands as if he is pulling a fence post.

It is loud in Mr. Monroe's part of the country. The green hills outside of Nashville seem determined to compensate for his reticence with a clamor of ducks, roosters, dogs, and birds.[10] Noting the sound, Mr. Robins, the visiting banjo player, recalled the time long ago when Mr. Monroe made a confession:

"He looked at me real funny and said: 'You know, I never wrote a tune in my life. All that music's in the air around you all the time. I was just the first one to reach up and pull it out.'"

Good Words for a Song

Strolling through his yard, Mr. Monroe began what promised to be an engaging description of the origins of "Blue Moon of Kentucky," perhaps his most famous song.

"I was coming from Florida to Virginia one time," he said. "I thought the words 'blue moon' would be good to put in a song."

But the story ended there.

"I thought it was a fine one," was Mr. Monroe's last word about the tune, which he first recorded in 1946.

The song was rerecorded in 1954 by one of the master's young fans, Elvis Presley, who sped it up and made it the flip side of his first single.

"He come and apologized for changing it the way he did," Mr. Monroe said. "I said if it'd help him get his start, I was for it 100 percent."

A long moment of silence ensued, and Mr. Monroe ended it by declaring, "I was baptized in the River of Jordan." The baptism occurred about a decade ago during a musical tour of Israel.

Mandolin-Shaped Clocks

Mr. Monroe's cabin is close and dark, with a hearth blackened by a century of fire. There are a dozen Stetsons of various hues adorning hall pegs, and a collectors' plate from every state hanging in the kitchen.

---

8. It is doubtful that Bill "cultivated" this image. He *was* a churchgoing patriarch.

9. An unknown reference. Bill's comments in "Bill Monroe: From Refined Oil to Slick Music," by Jack Hurst, had more to do with the Dirt Band's music than their hair.

10. Drowning out the crickets, no doubt.

There are mandolin-shaped clocks, a Bible, a ceramic puppy, and a jar of jelly beans. But there are no records in sight, no tapes, and no compact discs. "I haven't listened to them in so long, I can't remember what I've got," he said.

Mr. Monroe has boasted of his physical strength throughout his life, and he still tells the story of how he once balanced five men on a beam across his back.

His relentless touring made his family life, with two children, less sturdy. He has divorced twice, the second time after a brief marriage in 1985. Shortly thereafter someone broke into the cabin and shattered his treasured mandolin.[11]

"Oh, man, they tore it up," he said. "People that would break your mandolin, they really hate you."

Splintered into nearly 200 pieces, the instrument seemed unsalvageable. But a technician at the Gibson company spent three months reassembling the 1923 model with tweezers.

Dancing a Jig Onstage

Though his finances have soured in recent years because of some bad investments, Mr. Monroe said he declined an offer to sell the mandolin for $60,000.

When the visit ended, Mr. Monroe soaked his bruise, donned his hat, and departed for the Opry, where for 15 minutes he was again a younger man. He swapped licks with Ricky Skaggs, danced a jig, and disappeared backstage into a sea of sequins, pompadours, and autograph seekers.

Friends took him to the Opryland Shoney's[12] for dinner, where he nodded at fans and carped at the teenage waiter who served him apple pie in a foam-plastic container rather than on a plate. "Anybody don't know better's pitiful," he said.[13]

With three hours to kill before his second 15-minute show, which would end at midnight, Mr. Monroe returned to Dressing Room 2, where dozens of light bulbs danced off the mirrors and a bluegrass band seemed determined to raise the roof.

Bill Monroe didn't seem to mind. He tucked his hat over his eyes, locked his chin into his hand, and fell asleep.[14]

Originally published in *The New York Times,* June 9, 1994. © 1994 by *The New York Times.* Reprinted by permission.

EDITOR'S COMMENTS

By 1994 Bill's physical and financial problems began to catch up with him. Still weakened by his heart operation and often unsteady on his feet, he fell and frac-

---

11. The break-in occurred on November 13, 1985, before Bill and Della Monroe were divorced.

12. The Shoney's near Opryland. (The Shoney's Big Boy restaurant chain, mentioned in "Daddy Bluegrass and His Blues," by Martha Hume, has become Shoney's.)

13. It was common at this point for Bill to eat only one or two bites of pie. The waiter had probably been told to put it in this container so Bill could take the uneaten portion with him.

14. The publication of this article provoked widespread concern for Bill's plight. See the editor's comments, second paragraph.

tured his wrist on February 6. On March 7, he fell again and fractured his hip, and was immobilized for four weeks after hip replacement surgery. Then, on April 23, his farm was sold at auction to stave off creditors. (Asked at the end of the auction if there was anything he wanted to say, Bill sang a few lines of "Blue Moon of Kentucky," walked in the house, and shut the door.)

The publication of this less-than-flattering article in *The New York Times* on June 9 had a positive outcome: it aroused widespread concern for Bill's plight, especially in the bluegrass community. As a result, James Monroe was prompted to explain publicly with an "advertorial" in the September 1994 issue of *Bluegrass Unlimited.* It reassured readers that plans to sell the farm had always included a provision permitting Bill to live there for the rest of his life and claimed that James and his father, as business partners, were equally responsible for their financial woes.

Ralph Rinzler, born in Passaic, New Jersey, on July 20, 1934, died less than a month after this *New York Times* article was published, on July 2, 1994.

In 1995, Bill's fifty-sixth anniversary on the Grand Ole Opry, like his fiftieth, fell on the day and date he first performed on the show, Saturday, October 28. Unfortunately, Bill was ill with pneumonia and unable to perform on what would be his last Opry anniversary.

"Nobody Does It Like Bill"

JACK FLIPPIN

The first bluegrass festival I ever attended, Bill Monroe and the Blue Grass Boys were there; no greater introduction to festivals could I have known. The year was 1972 in crisp October; the venue was the public park of the village of Pioneer, Texas.

Earl Niemeyer and I had packed our clothes and banjos into his station wagon in Lubbock and driven 170 miles for the momentous event. Now we had arrived on this Friday evening and were waiting for the frosty-headed Bill to make his appearance on the wooden stage, adrenal excitement and palpitating anticipation building in my innards by the minute. For in a deeper sense, I had come an even longer way to experience this immortalized member of the Country Music Hall of Fame.

Twice over the years I had attended performances by Lester Flatt and Earl Scruggs and the Foggy Mountain Boys. Certainly they had not disappointed. But this time I was at an open-air bluegrass festival for the first time and, perhaps even more significantly, sensed I was getting back to the source, the core, the where-it-started: aware that the headliner of this fete had once employed Lester Flatt and Earl Scruggs as two of his Blue Grass Boys. And was known as the Father of Bluegrass.

✍

My first contact with the name Bill Monroe had been circa 1962, listening to Elvis Presley. My favorite of the King's recordings was "Blue Moon of Kentucky," and I had checked the label to see who had written such plaintive lyrics and soaring melody. Seeing the name in parenthesis, I had assumed Bill Monroe was a rhythm-and-blues songwriter—and an inspired one.

During the following year or two, I had seen Bill Monroe (surely not the same man who'd written the Elvis song) and the Blue Grass Boys regularly on Jack Linkletter's Saturday afternoon TV campus "Hootenanny" (Bill was one of the few Grand Ole Opry performers who could fit into the country and folk formats). He and his troupe had awed me with their twin-fiddle breakdown renditions of "Uncle Pen," "Footprints in the Snow," and other standards. Though not yet accustomed to his high-pitched singing, I sensed something true and real in this avuncular white-hat with the regal bearing and droll Appalachian twang. His expert, swift mandolin leads showed me from the get-go that here was no promo-hyped chord-strumming hack showman with a cadre of hired-gun fast-fingered fretmen bathing him in their pro sound to make him sound like a "musician." Raised on the sounds of Nashville, I was accustomed to seeing that deception and was picker enough myself to know the difference. To me it was evident that Bill himself was every bit the virtuoso that anybody backing him was. He had earned my respect.

Still, while Bill and his Boys were instrumental in dyeing my wool in the homespun hues of bluegrass, I remember apologizing to my friends while playing them Monroe's records: *Yes, I know, his voice is awful and they ought to get a good singer to handle the vocals, but just listen to that banjo; get a load of those twin fiddles: and that's ol' Bill himself on the mandolin. Isn't that something?* (Actually, as I was getting better acquainted with his authentic mountain singing, I was slowly developing an ear for his voice. In apologizing, I was merely attempting to accommodate to my pals' initial reactions to Bill.)

In time I became acquainted with affectionate jests about the legendary laryngeal stratospherics of the Grand Patriarch of bluegrass: ". . . that was so high it would take Bill Monroe to sing bass to it . . ." And, ". . . it matters not how high the moon. Bill Monroe can still sing tenor to it. . . ."

When I heard about a bluegrass group named the Monroe Doctrine, I sensed how deep is his mark, his signet on the whole genre.

And yes, ever so gradually, I had come to see (hear?) his voice as his trademark. To reject Monroe for his voice would be like turning down Louis "Satchmo" Armstrong for his gravelly scat-style intonations and disdaining Jimmy Durante because of his outsized schnozzola.

In 1970, southern journalist Paul Hemphill published his book *The Nashville Sound: Bright Lights and Country Music.* In recounting a Saturday night Grand Ole Opry performance, he reported, "The Blue Grass Boys positioned themselves behind the closed curtain, dressed in black tuxedos and ten-gallon hats, looking as grim as life-insurance agents delivering a death payoff—a mandolin, a banjo, a bass, a guitar, and two fiddles—Monroe holding his mandolin at the ready while he looked up at the glassed-in control booth for the signal to start. When the curtain swung open, the crowd hooted and stomped as the Blue Grass Boys flew into a classic bluegrass tune with the haunting sound of unamplified fiddle runs and a flying bass and a sprightly mandolin. . . ."

True enough. Bill didn't hire showmen. He hired musicians.

In the fall of that same year, both Bill and the Carter Family were formally inaugurated, in CMA ceremonies, into the Country Music Hall of Fame. The brief dedicatory tribute to Monroe said something to the effect that he had earned his place in the sun "without using electrified instruments." *Oh?* I remember thinking, *Is steadfastness to the old acoustical instruments suddenly experiencing a renaissance in Nashville?* And of course I knew it wasn't. Still, in the deep recesses of the essence of my fence-row being, I felt a warm sense of gratitude in that homage to Bill, discerning that country music, at least, hadn't forgotten where it came from.

⚘

A tour bus pulled on the grounds near the stage and a group of men carrying instrument cases came filing out. "That's him! That's Billy *Mun*-roe if I ever saw him!" gushed an old nester near me. I peered vainly into the semi-darkness, not recognizing anyone.

Soon Bill and his white-shirted, necktied, Texas-hatted crew materialized on the stage, placed themselves behind microphones, and jump-started into nimble motion on the lustrous Appalachian allegro that elevated Bill and others of his ilk to renown. Seeming to need no warmup, they mesmerized the crowd, performing such standards as "Mule Skinner Blues," "Blue Grass Breakdown," "Raw Hide," and one I particularly recall: "My Old Kentucky and You." If the attentions of anyone in the audience were diverted elsewhere, I failed to detect it, not that I was watching the spectators. For once, here was a performing group that didn't have to adhere to the tried-and-true show-biz axiom, "Leave 'em while they're still begging for more." I firmly believed (and still do) that had Bill & Co. played until midnight, no one would have left. *I* wouldn't have.

It was more than the music itself. We would be treated to bluegrass all weekend long, we knew: Jim and Jesse, the Stone Mountain Boys, the Goins Brothers, James Monroe . . . but in this unforgettable set, here standing before us was a larger-than-life legend, enhanced by his able minions. We concentrated on the moment, as if to etch it in bas-relief upon our consciousness forever.

He introduced his Blue Grass Boys: Kenny Baker on fiddle, Jack Hicks on banjo, Monroe Fields on bass, and Joe Stuart on guitar. There were winged creatures buzzing about the lights on the stage, causing some consternation among the group. "Boss, they sure got some big bugs down here in Texas," everyone heard Kenny Baker remark, swatting at one with his fiddle bow. Running through my mind upon hearing that was, *imagine being able to address Bill Monroe as "Boss": these fellows stand at the very pinnacle of bluegrass.* I stood in envy of them.

At one point, Monroe related to the audience, "One of Elvis Presley's first records was 'Blue Moon of Kentucky.' Now, I wrote that song, Elvis made a record of it, and . . . that's all right. He did it his own way and . . . that's all right."

Ah. Once and for all, the mystery was solved.

That night I slept in the back of Earl's station wagon while he sprawled on a seat. Others around us slept in even less commodious conditions. Earl and I noted one long-haired fellow making his "bed" on the running board of an automobile of some antiquity. *Welcome to bluegrass festivals,* I deadpanned to myself, adjusting the pillow under my head. Still I slept well, sweet music ringing in my ears.

I was enjoying myself, yes.

Monroe and his coterie performed some more the following day, as did other groups. I was privileged to meet such luminaries as Eddie Shelton, Wayne Harris, Jimmy Henley, Ronnie Gill, and others. It was a veritable honor roll of Texas bluegrass.

One of the entrepreneurs who put on the show drew a thunderous round of applause when he stood on the stage and postulated that, "Bluegrass is the soul of country music." Surely no one present would dispute that.

Earl and I left the following evening after sundown. As we departed, I took one last, lingering, longing look at the stage and noted Vic Jordan and his banjo accompanying Jim and Jesse in their nighttime set. When we were out of earshot, Earl asked me, "Can you still hear the banjos, fiddles, and mandolins ringing in your ears?"

Yes, I certainly could, I responded, and wanted that sonance to remain in my consciousness all the way back to Lubbock. But the sounds gradually faded as Earl and I drifted into conversation. We had much to talk about.

I told Earl that attending my first bluegrass festival had been an experience. But seeing the Great Man . . . hearing him perform . . . that was the most impressive of all.

✍

In the issue of *Time* that was published July 4, 1977, Roger Wolmuth submitted the following lines:

It is a sticky, hot night and several hundred people wait on hard wooden benches. Fireflies flicker, and on a small, lighted stage four country-suited musicians quietly fidget. In their midst stands an imposing figure in white and wearing a broad-brimmed hat. "I once played the mandolin all the way from Fort Wayne to Nashville without stopping," he thunders into a microphone. "Don't think I can't play all night if I want to!" As the crowd cheers, the big man leans forward and madly strums the opening riffs to "Orange Blossom Special."[1] Says a woman in the second row, "I just love it when Bill gets to roaring like that."

1. Bill seldom if ever played "opening riffs" for "Orange Blossom Special."

The roaring lion is Bill Monroe, 65, the patriarch of bluegrass music for more than three decades.

Make that five-going-on-six decades (Bill Monroe is now 84). In the meantime, sometime in the 1980s, the late Conway Twitty recorded "Boogie Grass Band," a driving, breakdown-rhythmed ode employing banjo and fiddle, among other stringed boxes. "I love to heeear . . . Bill sing about Kentucky," crowed this ex–rock 'n' roll country growler, as I listened in amazement. For once, Conway Twitty and I agreed on something.

✍

This feeling is reinforced in the current documentary film *High Lonesome*,[2] which engraves the persona of Bill Monroe once and forever upon the psyches of the partisans who behold him in his natural setting. At the beginning, there is a goose-pimply feeling of homecoming pathos as Bill takes us through the creaky-hinged door of his childhood old Kentucky home where "there's no light in the window." The melancholy scene would not be complete without the mourning doves lending their cooing dirges to the mood of the moment. That neglected frame shack must be haunted still by the ghosts of Bill's mother and uncle Pen, fiddles in hands, the faint spectral echoes of their shuffle-bowed catgut strings ringing along the bare walls.

It is apparent that Bill is not reading the words he utters, not from a teleprompter or anything else. They are just flowing from him as a rivulet from a mountain spring, spontaneous, unrehearsed, with no attempts at rhetoric. Yet poignant. The listener clings to every word. Leave the standardized timbre of a TV anchorman to the networks. It does not belong here.

High Lonesome accentuates the fact that Bill, like so many midsouthern ridge-runners in the 1930s, had to leave the nature-carved beauty of his native have-not precincts to go north to midwestern factories where the jobs were. Such reluctant emigrants as Bill and brothers Charlie and Birch were surely glad to be earning regular paychecks, even if it meant isolation from their familiar corrugated land and its people, which they, in their removed state, revered in song and story.

In tracing the origins of bluegrass, Bill gives us something to ponder which might surprise some of us. We banjo pickers like to think our five-stringed gourd is, instrumentally, what bluegrass is all about. Actually, we flatter ourselves. In *High Lonesome,* Bill sets the record straight: Bluegrass, in rhythm and structure, was built around the mandolin: Bill Monroe's own, to be exact. The banjo, fiddle, dobro, occasional lead guitar—they all followed the melodic path blazed by his mandolin. Now, it is true that ever since Earl Scruggs introduced the three-finger roll to the genre in about 1946, the five-string banjo has provided the signature sound of bluegrass. Indeed, while a bluegrass group can operate without a mandolin (as did Flatt

---

2. *High Lonesome: The Story of Bluegrass Music,* by Rachel Liebling, was released on video (Shanachie 604) in 1994.

and Scruggs)[3] or without a fiddle (the Dillards), a bluegrass group sans a banjo to many is like a circus without elephants: a contradiction in terms. Nevertheless, let not any vain five-string picker presume that from his instrument is where it all started. No, what Bill told us is true. Thus it is logical to conclude that the two greatest contributors to the sound of bluegrass are Bill Monroe and Earl Scruggs. In that order, yes.

✍

We of the bluegrass confraternity have words of only the highest esteem for the man who started it all.

Yet . . . when Monroe casually mentions that, over the years, "I've had 65 to 75 fiddlers," and about the same number for each instrument, then it appears that being a Blue Grass Boy carries about the same degree of permanence as being married to Zsa Zsa Gabor.

So what's with the high turnover? Any hired position with such a revolving-door aspect is enough to give a prospective staffer pause. Is Bill less charismatic with his charges than with his fans?

A few searching questions to musicians who could have played with him produce answers that imply that he can be a tough taskmaster to work with and to work *for:* that he can be demanding on his hirelings. Add this to the fact that life with him requires some gypsy blood: traveling, cramped conditions on the bus, sleeping in motels or on the bus, truck stop food—and you begin to get the picture. Some of the Boys have probably moved on up to bigger and better things: like being a studio musician in Nashville, or maybe playing in a show theater in Branson, where, in either case, they're home every night for a hot supper.

A young bass player named Ernie Sykes who has worked off-and-on as a Blue Grass Boy reports, "Bill is easier to work with now than ever before. The years have mellowed him. Those who know him have noticed that." And, to his credit, he has provided an upward avenue for many a raw, young picker, refining the fledgling performer en route.

In *High Lonesome,* one hears the voices of Bill and his group singing: ". . . Hey, goin' up Caney. Hey, ho, goin' up Caney." The voices are ghostly, shadowy, phantom-like, flitting in and out of the fiddle lead as a musical wraith: ". . . Hey, goin' up Caney. Hey, ho, goin' up Caney . . ." And they remind us of a fact we don't fancy to face: that one day our beloved Bill will, indeed, be "goin' up Caney," and we will be left without him. Of course, we'll certainly have what he leaves behind: his unique, singular, undefiled music.

Near the end of the film, a modern-day scene of Bill and his troupe is shown as a crowd thunderously welcomes them to a stage to perform. And there stands Bill, grinning and waving his white hat, showing his silver halo, a composite of General

---

3. During most of their twenty-one years together, Flatt and Scruggs's Foggy Mountain Boys included a mandolin player.

Ike, Brigham Young, and Papa Hemingway. Then he hoists his mandolin to the mike and gets down to business. That will remain on the earth to delight and enthrall us below. It must be a wondrous feeling for one to know that even after his soul has departed his body, his legacy shall yet endure for generations; perhaps perpetuity. And we who look forward to joining him in the Afterlife, even after he joins his uncle Pen there, we hope that, among the harps, etc., there will be mandolins also. . . .

🖎

It is interesting to speculate: even if Monroe had never lived, would there be bluegrass anyway? Was the advent of bluegrass inevitable, Bill or no Bill?

The hills of Appalachia have traditionally resounded with music—from the coming of the first Anglo-Saxons until the present. In Library of Congress recordings, one can hear the indigenous sounds of hill music.

But it was Bill Monroe, more than Ralph Stanley, more than Uncle Jimmy Thompson, more than Uncle Dave Macon, more than *anyone* . . . who bequeathed rhythm, substance, and voice to those sounds. Yes, who put them together into a listenable form, without which the genre would never have attained anything approaching the popularity that it has achieved. But for Bill, the word "bluegrass" wouldn't even exist in the English language, except to denote a type of pasturage in Kentucky. In the *Random House Webster's College Dictionary,* 1991 edition, the second definition of "bluegrass" is "country music, polyphonic in character, played on unamplified stringed instruments, esp. the solo banjo." Thus did Bill bestow upon American English a new word to denote the sound. Both the sound and the word have carried beyond our shores.

🖎

Yet another legacy he has given us is: himself. Born in 1911 in Rosine, Kentucky, he has taken such excellent care of himself that he is not only alive and robust today, but still *performing.*

Yes, Bill is with us presently. For years to come, we trust. We had best enjoy him while we may.

Yet, in a way, Mr. Monroe will never leave us.

Originally published in *Bluegrass Unlimited* 30:10 (Apr. 1996): 38–43. Reprinted by permission of the author.

EDITOR'S COMMENTS

This fine article by Houston-based writer Flippin appeared in the April 1996 issue of *Bluegrass Unlimited.* (This selection differs from the original in that several paragraphs from the author's manuscript have been added.)

By the time this article was published Bill had already given his last performance, at the Friday Night Opry on March 15 (the last song he sang that night was "True

Life Blues"). Dangerously high blood pressure levels before shows kept him from performing after that, and on April 5, he was admitted for observation at Baptist Hospital, where he suffered a stroke within a few days. He was then transferred to the Tennessee Christian Medical Center in the Nashville suburb of Madison on April 12, and a pacemaker was installed on April 24. The stroke affected his ability to speak clearly and to swallow, and he would show little reaction when visitors came, probably due to sedatives. On July 2, he was moved to the Northcrest Home and Hospice Center in Springfield, Tennessee, about thirty miles north of Nashville, where Bill spent his last days on earth, visited often by family and friends and attended to by a caring staff. He died there on Monday morning, September 9, 1996.

"The Father of Bluegrass"

JAY ORR AND MICHAEL GRAY

The night Bill Monroe was inducted into the Country Music Hall of Fame was an emotional evening for the bluegrass great.

Because of a petty disagreement he'd rather forget, Sonny Osborne had not spoken to Monroe for five or six years, despite the fact that Monroe had hired the banjo ace in 1952, at age 14, as the youngest ever of his Blue Grass Boys.

But on that night in 1970, Osborne spotted his former boss in a parking lot and called out to him.

"I rolled down the window of my truck and I said, 'Hey.'

"He looked over and I said, 'They couldn't have chosen a better person.'

"He walked over with big tears in his eyes, and mine, too. He put his hand on my arm in my pickup and said, 'You don't know what that means coming from you.'

"I said, 'Well, I know how I feel, and nobody deserves it any more than you.' We were very good friends from then on through 'til the end."

Monroe died Monday afternoon[1] at Northcrest Home and Hospice in Springfield. He suffered a stroke in March[2] and had been hospitalized in Baptist Hospital and Tennessee Christian Medical Center in Madison. He would have been 85 on Friday.

Osborne is one of many musicians who studied under the mentor at "bluegrass school" in the late legend's band before moving out on his own. Sonny Osborne and his brother, Bobby, went on to form the Osborne Brothers, an important bluegrass group in its own right.

"The Blue Grass Boys, more than any other band, was the incubator for all the

---

1. He died between 9:40 and 9:45 A.M.
2. April.

bands that followed in bluegrass and created this school of music which didn't really exist before him (Monroe). That was a major achievement," says Jim Rooney, who profiled Monroe in his groundbreaking book, *Bossmen: Bill Monroe and Muddy Waters.*

Early in his career as a leader, Rooney believes, it was sometimes hard for Monroe to accept the departure of a talented employee.

"He liked people in his band he could challenge. That's what attracted so many good musicians to him, even when the money and the conditions of playing were pretty grim.

"Throughout his career, he continued to attract some of the best musicians there were—the best fiddlers, the best banjo players, the best singers. That was because he was so challenging. If you could stand up next to him, you could stand up next to anybody."

Fathering a Musical Style

"I don't think there's another form of music that has experienced the presence of as dominant a personality as has bluegrass, through the impact of Bill Monroe," says Bill Ivey, executive director of the Country Music Hall of Fame.

Monroe was indisputably the "Father of Bluegrass Music." The style, which combines elements of old-time string band music, Anglo-American balladry, syncopated African-American dance music, and traditional gospel music, did not exist before he recruited and coached the musicians who would define the revolutionary sound.

The evolution of personnel in his Blue Grass Boys band, begun in 1939, led, in December 1945, to a unit that included guitarist and vocalist Lester Flatt, banjo innovator Earl Scruggs, bassist Howard Watts (known as Cedric Rainwater), and fiddler Chubby Wise.

The "original bluegrass band," as they would come to be known, made their first recordings on September 16 and 17, 1946—50 years ago this coming Monday and Tuesday—in Chicago for the Columbia Records company.

Among the most famous songs recorded by the original bluegrass band were "Blue Moon of Kentucky," "Will You Be Loving Another Man," "Molly and Tenbrooks," and "Footprints in the Snow."[3]

"I found him very easy to work with," Scruggs says, reflecting on the passing of his former boss. The banjo-picking innovator is the only surviving member of that band. "We put a sound together there that he had never had before. It was an exciting time for him.

"It was a new sound. Bill was the type guy—and I loved that—that if you pushed him, he played much better. The harder you played, the harder he'd work with you, and that was the first time I had ever worked with anybody who was like that.

---

3. "Footprints in the Snow" was recorded by Bill for the first time in 1945, prior to the formation of "the original bluegrass band."

"Somebody that would work hard against what I was working made me have more energy to pick and perform. It was just a battle between us pickers and singers, it seemed. It was an exciting time to see who could top each other. That's the way it seemed to work. You'd learn a lot like that, you could play stuff you never knew you could play."

Scruggs agrees that the sound Monroe and his band created will be the bluegrass legend's greatest legacy.

"I've heard him say so many, many times that he created that sound," Scruggs recalls. "I think he wants to be remembered as that. He created 'Bill Monroe' for sure. Nobody will ever take his place, in my opinion. I'm just glad to be a part of the sound he wanted to keep for the next 50 years after (we worked with him)."

"He Upped the Ante"

"Something that people tend to forget is that he raised the level of musicianship tremendously, especially in regard to string bands," says Charles Wolfe, country music historian and Middle Tennessee State University professor.

"When he came on the scene, they were kind of chugging along. He upped the ante. He said, 'If you're going to play with me, you're going to have to do better than that.' He would play songs in impossibly high keys and at impossibly fast tempos.

"One of the things that happened was that people who thought they were good mandolin players, good banjo players suddenly realized they had to get better. He's responsible for increasing, in a quantum way, the overall level of musicianship you hear in country music."

Before Monroe offered him a job with the Blue Grass Boys in 1963, former International Bluegrass Music Association (IBMA) male vocalist of the year Del McCoury was building a career as a banjo picker. During his yearlong tenure with Monroe, however, he emerged as a reputable vocalist and rhythm guitarist.

"(Monroe) auditioned (banjo innovator) Bill Keith and me on the same day," McCoury recalls. "He auditioned me playing guitar and singing lead. I had no idea what I was doing, but for some reason he figured I could do it. He told me I'd like it. I had been singing since I was a kid, but I was never serious about it because I liked the banjo.

"He was right, of course. I did like it. I never did go back to playing banjo seriously after that.

"As a teacher, Monroe never said anything about how to do things. I think he knew that you were learning from him just by playing with him. I know I learned a lot."[4]

"I just thought he had a wonderful voice and a good feel to his voice," says Ralph Stanley, who with Monroe's passing becomes the elder statesman of bluegrass.

"He knew how to sing a song, he knew what to put in it to make the people feel

---

4. Bill told many others "how to do things," but, in McCoury's case, he may have been more tolerant with the beginning guitarist.

it. He was a wonderful mandolin player. He loved his music and he kept it clean. He worked on it all the time and he always wanted it to be the best."

Bluegrass Hall of Honor[5] member Jimmy Martin first met Monroe in the alley behind the Ryman when he came down from Morristown, Tennessee, in 1949 to hear the bluegrass great at the Grand Ole Opry.

After an informal audition, Martin accompanied Monroe on a trip to Fort Smith, Arkansas, where he joined the master on stage. When Monroe and his band got back to Nashville, Martin had a job with the bluegrass great.

"He's the greatest thing that ever happened to bluegrass music, him, and Lester Flatt, Chubby Wise, Earl Scruggs, and you can count me in there if you want to, and the Osborne Brothers, and the Stanley Brothers," Martin said Monday.

"Bill Monroe is my idol and always will be. We have lost a great man of bluegrass music. If there was ever a man that worked with Bill Monroe that loved him, it's the King of Bluegrass, Jimmy Martin."

High Lonesome Sound

Monroe and his high lonesome sound appealed not only to country and mountain music fans, but also to folk music enthusiasts in cities and on college campuses.

"He was one of the rare country performers, and perhaps unique to his generation, in his ability to reach out to fans a lot younger than he and to reach out to people with very different backgrounds," Ivey says.

"His following was made up of people from the city long before that trend overtook country music in general. He was a great ambassador for the music."

Rooney, a Bostonian, has vivid memories of his first meeting with Monroe.

"I was actually trembling, I was so in awe of him," he recalls. "He was a serious person in my world. You got the impression from him right away that you better kind of be on your toes."

A lefty, Rooney plays the guitar in an unorthodox backward and upside-down style. When they first met, Monroe urged Rooney to pick a tune for him on a guitar that he shoved into Rooney's hands.

"I picked it up backwards and upside down and I tried to play something. I was just as nervous as I could be. But he said, 'You got a good lick there, and don't you change it.'

"In a way, I think that was his approach to life. If you had something original, he didn't believe in changing it. His steadfastness was something that was really impressive over the years. He would stick with his music through thick and thin and not go with the fashions."

"He had an air about him," McCoury says. "When he walked on stage—the way he stood and looked—you knew something good was going to happen. I mean something big. He was a complete musician and entertainer. He was an expert rhythm man, an expert lead (mandolin) man."

---

5. The IBMA's version of a Hall of Fame.

Bill's Classical Demeanor

Ivey echoes McCoury's sentiments.

"He had a great sense of how to be a star, when to give musically and personally, and when to hold back and be distant," the Hall of Fame exec says.

"Because of his manner—that dignified, austere, somewhat remote manner—I think he contributed a great deal to the perception of bluegrass as a fine art form within country music. Bill carried himself like an accomplished classical musician."

From 1939 through his last Grand Ole Opry appearance, March 15, 1996, the Father of Bluegrass maintained close ties to the venerable radio show on WSM-AM (650). His absence there had been felt already, in the six months since he suffered a stroke following his March 15 show.

"Bill Monroe's death brings to a close one of the most important chapters in the life of the Grand Ole Opry," said Opry president Hal Durham in a press release.[6]

"Bill was an active, supportive member of the Opry for 57 years, and brought a unique and distinctive kind of music to us and to the world. He was the epitome of the stately, reserved Southern gentleman, a shy and generous man who was justly proud of the acceptance of his bluegrass music, and of his role as the 'Father of Bluegrass.'

"The Opry will miss this Hall of Famer, not only for his music but also for what he represented in strength of character and the example he set for young performers."

"Bill was always proud to describe himself as a star of the Grand Ole Opry," says Ivey. "While I think he was proud to be the first bluegrass musician elected to the Country Music Hall of Fame, I think he was proudest of his long, long, and close association with the Grand Ole Opry."

"There's One More Left"

"I think, people like Ernest Tubb and Monroe, Minnie Pearl, and Acuff, when these guys go, let's face it, it's the complete end of an era," says Osborne. "There's one more left, Hank Snow. I know it's horrible to think about, but it's the end of an era.

"We'll miss his leadership," Osborne believes. "It's like an old guy on a baseball team. You know, Dressing Room 2 won't ever be the same again, as Dressing Room 1, after Acuff was gone, never will be the same again. In my mind they should have locked it."[7]

Monroe was religiously devout and frequently performed and recorded sacred numbers with his band.

"He always thought it was important for the Blue Grass Boys to perform gospel music and he always said the Blue Grass Boys performed gospel music to show they know the difference between right and wrong," says Ryman general manager

---

6. Durham was the manager of the Opry from 1974 to 1993. He retired as Opry president in 1996.

7. Dressing Room 1 at the new Opry House was exclusively Acuff's. Bill shared Dressing Room 2 with all of the bluegrass performers at the Opry.

Steve Buchanan, whose long association with the bluegrass great included produc-
ing two albums.[8]

Monroe would want to be remembered as having done the best he could and
for treating others honestly and fairly, Osborne feels.

Most important, though, was that he reconciled his spiritual life, says the banjo ace.

"He would want people to think that he got right with his Maker. He got right
in the last few years."

Originally published in the *Nashville Banner,* Sept. 10, 1996, A1–A2. Reprinted by
permission of the *Nashville Banner* and *The Tennessean.*

EDITOR'S COMMENTS

Bill's passing was reported by every news medium throughout the world on Tuesday, September 10. This article was one of two to appear on the front page of that
day's *Nashville Banner.*

"It's a Sad Day, Indeed, for Legend's Friends, Fans"

JOHN COMMINS

Scotsman Douglas McHattie hunched over the bar at the Station Inn and ordered
another draft, as a hodgepodge band of bluegrass pickers moaned "In the Pines"
from the tiny stage.

"Hand me a tissue, love," he asked bartender Lin Barber, dabbing the brimming
tears from his eyes. "It's a sad day, indeed.

"I came all the way from London to visit Mr. Monroe and wish him a happy
birthday," McHattie said, fingering his mandolin-shaped tie pin. "I was flying in
(Monday) afternoon and I got this terrible feeling. When I got to the taxi, the driver told me Bill Monroe had died."

McHattie, who first saw Monroe in 1966 at London's Royal Albert Hall, was one
of dozens of fans, friends, and musicians who passed through the crepe-decked door
of the Station Inn, Nashville's bluegrass mecca, to pay their respects in an impromptu wake Monday night for the recently-departed Father of Bluegrass.

---

8. *Live at the Opry: Celebrating 50 Years at the Grand Ole Opry,* MCA Records, MCAC/MCAD-
42286, released in 1989, and *Cryin' Holy unto the Lord,* MCA Records, MCAC/MCAD-10017, released in 1990.

Monroe died from heart failure Monday afternoon[1] at a Madison[2] nursing home. On Friday, he was to have celebrated his 85th birthday.

"I love Bill Monroe, so I just had to come here," McHattie said. "You Americans should know that you lost a hell of a man. There'll never be another person like that again."

In addition to McHattie, some of the best pickers in bluegrass were on hand to honor their mentor. The roster of musical mourners included Roland White, Doc Watson, Ronnie and Rob McCoury, Doug Dillard, Larry Cordle, Kathy Chiavola, Mike Henderson, David Grier, Mike Bub, and Terry Eldredge.

Reason "We're All Here"

"When I heard the news I just knew we had to do something," said J. T. Gray, owner of the Station Inn, 402 12th Avenue South, which is usually closed on Mondays. "Bill Monroe is the reason why this building is here. He's the reason why we're all here. Bill Monroe's responsible for all this.

"Whenever he walked in the door, every head in the place would turn. It was like God Himself had walked in. And he always came ready to play. I think everyone in here half expects him to walk through the door tonight."

Pickers and friends swapped songs and stories about the legendary octogenarian. Laughter and Monroe's music mingled in the smoky air.

"Bill would've wanted this. A lot of laughing," said mandolinist Roland White, a member of Monroe's famed Blue Grass Boys from 1967–69, who credits Monroe with "changing my life."

"I never knew what I wanted to do in music until I heard Bill Monroe."

Singer-songwriter Larry Cordle, with the band Lonesome Standard Time, laughed as he recalled how Monroe could "never, ever remember my name."

Lost Generation

"He'd get everybody else's name and he'd just get to me and forget," Cordle said. "I played with him for five or six years."[3]

"They don't make people like him anymore," Cordle added. "He was from a generation of people who have just disappeared from the planet. They didn't just say they were going to do something—they went and did it."

Ronnie McCoury, an award-winning mandolinist and the son of bluegrass legend Del McCoury, recalled the time Monroe brought him on stage during his Bean Blossom bluegrass festival in Indiana.

"I was just a shy little kid, peeking around the corner of the stage watching him play, and he saw me and came up and handed me his mandolin, that old, scratched-

---

1. Monday morning.
2. Springfield, Tennessee.
3. Informally, at the Bell Cove club in the Nashville suburb of Hendersonville.

up one. I was shaking just to hold it. He told me to go out and help him finish the set. I think at that moment right there we bonded.

"Tonight, we're all sad, but we're also celebrating the life of a great man and rejoicing in the great gift he brought us," McCoury said. "I know he's in a better place now and I know he's happy. He'd been singing about this day for many, many years."

Originally published in the *Nashville Banner,* Sept. 10, 1996, A1–A2. Reprinted by permission of the *Nashville Banner* and *The Tennessean.*

EDITOR'S COMMENTS

Sharing the front page of the *Nashville Banner* on September 10 with the previous selection was this report of the wake held at the Station Inn, one of Nashville's main bluegrass venues, on the night of Bill's passing.

Also on the front page of the *Banner,* under an accidentally reversed photo of Bill picking his mandolin, the caption informed, "There will be a funeral service at the Ryman on Wednesday prior to burial beneath the blue moon—and blue grass— of Kentucky on Thursday."

"Tears, Music Fill Bluegrass Legend's Final Ryman 'Show'"

JAY ORR

A long row of quarters lined the hinge of Bill Monroe's open casket as his friends and family paid their last respects to the giant of American music.

Monroe's favorite "Jesus" pin adorned the lapel of his suit. His right hand, crossed on his chest, held his glasses. On the edge of the casket a Bible lay open, presented by the local chapter of the musicians' union, and on an easel nearby sat a photo of Monroe caressing his beloved mandolin.

Once the casket was closed for his funeral service, an attendant placed Monroe's trademark Stetson hat atop the casket.

On the flower-filled stage, Monroe's manager Tony Conway, Grand Ole Opry officials Hal Durham and Bob Whittaker,[1] Ryman general manager Steve Buchanan, and Gaylord chief Bud Wendell uncovered a mandolin, mounted on a pedestal

---

1. Whittaker succeeded Durham as the manager of the Grand Ole Opry in 1993 and retired in 1998, succeeded, in turn, by Buchanan.

and spotlighted from above. The special decorative instrument was presented to Monroe in 1989, on the occasion of his 50th anniversary as a member of the Opry.

During an hour-long service, Monroe was honored with music, eulogy, and prayer. Some 1,500 friends, family, and colleagues attended the service in the Ryman, the building in which Monroe performed for many years as a mainstay of the Opry.

Pastor Paul Baggett of the Millersville Assembly of God, delivering his eulogy in the style of the old-time preachers Monroe heard in his youth, described him as a compassionate man who loved children.

Baggett explained that the quarters inside the casket recalled one of Monroe's customary gestures of affection toward kids.

"He loved to pat them on their head and give 'em a quarter to put them on their way," Baggett said.

Besides remembering the human side of Monroe, Baggett recalled that Monroe was a "country man" who "loved down-home living" and "never got above his raisin'."

The preacher also imagined what it would be like for Monroe in the hereafter.

"There are no cabins in Gloryland," he said, and predicted that there'll be no confusing heaven with Opryland.

"One day, I believe Bill Monroe will be the usher at the Golden Gate," Baggett speculated. "He'll invite all his friends and he'll be the welcoming committee."

In a second eulogy, later in the service, Pastor Roger Rush, of Holiday Heights Church[2] in Hendersonville, shared stories of attending church with Monroe during the past five years.

"I don't know if you know what it's like to sit at a church potluck with a giant," Rush said.

Rush told of one incident in which Monroe brought a birthday gift for a child in a needy family, instructing that the present be delivered on the child's birthday—not before or after.

To illustrate Monroe's strength and determination, Rush recalled that one Sunday morning, shortly after hip surgery, the bluegrass great stood and waited at his gate for Rush to pick him up for church.

Upon arriving for the service, Monroe shrugged off a wheelchair and the gradual incline of a ramp in favor of using the more challenging front steps of the church to go in and come out.

Calling him "a precious gift from God," Rush said, "He would have been the first to tell you his talent was a gift from God."

Just as moving as the spoken eulogies was the music, performed by Vince Gill, Marty Stuart, Ricky Skaggs, bassist Roy Huskey, Jr., and fiddler Stuart Duncan, with bluegrass great Ralph Stanley and Opry members Connie Smith, Alison Krauss, and Patty Loveless.

Gill, Stuart, Skaggs, Huskey, and Duncan followed a recording of Monroe's

---

2. Bill's church in his later years.

haunting instrumental, "My Last Days on Earth," with the gospel hymn "(I'm) Working on a Building."

Smith drew "Amens" and gasps of appreciation with her performance of "How Great Thou Art," accompanied by Gill, Stuart, Skaggs, Huskey, and Duncan.

Emmylou Harris sang the plaintive traditional number "Wayfaring Stranger," a favorite of Monroe's, with its lyric about going over Jordan.

Skaggs took the vocal lead on "Rank Stranger," with his former boss, Stanley, out front on the choruses in a moving display of mountain soul.

Krauss joined the group for the old traditional hymn "Angel Band," and Gill, Skaggs, Stuart, and Stanley put things on the sunny side with their rendition of "A Beautiful Life," recorded by Monroe in 1958. The song promises, "Each day I'll do a golden deed by helping those who are in need."[3]

Gill's eulogistic ballad, "Go Rest High on That Mountain," given a bluegrass treatment with Loveless joining Gill and Skaggs on vocals, seemed especially apt for the morning.

As the service drew to a close late Wednesday morning, Skaggs shared a couple of stories about Monroe and warned, "We could get into Mr. Monroe stories for the next hour."

Then, with the mildest of apologies to any who might be offended by the performance of a secular tune at the funeral, Skaggs, Gill, Stuart, and the rest launched into "Raw Hide," a showcase number usually played by Monroe at breakneck speed.

Three bagpipers marched in at the end of the service to usher Monroe's casket out of the old building to the strains of "Amazing Grace."

Among the Grand Ole Opry members paying their respects to their longtime colleague were Bill Anderson, Little Jimmy Dickens, Skeeter Davis, Jim Ed Brown, Jeanne Pruett, Grandpa Jones, Porter Wagoner, Bill Carlisle, John Conlee, George Hamilton IV, Jimmy C. Newman, Jan Howard, Jeannie Seely, Ranger Doug Green (of Riders in the Sky), Johnny Russell, Carol Lee Cooper, and DeFord Bailey, Jr., son of the late Opry harmonica pioneer.

Bluegrass greats Earl Scruggs, Jimmy Martin, Del McCoury, Mac Wiseman, and Jim and Jesse[4] were on hand, as were Amy Grant, Steve Earle, Billy Ray Cyrus, [Nashville] Mayor Phil Bredesen and his wife Andrea Conte, and former [Tennessee] Governor Ned McWherter.

Monroe—who died Monday afternoon,[5] four days short of his 85th birthday—was to be buried at 2 P.M. today in his hometown of Rosine, Kentucky.

Originally published in the *Nashville Banner*, Sept. 12, 1996, B1, B5. Reprinted by permission of the *Nashville Banner* and *The Tennessean*.

---

3. The verse continues, "My life on earth is but a span, and so I'll do the best I can."
4. Jim and Jesse are also Grand Ole Opry members.
5. Monday morning.

EDITOR'S COMMENTS

A memorial service was held on Wednesday, September 11, at Nashville's Ryman Auditiorium, home of the Grand Ole Opry from 1943 to 1974. *Nashville Banner* music critic Orr wrote this report for the September 12 edition of the newspaper.

"On the Death of William Smith Monroe"

ROBERT ASHLEY LOGUE

The air tonight, so soft and still,
is tinged with loss and pain;
upon its wings an early chill
and faint, unearthly strains—
the echoes of the angel band
that fill the skies o'er Dixie land;
celestial hosts on every hill
to lead the sweet refrain
and guide the spirit train.

Away, beyond these midnight skies,
in the light of everlasting spring—
beyond our sad and mournful sighs,
removed from every evil thing,
beyond the gaze of tear-dimmed eyes
and far from where his body lies
his spirit now forever sings;
his mandolin forever rings.

How they rejoice on that bright shore
while our hearts are lying low!
Our loved one's face we'll see no more,
nor meet him here below;
but the home for which our spirits long
is filled today with bluegrass song.

This day the angels waited for;
but how we hate to see him go!
This day they opened Heaven's door
and welcomed Bill Monroe.

EDITOR'S COMMENTS

Logue, a musician and brother of Debbie Logue, secretary of former Opry manager Hal Durham, wrote this poem on September 11, following the memorial service at the Ryman. That weekend he posted it backstage at the new Grand Ole Opry House, where he says he "practically grew up." There it was noticed by Sandy Rothman ("Bill Monroe's Birthday Party"), who was visiting Nashville following Bill's funeral in Rosine, and copies were available at the reception desk when he asked if he could make one.

"A Living Legend Dies"

DAVID McBRIDE

Bratcher's Grocery in Rosine was unusually quiet early Tuesday morning. What talk there was centered around a man whose name placed the small Ohio County community on a multi-nation map.

Gilbert Pharris sat in one of two chairs near the rear of the store. He flipped cigarette ashes into a styrofoam cup and talked about Bill Monroe.

"Bill was a good person and never really changed much after he got famous," Pharris said. "He's been in this place several times and I talked to him when he visited his sister just down the road."

Pharris couldn't remember the last time he talked with the fabled musician and he realized that opportunity would never present itself again.

Monroe died Monday at the Northcrest Home and Hospice Center in Springfield, Tennessee. He was 84 years old and just a few days shy of his 85th birthday.

"Bill didn't spend a lot of time around Rosine in later years, but he did give a free concert at the old barn (Ole Barn Jamboree) not too many years ago and everybody really appreciated that," Pharris said.

Eleanor Bratcher, co-owner of the grocery store with her husband, Hoyt, wasn't behind the counter Tuesday as she normally would be. Instead, she was in Paducah to be with a sister who was undergoing major surgery.

"I was never around Bill Monroe that much, but I'll miss him just like all lovers of bluegrass music will miss him," she said by telephone. "His name and the name of this little town will forever go together."

The Bratchers converted the former barn next door to their business into a haven for bluegrass and country music. Monroe was the biggest name, by far, to entertain there.

"That was some kind of night," Ms. Bratcher recalled. "A person like myself just doesn't get the opportunity to be involved in something like that more than one time in a lifetime."

Born September 13, 1911, Monroe was widely recognized as the Father of Blue-grass Music. He liked to say his particular brand of music contained something for a variety of music lovers.

"It (bluegrass) has a little blues and some gospel in it," he once said during a visit to Rosine. "It also has a little jazz. People wanted it to have a little jazz."

Monroe's death reportedly was brought on by complications from a recent stroke. He also had open-heart surgery in recent years, but recuperated sufficiently to resume his career on a limited basis.

Herbert Napier, 64 and a native of Rosine, recalled working on the Monroe farm.

"I was just a young boy, maybe 14, and I remember I didn't get paid much," Napier said.

While he respected the Monroe name and the role Bill Monroe played in the creation and cultivation of bluegrass music, Napier said he did not look at the entire picture through rose-colored glasses.

"If he had done for Rosine what some of the people of this community had done for him, Rosine could have really been some kind of a place," Napier said.

Stoy Geary, Rosine's fire chief and staunch Monroe supporter, didn't take issue with Napier, but he did voice his own thoughts and opinions.

"The people who didn't like Bill really didn't know the man," Geary said while standing in front of the Rosine Post Office. "You have to know a person for what he is in order to really appreciate him."

Geary said Monroe afforded him a thrill that not many people will ever experience.

"I was at the Grand Ole Opry and Bill invited me to come up onto the stage," Geary recalled. "He introduced me as one of the boys from Rosine. That's a time in my life I'll never forget."

Geary said he couldn't buy the notion by some that Monroe never did anything for Rosine.

"If that's the case, then it's everybody's fault," he said. "Different people have different thoughts and attitudes and some never really appreciated the man for who he was."

And Geary added:

"If for no other reason, you have to appreciate the fact that when people mention the name Monroe, they also mention the name Rosine in the same breath," Geary said. "That's meant a lot to this town."

Geary said there has been a lot of talk about doing a lot of things in Rosine, including building a recording studio. But that never materialized.

A former deputy sheriff, Geary said he is sure of one thing.

"Bill Monroe's music, especially his gospel music, touches the soul," he said. "That's what music's supposed to do."

James Pharis, a former Ohio County Courthouse custodian and country music buff, was a proclaimed Monroe fan.

"I was a great friend of Bill's and loved him dearly," Pharis said. "He will be missed by many people and his songs will always live in my heart."

Rosetta Kiper, a lifelong resident of Rosine, is the daughter of Bill Monroe's brother, the late Speed B. Monroe.[1] She too was outside the Rosine Post Office Tuesday morning.

"We were always pretty close," Kiper said. "The last time I saw him was at his daughter's funeral in Nashville a couple of years ago."[2]

Kiper said her uncle never lost touch with Rosine.

"Ohio County has lost a great man and he loved his hometown of Rosine enough that he requested to be buried here," she said.

Bertha Kurth, 88, a sister of Monroe's and a resident of Rosine, was not available to be interviewed Tuesday morning.[3]

Originally published in the Ohio County, Kentucky, *Times-News,* Sept. 12, 1996. Reprinted by permission of the author.

EDITOR'S COMMENTS

This article was written by the editor of the Ohio County, Kentucky, *Times-News.* It appeared on the front page of the weekly newspaper's edition of Thursday, September 12, the day of Bill's funeral at the Rosine Methodist Church and burial in the Rosine Cemetery. (A brief review of Bill's career is not included here.)

"Tears Fell on Rosine"

MARYE YEOMANS

There just never seems to be enough time to do all you would like to; all those little things that mean so much to those around you; all the good intentions that never get acted upon. To have meaningful conversations with all the people you want to at a gathering such as the IBMA or, in this case, at the funeral of Bill Monroe in Rosine, Kentucky, on Thursday, September 12, 1996, just one day shy of what would've been his 85th birthday.

With a heavy heart I left Nashville in the morning after working a few hours, hoping to arrive in Rosine early enough to make some photographs of the folks I knew would be gathering outside the little white country churchhouse, hoping to visit with some friends.

---

1. Speed V. Monroe (mentioned by Ralph Rinzler in *Bill Monroe and the Blue Grass Boys: Live Recordings, 1956–1969*).

2. Melissa Monroe's funeral was held on December 5, 1990.

3. Bertha Monroe Kurth, born July 17, 1908, died about six months later, on April 1, 1997.

It was a gorgeous sunny morning in Tennessee, a beautiful day to be out on the road, windows rolled down, "Kentucky Mandolin," "Jerusalem Ridge," "The First Whippoorwill," and, yes, "My Last Days on Earth" fortifying me as each moment brought me closer to my last glimpse of the man I saw as a pioneer, and counted among my dear friends, a man who had paid his dues, lived a good long life, had resolved his quarrels, and was finally ready for that better life.

I felt so strange. There was the overwhelming sense of loss, the feeling that things would never again be quite the same, yet there was a feeling of peace and quiet, too. I found my appreciation for the man and his music had actually grown more intense with his death; I'd spent the past several days, late at night, listening only to the music of Bill Monroe, true life music, white man's blues. In the rare moments when I wasn't listening to Bill, I was thinking about him, reliving precious moments frozen in time, or I was talking with friends about him, or e-mailing people I'd never met, whose voices and faces I wouldn't recognize, acquaintances who'd reached out to me through BGRASS-L, something that might never have existed if Bill Monroe had not been born in 1911 to J. B. and Malissa Monroe in Kentucky, if he hadn't been a cross-eyed child who felt rejected and hid in the barn when company came to the house, if he hadn't been the man who persevered against all odds to become the legend we all miss so much, if he hadn't been the man who never quite believed in his worth, who always seemed to need to prove himself, his strength, his power, his endurance; the man who pushed himself to greater accomplishments, a real-life inspiration.

What if he'd been born in India or Africa? Would there have been bluegrass as we know it today? Would "Jerusalem Ridge" have been written? What if Bill had not had such a commitment to his vision of what the bluegrass music should be, how the instruments should sound, how the parts should be sung? What if he hadn't insisted it be done over and over until it was right? What if he'd succumbed to rock and roll and turned his back on old-time music and the blues, two of his greatest musical influences? Bill gave his life, his energy, his body and soul to keep the bluegrass music alive, and at a tremendous cost to him and his family. It is my belief that there are no coincidences, and that all these things occurred because it was the time and the place, the destiny of Mr. Monroe, to do just exactly as he did; to unite us in a music we love so dearly.

Not that Bill was solely responsible for what has brought us to this forum, but, as so many have said, if it weren't for bluegrass, what would we be doing with all of our vacation time? Who would our friends be? I doubt I'd have friends in Japan, the Czech Republic, and Russia; friends in virtually all of the United States.

Anyway, my thoughts on the way to Rosine were strange and wonderful, sad and happy all at the same time. The music I'd been listening to for so many years had a new meaning for me; I think I was just listening much more closely than I ever had before; and it was as if I'd never heard it. I found my admiration for the man I'd called friend growing exponentially as I listened to the lyrics he'd penned, to the lonesome tunes he'd written, while my eyes perceived the territory he'd often traveled by horse or mule, hauling railroad ties or going to play at a dance with Uncle Pen.

It's only about 40 miles from Nashville to the Kentucky border. In that span, the day went from radiant sunshine to cloudy and overcast. In Kentucky, it seemed that all the clouds were gathering and moving together in the same direction as you and I . . . toward Rosine. Soon there was a strange light in the darkness of the day, an occasional ray of sunshine finding its way through the dark, thick, stormy sky. It seemed like a gospel kind of day to me; I wanted to sing and shout, I wanted to cry. It was my need to drive the distance alone, with only my thoughts and the music of Bill Monroe as my company; it felt so right that way.

Approaching Hartford, Kentucky, just 10 miles down the road from Rosine, a soft, light rain began to fall, I thought, like the teardrops rolling down my face, as I listened to Mr. Monroe singing "Kentucky Waltz," cloud drops were falling down my window. It seemed fitting that the clouds, surrounding the hills and hollers Mr. Bill loved so well and immortalized in song that they would live forever in our hearts, had been gathered together over the little community churchhouse, watching over the friends and family clustered there, shedding their tears at this bittersweet goodbye.

Arriving in Rosine 30 minutes before the service, I started seeing longtime friends. Though it had clearly been raining in Rosine, the sun starting to peep through created a warm light; the sky was smiling as I walked toward the little Methodist church[1] and the kindred spirits congregated there, talking quietly. There were cars everywhere, TV cameras, reporters with pads, pens, and cameras running about, people of all ages, Volvos and beat-up pickup trucks parked alongside each other.

A line of people moved solemnly up the steep church steps, stuffing themselves through the narrow doors, signing the guest register, standing patiently in line to catch a last glimpse, return a quarter to Mr. Bill, say a prayer, to weep. There wasn't time to linger, the line advanced and moved to the back door. The church was chock-full of people; probably far more than it had ever welcomed on Easter Sunday. The gaiety of Easter was absent; they all needed to be there.

The quarters had multiplied since yesterday's Ryman service, like the loaves and fish? Today there were two long and glistening rows of quarters adorning the casket lid. While the Ryman service was done with a closed casket, Mr. Bill was visible to those inside throughout the country-style service.

There's no point in saying who was there; we were all there. I saw more bluegrass people there than at the Ryman, and also more people I didn't know. Lots of former Blue Grass Boys were there; Bill would've liked that.

While the sanctuary was overflowing with people, many of whom stood throughout the hour-and-a-half service, there were three or four times as many people on the lawn behind and around the church listening via speakers which had been placed there. One policeman estimated 1,000 people attended Bill's funeral; another person reported 1,200.

---

1. The Rosine Methodist Church.

The service began with Ricky Skaggs singing "Amazing Grace." A woman with a beautiful voice seated near me at the back of the church joined in, and, soon, many of us in the crowd became the choir and raised our voices in memory of Mr. Monroe. The final verse had two words, "Praise God," and most present seemed to pick up on that verse rather easily. Maybe it was the stifling heat, maybe the sadness of the moment, but a woman near me, face soaked with tears, left the building shortly after the service commenced.

Representatives of the state of Kentucky and Ohio County said a few words and offered their sympathy. The family was seated in the front of the church at a 90-degree angle from the crowd, the head of Bill's casket just a couple of feet from their pew. Somehow it seemed that James and Jimbo[2] were less distraught today, though it probably wasn't so. It was a hard time for them.

Ralph Stanley got up and sang one of my favorite Stanley numbers, "Two Coats," with Ricky playing mandolin and singing with him. I will forever associate this song with the last time I saw Bill, and love it even more than before. A very emotional Ralph moved us all beyond tears and beyond words with his heartfelt vocals.

Ricky then sang "I Was Standing by the Bedside of a Neighbor." Ricky broke down during the first couple of verses, so emotional, at such a loss, he could barely whisper the words through his sobs; it was the time I've felt most in tune with Ricky in all these years; my spirit was right there with him, my heart crying, urging him on.

A beautiful African-American woman named Alma Randolph from Ohio County, Kentucky, blessed with a sweet, soothing, uplifting voice, sang "Take My Hand, Precious Lord," and I felt that Bill would've really liked that. It certainly wasn't bluegrass or blues style, but with the tremendous influence of Arnold Shultz always so evident in Bill's music, it seemed right that she would be such a wonderful part of the service, of the circle of life present there.

Various Blue Grass Boys got up, led by Wayne Lewis, with Art Stamper and Robert Bowlin on fiddles, Dana Cupp on banjo, Skaggs singing tenor, and Wayne on guitar, and did "Little Community Church." Del McCoury then sang "The Old Crossroad" with Ricky and others.

The Blue Grass Boys were then recognized. Some of the [other] Blue Grass Boys in attendance (my advance apologies; I'm sure there were many there whom I did not recognize): Kenny Baker, Bob Black, Carlos Brock, Jimmy Campbell, David Deese, Glen Duncan, Lamar Grier, R. C. Harris, Doug Hutchens, Dan Jones, Ralph Lewis, Butch Robins, Billy Rose, Sandy Rothman, Guy Stevenson, and Tater Tate. Undoubtedly a few who were present went unnoticed. No slight intended.

"I Saw the Light," sung by Brock, was next, followed by "Life's Railway to Heaven," sung by Jones. Hutchens was then introduced. A very emotional Wayne Lewis, voice cracking, pausing every few words to take a breath, fighting his grief, then announced that Hutchens had documented 175 full-time Blue Grass Boys, people who had worked with Bill on a regular basis over a period of time . . . trying to follow in his footsteps.

---

2. James Monroe and his son, James "Jimbo" Monroe II.

Wayne Lewis came up to sing and said, "This is probably the second hardest time it's ever been for me to sing this song. The first time was when I sang this at Jimmie Skinner's funeral, and I thought probably that was the hardest thing I'd ever done in my life, but this time might prove to be harder." He then asked everyone to join in and sing "Precious Memories" with him. He said Bill always liked for the people to join in and sing it with them at the festivals. Everyone then wholeheartedly sang the choruses.

James Monroe got up and said a few words about his father. He said "he had friends all over the world . . . they came from all over the country to the Ryman yesterday . . . he's here with us today; he's looking at us and hears us; and I think he appreciates every one of you folks; good singers here, some of the best in the country; I know he's in a better place."

Several Opry members were present. Skeeter Davis said that through the years she always had such a love and attachment to Mr. Monroe; was so impressed with him. "What a testimony he's left behind." She mentioned Ricky, Vince [Gill], and all the Blue Grass Boys, and all he's given them and left behind for them. She said, "What a big birthday party there'll be in heaven for Bill tomorrow, while he celebrates with Jesus and Minnie [Pearl] and Roy [Acuff]. We love you, Bill. Happy Birthday in heaven!"

Margie Sullivan[3] then said, "I can't really tell him goodbye, James. I just have to say goodnight. I have had many occasions to talk with Bill about the Lord; shared many wonderful experiences with him. He was a man who loved his friends, he loved everybody, but, more than that, he loved the Lord. I feel that today he's looking down on us all; he sees us all and he hears us all, but there is rejoicing in heaven because one more has entered, and he'll be playing that mandolin and he'll be walking the streets of gold and he'll be waiting for all of us."

Several other colleagues got up and said a few words about Bill. Bobby Osborne got up and said, "There's so many things I could say about Bill Monroe, it would probably take me three or four days to tell you all of it. I never was a Blue Grass Boy, not because I didn't want to be, but I always sang the same part that he did, and played the same instrument. He and I both knew that there wasn't room for two of us in the same band. The last 15 or 20 years, Sonny and I have been very close to Mr. Monroe. We have shared the same dressing room with Bill Monroe and the Blue Grass Boys and Jim and Jesse . . . and I want to say once again that I am so thankful that I lived in the days of Bill Monroe."

Alma Randolph then sang a very beautiful song, "Don't Cry for Me." Here are some of the words, a beautiful message:

> Here we are again, that old familiar place,
> When the wind will blow, no one ever knows the time or place.
> Don't cry for me, don't shed a tear,

---

3. Of the gospel-singing Sullivan Family.

The time I spent with you will always be,
And now that I am gone,
I want you to carry on,
But don't cry for me . . . .

Disobedient souls that we are, everyone cried.

Preacher Baggett, pastor at James Monroe's Assembly of God church in Goodlettsville,[4] then gave a lengthy sermon in the sweltering heat. The service finally drew to a grateful close.

It seemed that the crowd had grown exponentially since I'd last felt the fresh, cool air of Rosine on my face. Everywhere the eye could see were upturned faces of all ages, awaiting the appearance of the procession of pallbearers carrying Bill Monroe home. The seconds ticked slowly by as we all waited for them to arrive, carrying our beloved leader down his final flight of steps to the long, black limousine which waited quietly to transport him to his final resting place. The casket lifted into the vehicle, the door closed, the crowd of friends, and Blue Grass Boys, neighbors, and the curious, all made their way up the road, just a short distance to the lonesome old cemetery and the newly-dug grave which waited to hold the remains of our father, our grandfather, our friend, our mentor, our Bill Monroe.

The flowers everywhere. Lots of roses. The large, white clouds, the fall blue sky. The sun. Alma Randolph began to sing, "The sun shines bright on my old Kentucky home . . . Weep no more, my lady, oh, weep no more today. We will sing one song for our old Kentucky home, for our old Kentucky home far away." Lonesome. Together. Sobbing. Touching. Ricky and Ralph sang the Stanley number, "Gloryland," the chorus of which is "Weep not, friends. I'm going home . . . up there we'll die no more . . . no coffins will be made up there, no graves on that bright shore."

Ralph and Ricky then led us in "Swing Low, Sweet Chariot," some silence, then a spontaneous "Blue Moon of Kentucky" was softly sung. A prayer. The crowd moved slowly. The tent surrounding the grave was peeled away, light shining on the small box that contained the earthly remains of the larger-than-life man, Bill Monroe.

Jimbo Monroe later told me that before the casket was lowered, Ralph Stanley put his hand on Bill's casket and said, "We'll meet again someday." He turned to Jimbo and told him that Bill had been at Carter's funeral and had gone to Carter's casket and said, "We'll meet again someday." It meant a lot to me.

Two men with shovels began to do the job some of us couldn't bear to observe; others chose to add a handful or two to the grave. Many picked up a rock-like hunk of clay from the graveside to carry home with them. I could imagine the stories they might tell to their children or grandchildren . . . stories of a great man, the man who was so powerful, the man who was so real, so close to the earth, as one with the soil, the trees, the creatures, the little children.

What would I tell people one day, maybe not so far off, when they would stand

4. In Millersville, Tennessee.

breathlessly, holding on to every word, as I told of seeing Mr. Monroe on stage, how he always looked so much bigger than he really was in front of a crowd, of hearing him play "Dusty Miller," sing "Body and Soul," or "Close By," or "Kentucky Waltz," watching him dance with Emmylou, what would I tell them? Could they possibly understand what that meant to me, to all of us? How could they ever know what a force he was, how he had more presence than a room full of rich, well-educated men? How to put into words what I'm having such a difficult time feeling? I'm trying and I'm crying. How to type from memory because your eyes are too blurred to see the letters on the keys?

Blue Grass Boys reunion photo by the statue of Uncle Pen.[5] Many hugs, fellowship, silence. The wind blowing, warm and soft on that old cemetery mound. As the sun set, as the last goodbye was said, the road back out of Rosine seemed so different than the one I'd driven in on. A peace. I turned on my tape player and then, as I drove past the house where Charlie Monroe had lived, a house just a half mile or so below the house where J. B. and Malissa and Bill and all the Monroe kids had been raised, I swear to God, "My Last Days on Earth" began to play. It was meant to be that way.

Goodbye, Mr. Bill. Goodnight. Rest in peace. We love you. We'll meet again someday.

Originally posted on the Internet discussion list BGRASS-L on September 17, 1996. Reprinted by permission of the author.

EDITOR'S COMMENTS

Photographer Yeomans posted her account of the funeral service and burial ceremony in an e-mail message to BGRASS-L subscribers on September 17, 1996. It was later published in *Bluegrass Unlimited* 31:5 (Nov. 1996): 22–23. (This selection differs from the original mainly in matters of punctuation.)

"The Passing of a Patriarch"

MALCOLM JONES JR.

It is a rare thing to be able to credit one person with the creation of a musical genre. Everything from the symphony to the 12-bar blues were wrested into shape by many hands, by hacks and geniuses alike. Bluegrass is the one uncontested exception. One of the most electrifying genres in American popular music, it was the single-hand-

---

5. Actually, a large monument honoring Pendleton Vandiver, not a statue of him.

ed creation of Bill Monroe. He invented and refined it in the mid-1940s and thereafter performed it with zeal and exemplary skill almost until his death last week in Springfield, Tennessee; he was 84 and had had a stroke earlier this year. Even Monroe, a man not given to false modesty—or modesty of any kind,[1] for that matter—sounded flabbergasted by his creation. "I never wrote a tune in my life," he once said. "All that music's in the air around you all the time. I was just the first one to reach up and pull it out."[2]

The truth is, Monroe listened harder than most people, and he listened everywhere—to the guitars and fiddles of his brothers and mother and uncle, to the choirs he heard in church and to the radio that brought Tin Pan Alley all the way to the Rosine, Kentucky, farm where he grew up. In songs like "Blue Moon of Kentucky" and "The Gold Rush," the mature musician would fuse Gaelic fiddle tunes with blues, stir in the syncopation of swing and acrid gospel harmonies and then accelerate this hybrid to a breakneck tempo.

Monroe's "high, lonesome sound" was both ancient and contemporary, a true reflection of its creator's divided sensibilities. He depended on technology—Grand Ole Opry radio broadcasts, the recording studio, buses for touring—to become a household name across the nation. And yet, he viewed the modern world with grave suspicion. All his life he kept looking back, cherishing songs he'd learned from his uncle, the fiddler Pen Vandiver, adamantly refusing to hear his music played on anything but acoustic instruments. His genius lay in his ability to express his divided loyalties in his music. The exquisite tension in bluegrass—the sound of something threatening every second to fly apart—was put there by a man trying his damnedest to negotiate a truce between past and present.

Monroe influenced everyone from Elvis Presley to the Grateful Dead.[3] And while bluegrass may sound a bit antique six decades after its invention, it has lost none of its ferocity—until now. For the unmatched performer of this music was always Monroe himself, a brilliant composer, an intrepid instrumentalist, and a wonderful singer. No one who saw him in his prime could forget the sound of that near-psychotic falsetto soaring over the sound of a mandolin played so fast that one critic said Monroe was not playing his instrument so much as piloting it.[4] Pyrotechnics, however, were only part of the point. "It's played from my heart to your heart," Monroe declared. Even near the end, when the famously fierce voice had thinned to transparency and the fingers were no longer so fleet, Monroe never lost his ability to touch your heart, or make the hair rise on the back of your neck.

1. Bill *was* modest, especially about his playing, but not about the music he fathered.
2. This quotation is derived from banjo player Butch Robins in Jason DeParle's "Bill Monroe Has Lots to Sing but Little to Say."
3. Bill had little if any influence on the Grateful Dead, other than on the late Jerry Garcia. See the editor's comments, second paragraph.
4. Robert Cantwell in *Bluegrass Breakdown*.

EDITOR'S COMMENTS

Jones Jr., the cultural editor for *Newsweek,* wrote this tribute for the September 23, 1996, issue of the magazine.

The late Jerry Garcia and his friend Sandy Rothman ("Bill Monroe's Birthday Party") came east from California in 1964, hoping to work with Bill. Rothman stayed and was eventually hired, but Garcia decided to return to California and later helped form the Grateful Dead. Although Garcia continued to be a fan (about a year before his death, in the booket for MCA's *The Music of Bill Monroe,* he was quoted as saying "I still want to be a Blue Grass Boy"),[1] Bill had little if any influence on the rest of the famous rock band. (Bill's influence *was* wide, but among rockers it was probably strongest among the first generation of white performers, including Buddy Holly, Carl Perkins, and Elvis Presley.)

Note

1. Booklet compiled by John W. Rumble for *The Music of Bill Monroe: From 1936 to 1994,* MCA Records, MCAC/MCAD4-11048, released 1994, 43.

"Cross-eyed Child"

JOHN HARTFORD

The cross-eyed child is left alone, alone with his lonesome eyes,
While older brothers ride away in boots and clothes so fine.
He walks the hills and the railroad track, singing in a voice so high,
A voice so wild it will freeze your heart, like the heart of the cross-eyed child.

Behind the house, behind the barn, behind the white oak tree,
Underneath the old back porch, where he may not be seen,
He hides that they not laugh at him as they go riding by,
And know the tears that feed the pain in the heart of the cross-eyed child.

Back inside the darkness there he hears the fiddle tune.
She takes his hand and pulls him out and leads him into the room.
Where brothers drink and uncles play and sisters dance in style.
No drop to stain his determined lips, the vow of the cross-eyed child.

He wills himself to persevere as strong he upward grows.
They come to match him, fist and note, then on their way they go.
He does what he does the best he can, some say it is his style,
But they can't see old Kentucky in the heart of the cross-eyed child.

Still proving himself to people gone, his pride must have its way.
They're long since down in the churchyard ground on the hill so far away.

He sings his song to the midnight sky, a wail on the radio dial,
And around the world they hear the blues in the heart of the cross-eyed child.

And no one grins, we all chime in to pick with the cross-eyed child.

Originally published in *Bluegrass Unlimited* 31:4 (Oct. 1996): 33. © 1995. Reprinted by permission of the author.

EDITOR'S COMMENTS

The lyrics of Hartford's song accompanied Bill's obituary in the October 1996 issue of *Bluegrass Unlimited*. Hartford has since recorded this poem set to music for a Rounder Records project titled *Good Old Boys* (0462). On the recording and in live performance, he includes spoken reminiscences about Bill between the verses.

Bill's early vision affliction wasn't discussed in print until the 1970s. In his monograph for *Stars of Country Music,* Ralph Rinzler was the first to relate it to Bill's adult personality:

> It was not musicianship alone that enabled Monroe to establish a new, yet conservative, music in Nashville at a time when all trends pointed in directions other than those he chose. He could stand alone because that was his wont from earliest childhood. . . .
>
> The youngest of eight children, Bill was hampered by critically poor vision throughout his childhood. He was excluded from playing with his much older brothers both by the considerable gap in age . . . and by his inability to participate actively in the most popular sport, baseball, because of his bad eyesight. Not only was Bill left out of competitive play of his age group, he also avoided the gaze and jibes of elders, especially strangers, who were apt to comment on his crossed eyes. The Monroe family place, where Bill was born and raised, was on the wagon road into town. When passers-by stopped to visit, Bill recalls slipping off to the barn a few yards behind the house.[1]

Note

1. Ralph Rinzler, "Bill Monroe," in *Stars of Country Music: Uncle Dave Macon to Johnny Rodriguez,* ed. Bill C. Malone and Judith McCulloh (Urbana: University of Illinois Press, 1975), 205.

"The Bill I Loved"

HAZEL SMITH

I told George Fletcher[1] I could not write an obit for Bill Monroe. It hurts too much. Let me share a few personal incidents. I recall a time when it snowed 18 inches deep. We lived in a three-room shack in the middle of a cow pasture on Dickerson Road. It was so cold, and I was sick in bed with the flu and had a 104 temperature. Here Bill comes up that steep hill driving that old blue Chevrolet station wagon with groceries for my eight-year-old son, Terry, and myself, went in the kitchen and cooked our supper of roast, baked beans, and fried potatoes, and made a salad. Another time I remember he and Terry went to town and bought me a makeup mirror for Mother's Day.

When my sons were 14 and 17, they began working on Bill's Goodlettsville farm. The stories they have from that time would fill a book. One Thanksgiving the Monroe brothers (Bill and Birch) and my two sons, Billy and Terry, came in from working the farm. They had me sit in the living room while they harmonized a hymn a cappella before they ate lunch. When my first grandchild, Adam, was born, Bill got to the hospital with flowers for Billy's wife, Takako, before anyone else. Billy asked Bill to be Adam's godfather. Bill was honored.

Once I fell on ice at Christmas and almost broke my leg off on mama's steps in North Carolina. After surgery, my leg wasn't healing, my temperature was dangerously high, and so was my blood pressure. Bill called. I explained to him the diagnosis and told him I was going to die if something wasn't done, and asked him to pray for me. When I heard his knees hit the floor and heard the prayer he was praying, begging the Lord to heal me, I had no doubt in my mind what the outcome would be. Sure enough, when a shocked doctor came into the room the next morning, my brother Henry and Terry were there. The doctor came in shaking his head. "It's amazing," he said. "Your temp. is normal, your blood pressure is down, and let me look at that leg." I told him there was no use to look, it was scabbed over. Of course it was. The doctor didn't understand when I flat told him I had a miracle healing. When I finally flew home from the hospital, I'd sit in the living room in my recliner and stare out the storm door at the snow. Every day I'd see that big white hat walking up the hill I live on in Madison, and it would be Bill with a plate of food for me from a restaurant.

Then there was the time 30 Japanese bluegrass students and their escort were at my house. I secretly called Bill. He came with his mandolin, walked around to

---

1. The senior editor of *Country Music* magazine at the time.

the back door and knocked. When he walked in, they screamed in excitement as he took out his mandolin, and played and sang. There wasn't a dry eye in the room. Another time he stopped on I-65[2] to help this couple with three kids in an old car that had a flat tire. Bill had the poor, sunburned farmer and his family get in his car. He drove them to a filling station and paid for having the tire patched. He let them out of his car and watched the man put the tire on, then he told them to meet him in an hour at the filling station. He took that family backstage at the Opry that night. That day I'd watched as a big shot with a big mouth, driving a shiny new Cadillac, was bragging about his Texas oil wells and all his money. He got in Bill's face and asked him how to get in the Opry. Bill looked the other way with that look he could have, and said he didn't know anything about it. To Bill, it was the little man that mattered.

Both Bill and my son Billy went to Holiday Heights Baptist Church,[3] and many times on Sunday night the two of them would sing from the same hymn book. This meant a lot to Bill, and he'd always call and tell me about it. He always had quarters for the kids at church. There's no telling how many quarters he's given children through the years, including my grandsons Adam and Jeremy.

After getting permission from MCA, the boys and I drove out to Bill's log cabin and told him that K-tel wanted Billy and Terry[4] to record a tribute album to him. Bill was thrilled and asked if they'd "let" him play and sing on it. On February 21st, just weeks before his stroke, I drove Bill to the studio. I've never seen him happier. Bill said it was like old times being with Billy and Terry and me. As it turned out, Bill's last recording was done in my presence and with my sons. Bill played mandolin and sang "Blue Moon of Kentucky," played the mandolin riff on the beginning of "Mule Skinner Blues,"[5] and played mandolin and sang harmony on the last chorus of "Walk Softly on This Heart of Mine." Then he asked to hear the entire album.

"That's fine, right there," Bill allowed. "Billy, you and Terry should be on the Opry. You done it the way it's supposed to be," he concluded. Inside the CD[6] is a priceless photograph, taken in the studio that day by Terry's wife, Sharon, of Bill with Billy and Terry. And wouldn't you know, Bill gave Tyler and Tara (Terry and Sharon's kids) each a quarter that day.

Bill Monroe is the ONLY person who created his own music in the 20th century. Even Bob Dylan told Bill this when he came to see him perform at the Troubadour in Los Angeles some years back. The music speaks for itself.

I will let writers with minds greater than mine tell the story of bluegrass and how an almost-blind-from-birth, uneducated genius created this marvelous music. Tonight, the night of his death, I can only speak from my heart and share with

---

2. The main north-south interstate through Nashville.
3. Bill's church is located near the Bell Cove club. See the editor's comments, second paragraph.
4. Both of Smith's sons are active in bluegrass. See the editor's comments, third paragraph.
5. Which Billy Smith sang.
6. *Bill Monroe Tribute*, K-tel, 3642-2, released 1996.

you these personal moments I spent with the Bill I loved . . . times like these, when
I would forget he was a legend and in the Country Music Hall of Fame.

Originally published in *Country Music* 182 (Nov.–Dec. 1996): 4. Reprinted by permission of Sussex Publishers, Inc.

EDITOR'S COMMENTS

For her column in the November–December 1996 issue of *Country Music,* Smith
wrote of a different side of Bill—the caring friend who would go out of his way to
help whenever help was ever needed.

Holiday Heights Baptist Church in Hendersonville is located near the Bell Cove
club, and it was there, on Wednesday nights after church, that Bill would sit in with
the Larry Cordle band at "the Cove."

Both of Smith's sons are active and successful in bluegrass music. Billy (born
November 11, 1956), a talented singer and guitarist, has written songs recorded by
Bill ("He'll Take You In"), Alison Krauss, and the Lonesome River Band, among
others. Terry (born June 15, 1960), one of the music's finest bassists, has worked with
the Osborne Brothers since June 1989.

"Bill Monroe: An Appreciation"

RICHARD SPOTTSWOOD

With Bill Monroe's death, the world seems different. Sure, his health had been slowly
declining, and his voice had been a less than perfect instrument for years, but the
overdue acknowledgements and accolades of the 1980s and 1990s[1] and, most of all,
his continued presence among us, kept him with us both as a friend and as an artistic witness to everything he stood for in American music. His frailties may have
revealed his humanity, but through his artistry he was like a God to us, his flock,
representing a creative genius we've come to understand was truly great. The stature and accomplishments of Bill Monroe invite comparison with those of any other artist you care to name.

Other attempts to establish Monroe's proper place have inspired comparisons
with performers and composers from Charlie Parker to Charles Ives, from Mozart
to Ellington. These seem just, if subjective, and acknowledge that appreciation of
the impact and true worth of Monroe's art has steadily grown since the 1960s, when

---

1. Some of these not previously mentioned are noted in the editor's comments, second paragraph.

SPOTTSWOOD ✍ "An Appreciation" 259

his friend, manager, and fan Ralph Rinzler first coined the phrase "Father of Blue-grass,"[2] which implicitly crystallized his role as founder of a new music which owed its flowering to root elements of the blues, minstrelsy, gospel songs, fiddle tunes, and country music.

It's not that Monroe's musical revolution was part of any conscious scheme. Throughout his career, he went out of his way to celebrate his and our musical past, both as it really was and as his fertile imagination remembered and recreated it. With his older brother Charlie, the Monroe Bothers revived and recast traditional songs, songs from the 19th and early 20th centuries, old and new gospel tunes, songs from the Carter Family and Jimmie Rodgers repertoires,[3] and anything else which lingered from earlier days that could fire their imagination. The Blue Grass Boys of 1940 and beyond worked in new circumstances created by the recent formation of BMI (Broadcast Music, Incorporated), which sought new country music, rewarding composers with copyright protection and royalty payments. Though the system and its new economics didn't cast traditional music aside, it soon became clear that an important part of a country musician's livelihood would be the creation and publication of original material.

Monroe records of the time (1940–45) extended the Brothers' mixture to include new music which fit the Blue Grass Boys' sound. Bill's earliest "compositions" consisted of two blues-flavored mandolin features, the western-flavored "Honky Tonk Swing" and the supercharged "Tennessee Blues," whose accelerated tempo and high energy foretold much that would be characteristic of bluegrass. By 1945, he had composed enough original songs to feature them on most of a recording session. He kept creating memorable original songs through the early 1950s and astonishing instrumental tunes practically to the end.

Monroe's songs came to define bluegrass as much as the sound of the mandolin or banjo. Except for his songs of faith, most were somber, some were tragic and, as Robert Cantwell has observed, there were few which didn't carry a sense of deep nostalgia and distance in time or in place from home, family, a loved one, a community, cherished memories, or cherished values. These qualities, as much as Bill's arresting tenor voice, gave us the notion of the "high, lonesome sound."

Despite his proclaimed "ancient tones," Monroe was no antiquarian. He came of age with personalities like Alan Lomax and Burl Ives, whose specialty was preserving and recreating the past; Bill Monroe celebrated the past instead by using it as a key reference point within the context of a music as contemporary—and revolutionary—as that of Igor Stravinsky or Miles Davis. Unlike them, he rarely used dissonance for its own sake; Bill's melodic and harmonic language rarely strayed beyond those in Baptist hymnals. Instead, his musical revolution was created by a new ensemble style which deliberately turned its back on the prevailing honky-tonk sound of electric guitars, keeping for rhythm only the guitar and jazz-derived string bass.

---

2. It was not Rinzler who coined the phrase.

3. The Monroe Brothers recorded only one Rodgers song, "Dear Old Sunny South by the Sea," which they titled "In My Dear Old Southern Home."

Bill kept the fiddle for those ancient tones. Its association with 18th century Scots-Irish pioneers let us know that even his new music bore deep roots. His mandolin music echoed the fiddle, which, in Bill's childhood, had been his first inspiration, as he created new possibilities for an instrument historically thought of as little more than a toy. Finally, though Earl Scruggs brought his novel banjo techniques to the Blue Grass Boys in a state of high development, it's hard to think of any other kind of ensemble Earl could have blended with so perfectly. And, as Stephen Wade notes, the banjo, with its head of stretched hide, not only replaced the jazz drum, but added those exciting, displaced syncopations which reproduced African-American rhythms in a white mountain band.

Had Bill Monroe not been such an accomplished, aggressive musician in his own right, an Earl Scruggs would have upstaged him and everyone else around, leaving only a backup role possible for others. But it proved a major final touch for Monroe, adding another level of excitement, as Scruggs and his successors placed rhythmic accents where they'd never been before and provided a lead voice which could blend with and compete with the fiddle and mandolin. The banjo brought its own historical symbolism along too. Fiddle and banjo had been the African-American instruments of choice from slavery days through the early 20th century. They'd also been the vehicles for minstrel and mountain music in the 19th century; their inclusion in bluegrass kept still one more ancient tone alive and well in our own time.

Bill's vision and imagination allowed him to mold his music from his ingredients and create something instantly recognizable and distinct from anything preceding it. Even after his music was emulated to the point where it received the name "bluegrass," he continued to develop and extend it in accord with his inner voices. One fiddle became multiple fiddles in the 1950s and, when Kenny Baker became more or less a permanent adjunct, Monroe's compositions became primarily instrumental and increasingly fiddle-dominated. His 1954 "Get Up John," based on one of his uncle Pen's fiddle tunes, became something of a model for Monroe pieces in the 1970s and 1980s, which explored various modalities and minor keys, exploring those ancient tones at the expense of the hotter, more flamboyant sensibilities of "Raw Hide" or "Blue Grass Breakdown." Suitably sprinkled amongst the new/old tunes were some archaic polkas and waltzes, further recalling a real and imagined past. With the exception of "Jerusalem Ridge" and "My Last Days on Earth," much of this large body of instrumental music has gone unappreciated in our time; I don't think it will forever.

This all-too-brief appreciation hardly begins to tell the tale of this incomparable man and his music. For me, it's only an inadequate testimonial to someone who, though I never knew him well, has touched me again and again from my own youth on to advancing years. I always felt a touch of shyness in his presence, since even in the flesh he seemed so much larger than life.

For the moment I mourn his death while I celebrate his long, exciting life. Even if he hadn't survived to create a musical landscape beyond that which he assembled in the 1940s, he would still be a household name. How fortunate we are that he did survive, that his vision, his sense of possibilities, and his artistic resolve compelled him to renew and redefine for so many years the music we call bluegrass.

Originally published in *Bluegrass Unlimited* 31:5 (Nov. 1996): 16–17. Reprinted by permission of the author.

EDITOR'S COMMENTS

This thoughtful commentary appeared in the November 1996 issue of *Bluegrass Unlimited*. In contrast to the personal tribute of Hazel Smith ("The Bill I Loved"), Spottswood expressed the sense of loss felt by those who had admired Bill from afar, who had studied and analyzed his music, yet who claimed that they "never knew him well."

Among the many other awards and recognitions not previously mentioned that were given to Bill in the 1980s and 1990s: In 1982 he was one of the first recipients of the National Heritage Fellowship Award from the National Endowment for the Arts; his "Blue Moon of Kentucky" became a state song of Kentucky in 1989; in 1991 he was inducted into the International Bluegrass Music Association's "Hall of Honor"; he received the Lifetime Achievement Award in 1993 from the National Academy of Recording Arts and Sciences; and in 1995 President Clinton awarded him the National Medal of Arts in ceremonies at the White House, after which he sang the aforementioned song of the Blue Grass State.

"I Hear a Sweet Voice Calling"

TOM WOLF

I'm back here in Nairobi[1] where I came first in the Peace Corps in 1967, and I remember finding a Bill Monroe LP in a local record shop (*The Father of Blue Grass Music*, with the old RCA cuts, including "Six White Horses," "Orange Blossom Special," "No Letter in the Mail," "Dog House Blues," etc.)[2] and writing to *Bluegrass Unlimited* about it.

So it's here again where I hear about his passing. I feel the need to share my thoughts and a few memories with you folks, along with some other friends who have helped sustain me over these years and done so much for the music, especially 30 years ago when it was considerably more "fringe" than it is now. I remember

---

1. Capital city of the east African country of Kenya.
2. Bill Monroe and His Blue Grass Boys, *The Father of Blue Grass Music*, RCA Camden, CAL-719, released Oct. 1962.

taking out my subscription with the second issue, about a year after my brother, a couple of friends, and I from Michigan went down to Fincastle[3] for that first Life-Marking event. I've still got my color (silent) movies of that, with Bill and Jimmy Martin, the Stanleys with Shuffler,[4] and all. Quite a weekend. And that was just over a year since first seeing Monroe (with Doc Watson) at our college (Oberlin), when Ralph Rinzler was really doing everything he could to get Monroe onto parts of the American map he hadn't got to before.

I've got two little stories. The first is of just a few weeks ago. I was home last July,[5] and heard Bill was quite sick, hospitalized after a stroke. At one show in Michigan, Sonny Osborne reported that a month or so earlier he had been to visit Bill, but didn't get much of a response in terms of recognition. That didn't sound good.

So I guess it wasn't surprising that on a Thursday recently I dreamed he had died. I woke up very anxious, and the following weekend when I tried to phone my mother, I wanted to ask her if she had heard anything about his condition. Due to the clogged phone lines, I didn't get through until the following Monday. She assured me nothing had happened, saying that if he had died, it surely would have been on the news. So I relaxed. The next day I received an e-mail message from one of my old college corridor-mates (now a USAID director in Rwanda)[6] which said simply: "Subject: Bill Monroe; Message: R.I.P." Later the same day another e-mail came in from my brother saying Bill had died the very day I had that conversation with my mother, just four days after my dream.

The other story has two parts. The first goes back to 1975, when the Blue Grass Boys were in London, England, and so was I, as a student. People had been hoping that after his appearance at Wembley Stadium, Bill would feel like picking some in his basement dressing room. I walked to my car to get my brother's old Gibson Jumbo I had with me there, but by the time I got back, everyone (including Bill Keith, who was touring in Europe, and Bill Clifton, who was then living in England) had left. Bill was sitting there by himself, listening to a young English guy playing Irish tunes on a mandolin, very well. After each tune, Bill would say, "That's very good. Play me another." This went on for some time, until the English guy said that was about all the tunes he knew, so he put his mandolin away.

So I took out the old Gibson, and right away Bill sort of snapped, and said, "That's just like the guitar my brother Charlie had when he started recording." So I asked Bill if he remembered one of those early songs, "What Would You Give in Exchange for Your Soul?" He said sure, and before I was through the first verse, he was singing it with me. Then he picked up his mandolin and we did a few more, including "The Old Crossroad." The main thing I recall is how incredibly powerful his voice was. It wasn't so loud, just POWERFUL. You really had to work to keep

---

3. Fincastle, Virginia, near Roanoke, the site of the first bluegrass festival in 1965.
4. George Shuffler, lead guitarist for the Stanley Brothers.
5. 1996.
6. The United States Agency for International Development, for which both the author and his friend work. Rwanda borders Kenya in east Africa.

up with him, and the same for the rhythm on the guitar. That mandolin of his would just wipe you up if you didn't stand your ground. I struggled. Bill paid no mind; he just sang and played.

Once I almost lost it. I thought: "Here I am singing with Bill Monroe," with no one else but the now-silent English mandolin player around, watching Monroe in awe. I tried to stop thinking, and just sing. And then our other friends started drifting back in, and before long we had an incredible session with Bill Keith on banjo joining Kenny Baker and the rest of Bill's band to fill things out. I still remember Kenny's break on "Highway of Regret," as we pinched songs from the Stanleys, and elsewhere. But the main thing was, Bill was playing, and singing, for himself. He didn't care about not being on stage. He probably didn't care that much about the rest of us. He was doing his thing, playing his music. I can't remember how long we went on for. Nobody wanted it to stop.

The second part of the story took place about a year later when I met Bill at a festival in Indiana. Right away he said, "I hope you'll come up on stage and sing one of those songs we sang in London last year." And we did (once I followed his instructions to change my shorts for long pants and "put on a real shirt, O.K.?"), after Bill introduced me as "one of our friends we got to know over there in England, though he comes from Michigan." So we did "The Old Crossroad" (but this time he made me a lot more nervous by making me sing solo lead and then coming in with three harmony parts on the chorus, not quite as exciting as a duet all the way through. And he had raised it from G to B-flat!).

Why would Bill take the trouble to give recognition to somebody no one else knew? To someone who was not *that* great a guitar player, or singer, really? He gained nothing for himself by doing that. But he made the day—and more—for his admirer. I guess that was just his way of showing his appreciation for somebody who had shown appreciation for *his* music, and who had had the chance to show it in rather unusual circumstances.

There will come a time when there won't be anyone alive who saw Monroe, listened to him talk, watched him play, heard him sing. Sure, there will be the films, the recordings, the videos, the books. But will they begin to convey the strength of the man, his bursting talent, his pride—even arrogance—and the sheer power of his creativity and presence? It's hard to say. But for those of us who witnessed it, however distantly, or however briefly, it's something we will never forget, or ever get completely out of us.

Two final notes: First, who can tell me why Bill had the bass stop playing during all the choruses he sang with Lester Flatt on "I Hear a Sweet Voice Calling"? It puts such an incredible focus on those words and voices. Did anyone ever ask Bill?[7]

Second, last Friday I walked into the bar area of a big hotel here in Nairobi and his 1939 version of "Orange Blossom Special" (off that same LP I had seen in a music

---

7. I never asked Bill, but it's my guess that bassist Howard Watts stopped playing to concentrate on making his harmony singing perfect, which it is.

store my first week in the country in 1967) was playing on the P.A. I asked one of the (African) waiters, "Where in the world did that tape come from?" He smiled and said, "It's the bar man's personal tape, not the hotel's!"

Originally published in *Bluegrass Unlimited* 31:9 (Mar. 1997): 10–11. Reprinted by permission of the author.

EDITOR'S COMMENTS

This selection, an open letter to readers of *Bluegrass Unlimited,* was published in the "Reader's Forum" section of the March 1997 issue. When Wolf wrote his first letter to *Bluegrass Unlimited* in 1967, after finding one of Bill's albums halfway around the world in Kenya, the magazine was still being printed on a mimeograph machine.

"Thirty Years of Bean Blossom Recollections"

JIM PEVA

It is hard for me to believe that over thirty years have passed since the first outdoor festival at Bean Blossom.

Our family first attended indoor shows at Bean Blossom in 1961, when they were held each weekend in the Brown County Jamboree Barn, now torn down.[1] It was located on the site of the present museum. There was usually a square dance on Saturday night, and afternoon and evening shows on Sunday. Only part of the barn floor was concrete in those days, each side and part of the rear was covered with cinders. The show season at the barn lasted from Easter Sunday well into November. During some of those November shows, snow covered the ground outside and the old wood stoves along the sides of the barn had to be fed to keep the place warm. Bill Monroe and his Blue Grass Boys almost always opened the season and played four or five times during the year. In all that time, we only missed one of Bill's shows.

The first outdoor festival I attended was in 1967.[2] At that time I had a fold-down camper and we pulled it to Bean Blossom with C. D. McClary's pickup truck. There were just three of us that trip, C. D., Bud Freedman, and myself.[3] We put up the camper right out in the open field between the barn and the dip in the road that leads to

---

1. It was torn down in 1986.

2. The first *outdoor* festival at Bean Blossom was held in 1968. See the editor's comments, second paragraph.

3. Peva and McClary were part of a group that managed the park in 1965. See the editor's comments, third paragraph.

the present stage area. We had no electricity or water, and carried our water in jugs from a tank truck parked near where the concession stands are now located.

I will never forget the arrival of Bill "Saginaw" Richmond at the start of that festival. This may sound like an exaggeration, but I swear it is true. We had just got our camper set up when a pickup truck camper rolled to a stop beside us. A large, portly man with a wild look in his eyes jumped out of the passenger side of the truck with his fiddle and bow in his hand, literally, before the truck came to a stop—looking for a jam session. Jam sessions were not hard to find, and every few yards there would be a knot of musicians "swatting it out," surrounded by a ring of spectators four or five deep. Saginaw's brother, his driver, immediately set about his task of relaying refreshments to whichever jam session Saginaw was participating in. They arrived at noon, as I recall, and the sun was hot. Saginaw carried a white bath towel draped over his shoulder to wipe sweat with. He was still jamming when the sun came up the next morning.

One evening, C. D., Bud, and I were strolling through the campground (the whole place was a campground, just about, except inside the old barn), when out of the darkness came the sound of this beautiful, precise guitar, accompanying a fiddle player. We listened to the music for several minutes, not knowing who the players were, because of the large group of spectators blocking our view. As we worked our way through the crowd, we discovered that the flawless guitar work was being performed by Red Smiley, who was accompanying an unknown fiddler who claimed to have just composed the number they were playing. If that was true, it must have been a tune very similar to one Red knew by heart, because he anticipated every chord change effortlessly.

That was some of the magic of those early festivals at Bean Blossom—unexpectedly discovering the real stars of bluegrass—people whose records you had, but had never seen in person before, nonchalantly jamming with their fans.

One late afternoon, a day or so before the festival started, Bill Monroe and a small group of four or five fans were having a little picking session in the barn. They were seated in a circle on folding chairs and only a few people were there, listening. Bill was dressed in work clothes, denim pants and jacket and a ball cap. He had probably just come in from a fence-row clearing or fence-stretching session with the Blue Grass Boys, who were expected to help with the chores around the festival grounds in those days. Just then, a "hippie" girl walked into the barn, carrying all her belongings and her instrument case. As I recall, she was from California, and she said it was her first time at Bean Blossom. She politely asked if she could join the session, and somebody pulled up another chair. She played one or two songs with the group, until Bill took a mandolin break, and then she turned pale, stopped playing, and said, "OH, MY GOD—YOU'RE BILL MONROE!!" Bill didn't say anything, but chuckled and kept playing. He always seemed to get a kick out of things like that.

In the 1970s, on rare occasions before the festival started, Bill would bring his mandolin and pick around our campfire late at night. I especially remember one

Tuesday night when he played "Evening Prayer Blues," telling us beforehand what to listen for in each part. Magic moments, and no tape recorder.

The events of the various festivals that stick in my mind sort of blur together and I can't remember precisely at which festival a particular thing happened in most cases. And my memories of Bean Blossom are centered more around jam sessions and friendships made around campfires than what took place on the stage. One big exception to this was the year that Lester Flatt came to Bean Blossom for the first time.[4] Bill was on stage and he welcomed Lester with a handshake and performed several songs with him, ending their 20 some-odd years of ignoring each other. The crowd went wild. Everybody wanted to see this and the backstage emptied out, all of the entertainers rushing around in front. I was sitting in a folding lawn chair in the second row. Even though there were wooden-plank benches, because the benches were uncomfortable, a lot of people in those days brought chairs. There was an empty lawn chair beside me and Don Reno spotted it and, in the excitement of the moment, sat down too hard and the aluminum frame broke, slowly settling him to ground level. Don didn't seem to notice, being overcome with the emotion of the moment—the reunion of two of the greatest performers bluegrass music will ever know.

The uncrowned king of the post-midnight jammers from the Blue Grass Boys has to be Kenny Baker. During one of the early festivals, Kenny and Bob Black, later to become a Blue Grass Boy himself, jammed for several nights until the sun came up. Bob's unique banjo style, and his ability to play fiddle tunes note-for-note on the banjo, suited Kenny to a T. Out of those jam sessions came several Kenny Baker albums featuring Bob Black on the banjo. During the later festivals, Kenny would jam at the campsite of Hazel and Doc Ward, just at the edge of the woods. Raymond Huffmaster was a regular there too, along with Dana Cupp, Jack Zell, and many other amateur and professional musicians who played around the campfire many a night until dawn for the pure pleasure of making music.

During the early Bean Blossom festivals, Calvin Robins (Butch Robins' father) was the electrician-handyman for the festival grounds and also served as the goodwill ambassador to the Japanese fans who attended the festival. (Calvin later paid a visit to Japan, resulting from the friendships made at Bean Blossom.)

After Calvin's death,[5] my daughter Cathy and grandson Shelby unofficially assumed Calvin's role, and we would store the tents used by the Japanese fans at our house during the year and put them up, or reserve space for them to be put up, near our camper when festival time came around. They would usually arrive late on Friday afternoon, from Nashville, in a chartered bus. Two brothers, Saburo and Toshio Watanabe, who have a music business in Japan,[6] would be the tour guides, usually one of them every other year. Some of the groups were quite large, 20 or 30 people, most of them college-age, and nearly all were musicians. Saburo played banjo and

4. 1971.
5. Calvin Robins died on May 21, 1980.
6. B.O.M. Service, Ltd., Hyogo, Japan.

Toshio played bass with the Bluegrass 45, which performed at one of the early Bean Blossom festivals,[7] becoming the first Japanese bluegrass band to play in the U.S.

It became a tradition that we would have a hamburger cookout over the campfire on our grill for the Japanese folks. They couldn't get their fill of beef—a very expensive commodity in Japan. One year the group surprised us by cooking for us—teriyaki steak with vegetables—and it was delicious!

We were always amazed at how many Japanese musicians could sleep in a small tent. Cathy had an aluminum-frame four-person tent which they used when their tents were full. You could tell how many people were occupying a tent by counting the shoes outside and dividing by two. We counted sixteen shoes outside this four-person tent.

The Friday evening "Sunset Jam" was a tradition at the June Bean Blossom festival up until a few years ago. After the afternoon supper break, a sound system would be set up between the barn and the road, near the entrance. Everybody with an instrument, professional entertainers and fans alike, was invited to come and take part in the jam. Bill was the emcee and he would invite individuals up to the mike to perform with him and they would play until the sun went down. Many people who were later to make their own professional bluegrass and country music debuts played in these jam sessions. Sometimes the jam would last until the evening show had already begun back on the stage. Bill would have a count made of those participating, and, as I recall, sometimes there were over 200 musicians playing in the Sunset Jam.

Birch Monroe was a fixture at Bean Blossom up until the time of his death in 1982. Bill would usually invite "Brother Birch Monroe" up to the stage sometime during his show to fiddle a tune or two and sing a gospel song with the Blue Grass Boys. Birch lived in Martinsville, Indiana, and took care of the Bean Blossom property for Bill. He mowed the grass, fixed the plumbing, split firewood for the woodstoves in the barn, and did every other chore around the barn and the festival that needed to be done. But you never saw Birch without his white shirt and tie. It didn't matter what he was doing, digging a ditch, or performing on stage, he always wore a white shirt and tie. One time I asked Birch where he got the particular tie he was wearing, and he answered without the slightest hesitation, "I got that tie in Gary, Indiana, in 1930."

Birch was a friendly man, a good old-time fiddler, and he was very proud of Bill's success. Bill liked to kid Birch, and he always took it good-naturedly. Almost without exception, when Birch would emcee a show in the barn, his first words were "Howdy, howdy, friends and neighbors." He sang the bass parts in the quartets and you can hear his distinctive voice on some of Bill's recordings made in the 1940s and 50s.[8]

The trademark of the early Bean Blossom outdoor festivals was music, music, continuous music. About the only quiet time was between sunrise and 10 A.M. Jam

---

7. 1971.

8. Birch sang bass on four of Bill's recordings: "The Shining Path" and "Wicked Path of Sin" in 1946, and "I'll Meet You in Church Sunday Morning" and "Boat of Love" in 1950.

sessions were everywhere and the heavy thump of the upright bass permeated everything. The shows on stage were incidental to the jam sessions, and many of those (like Bill "Saginaw" Richmond) who came only to jam never went down to see a show. After one of those festivals, my wife Ailene and I came home to a quiet house. I asked her, "Can you hear it—the music in your head?" And she could hear it too!

So why would anyone go to Bean Blossom festivals 30 years in a row? I think I know the answer—a vain attempt to recapture the past—the hope that the jam sessions will be back in all their glory—that old friends from far away, not seen in years, will miraculously show up to help relive the good times of years gone by. And sometimes it happens—Bill Richmond shows up after an absence of several years, this time playing fiddle with the band Blue Velvet—but he still finds time to jam. Tex Roberts from Pennsylvania appears with his guitar after a 10-year absence and again sings "40th and Plum" at the campfire. But Tex will be dead of a heart attack before the next festival comes around. And so many others won't be back either, because they have gone on to a greater festival with their Maker. Farmers, carpenters, truckers, physicians, teachers, lawyers, laborers, all drawn together by their love of an original style of American music—bluegrass—and, at Bean Blossom, they could shake hands with and marvel at the artistry of the man who put it all together—the man who started this great annual gathering over 30 years ago—truly a legend in his own time and an American Treasure, Mr. William Smith Monroe. And they knew that Mister Bill would be genuinely glad to see them.

But now Bill Monroe, too, has moved to a better place. Bluegrass music will continue, and, hopefully, James Monroe will continue the festivals at Bean Blossom for many years to come.[9] And as time passes, I believe those of us who were regulars at Bean Blossom will come to realize how very privileged we were to share the unique experience of being friends of Bill Monroe; to help him load his cows on a truck down by the lake; to help get the bean pot ready for Tex Logan's barbecued beans; to take charge of the gate for him at his request when James Monroe was involved in a serious accident en route to Bean Blossom, while Bill was in Oklahoma.[10] All of these, and hundreds of other memories, make Bean Blossom a very special place.

But one memory will always have an honored place on my wall. When Bill arrived at Bean Blossom from Oklahoma after James' accident, he insisted on paying me for supervising the ticket sales at the gate. I refused payment, telling him I was glad to do him a favor. Several days later at the festival, I was sitting by my campfire, and Bill and all of the Blue Grass Boys walked up, with their instruments. They played a song, and then Bill had a framed certificate in his hand, which he handed to me.

9. James Monroe sold the Bean Blossom park in 1997. See the editor's comments, fourth paragraph.

10. This 1977 accident is discussed in "Monroe, the Father, Monroe, the Son," by Don Rhodes.

Bill Monroe's famous bluegrass festival at the
Brown County Jamboree Park, in Bean Blossom,
Indiana, is held every year in the month of June.
The friendship of Jim and Ailene Peva and
their daughters Mary, Becky and Kathy has
meant so much to me down through the years
here at Bean Blossom, that I want them to have
a pass to this festival for as long as I live.

The Father of Bluegrass music,

Bill Monroe.

Originally published in *Bluegrass Unlimited* 32:7 (Jan. 1998): 34–38. Reprinted by permission of the author.

EDITOR'S COMMENTS

Peva's recollections were featured in the January 1998 issue of *Bluegrass Unlimited.*

The first festival at Bean Blossom was held inside the Brown County Jamboree Barn on June 24 and 25, 1967. The first actual *outdoor* festival at Bean Blossom was held in 1968, on June 21 through 23, and it is this time that Peva recalls in the first part of his article.

A retired colonel in the Indiana State Police, Peva and three friends (including C. D. McClary) formed the Brown County Music Corporation in 1965, and took over management of the Brown County Jamboree for that year. The corporation made many improvements to the facility, helping to prepare the site for the 1967 festival.

Just prior to the publication of this article, in late 1997, James Monroe sold Monroe's Festival Park and Campground at Bean Blossom to former Blue Grass Boy Dwight Dillman, who picked banjo with Bill in 1974. Dillman has made extensive improvements and continues to hold festivals there.

"The Man in the White Hat"

JOEL M. VANCE

My son told me that Bill Monroe had died; it had just been on the news. I was down-stairs listening to bluegrass.

It was as if we'd gotten a call deep in the night saying, "I have bad news." It was as if a member of the family had died.

One I revered.

I "met" Bill Monroe only once—at a concert when I held out an album, in a sweaty hand, for an autograph. "Best Wishes, Bill Monroe," he wrote. Hardly an intimate relationship.

But my association with Bill Monroe was connected, over 48 years, like the beads of a rare necklace.

We all die; we knew Bill Monroe would die. I was amazed each time he got sick and survived, this old man who looked as if he'd stepped out of Canaan Land, doffed his Biblical robes in favor of an elegant cream-colored suit. He'd been reported ill with some dread disease, then he was back on stage, touring with that killing sched-ule. How could he go on and on?

He was 84 years old when he died, just four days short of 85. Most people ARE dead by then. But Bill Monroe was ageless. He'd beaten cancer, heart problems, and God knows what-all, had continued to perform, had continued to be . . . well, age-less. Other legends peeled off and crashed in the hills, one by one.

Roy Acuff died. Ernest Tubb died. Uncle Dave Macon, Sam and Kirk McGee, the Fruit Jar Drinkers . . . they all died. Bill Monroe? He'd be onstage at the Opry next Saturday night, just as he had been since 1939.

"Bill Monroe died," my son said.

I wanted to cry.

I don't cry much about people who die unless they are heroes, and few are. "Hell, he puts his pants on one leg at a time," was what Cal Hubbard told me about Stan Musial just before he introduced me to The Man. Cal Hubbard made both the base-ball and football Halls of Fame, and Musial was the greatest St. Louis Cardinal of all, also a Hall of Famer.

But I wasn't intimidated because I knew Stan the Man put his pants on one leg at a time and that helped me shake hands and not be daunted.

Bill Monroe? I was inarticulate and shaky-nervous when I handed him my al-bum, sweat stains from my hand on the cover. Few people transcend one leg at a time. Bill Monroe did.

We started the association that he didn't know we had back in 1947 on a sultry summer night before air conditioning, at least in Brunswick, Missouri.

Mr. Monroe and his Blue Grass Boys were barnstorming through the Midwest and Brunswick's El Jon Theater was a brief stop along an endless string of little towns going nowhere.

There was a movie and a stage show. I don't remember the movie, but I will never forget the music.

I was 14 years old. I watched the Blue Grass Boys work the single microphone like a synchronized athletic team, the instruments weaving around each other with cobra-like precision as the Boys stepped up for instrumental solos or merged for harmony singing.

This must have been the classic band with Flatt and Scruggs, Chubby Wise, Monroe, and Howard Watts, though they were to break up that same year.[1] I didn't realize I was watching history. But I did realize that I was listening to something exciting and enduring.

Bluegrass was new music in 1947. The Blue Grass Boys in their classic form first recorded only two years before,[2] though you could argue all the elements of the bluegrass sound had been around since the 1930s.

Few had heard music like it before. No one understood that a world was being created. It was something entirely new. Few are blessed with prevision and can realize they are witnessing history as it happens.

Bill and Charlie Monroe had all the elements of bluegrass in the 1930s, but there were only two of them; there were five Blue Grass Boys and one was Earl Scruggs with his magic banjo. Another was Lester Flatt, playing the G run . . . but if you listen closely to Bill and Charlie, you'll hear Charlie do nearly the same thing.

Dead . . . the Monroe Brothers all are dead now, and there is no one to take their place because the ones who came first are unique. They are pioneers and there can be only one generation of pioneers. Everyone else builds on that. When the elders of the tribe vanish, the genesis is gone and can never come again.

I spent my teenage Saturday nights glued to an old Zenith radio, listening to the Grand Ole Opry. I listened through endless Carl Smith and Faron Young and Kitty Wells sets just hoping I'd hear that hyped acoustic sound that Bill Monroe and his Blue Grass Boys created.

They tore through the "Mule Skinner Blues" and Jimmie Rodgers must have stirred in HIS grave to hear his eighth blue yodel gone so frantic.

There was nothing like it on the Opry. Bluegrass was a cautiously-approached music, like a snake you weren't sure about. Maybe it was venomous, maybe not. I suspect mainstream country was a little afraid of what would be called "folk music in overdrive."

Bill Monroe music was frenetic. It was like Elvis's recorded introduction to the "Milk Cow Blues"—"Wait a minute, fellas . . . that don't move!" And Elvis then launched a quintessential rockabilly treatise.

Elvis paid his own tribute to Mr. Monroe when he recorded "Blue Moon of Ken-

---

1. The band that Vance saw in the summer of 1947 broke up in early 1948.

2. This band had recorded for the first time less than a year earlier, in September 1946.

tucky" and Mr. Monroe said it was all right with him if that young feller shot adrenaline into his song. After all, that's what Mr. Monroe had done to country music.

I was down in the Missouri Ozarks 30 years later at the Eminence Bluegrass Festival. My car overheated and threatened to falter off to Automotive Heaven, but I could not have cared less. The music was what I came for and if I had to walk 150 miles home, so be it.

The Country Gentlemen were there and so was Mac Wiseman. And there was a big bus in the parking lot with Bill Monroe's name on it and I got dry in the mouth when I thought about that. I hadn't seen him since the El Jon, which had closed long before, for lack of business.

"And now, ladies and gentlemen, Bill Monroe and the Blue Grass Boys!"

We waited all day for that.

A little girl stood at the stage apron, patiently waiting for the song to end. Mr. Monroe, immaculate in white, looking like God had taken up the mandolin, finished his song, then he bent down on his knee, and listened to the little girl for a moment.

He straightened up and said, "The little lady wants to hear 'Footprints in the Snow.'" He smiled at her and the band swung into the song. Not "the kid" or "I have a request," but "the little lady," which is the way he saw this tiny child—a lady to whom he could only be courtly because that was his raisin'. I had a lump in my throat, not from the old weeper he sang, but because of his grace.

And then came that spooky album *Master of Bluegrass,* with the eerie instrumental "My Last Days on Earth." I listened to the sea gulls crying and the minor key moan of Mr. Monroe's famed F-5 and I thought "Oh God, he's going to die! He's writing his elegy. This is what he wants them to play at his funeral!"

The album came out in 1981 and Mr. Monroe strode the earth like a giant for another 15 years. Both he and God were wrong, I guess.

I have that album autographed. He was doing several shows a day at the Missouri State Fair and I was working the Conservation Department booth, answering the most-asked question, "Where's the john?"

I skipped out of work three times a day to see the Bill Monroe show. Over at the grandstands they were getting ready for Willie Nelson, the featured act, and tickets cost a small fortune. But Mr. Monroe and his band were free, in a small tent, sponsored by a benevolent corporate entity.

Mr. Monroe was limping from some infirmity or another and was helped onto the stage by his solicitous band members. He looked a thousand years old. He looked like Moses come down from the mountain with the commandments of life: "Live, love, and enjoy bluegrass."

When he struck up "Uncle Pen," there was no infirmity in those two hands. He ate the mandolin alive. It sang and cried and shouted every emotion. It was alive and so was I, sweating in the August heat and wondering why other people were the headliners and this old man was not. Hell, the El Jon headlined him when Willie Nelson was 15 years old.[3]

---

3. Willie Nelson was born on April 30, 1933. See the editor's comments, second paragraph.

Back at the booth where I worked, a woman conservation agent stopped by and said that Bill Monroe was an old family friend.

"He used to fox-hunt with my daddy," she said. He had stayed with them and they'd had a parlor pickin' session just the night before. "Oh, yeah," she said. "We sit around in the front room and pick some." She played bass and I guess all the neighborhood pickers came by to play with The Man.

"I'll let you know the next time he stays with us and you can sit in," she said. For years after I would sit outside our house in the dark and sing "Blue Moon of Kentucky" and dream of the day I might get to pick with Bill Monroe. I was afraid, but willing to try because I'd heard that while Bill Monroe was tough on his band, he was gentle with thumb-fingered amateur pickers like me.

I never got the chance. I never will.

Originally published in *Bluegrass Now* 8:1 (Jan. 1998): 46–47. Reprinted by permission of the author and the publisher.

EDITOR'S COMMENTS

Bluegrass Now, a relatively new bluegrass magazine published in Missouri, included this article by Missouri author Vance in its January 1998 issue.

Double-checking Willie Nelson's birthdate, I found that he was born on April 30, 1933. In the summer of 1947, when Bill and the Blue Grass Boys appeared at the El Jon Theater in Brunswick, Missouri, both Nelson and the author were fourteen years old!

"Bill Monroe's Rosine Home"

JAMES NOLD JR.

Rosine, Kentucky, had never seen a day like September 12, 1996.

The hearse carrying its most famous native son arrived from Nashville, speeding up U.S. 62 with a police escort. This highway came through in 1930, the year after Bill Monroe left Rosine to join his brothers working in the Sinclair Oil refinery east of Chicago—an inauspicious beginning that led quickly to a recording career, a spot as one of the bulwarks of the Grand Ole Opry, and recognition as perhaps the only American to have invented a musical form: bluegrass, named after his backup band, the Blue Grass Boys.

But while Monroe stopped living in Rosine during Herbert Hoover's administration, Rosine never stopped living in him.

He named these hills "the fondest spot in my memory" in his song "I'm on My

Way Back to the Old Home." The idea of "the folks back home" was a touchstone for all of his music.

Monroe's niece, Rosetta Kiper, a shy woman who nevertheless projects an astonishing radiance, is said to have been the inspiration for his song "My Rose of Old Kentucky." The tiny white church where the funeral took place was built in 1953 to replace the chapel where the Monroes had worshipped, a building that inspired one of his most touching religious songs, "Little Community Church."

Across the highway (named "Bill Monroe Avenue" as it passes through Rosine) was a space waiting for him in the "little lonesome graveyard" he described in "Memories of Mother and Dad." A few rows away from Monroe's grave (and those of his mother, father, and brothers)[1] is the monument to Bill's uncle, Pendleton Vandiver. One of Monroe's most famous songs turned "Uncle Pen" into a mythical figure, celebrating the old-fashioned fiddle tunes such as "Sally Goodin" and "Soldier's Joy" that uncle and nephew played for dances throughout these western Kentucky hills.

And the hill where the Monroes lived, Jerusalem Ridge, gave its name to one of Monroe's greatest instrumentals—a tale told by the fireside about the wild, free new world settled by the Scots-Irish and the music they brought with them.

"My father was a sentimental person," James Monroe said in a telephone interview several months after the funeral. "Things that happened in the past to him meant a lot to him. . . . Bill Monroe was a true Kentuckian—that's where his heart really was."

People standing outside waiting for the funeral to begin offered reporters their bits of contact with Monroe. One man played baseball against the team that traveled as part of his tent show in the 1940s; another recollected a profession of friendship Monroe made; another recalled how Monroe would visit people bearing gifts of a rooster and a hen—the rooster being a played-out gamecock, the hen a possible source of new fighters.

They heard him on the Opry; they saw him come to town in one or another impressive car. They go hunting near the family's house—boarded up, sagging, surrounded by coal pits, but still standing. One local man, Otis Stogner, has a fiddle he says belonged to Uncle Pen, a relic that would be the bluegrass equivalent of water used by John the Baptist.

"The truth is, this town is a shrine to Bill Monroe because he wrote all of his music about the stuff in this town," says Aaron Hutchings, the Louisville-based unit leader of television station KET2, and chair and founder of the Rosine Association, the group that is planning a monument in Rosine—and other things to follow—to honor Monroe.

And yet the relationship between Monroe and Rosine was not entirely happy. He was painfully shy as a child—he'd hide in the barn when company came, because he was afraid they'd taunt his cross-eyed appearance. And after Bill Monroe

---

1. And sisters.

became famous, his hometown took an amazingly long time before it ever honored him.

According to who you ask, anywhere from 500 to 2,000 people came to Rosine the day Monroe was buried. There was a block-long, two-hour line waiting to go inside and view the body, in a powder-blue casket, the inner edge lined with quarters—Monroe's trademark gift to any child he met.

After everyone who wanted to view the body had gone through, the service began, broadcast on speakers set up behind the church.

Planning for the funeral had begun almost immediately after Monroe died three days earlier. It involved not just Monroe's family, the undertaker, and the church, but also Ohio County Judge/Executive Dudley Cooper, the state police, and businesses from nearby Beaver Dam and Hartford. They brought in portable toilets; volunteers in Rosine mowed grass and cleaned the town; local restaurants donated food.

Rosine has seen large crowds before, for various bluegrass festivals—one of them Monroe's unsuccessful attempt in the 1970s to get his own going there.[2] But it had never had so much attention. There were satellite trucks from a whole host of television stations, and so many reporters it seemed as if every fourth person was scribbling in a notebook.

While most of country music had paid its respects the day before at a memorial service in Nashville, there were still many famous faces and voices present—Ricky Skaggs, Ralph Stanley, Bobby Osborne, Skeeter Davis, Del McCoury, the great dobro player Josh Graves, the young fiddle player and singer Laurie Lewis, and a good many of the 175 or so individuals who played in the Blue Grass Boys. Some of them gathered before the service to play bluegrass spirituals on the bandstand of the little community park behind the church. The music had a soft, ruminative quality—a smiling fellowship tinged with regret and respect.

It was a tearful service, and even for those standing outside in the bright sunshine, a moving one. A sobbing Ricky Skaggs addressed James Monroe, saying that he knew how much James had to sacrifice so that his father could share his music with the world. There was a touching measure of respect in the slow, purposeful procession from the church to the graveyard on the other side of the highway. There was admiration, love, and sorrow mingled in the soft version of "Blue Moon of Kentucky" the assembly sang at graveside.

But there was also a powerful touch of the strangeness celebrity creates. Many in the crowd had clearly come to gawk rather than mourn. Some posed for photos leaning against the hearse. On the way out of the church, someone rushed up to the minister who had preached the sermon and got his autograph; after Monroe was interred, people were taking handfuls of the dirt from his grave.

People were still coming into Rosine the evening following the funeral—and they're still coming: A dozen or more come every day to see Monroe's grave. Most are from other countries, especially Japan.

---

2. Bill held festivals there from 1973 to 1975.

There wasn't a lot else to see in Rosine that fall. It's tiny—the signs on U.S. 62, welcoming visitors from the west and the east, are about .3 miles apart. The center of town consists of a few blocks on either side of 62, which include the Methodist and Baptist churches, the community park (which hosts two yearly festivals), and the graveyard. Neither the general store nor the Country Kitchen restaurant was open for business. The only places into which a stranger could walk without knocking were the tiny post office; the old barn across the parking lot from the general store (which holds a Friday night bluegrass jamboree); and, on Sunday, the two churches.

The town is no longer incorporated. Nobody knows how many people live in Rosine, but 250 is a common guess. Residents have to drive eight miles down the road to Beaver Dam for groceries, gas, or any other consumer good. It's not dilapidated, like those ramshackle communities you occasionally see that look as if they'd have to rally to be ghost towns. But to a new arrival, the town seems to lack a focus—some organizing principle.

"Rosine was supposed to have been a big town," says Frances Johnson Harvey, one of Rosine's more active local boosters. It was laid out in 1872 along the Elizabethtown and Paducah Railroad line by Col. Henry D. McHenry, a local lawyer and politician who served in the U.S. Congress. The area's original name, Pigeon Roost, was changed to Rosine, the pen name McHenry's wife, Jennie, used for her 1867 book of poems, *Forget Me Not*.[3]

Businesses and hotels lined Front Street until a 1900 fire destroyed them. Still, the town continued to be a commercial center into the 1940s. In the years just after World War II there were nine groceries, and on Saturdays you could see as many as 35 or 40 teams of horses and mules hitched up to wagons and tied outside the stores.

Ohio County is in the Western Coal Field region, and coal remains significant there—among the most arresting sights of the drive from Beaver Dam to Rosine are the towering draglines of the Zielinski coal operation, and you're likely to see strip pits as you drive around the hills above the town. "Coal falls out of the ground in Rosine," says Hutchings, who was digging recently on his grandfather's farm and struck coal within the first foot.

But the coal boom of the 1960s and 70s had subsided because of the limited demand for high-sulfur coal. Another long-standing industry, timber, remains strong: County Judge/Executive Cooper estimates that wood-related products account for between a fourth and a third of the county's jobs. And in 1995, Perdue Chicken opened a $65 million plant in nearby Cromwell that employs 800 people.

One thing hasn't changed since Bill Monroe's day—there aren't many jobs there. "I never had a job in Ohio County making over $1 an hour in my life," says Billy Logsdon, a Monroe family friend who spent some time driving the bus for Bill and the band. "When I came back out of the service, there wasn't nothing here then—

---

3. Pigeon Roost was renamed Rosine in 1873 by Col. McHenry, a lawyer, banker, and state legislator. See the editor's comments, second paragraph.

sawmill; drive a truck, 90 cents an hour." He moved up to East Chicago, Indiana, in 1959 to work in the steel mills there.

According to statistics from the state Cabinet for Economic Development, Ohio County had 8.8 percent unemployment in 1996, compared to a state rate of 5.6. Weekly wages have improved since Logsdon's experience, but are still $110 below the state average.

As a result, Rosine is a place young people are likely to leave, to look for jobs and out of boredom: "Activities for younger people are just about nonexistent," says Chad Taylor, a 23-year-old who commutes to work as an electrician in Madisonville. In the three trips I made to Rosine to research this story, Taylor and his wife April were the youngest people I spoke to; every other resident I met was 59 or older, many of them retirees who'd spent their lives working in Louisville, Chicago, Nashville, or some other, larger place.

But their hometown kept a powerful claim on them. Harvey recalls living in Mississippi and seeing network news coverage of the funeral of Charlie Monroe,[4] Bill's brother and original recording partner. When it showed the hearse turning a familiar curve, she burst into tears. Her in-laws asked what was the matter. She said, "I said, 'I just saw Rosine—I just saw home.'"

Towns throughout Kentucky have been gutted by the same set of forces—the move to the cities, the decline of family farms, the boom-and-bust cycle of coal, the replacement of traditional social life by television.

Two things distinguish Rosine from other small towns stranded by the flood of events: the strong musical tradition, which found its most famous exponents in Bill, Charlie, and Birch Monroe; and a plan for the future, built upon that tradition.

Along with the tourists, the media has persisted in visiting Rosine. *The New York Times* came several weeks after Monroe's funeral. Its reporter wrote about the sound of music drifting on the night air, playing up a purported local superstition that the music was played by the ghost of Uncle Pen wandering the hills. After Monroe's funeral, the ghostly fiddle was supposedly joined by the sound of a mandolin—the instrument Bill Monroe played.

Hutchings has a more pragmatic explanation: Sound carries across these ridges, and there's almost always someone playing in their house somewhere.

"The tradition is so great that they're probably playing up there tonight"—it's a Saturday afternoon as he points at a house several hundred yards away—"and they're probably playing up on that hill, and you hear all this music, and you think, 'Man, this is really weird,' if you're not from Rosine and you hear all this music around here—you think the trees are playing music, you know?"

Wendell Allen, chair and founder of the Rosine Community Park Association and leader of the Rosine Area Community Choir, calls music "the thread that held everything together. We would be like so many other little places if not for the music that continues here," he says. "That's what kept Rosine alive, and a viable community."

---

4. In 1975.

Sixty-four-year-old Logsdon remembers music as the center of social life when he was growing up. There were square dances somewhere in the area almost every Saturday night. They weren't barn dances, but living room parties—50 or 60 people in a parlor that had been cleared of furniture. Invitations were via word of mouth.

"We'd start for a party somewhere, and the only way we had to get there was to walk," Logsdon recalls. "We'd start out from Rosine, maybe going to Mount Pleasant, or Baizetown"—three and seven miles south, respectively—"on these back roads, and (the musicians) would play all the way up, as we walked along." Hutchings adds that Uncle Pen rode a mule that knew the roads, so Pen could let go the reins and play the fiddle on his way to the next dance.

"It's always been a strong music community," Logsdon says. Bill Monroe "just happened to be the one that pushed it further than what everybody else (did)."

Rosine's music is the basis of Monroe's. He combined Uncle Pen's fiddle tunes with the other music he heard as a boy and young man, such as the "shape note" singing in the churches and the blues played by itinerant guitar player Arnold Shultz.

But Monroe added his own personal touch. There was drive to his playing, and an originality in the way he composed and arranged the music—pitched higher than other country music, and played faster than anything heard before rock 'n' roll—that came from his own character: his willingness to work hard, his fierce pride, his competitiveness. When he drove Monroe's bus, Logsdon got an insight into how much work Monroe put into his music—and how hard he drove his musicians: "You wouldn't believe. We'd be going down the road on that bus, and he'd get some of them musicians and they'd go over one line in a song for an hour at a time."[5]

Monroe's music came to full flowering in the years just after World War II, when the Blue Grass Boys included Lester Flatt and Earl Scruggs. The business side of Monroe's music took a hit when rock 'n' roll came through—although a super-charged version of "Blue Moon of Kentucky" was one side of Elvis Presley's first single—but the Blue Grass Boys came to be known as a school for excellent musicians, among them Don Reno, Mac Wiseman, Jimmy Martin, Del McCoury, Peter Rowan, and Vassar Clements.

Monroe never changed his music to cater to trends—it stayed acoustic when most country music went amplified (he did change the tempo of "Blue Moon of Kentucky" to match Elvis's rendition). In the folk revival of the early 1960s, college audiences and young suburbanites came to realize what an accomplishment creating bluegrass had been, and bluegrass festivals became a new venue for Monroe and the other musicians he inspired.

Monroe mentioned his hometown, its places and people, in his songs and interviews. But the town took its time honoring him. While he proudly guarded the title "Father of Bluegrass Music," for years road signs into Rosine identified the town as the birthplace of the music without mentioning his name at all.

"Ohio County never got down to what they should have," Monroe told the

---

5. Logsdon drove the Blue Grass Special off and on during 1973 and 1974.

Louisville Courier-Journal in 1983, when asked about the road signs. "They've never helped me out. You have the feeling that people are jealous, or that they don't want to spend a dollar. I don't know. I stand like a man should."

Some of this disregard was standard prophet-without-honor-in-his-own-country stuff. "He was just another person to me," Logsdon says. "I never realized what his music was doing until I went with him."

There were complaints that the $5 gate price for Monroe's 1974 festival—at which he was joined by most of the big names in bluegrass—was too high. And folks in Rosine will mention that some people were upset that he left so soon after finishing his shows in Rosine, rather than staying around to visit longer.

Logsdon says people who weren't met and greeted shouldn't have felt singled out or insulted: "Bill never did stand and talk to anybody. He'd talk, but he'd cut words and everything so short. Lot of people thought he was mad whenever he talked to them—they didn't realize the whole family is the same situation . . . that's just the way they talk—the whole family was that way."

"I've heard the comment a couple of times, 'What's Bill ever done for Rosine?'" says Billy Burden, an Ohio County magistrate who also plays in a bluegrass group called Jerusalem Ridge. "I always say, 'Well, what's he supposed to do for Rosine? Is he supposed to send money back?' What he's done, Rosine has nothing to do with at all. His fame didn't come from Rosine; it came from Bill Monroe. Rosine's fame come from Bill Monroe."

And yet Monroe made two contributions to Rosine anyway. His music gave the town a gift that many a larger place doesn't have—the knowledge that its everyday places have the capacity of inspiring great art.

"It means a lot to all of us to have Bill Monroe write songs about Rosine," says Burden. "It's always had a place in my heart that he has written things that would go on forever—everything else might leave, but these songs, the memories, the history, will still be here."

And by being buried in Rosine, he gave the town something to build on—a location for bluegrass pilgrimages.

Friday nights, the music borne on Rosine's night air has a definite source—the Rosine Barn Jamboree, a weekly jam session run by the Rosine Association (TRA) as a fund-raiser.

The jamboree began in the general store around 1990, with a group of people who gathered there one weekend to sit around picking. It soon began to draw so many people they moved out onto the porch, then to the barn. The barn holds 100 people; in warm weather, they open the doors to allow more people to hear the music. Musicians come from Owensboro, Evansville (Indiana), and other cities— so many that the folks running the show form them into spur-of-the-moment bands to make sure everyone gets a chance to play.

Members of TRA, formed in 1995, collect donations at the door. The mission of TRA is to educate people about Rosine's history and the history of bluegrass music. Shortly after Monroe's death, it began raising funds to build a monument to Monroe. They're selling bricks—or, more accurately, the space for an inscription on the bricks—in a set of radial walls that will extend from the monument's central statue. The project received a major boost this winter when Governor Patton[6] gave the county $800,000—the first of a promised $2.5 million over four years—to build an interpretive center which may also include a 1,000-seat performance space.

The monument and museum will be on a 20-acre plot of ground called Everett Park, the same location where Monroe played his 1973 return concert.[7] Judge Cooper estimates that construction should begin in 1999. And other developments in Rosine are moving even more quickly.

Ohio County paid for a giant obelisk that was erected on Monroe's grave last summer.[8] Highway 62 has been officially renamed the Blue Moon of Kentucky Parkway. Ohio County native Pal Goff renovated the general store and reopened it as Rosine General Merchandise, with a restaurant that's already gained widespread fame for its Pal Burger and Mony Fries (named after Goff's wife, Ramona). The barn finally has its own heating system—replacing a scantly effective series of space heaters—and a new sound system.

James Monroe says if everything goes well he plans to move the Bill Monroe Museum currently at Bean Blossom, Indiana, down to Everett Park. He also plans to restore Uncle Pen's cabin (also in Bean Blossom) to its three-acre tract, which has remained in family hands. And Bill Monroe's boyhood home—the tumbledown shack he can be seen walking through in the movie *High Lonesome*—may also be moved to Everett Park.

Hutchings envisions Rosine becoming a more tasteful version of Branson, Missouri, with the center of town coming as close as possible to how it appeared in 1939.

The true memorial to Monroe is in private hands, in the memories of the people who knew him throughout his long, difficult, and accomplished life. Talking three months after Monroe's funeral, Rosetta Kiper's face still changed when she talked about his death. "You know, I can hardly stand to know that he's gone," she said. "It hurts me awful bad."

But at the same time, Monroe's legacy is accessible to anyone who ventures into this small patch of Kentucky with receptive eyes, ears, and imagination.

There is something wonderful about walking outside the old barn during the Friday night jamboree and hearing the music filtering out into the still, cold night. Or to be listening to one of Monroe's powerful, haunting instrumentals like "Kentucky Mandolin" as you crest a rise in the road, and to see the landscape of his youth spread darkly around you, lit by only a few lamps on the highway, some houselights, and a thin wedge of purple and amber cracking through the black at the horizon. There is a fit between the sounds and the scenery that goes deeper and seems uncannier than anything evident would suggest.

---

6. Paul Patton, governor of Kentucky, 1995 to the present.
7. During Rosine's bicentennial celebration; the Uncle Pen monument was dedicated at this time.
8. In 1997.

Monroe captured how far he had traveled from Rosine when he sang these haunting words in "I'm on My Way Back to the Old Home":

> I'm on my way back to the old home.
> The road winds on up the hill,
> But there's no light in the window
> That shined long ago where I lived.

But he—and a number of dedicated people in his hometown—have hung a new lantern there for anyone who cares to come by.

Originally published in *Kentucky Living* 52:5 (May 1998): 28–33. Reprinted by permission of the author.

EDITOR'S COMMENTS

Journalist Nold Jr.'s look at Bill's hometown appeared in the May 1998 issue of *Kentucky Living,* a publication of the Kentucky Association of Electric Cooperatives. (Several paragraphs from the original manuscript have been added.)

Pigeon Roost, Kentucky, was officially renamed Rosine in 1873 by Colonel McHenry, a lawyer, banker, and state legislator (not U.S. congressman), who had invested heavily in the development of the area. The new name was chosen to honor his wife, Jennie Taylor McHenry (1832–1914), who used it as a pen name six years earlier for her (possibly self-published) book of poems.

Copies of the original *Forget Me Not* have apparently not survived, but the book was republished in 1907, under McHenry's own name, by Louisville publisher Ben LaBree Jr., and a copy was located at the archival library of the University of Kentucky in Lexington. It contains Mrs. McHenry's touching reflections on love, death, and the seasons, including several poems inspired by and dedicated to her family and friends. The title poem, "Forget Me Not," presumably the same in both editions of the book, is found on the next-to-last page of the 1907 edition.

Reminiscent of Bill in many ways to me, with its mention of friends and sunset and even "all my faults," "Forget Me Not" is reprinted on the following page. Although it's not likely that we will ever forget Bill, I hope that this poem will be a fitting conclusion for *The Bill Monroe Reader.*

"Forget Me Not"

JENNIE T. McHENRY

When morning springs with laughter sweet,
The glowing god of day to greet,
When friends each other gladly meet,
Forget me not.

When eve with gentle step steals on,
When all the cares of day are done,
When in the west slow sinks the sun,
Forget me not.

When night her sombre mantle wears,
Gemmed with her countless glittering stars,
When every flower a diamond bears,
Forget me not.

When pleasure's cup foams to the brim,
When no dark clouds your pathway dim,
When life swells in one glorious hymn,
Forget me not.

If sorrow on your heart should shed
Her baneful glow, if hope lie dead,
If all your thoughts to grief are wed,
Forget me not.

When Sabbath bells fall on the air,
Then softly swells the morning prayer,
With all my faults, sweet friends, oh, there,
Forget me not.

Originally published in Jennie T. McHenry, *Forget Me Not* (Louisville, Ky.: Ben La-Bree Jr., 1907), 101.

Selected Bibliography

BOOKS ABOUT BILL MONROE AND BLUEGRASS MUSIC

Artis, Bob. *Bluegrass.* New York: Hawthorn Books, 1975.

Cantwell, Robert. *Bluegrass Breakdown: The Making of the Old Southern Sound.* Urbana: University of Illinois Press, 1984.

Dawidoff, Nicholas. *In the Country of Country.* New York: Pantheon Books, 1997. (Includes a chapter on Bill Monroe and Ralph Stanley.)

Hill, Fred. *Grass Roots.* Rutland, Vt.: Academy Books, 1980.

Hood, Phil, ed. *Artists of American Folk Music.* New York: Quill/A Guitar Player and Frets Book, 1986. (Includes the May 1979 *Frets* interview with Bill Monroe by Dix Bruce.)

Kingsbury, Paul, ed. *The Country Music Reader: Twenty-five Years of the Journal of Country Music.* Nashville: Country Music Foundation Press and Vanderbilt University Press, 1996. (Includes Thomas Goldsmith's 1989 article about Bill Monroe, "50 Years and Counting.")

Kochman, Marilyn, ed. *The Big Book of Bluegrass.* New York: Quill/A Frets Book, 1984. (Includes the May 1979 *Frets* interview with Bill Monroe by Dix Bruce.)

Lambert, Jake, with Curly Sechler. *A Biography of Lester Flatt.* Hendersonville, Tenn.: Jay-Lyn Publications, 1982.

Lewis, George H. *All That Glitters: Country Music in America.* Bowling Green, Ky.: Bowling Green State University Press, 1995. (Includes Robert Cantwell's "Mimesis in Bill Monroe's Music.")

Malone, Bill C. *Country Music, U.S.A.* Austin, Tex.: American Folklore Society, 1968; rev. ed., Austin: University of Texas Press, 1985. (Includes a chapter on bluegrass.)

Malone, Bill C., and Judith McCulloh, eds. *Stars of Country Music: Uncle Dave Macon to Johnny Rodriguez.* Urbana: University of Illinois Press, 1975. (Includes Ralph Rinzler's "Bill Monroe.")

Nash, Alana. *Behind Closed Doors.* New York: Alfred A. Knopf, 1988. (Includes a 1986 interview with Bill Monroe by the author.)

Price, Steven D. *Old as the Hills: The Story of Bluegrass.* New York: Viking Press, 1975.

Rooney, James. *Bossmen: Bill Monroe and Muddy Waters.* New York: Dial Press, 1971; 2d ed., New York: Hayden Book Co., 1971; 3d ed., New York: DaCapo Press, 1991.

Rosenberg, Neil V. *Bill Monroe and His Blue Grass Boys: An Illustrated Discography.* Nashville: Country Music Foundation Press, 1974.

———. *Bluegrass: A History.* Urbana: University of Illinois Press, 1985.

Wesbrooks, Willie Egbert, with Barbara M. McLean and Sandra S. Grafton. *Everybody's Cousin.* New York: Manor Books, 1979.

Willis, Barry R., ed. *America's Music: Bluegrass.* Franktown, Colo.: Pine Valley Music, 1997.

Wolfe, Charles K. *Kentucky Country.* Lexington: University Press of Kentucky, 1982.

————. *Tennessee Strings: The Story of Country Music in Tennessee.* Knoxville: University of Tennessee Press, 1977.

Yates, Jeff. *Bill Monroe: 200 Bluegrass Specials.* Miami Beach: Hansen House, 1983.

Index

Numbers in **boldface** refer to pages that contain quoted comments by Bill Monroe on specific topics. Numbers followed by an asterisk refer to pages that include quoted comments about him.

TOM EWING attended Ohio State University in his native Columbus, earning degrees in journalism (1973) and education (1979). Between degrees he played and recorded with Earl Taylor and the Stoney Mountain Boys in Cincinnati and founded an ongoing bluegrass radio show on Ohio State's WOSU-AM. Beginning in 1979, he taught for the Columbus Public Schools, leaving to join Bill Monroe and the Blue Grass Boys in 1986. He has written the "Thirty Years Ago This Month" column for *Bluegrass Unlimited* since 1994. Following Monroe's death in 1996, Ewing has played with David Davis and the Warrior River Boys and with Jim and Jesse and the Virginia Boys.

MUSIC IN AMERICAN LIFE

"My Song Is My Weapon": People's Songs, American Communism, and the Politics of
 Culture, 1930–50   *Robbie Lieberman*

Chosen Voices: The Story of the American Cantorate   *Mark Slobin*

Theodore Thomas: America's Conductor and Builder of Orchestras, 1835–1905
 Ezra Schabas

"The Whorehouse Bells Were Ringing" and Other Songs Cowboys Sing   *Guy Logsdon*

Crazeology: The Autobiography of a Chicago Jazzman   *Bud Freeman, as Told to
 Robert Wolf*

Discoursing Sweet Music: Brass Bands and Community Life in Turn-of-the-
 Century Pennsylvania   *Kenneth Kreitner*

Mormonism and Music: A History   *Michael Hicks*

Voices of the Jazz Age: Profiles of Eight Vintage Jazzmen   *Chip Deffaa*

Pickin' on Peachtree: A History of Country Music in Atlanta, Georgia   *Wayne W. Daniel*

Bitter Music: Collected Journals, Essays, Introductions, and Librettos   *Harry Partch;
 edited by Thomas McGeary*

Ethnic Music on Records: A Discography of Ethnic Recordings Produced in the United
 States, 1893 to 1942   *Richard K. Spottswood*

Downhome Blues Lyrics: An Anthology from the Post–World War II Era   *Jeff Todd Titon*

Ellington: The Early Years   *Mark Tucker*

Chicago Soul   *Robert Pruter*

That Half-Barbaric Twang: The Banjo in American Popular Culture   *Karen Linn*

Hot Man: The Life of Art Hodes   *Art Hodes and Chadwick Hansen*

The Erotic Muse: American Bawdy Songs (2d ed.)   *Ed Cray*

Barrio Rhythm: Mexican American Music in Los Angeles   *Steven Loza*

The Creation of Jazz: Music, Race, and Culture in Urban America   *Burton W. Peretti*

Charles Martin Loeffler: A Life Apart in Music   *Ellen Knight*

Club Date Musicians: Playing the New York Party Circuit   *Bruce A. MacLeod*

Opera on the Road: Traveling Opera Troupes in the United States, 1825–60
 Katherine K. Preston

The Stonemans: An Appalachian Family and the Music That Shaped Their Lives
 Ivan M. Tribe

Transforming Tradition: Folk Music Revivals Examined   *Edited by Neil V. Rosenberg*

The Crooked Stovepipe: Athapaskan Fiddle Music and Square Dancing in Northeast
 Alaska and Northwest Canada   *Craig Mishler*

Traveling the High Way Home: Ralph Stanley and the World of Traditional
 Bluegrass Music   *John Wright*

Carl Ruggles: Composer, Painter, and Storyteller   *Marilyn Ziffrin*

Never without a Song: The Years and Songs of Jennie Devlin, 1865–1952
 Katharine D. Newman

The Hank Snow Story   *Hank Snow, with Jack Ownbey and Bob Burris*

Milton Brown and the Founding of Western Swing   *Cary Ginell, with special assistance
 from Roy Lee Brown*

Santiago de Murcia's "Códice Saldívar No. 4": A Treasury of Secular Guitar Music from
 Baroque Mexico   *Craig H. Russell*

The Sound of the Dove: Singing in Appalachian Primitive Baptist Churches
 Beverly Bush Patterson

Heartland Excursions: Ethnomusicological Reflections on Schools of Music   *Bruno Nettl*

Typeset in 10/12.5 Adobe Minion
with Sassafras display
Designed by Copenhaver Cumpston
Composed by Jim Proefrock
at the University of Illinois Press
Manufactured by Thomson-Shore, Inc.

University of Illinois Press
1325 South Oak Street
Champaign, IL 61820-6903
www.press.uillinois.edu